MULTILATERAL DIPLOMACY AND THE UNITED NATIONS TODAY

MULTILATERAL DIPLOMACY AND THE UNITED NATIONS TODAY

SECOND EDITION

Edited by

James P. Muldoon, Jr.

JoAnn Fagot Aviel

Richard Reitano

and Earl Sullivan

A Member of the Perseus Books Group

Copyright © 2005 by Westview Press, a Member of the Perseus Books Group.

Published in the United States of America by Westview Press, A Member of the Perseus Books Group.

Find us on the world wide web at www.westviewpress.com

Westview Press books are available at special discounts for bulk purchases in the United States by corporations, institutions, and other organizations. For more information, please contact the Special Markets Department at the Perseus Books Group, 11 Cambridge Center, Cambridge, MA 02142, or call (617) 252-5298, (800) 255-1514 or email special.markets@perseusbooks.com.

A Cataloging-in-Publication data record for this book is available from the Library of Congress.

ISBN 0-8133-4310-0 (paperback)

The paper used in this publication meets the requirements of the American National Standard for Permanence of Paper for Printed Library Materials Z39.48-1984.

10   9   8   7   6   5   4   3   2   1

CONTENTS

PREFACE TO THE
SECOND EDITION

Much has changed in the world of multilateral diplomacy and the United Nations in the six years since this book was first published. Unfortunately, too few of the changes have been positive. The challenges of globalization have grown more pronounced and complex. The demands on the United Nations continue to rise while the financial and human resources available to the organization to meet these demands continue to decline. The "crisis of multilateralism" that emerged in the wake of the Cold War has worsened, especially since the terrorist attacks of September 11, 2001, and the launch of the U.S.-led "war on terror." And yet the United Nations soldiers on, adapting and adjusting to the difficult environment of the post–9/11 world.

When we started working on this new edition two years ago, it was quite clear that the challenges confronting multilateral diplomacy and the United Nations at the start of the twenty-first century were not very different from those at the end of the twentieth century. In other words, what we had covered in the first edition was still salient. At the same time, we recognized that the diplomatic dynamics at the United Nations have changed more than a simple update of the text could capture. Hence, we not only asked the contributors to the first edition to revise their essays but also added new essays to the mix, bringing new perspectives and insights to the subject. Although this book was originally conceived to expand the resources available to students and faculty in the Model UN program, we are confident that this new edition will also be useful for courses on international relations, international organizations, and contemporary foreign policy, as well as for diplomatic training programs, and to practitioners currently in the profession.

This new edition would not have been possible without the generous participation of the contributors. It has been a privilege to work with them on this project. We would also like to express our gratitude to the many colleagues and friends who have supported this project and our individual efforts over the last six years. We are also grateful to Ecoforum Ltd/Strategic Advisory Board of Hungarian Development Bank for permission to reprint from their journal, *Quarterly Hungarian Economic Review*, Jacques Fomerand's article that appears in Chapter 5. Finally, we are particularly indebted to Steve Catalano and the rest of the Westview editorial team for their guidance, assistance, and, most of all, confidence in this enterprise.

James P. Muldoon, Jr
JoAnn Fagot Aviel
Richard Reitano
Earl (Tim) Sullivan

July 2004

INTRODUCTION

James P. Muldoon, Jr.

Whether the terrorist attacks on the United States were a massive earthquake or a passing tremor, September 11 has changed much in world politics. It is not just the perception of the world that has changed: The structure of relations between and among nations has been affected, perhaps profoundly, for years to come. The post–September 11 world opens a new chapter in international politics. Pariahs have become partners and marginalized institutions have become major players.

William H. Luers, President of the United Nations Association of the USA

The fortunes of multilateral diplomacy and the United Nations have waxed and waned since the launch of the US-led "war on terror"—the "first twenty-first-century war" according to US President George W. Bush. But there is nothing new about this situation. The UN has long been the whipping boy of its most powerful member. So, it was not unexpected (at least among students of diplomacy and international organizations) when the world body was beseeched by the world's only "hyperpower" for support and assistance in fighting the world's evildoers and rogues and was then derided as irrelevant and inept for refusing to blindly "rubber-stamp" Washington's grand strategy for winning the war on terror. However, the viciousness of the criticism and the sustained effort to discredit the United Nations by the neoconservative faction of the Bush administration in the run-up to the war on Iraq were both extraordinary and effective.[1]

The fate of the United Nations has been a serious concern of many schol-
ars and policymakers for some time, in particular its role in a post–Cold
War international order dominated by the world's sole superpower, the
United States. The end of the Cold War "engendered hopes that the
United Nations might finally be able to meet the tasks and aims set out in
its Charter, above all peacekeeping and the protection of human rights.
. . . [However,] at the beginning of the new century a 'unipolar world order' seems to have arisen from the ruins of the bipolar world order," a
"power-based hierarchical order of the world's states" with the "US as
the only world power capable of global action, and the US, under the
Clinton administration, resolutely pursu[ing] a policy of hegemony"
(Messner and Nuscheler 2002, 125 and 134). Instead of the United Nations and reinvigorated multilateralism being the cornerstone of the "new
world order,"[2] a Pax Americana has gradually taken hold, which depends
on the durability of American preponderance and preeminence (militarily,
economically, and culturally) in the world.

The current talk of American "empire" and "imperialism" reflects the
growing disenchantment with the way the United States has managed the
post–Cold War international order. Charles Kupchan points out:

> America today arguably has greater ability to shape the future of world poli-
> tics than any other power in history. The military, economic, technological,
> and cultural dominance of the United States is unprecedented. . . . Despite the
> opportunities afforded by its dominance and by the end of the cold war,
> America is squandering the moment. . . . Washington's swaggering brand of
> global leadership and its dismissive attitude toward international institutions
> have succeeded in alienating much of the world and straining to the breaking
> point many of America's key partnerships. Rather than rallying behind the
> United States, countries around the world are distancing themselves from
> Washington and locking arms to resist a wayward America. . . .
>
> The failure of the United States to manage more successfully the post–cold
> war international order is a direct by-product of Washington's misperception
> of the world's geopolitical landscape. Backed up by repeated scholarly pro-
> nouncements about the longevity of unipolarity, successive administrations
> have operated under the assumption that U.S. primacy is here to stay.
> . . . Such confidence in the durability of U.S. preponderance bred the compla-
> cency of the 1990s. Washington believed that order would devolve naturally
> from hierarchy; there was no pressing need for institutional innovation. The
> blustery policies of the Bush administration have similarly been based on the
> presumption that a combination of preeminence and uncompromising leader-
> ship will induce the rest of the world to get in line. . . .

The America era is alive and well, but the rise of alternative centers of power and a difficult and diffident U.S. internationalism will ensure that it comes undone as this new century progresses—with profound geopolitical consequences. The stability and order that devolve from American preponderance will gradually be replaced by renewed competition for primacy. The unstoppable locomotive of globalization will run off its tracks as soon as Washington is no longer behind the controls. Pax Americana is poised to give way to a much more unpredictable and dangerous global environment. And the chief threat will come not from the likes of Osama bin Laden, but from the return of traditional geopolitical rivalry. (Kupchan 2003, 205–206 and 208)

There are profound implications for the United Nations and multilateralism in this dramatic return of "Great Power" politics to the world stage. Michael Glennon argues that the Iraq war brought the UN's "Gothic edifice of multiple levels, with grand porticos, ponderous buttresses, and lofty spires" crashing down—"The terrain on which the UN's temple rested was shot through with fissures. The ground was unable to support humanity's lofty legalist shrine. Power disparities, cultural disparities, and differing views on the use of force toppled the temple." Glennon warns that the "greater danger after the second Persian Gulf War is not that the United States will use force when it should not, but that, chastened by the war's horror, the public's opposition, and the economy's gyrations, it will not use force when it should. That the world is at risk of cascading disorder places a greater rather than a lesser responsibility on the United States to use its power assertively to halt or slow the pace of disintegration" (Glennon 2003, 30 and 34). This warning is echoed by historian Niall Ferguson: "Anyone who dislikes U.S. hegemony should bear in mind that, rather than a multipolar world of competing great powers, a world with no hegemon at all may be the real alternative to U.S. primacy. Apolarity could turn out to mean an anarchic new Dark Age: an era of waning empires and religious fanaticism; of endemic plunder and pillage in the world's forgotten regions; of economic stagnation and civilization's retreat into a few fortified enclaves" (Ferguson 2004, 34).

For most scholars, whether "realists" or "internationalists," the central issue in world politics today is not the relevance of the United Nations or multilateralism but the legitimacy of American power and how it is exercised. Indeed, the realists have long dismissed the UN as irrelevant and a convenient fiction that masks the true essence of international politics, namely, power. Internationalists, by contrast, have long maintained that the United Nations "provides a vital political and diplomatic framework for the actions of its most powerful member, while casting them in the context of international law and legitimacy (and bringing to bear on them the perspectives and concerns of its universal membership)," thereby embedding American power as well as the power of other states "in international institutions, where the use of force would be subjected to the constraints of international law" (Tharoor 2003, 78–79). What has internationalists most concerned and frightened is the aggressive unilateralist proclivities of the United States, especially during the administration of George W. Bush, which have alienated the entire international community and, if they persist, will surely do irreparable damage to the United Nations and undermine the multilateral system. It is not that the United Nations and multilateralism are faultless—the problems and weaknesses of the United Nations and multilateral diplomacy are well known—rather, it is the principles and values of the international order, the universally upheld rules and norms that the UN and multilateralism embody, that are at stake. "Being the indispensable power can tempt one into being indisposed to accept the constraints of multilateral diplomacy. But being indispensable does not confer the authority to dispense with the legitimacy of the United Nations as the only entity that can speak in the name of the international community. The reason for much disquiet around the world with the precedent of NATO action in Kosovo was not because their abhorrence of ethnic cleansing was any less. Rather, it was because of their dissent from a world order which permits or tolerates unilateral behavior by the strong and their preference for an order in which principles and values are embedded in universally applicable norms and the rough edges of power are softened by institutionalized multilateralism" (Thakur 2002, 282–283).

The Institution of Diplomacy

Diplomacy is the method by which nation-states, through authorized agents, maintain mutual relations, communicate with each other, and carry out political, economic, and legal transactions. Although the roots of diplomacy reach back to the beginning of organized human society, the Peace of Westphalia of 1648 is generally believed to be the origin of diplomacy as an institution, since it marked the beginning of the European nation-state system (which initially consisted of twelve well-defined sovereign states) and codified the rules of conduct among sovereign and "equal" states. The Westphalian principles of sovereignty and the territorial state that were established in the seventeenth century are the foundation of today's multilateral diplomatic system. But since the end of the Cold War, this foundation appears to be crumbling under the pressure of globalization, a circumstance giving rise to serious questions about the emerging new world order and the future of multilateral diplomacy and the United Nations. Are the Westphalian nation-state system, multilateral diplomacy, and the United Nations increasingly passé? Is the international system of the twenty-first century to be, as Henry Kissinger maintains, "more like the European state system of the eighteenth and nineteenth centuries than the rigid patterns of the Cold War" (Kissinger 1994, 23)?

From "Old" to "New" Diplomacy

The history of diplomacy is commonly divided between the "old diplomacy," which reached its zenith in the nineteenth century, and the "new diplomacy" of the twentieth.[3] The "old diplomacy" or, as it is more commonly known, "bilateral diplomacy" was dominated for almost three hundred years by the "French system of diplomacy," which established and developed several key features of contemporary diplomacy: resident ambassadors, secret negotiations, ceremonial duties and protocol, honesty, and professionalism (Berridge 1995, 1–9). Old diplomacy was predominantly limited to the conduct of relations on a state-to-state basis via resident missions (embassies) with the resident ambassador as the key actor. The "new diplomacy" that emerged in the nineteenth century and found its fullest expression in the twentieth is distinguished from the "old" by two themes: "first, the demand that diplomacy should be more open to public scrutiny and control, and second, the projected establishment of an international organization which would act both as a forum for the peaceful settlement of disputes and as a deterrent to the waging of aggressive war" (Hamilton and Langhorne 1995, 137).

The vestiges of the "old diplomacy" began to fade into the background after World War II, when the "standing diplomatic conference" and multilateral diplomacy blossomed. By the middle of the twentieth century, the international arena had become too big and too complex for traditional bilateral diplomacy, unleashing the unprecedented drive of the past fifty years to build international and regional organizations with defined rules of procedure, permanent secretariats, and permanently accredited diplomatic missions,[4] and gradually shifting the emphasis in diplomatic method from traditional bilateralism to multilateralism. This was a particularly important development in international relations as John Gerard Ruggie points out:

A completely novel form was added to the institutional repertoire of states in 1919: the multipurpose, universal membership organization, instantiated first by the League of Nations and then by the United Nations. Prior international organizations had but limited membership, determined by power, function, or both, and they were assigned specific and highly circumscribed tasks. In contrast, here were organizations based on little more than shared aspirations, with broad agendas in which large and small had a constitutionally mandated voice. Moreover, decision making within international organizations increasingly became subject to the mechanism of voting, as opposed to treaty drafting or customary accretion, and voting itself subsequently shifted away in most instances from the early unanimity requirement that was consistent with the traditional mode of conducting international proceedings. Finally, the move [to formal organizations] amplified a trend that had begun in the nineteenth century, a trend toward multilateral as opposed to merely bilateral diplomacy, especially in the form of "conference diplomacy." (Ruggie 1993, 23)

Characteristics of Multilateral Diplomacy

As a consequence, the "new" diplomacy, especially as it is manifested in the United Nations, broadened the tasks of the profession, subtly changing how diplomats conduct their trade. Today, the tasks of a diplomat include

1. formal and substantive representation (the former involves presentation of credentials, protocol, and participation in the diplomatic circuit of a national capital or an international or regional institution, while the latter includes explanation and defense of national policies and negotiations with other governments);

2. information gathering (acting as a "listening post");

3. laying the groundwork or preparing the basis for a policy or new initiatives;

4. reducing interstate friction or "oiling the wheels of bilateral or multilateral relations";

5. managing order and change; and

6. creating, drafting, and amending international normative and regulatory rules. (Barston 1988, 2–3)

Multilateral diplomacy emphasizes diplomats' public speaking, debating, and language skills because interactions are conducted "principally by means of verbal, face-to-face exchanges rather than in the predominantly written style of bilateral diplomacy" (Berridge 1995, 56).

The expansion and intertwining of political, economic, and social issues and concerns on the agenda of multilateral diplomacy have pushed diplomats toward greater specialization and have "increased involvement in external affairs of domestic ministries, such as those concerned with agriculture, civil aviation, finance and health" (Hamilton and Langhorne 1995, 217). As Sir David Hannay, former Permanent Representative of the United Kingdom to the United Nations, points out, "You have to have a reasonable spread of specializations. You now certainly have to have military advice. And on the development side, you have to have people who know something about the environment, who know something about population control, who know something about wider development policies" (Crossette 1996, A8). Also, multilateral diplomacy has overlaid the task of managing the international system on the diplomats' traditional function of advancing or protecting national interests within the system.

While the new diplomacy put greater emphasis on the multilateral side of diplomatic practice, bilateral diplomacy continued to be a feature of international relations after 1945. Indeed, much of the activity in the United Nations and other international organizations is essentially bilateral (Berridge and Jennings 1985, xiv). Therefore, diplomats have to move from one context to the other no matter where they happened to be posted—at the United Nations in New York or at the Court of St. James in London. For example, at the United Nations a diplomat will conduct bilateral discussions with several countries before attending a meeting of the General Assembly, where he or she will then negotiate with groups of countries on an issue. The challenge for diplomats is to determine when and how to perform these functions most effectively.

Diplomats have available to them in this regard a large body of literature that dissects and analyzes the institution and practice of modern diplomacy. The annals of diplomacy are replete with the stories and reminiscences of those charged with the task of representing states and negotiating on behalf of state interests. The technicalities and minutiae of the day-to-day duties and responsibilities of the diplomat are chronicled in numerous manuals, memoirs, and biographies of practitioners, providing substantial fodder for historians to chew on and analyze, while scholars and analysts produce countless articles, monographs, and books on the broad and complex exigencies the men and women in the diplomatic profession face in a world of increasing interdependence and rapid global change.

But as we go forward in the twenty-first century, multilateral diplomacy in the United Nations faces some difficult challenges. The institution of diplomacy, after coping with and adjusting to the East-West rivalry of the Cold War, the expansion of the international community from 51 states in 1945 to 191 today, and the increase of transnational and global issues on the diplomatic agenda, must now find its way and place in a world where, according to John Stempel, "the parameters of the international political environment have shifted, producing an altered spectrum of issues, rapid communication and faster transportation, a blurring of the distinctions of sovereignty as transnational and subnational [actors] challenge the monopoly of a geometrically-expanded number of nation-states, and a breakdown of the intellectual categories by which diplomacy has heretofore been understood" (Stempel 1997, 2).

The United Nations and Multilateral Diplomacy as Global Governance

Shashi Tharoor, UN Under Secretary-General for Communications and Public Information, reminds us "The United Nations is the preeminent institution of multilateralism. It provides a forum where sovereign states can come together to share burdens, address common problems, and seize common opportunities. The UN helps establish the norms that many countries—including the United States—would like everyone to live by" (Tharoor 2003, 67–68). Although this depiction of the United Nations is fundamentally correct, it is incomplete. Since the end of the Cold War, the UN has progressively opened itself up, allowing nonstate actors to participate in the process of deliberation and policy formulation at the UN. In 1997, Secretary-General Kofi Annan initiated sweeping reforms of the organization's management and culture. He saw that "most of the policy issues in which the UN is involved have become, or are now better understood to be, intersectoral or transsectoral in character. . . . Information age technologies have transformed the temporal context of policymaking [and] the institutional context in which all international organizations now operate is much more densely populated by other international actors, both public and private, than it was in the past. . . . The very organizational features that are now most demanded by the UN's external context in some respects are in shortest supply: strategic deployment of resources, unity of purpose, coherence of effort, agility and flexibility. The current reform effort aims at redressing this imbalance" (Annan 1998, 128–129). The UN has launched a number of international initiatives, such as public-private partnerships and multisector policy networks that bring together governments, businesses, and nongovernmental organizations to tackle an array of global problems. The UN is technically an intergovernmental organization, an association of sovereign states, but as these international initiatives and reforms are formalized and institutionalized into the UN structure, the UN practically becomes a "global" organization.

The UN of today is clearly not the UN of 1945. It has adjusted its procedures, operations, and management to the changes in the world's political, economic, and social landscape with innovation and ingenuity. New structures are being built, such as the UN Global Compact, bolstering the existing infrastructure and increasing the capacity and capability of the UN system. This "quiet revolution at the United Nations" has moved forward under the steady and patient leadership of Kofi Annan, who has carefully guided the organization's transformation during one of the roughest periods in the UN's history. In fact, it is Annan's clear vision of the UN's role and purpose in the twenty-first century that has enabled the UN to withstand (and outlast) American criticism and unilateralist, "go-it-alone" policies.[5] Today, it is widely recognized that diplomacy is the key instrument for peacefully managing change and the many problems of the post–9/11 world; that the multilateral institutions erected throughout the twentieth century, most notably the United Nations, are indispensable to the effective practice of diplomacy as well as important actors in their own right in contemporary international relations; and that both are essential for good global governance.

The effect of globalization, nonstate actors, and new transnational concerns on the practice of multilateral diplomacy and the United Nations is the central theme of this book. In the chapters that follow, diplomats, scholars, UN officials, and leaders of nongovernmental organizations (NGOs), representing a wide range of perspectives and views reflect upon the current and future state of the United Nations and where multilateral diplomacy is heading. The first three chapters explore the changes that have occurred within three broad categories of multilateral diplomacy—UN diplomacy, international peace and security, and international economic relations—and shed some light on how the international system is faring. The next two chapters examine emergent aspects of contemporary multilateral diplomacy: nongovernmental diplomacy and multilateralism. The concluding chapter brings the discussion back to the central theme of the book with an examination of the prospects of multilateral diplomacy. In the end, we hope that this collection of essays will illuminate both the challenges and the possibilities of multilateral diplomacy as an institution and a profession in the twenty-first century and will make a modest contribution to a better understanding of how diplomacy is practiced, the enduring value of multilateralism, and the important role of the United Nations in today's world.

Notes

1. But, in the end, the real loser in this latest round of UN-bashing has been the United States. As James Rubin pointed out recently: "A war with greater legitimacy would have minimized the resentment toward American forces in Iraq. With a UN blessing, it would have been much easier to recruit peacekeepers from around the

world to serve under American command, helping to share the burden and growing risk of policing chaotic Iraq and building new institutions there. When it comes to occupying a country, there is simply no substitute for a UN stamp of approval. Past peace operations in Bosnia and Kosovo show that U.S. troops operating under a UN mandate are far less likely to be regarded as invaders by the local population. Had Washington considered the diplomatic consequences of war as carefully as the military components, much of the collateral damage could have been avoided. The Bush administration deserves credit for mustering the international will to end Iraq's ten-year defiance of the UN. America's willingness to exercise its power alone if need be convinced the world last fall to finally confront the Iraqi dictatorship. But exercising power without careful diplomacy has left the United States' reputation in tatters" (Rubin 2003, 66).

2. In the immediate post–Cold War period, the UN Security Council mandated Secretary-General Boutros Boutros-Ghali to prepare a report detailing the post–Cold War role for the United Nations in the maintenance of international peace and security. This resulted in Boutros-Ghali's *Agenda for Peace,* which was quickly dismissed by the "big powers"—most vehemently by the US Ambassador to the UN, Madeleine Albright, who argued at the time that the Secretary-General was simply "arrogating more power to himself"—indicating that the United States was not really prepared to give the UN the necessary means to play the lead role in dealing with post–Cold War conflicts. See Luck 1999, 189–190, and Messner and Nuscheler 2002, 129.

3. For a thorough and detailed account of the evolution of diplomacy, see Hamilton and Langhorne 1995.

4. According to Professor Martin Rochester, "The number of IGOs [intergovernmental organizations] has increased over twenty-fold since 1900. Of all IGOs presently in existence, some 95 percent were created in the past fifty years" (Rochester 1993, 42).

5. Annan's vision for the UN in the twenty-first century is detailed in his report for the UN Millennium Summit: *"We the Peoples": The Role of the United Nations in the 21st Century,* UN document A/54/2000.

References

Annan, Kofi. (1998) "The Quiet Revolution," *Global Governance,* Vol. 4, No. 2, April-June, pp. 123–138.

Barston, Ronald P. (1988) *Modern Diplomacy* (Essex, UK: Longman Group UK).

Berridge, G. R. (1995) *Diplomacy: Theory and Practice* (Hertfordshire, UK: Prentice Hall/Harvester Wheatsheaf).

Berridge, G. R. and A. Jennings, eds. (1985) *Diplomacy at the United Nations* (London: Macmillan).

Crossette, Barbara. "The World That Awaits U.N. Envoy," *New York Times,* December 16, 1996, p. A8.

Ferguson, Niall. (2004) "A World Without Power," *Foreign Policy,* July-August, pp. 32–39.

Glennon, Michael J. (2003) "Why the Security Council Failed," *Foreign Affairs*, Vol. 82, No. 3, May-June, pp. 16–35.

Hamilton, Keith and Richard Langhorne. (1995) *The Practice of Diplomacy: Its Evolution, Theory and Administration* (London: Routledge).

Kissinger, Henry. (1994) *Diplomacy*. (New York: Simon and Schuster).

Kupchan, Charles A. (2003) "The Rise of Europe, America's Changing Internationalism, and the End of U.S. Primacy," *Political Science Quarterly*, Vol. 118, No. 2, Summer, pp. 205–232.

Luck, Edward C. (1999) *Mixed Messages: American Politics and International Organization 1919–1999*. (Washington, D.C.: Brookings Institution Press).

Messner, Dirk and Franz Nuscheler. (2002) "World Politics—Structures and Trends," in *Global Trends & Global Governance*, edited by Paul Kennedy, Dirk Messner, and Franz Nuscheler (London: Pluto Press), pp. 125–155.

Rochester, J. Martin. (1993) *Waiting for the Millennium: The United Nations and the Future of World Order* (Columbia: University of South Carolina Press).

Rubin, James P. (2003) "Stumbling into War," *Foreign Affairs*, Vol. 82, No. 5, September-October, pp. 46–66.

Ruggie, John Gerard, ed. (1993) *Multilateralism Matters: The Theory and Praxis of an Institutional Form* (New York: Columbia University Press).

Stempel, John D. (1997) "Contemporary Diplomacy and Conflict Resolution: The Intertwining." Paper presented at the International Studies Association Annual Conference, Minneapolis, Minn., March 1997.

Thakur, Ramesh. (2002) "Security in the New Millennium," in *Enhancing Global Governance: Towards a New Diplomacy*, edited by Andrew F. Cooper, John English, and Ramesh Thakur (Tokyo and New York: United Nations University Press), pp. 268–286.

Tharoor, Shashi. (2003) "Why America Still Needs the United Nations," *Foreign Affairs*, Vol. 82, No. 5, September-October, pp. 67–80.

Chapter ONE

UNITED NATIONS DIPLOMACY

THE EVOLUTION OF
MULTILATERAL DIPLOMACY

JoAnn Fagot Aviel

The evolution of multilateral diplomacy and organization is closely linked to the evolution of the nation-state system, which can be traced back to the Treaty of Westphalia in 1648 as described in the Introduction. Changes have usually occurred through war or technological innovations. The Napoleonic wars led to the creation of the Concert of Europe, World War I to the League of Nations, and World War II to the United Nations, as the victors in each war attempted to set up a system or organization to preserve the gains they had achieved and prevent future wars. With the end of the Cold War, multilateral diplomacy is currently at another transition point.

At the Congress of Vienna in 1815 occurred the first attempt to institutionalize the regular calling of conferences to help manage relationships among the most powerful states. In Vienna the victors over Napoleon (England, Austria, Prussia, and Russia, joined later by the vanquished France) created the Concert of Europe, an informal agreement to preserve the status quo in Europe. They codified the status and functions of diplomats and established the principle that any member could initiate a call for a conference with the others. Although thirty conferences were called, bilateral diplomacy remained the normal form of negotiation. However, technological progress did lead to the development of other forms of multilateral diplomacy. With the invention of the steamship, for example, individuals and goods began moving from nation to nation with considerable ease and speed, the result being the expansion of commercial and other relations among the nation-states of Europe. This particular development gave rise to Europe's first institutions for international cooperation, in the form of commissions to oversee river traffic, operate navigational facilities, and settle violations of rules. Later in the century came the International Telegraphic Union (1865) and the Universal Postal Union (1874)—the first of the international institutions with permanent staff, a conference with the power to pass legislation, and an executive council. Both state and nonstate parties sent representatives. This institutionalizing of multilateral diplomacy initiated new forms of collective decisionmaking, such as weighted voting, where each nation's voting power is determined by the size of its budget contribution.

Advances in weapons technology as well as in communication and transportation led to the organization of peace societies in many countries. Their call for the limitation of armaments and the arbitration of international disputes influenced Czar Nicholas II of Russia in 1899 to call for a conference at The Hague. The twenty-six primarily European states that attended established the first Permanent Court of Arbitration, which, however, consisted only of a list of jurists whom parties to a dispute might select as arbitrators. A second Hague Conference in 1907, which attempted to limit or reduce armaments, was noteworthy for its inclusion of a substantial number of non-European states among the forty-four attending. Delegates at these two Hague Conferences recommended setting up permanent headquarters and holding regular conferences there, and they experimented with such organizational arrangements as chairmen, committees, and roll call votes. For all the efforts to institutionalize the workings of multilateral diplomacy, the domestic dynamics of the nation-state system reinforced internal integration at the expense of transnational ties. When a crisis broke out in the Balkans in 1914, there was no permanent conference or machinery to try to settle the dispute, which quickly escalated into World War I. Its victors, recognizing the need for permanent institutions to stabilize the international system and prevent future wars, set about establishing such bodies after the peace. Among the victorious allies was a non-European country, the United States, which joined the ranks of Great Powers and whose president was a primary drafter of the Covenant of the League of Nations. However although US President Woodrow Wilson saw the need to establish a collective security system, the US Senate did not, refusing to ratify the Covenant. Whenever the Great Powers wanted to get together, they would have to meet outside the League, and the League's decisions did not have the weight of all the Great Powers behind them. The League's inability to stop the expansion of the Axis Powers—Germany, Italy, and Japan—in the 1930s and 1940s led to a second world war.

The Allies of World War II, drawing from the experience of the League, developed the United Nations system. This time, though, the coalition did not wait for victory to establish an international organization. The Charter of the United Nations was drafted at conferences attended by the leaders of the United States, Great Britain, the Soviet Union, and occasionally other Allied nations, even as the fighting went on. With victory in sight, the "Big Three," along with the governments of China and France, invited all nations that had declared war on the three Axis powers to attend a conference in San Francisco and finalize agreements on the draft. It was at this conference in 1945 that the UN Charter was adopted. It was here, too, that conference delegates established a preparatory committee to organize the first meetings of the United Nations' major organs.

The United Nations is composed of five organs similar to those of the League—the Security Council, the General Assembly, the International Court of Justice, the Secretariat, and the Trusteeship Council—although the founders changed some of the names and rules of procedure. For example the League's Council had five permanent members representing the principal Allied powers, as does the United Nations' Security Council. However, whereas decisions of the League required a consensus of all members, in the UN Security Council a consensus is required only of the five permanent members (China, France, Russia, the United Kingdom, and the United States); thus they are given a veto over decisions. The inclusion of a sixth principal organ, the Economic and Social Council (ECOSOC), reflected the increasing importance attached to these issues not only by governments but also by nongovernmental organizations (NGOs), some representatives of which took part in the San Francisco conference as members of the US delegation or as observers. The ECOSOC nominally supervises the many specialized agencies of the United Nations, although most function quite independently and some, such as the Universal Postal Union, are older than the United Nations itself.

With the transformation of the Allied coalition of World War II into two rival blocs, multilateral diplomacy also changed. Instead of being partners in the effort to defeat a common enemy, the major international players now tended to see most issues in terms of their effect on the power of each bloc. Looking back, former Israeli Ambassador to the United Nations, Abba Eban, noted one positive effect of a bipolar world, if not necessarily appreciated at the time: "The Cold War, with all its perils, expressed a certain bleak stability; alignments, fidelities, and rivalries were sharply defined" (Eban 1995, 50). However, the Cold War had a stultifying effect on multilateral diplomacy, which was often forced into a political and ideological straitjacket, writes former Jamaican UN Ambassador Don Mills later in this chapter. Even the admission of new UN members was affected, no new member being admitted from 1950 to 1955 as each side rejected potential members of the other's voting bloc until a package deal to admit sixteen nations including members from each bloc was negotiated in 1955.

Although multilateral diplomacy successfully managed to keep under control many of the conflicts that attended the decolonization process, almost all issues that the two great military powers (the United States and the former Union of Soviet Socialist Republics) considered important were negotiated bilaterally outside the United Nations system. At the same time, the two sides often used multilateral diplomacy to score propaganda points against the other side by making speeches and passing resolutions condemning the other. However, the United Nations was not just a propaganda forum, since the increasing "Third World" majority in the UN General Assembly was able to focus the UN's work on the economic and social problems of poor countries.

The UN's focus has shifted from development activities with the ending of the Cold War. Greater consensus among the permanent members of the Security Council made it possible for the United Nations to increase its peacekeeping and peace-related activities as noted by Ambassador Mills. A recent study reveals that, during the Cold War, multilateral organizations had some effect on preventing or resolving conflicts in about 25 percent of the conflicts that they considered. In 1985–1990, as the Cold War waned, the "success rate" increased to 36 percent (Holsti 1995, 354). During the period 1987–1993, the number of resolutions passed by the Security Council went from fifteen to seventy-eight, the number of peacekeeping missions from five to seventeen, the number of peacekeepers from 12,000 to 78,000, and the number of countries contributing troops to UN peacekeeping missions from twenty-six to seventy-six (Goldstein 1996, 276). However, the immediate post–Cold War era may have seen the peak of UN peacekeeping activity. Failures in Bosnia, Somalia, and Rwanda and budgetary difficulties have made members more reluctant to be involved in peacekeeping efforts. The United Nations was called in to replace regional peacekeeping forces in Sierra Leone in 1999. Of the fourteen peacekeeping missions in 2003, five were in Africa. After the 9/11 terrorist attack in 2001 on the United States, the UN Security Council unanimously passed a resolution condemning the attack and sanctioning a US response. However, after the defeat of the Taliban government in Afghanistan, NATO forces, instead of United Nations forces, were invited to help keep the peace although a UN Assistance Mission does operate in Afghanistan under the direction of the UN Department of Peacekeeping Operations. After the United States failed to obtain UN support for its attack on Saddam Hussein's government in Iraq, debate has ensued over what the UN role in Iraq should be(www.un.org).

Although UN peacekeeping activity may diminish in the immediate future, multilateral diplomacy will continue to be important. Multilateral institutions such as the World Trade Organization, the International

Telecommunications Union, and the International Monetary Fund, combined with the competitive spread of standardized systems and technologies of production, have significantly increased the ease, speed, and security with which goods, capital, and knowledge flow across national boundaries, transforming the international economy and diplomacy itself (Sjolander 1996, 605–608). As interaction across national boundaries increases, so does multilateral diplomacy in order to help manage these interactions and attempt to settle conflicts that arise. Progress on technological fronts allows faster and more frequent contacts among governments as well as among groups within countries. There is a growing realization that when problems that are caused by many actors affect many others—problems of the environment, for example—the attempts at finding a solution should involve everyone. Furthermore, the problems themselves are increasingly complex, overlapping many different issue areas and likely to mobilize a variety of interest groups to influence the actions taken. The existence of many multilateral agreements and organizations raises expectations that decisions about important international actions will be taken within the framework of a multilateral organization or conference (Rourke 1995, 311).

Multilateral negotiation is thus characterized by multiparties, multi-issues, multiroles, and multivalues. The level of complexity is far greater in a multilateral conference than in bilateral diplomacy, as is the level of skill needed to manage that complexity. Application of legislative as well as diplomatic skills is needed because of the importance of knowing how to use the rules of procedure to advance a diplomat's goals. Sheer numbers also contribute to increasing the complexity. Ambassador Don Mills writes later in this chapter that although the practice and character of multilateral diplomacy at the United Nations is generally the same as it was when there were 50-plus members, the presence today of 191 members has "brought new dimensions and pressures to international affairs and the multilateral organizations, with significant impact on the UN and its agenda." Among these new dimensions is a greater diversity of issues and actors including nonstate actors, as issues previously thought to be primarily domestic become subjects of international negotiation and issues previously thought to be primarily international increasingly affect domestic interests. Ambassador Mills discusses the wide range of current issues in multilateral diplomacy and describes the new multilateral milieu this way: "The community in which the UN diplomat operates is composed of the representatives of other governments, UN staff at all levels, and representatives of the media and of NGOs."

The only way for anyone to deal with this complexity is to build coalitions involving states, nonstate actors, and international organizations and to privately develop an informal consensus on how to deal with a problem before presenting a decision for a vote in the formal institutional structures.

Later in this chapter Ambassador Sergey Lavrov, drawing on his experiences as Russia's Permanent Representative to the United Nations, describes some of the mechanisms of collective decisionmaking in the Security Council, where the importance of a consensus among the permanent members results in their meeting informally before decisions are made. Mutual interests among the nonaligned members of the Council have often led them to meet informally as well. If a "group of friends" has gathered around a particular issue such as Afghanistan or the Western Sahara, its members will meet informally before submitting a draft of a resolution to other Council members. To pass a resolution, coalitions in the Council need to involve both permanent and nonpermanent members, but these coalitions change according to the issue.

Multilateral diplomacy involves the art of building and managing these coalitions before, during, and after negotiations on a particular issue. In complex and lengthy negotiations, such as those involved in drafting the UN Convention of the Law of the Sea, coalitions must often be formed not only between nations but also within nations—among ministries dealing with fisheries, defense, the environment, and foreign affairs as well as with nongovernmental organizations and private enterprises. The latter may have already formed coalitions among themselves, some of which may include individual ministries as well as nongovernmental organizations in other countries. After hammering out a unified position in often lengthy negotiations among its members, the coalition often must attempt to change this position in response to other proposals and changing conditions, both domestically and globally, if it is to be successful in meeting its goals. One of the principal challenges for those wanting to pass a resolution or obtain a multilateral agreement is to design the negotiations in such a way that they encourage the creation of coalitions supporting agreement and minimize the possibility of coalitions opposing it. The issues themselves have to be packaged in such a way as to promote linkages and trade-offs among the issues. Ambassador Lavrov points out that tactical flexibility is even more important at the United Nations than in bilateral diplomacy. Ambassador Mills emphasizes that for those who work in the United Nations "ability to speak convincingly at meetings and to prepare statements for oneself or for one's seniors is essential for diplomats at the United Nations, as are negotiation and arbitration skills, since these are the dominant activity of multilateral diplomacy today."

Another important skill in multilateral diplomacy discussed by Ambassador Lavrov is the ability to cultivate good relations with the media, especially the US media. Ambassador Mills notes that skill in making use of new telecommunication technologies is also essential. Owing to such technologies, "sovereign" states are less able than before to control the transborder movement of money and of information. Other modern developments add new dimensions to the diplomat's traditional role as representative of a sovereign state. As the twenty-eight world leaders who composed the Commission on Global Governance point out in their report on the opportunities for global cooperation on issues requiring multilateral action, nation-states and their representatives must deal not only with the problems of an increasingly globalized world on one level, but also with the demands of grassroots movements which may even include demands for devolution, if not outright secession, on another level (Commission 1995, 11). At a time when city and state officials and private citizens themselves are entering into negotiations with foreign governments, businesses, and nongovernmental organizations, diplomacy is also increasingly called for at the subnational level.

Traditionally, international political theory has been concerned with the interaction of nation-states, whose increasing interdependence is said to be a mark of the current international system. States in an interdependent world are still seen by many theorists as well as diplomats as operating as individual actors that can rationally formulate and act upon their national interests. According to this view states are drawn into multilateralism and the construction of interstate institutions or regimes in pursuit of their national interests, and the task of the diplomat is thus seen as protecting the country's national interests (Cerny 1996, 622–623). However according to a competing view, globalization has gone so far as to render state structures incapable of managing complex issues involving local, regional, national, and transnational relationships, and thus the diplomat must work to construct multilateral institutions and agreements to help manage these relationships (Cerny 1996, 628). Ambassadors Amer Araim, Sergey Lavrov, and Don Mills all agree that today's diplomat has a dual responsibility: to promote his or her country's interests and to advance the interests of the global community.

Although not all diplomats may agree that there is a dual responsibility, for those who do, tension can exist over reconciling these two responsibilities, which sometimes conflict, while engaging in multilateral diplomacy. Tension also exists between those who feel that there can be consensus on what would be good for the global community, such as preserving the environment and protecting human rights, and those who are suspicious even of the term *global community*. The latter vary between those who see the advocating of global goals as a way for the West, especially the United States, to assert its dominance and others, especially conservatives in the United States, who see support for a global community and often multilateral organizations themselves as a way to subvert national sovereignty.

There is currently a crisis for multilateral diplomacy, as influential figures in the dominant power debate the extent to which the United States should make use of it or act unilaterally. The United States is reluctant to pay for multilateral organizations or actions that it cannot control to its satisfaction, and other nations are reluctant to merely acquiesce in actions controlled by the United States. Later in this chapter, Ambassador Amer Araim recounts his experience while a member of the Iraqi delegation to the United Nations with the attempt of the US Ambassador to have him withdraw a resolution on Puerto Rico and his opposition to US policy on Iraq and Palestine. He states that "the second Gulf War represented the total failure of the Organization" and suggests certain reforms which are needed. Ambassador Sergey Lavrov states later in this chapter that there is agreement on the need for reforming the United Nations to meet the challenges of the new millennium, but not on the specific reforms needed. He states, "It will take intense negotiations to reduce these various ideas to a common denominator and reach agreement on optimal approaches to strengthen the UN system." Although he does not criticize the United States directly, he does criticize unilateralism, pointing out that "a consensus among the UN's members would be worth much more than any unilateral action since it promotes a global approach to the solution of the modern world's inescapably global problems." Multilateral diplomacy will not disappear, since technological and environmental changes and the growing number of both state and nonstate actors in the post–Cold War era require its use. The changing realities of the post–Cold War era, however, will necessitate further restructuring and reform of multilateral organizations and even greater skill in multilateral diplomacy.

References

Cerny, Philip G. (1996) "Globalization and Other Stories: The Search for a New Paradigm for International Relations," *International Journal*, Vol. 51, No. 4, Autumn, pp. 617–638.

Commission on Global Governance. (1995) *Our Global Neighborhood* (New York: Oxford University Press).

Eban, Abba. (1995) "The U.N. Idea Revisited," *Foreign Affairs*, Vol. 74, No. 5, September-October, pp. 39–55.

Goldstein, Joshua. (1996) *International Relations* (New York: HarperCollins).

Hampson, Fen Osler with Michael Hart. (1996) *Multilateral Negotiations: Lessons from Arms Control, Trade, and the Environment.* (Baltimore: The John Hopkins University Press).

Holsti, K. J. (1995) *International Politics, A Framework for Analysis* (Englewood Cliffs, N.J.: Prentice Hall).

Rourke, John T. (1995) *International Politics on the World Stage.* (Guilford, Conn.: Duskin).

Sjolander, Claire Turenne. (1996) "The Rhetoric of Globalization: What's in a Wor(l)d?" *International Journal*, Vol. 51, No. 4, Autumn, pp. 603–616.

The Diplomat at
the United Nations:
Yesterday and Today

Ambassador Don Mills

The founding of the United Nations system over fifty years ago, its evolution, and its wide-ranging interests and activities have no parallel in human affairs. The United Nations occupies a central and unique place in world politics, and it plays a leading role on the world diplomatic stage with an expanding cast of players, which now includes multilateral organizations, regional institutions, governments, commercial interests, nongovernmental entities, and individuals. More than two generations of diplomats have now served their countries at the United Nations, learning through experience the ins and outs of multilateral diplomacy and how to work in a very challenging and demanding environment.

One of the most significant changes in multilateral diplomacy has been the increase in UN membership, growing from 51 member states in 1945 to today's 191. The United Nations played a major role in the decolonization process, and this brought a large number of developing countries, which had been colonies, to independence and membership in the United Nations—the lion's share of them gaining independence between the mid-1950s and the mid-1970s.[1] This expansion of the nation-state system after World War II dramatically altered the diplomatic scene both inside and outside the United Nations, as a large number of relatively inexperienced diplomats began to take part in UN meetings and negotiations. These new member states—representing new cultures, languages, interests, and social conditions—brought new dimensions and pressures to international affairs and the multilateral organizations, with significant impact on the UN and its agenda. In line with these developments more and more people from the newly independent countries came to occupy positions on the staff of the United Nations and its various agencies.

More recently, the United Nations admitted some twenty newly independent states of Central and Eastern Europe, Central Asia, and the Baltic region, formerly part of the Soviet Union, altering once again the diplomatic scene at the United Nations. This latest wave of new members is one of the major consequences of the dramatic events of the early 1990s following the breakup of the Soviet Union and the end of the Cold War. Even though a fairly large number of inexperienced diplomats have joined in UN meetings and negotiations, the impact of this influx of new member states on the dynamics of diplomacy in the UN was not as great as that of the earlier wave of new members.

Likewise, the process of regional cooperation, which had been set in motion in the early postwar years with the European Communities and was later imitated by some newly independent countries, continues its forward march. This trend toward regionalism appears to be encouraging the formation of trading blocs in different parts of the world. The implications of this development for the nation-state system, for international trade, and for the UN system are not yet entirely clear, although it has been speculated that one result might be a return to protectionism, this time on a regional scale. But there is no doubt that, given the growing importance of regional arrangements in the post–Cold War world, they will inevitably impact on the multilateral system and on the practice of diplomacy at the United Nations.

The post–World War II years saw major developments in many aspects of human and world affairs, increasing the complexity of multilateral diplomacy and its content. The end of the Cold War has been marked by considerable uncertainty in some aspects of international relations, as well as the emergence of new concerns, adding to an already overcrowded international agenda. Some of these, such as the issues of human security, international terrorism, inter- and intrastate conflicts, the AIDS epidemic, advancing globalization, and sustainable development, have contributed to the complex situation confronting diplomats today, especially those working in the United Nations system.

The Cold War and After

The Cold War had a considerable impact on the UN system itself, infecting a number of important issues and affecting relations between states. The Security Council in particular was often the site of tension and confrontation, as demonstrated by the frequent use of the veto by the permanent members (particularly the USSR and the United States). The polarization of international relations between East and West created something like a balance of power between two political camps, each led by a nuclear superpower, and multilateral diplomacy was frequently forced into a political and ideological straitjacket.

Entering the United Nations and the fields of international relations and diplomacy in great numbers, the representatives of the new member states of the South encountered a world sharply divided on ideological lines between East and West. This proved to be a difficult and sometimes dangerous environment, especially in the light of their lack of diplomatic experience and of political, economic, and military resources in the face of intense pressures emanating from the rivalry between the superpowers.

The developing countries, as new entrants into the arena of world affairs, sought to challenge and to change some of the structures of the UN system as well as the relations between states. They argued that the international political and economic order had developed in circumstances that rendered the institutions of the international system, in important respects, unrepresentative of their interests and aspirations. To further their cause they formed their own organizations, notably the Non-Aligned Movement (NAM) and the Group of 77 (G-77), the latter being the main caucus group of these countries in the UN system that prepares their initiatives and positions, particularly with respect to international economic and social issues. The concept of the NAM was launched by twenty-nine African and Asian countries meeting in Bandung, Indonesia, in 1955 and now includes nearly all developing countries.[2] The G-77 started in 1964 with 77 members, and has over 135 today. The developing countries also succeeded in their initiative toward the establishment of the UN Conference on Trade and Development (UNCTAD), a major negotiating organization within the UN system. In addition, they have worked over the years for the reform of the international monetary system and the structure of the International Monetary Fund (IMF), as well as for changes in the composition of the UN Security Council and the use of the veto power.

For most of the 1970s developing countries were engaged in negotiations with the industrialized countries in the United Nations, seeking to bring significant changes in the international economic system. These negotiations focused on the developing countries' proposal for the new international economic order (NIEO), which was tabled by the G-77 in the UN General Assembly in 1974 and attracted considerable interest outside the UN system in universities and the nongovernmental sector. In these and other ways the new countries sought to counterbalance their disadvantages of size and economic and political leverage. They created, in effect, a third force in the multilateral system—a system which at that time was deeply affected by the confrontation between the superpowers.

The diplomats of the United Nations on all sides were faced with a complex agenda as well as many hidden factors and motives, all generating considerable political pressures. During the Cold War period, developing countries often received the political support of the Soviet Union and its allies in the Soviet bloc in the United Nations on certain critical issues that were of greatest importance to them. It was common for the Soviets and their allies to vote with the G-77 countries on resolutions calling for the NIEO, the liberation of a number of countries still under colonial rule, especially in Africa, and the elimination of white minority rule in Rhodesia (now Zimbabwe) and in South Africa. Although it was quite evident that at times such support was a deliberate strategy on the part of the Soviet bloc against the major Western powers, many developing countries appreciated the backing. This situation led some Western diplomats to believe that there was a virtual conspiracy at the United Nations between the Soviet Union and the NAM countries—newly independent countries in Africa, Asia, and Latin America and the Caribbean that claimed to be in neither the American nor the Soviet camp. It is true that a few developing countries had a formal political association with the USSR, but for most the relationship with the Soviet Union was very limited.

It has also been argued that some developing countries attempted to play the two superpowers off against each other during the Cold War to gain support and additional aid. A number of countries negotiated formal trade agreements with the Soviet Union and other Eastern European states, in some cases with mutually beneficial results; and some countries entered into agreements involving technical cooperation. But the view that all or most developing countries were "in the pocket" of the Soviets is unfounded and unfair.

The Dawning of the Post–Cold War Period

The assembling of an international force under the auspices of the United Nations and led by the United States to roll back Iraq's annexation of Kuwait in 1991 was emblematic of the dramatic changes that were to sweep the international community at the dawn of the post–Cold War era. In the United Nations, this action was initially viewed as a great opportunity to reinforce the UN's role in combating aggression and maintaining international peace and security. But as the action proceeded, many member states, as well as observers, began to feel that the United Nations had become an instrument of the major powers and had given a license for the waging of unlimited war against Iraq.

The extraordinary situation—in which the Soviet Union cooperated openly with the United States and gave full endorsement to the military action by other countries during the build-up to "Desert Storm"—led President George H.W. Bush to proclaim that a "New World Order" had emerged. Addressing the US Congress in September 1990, he spoke of "a new era . . . freer from the threat of terror, stronger in the pursuit of justice . . . , an era in which the nations of the world, East and West, North and South, can prosper and live in harmony" (Bush 1990). These sentiments were echoed by other European leaders. Former Prime Minister Margaret Thatcher of Great Britain, for example, held out the prospect of a wider community, centered on the European Community, reaching from North America to the Soviet Union. Former Soviet President Mikhail Gorbachev saw the reunification of East and West Germany as facilitating the desire for a "common European home." The "Charter of Paris for a New Europe," adopted at a historic summit meeting of the Conference on (now Organization for) Security and Cooperation in Europe, spoke of "a new era of democracy, peace and unity in Europe." The late President of France, François Mitterand, proclaimed, "Thirty-four states share from now a common vision of the world and a common heritage of values." This view of the world was seen by some as a triumph of Western values and power in the Cold War's ideological battle between East and West. But other leaders from both East and West drew attention to a new danger that was emerging, namely, a Europe divided no longer along political or ideological lines, but between rich and poor. Clearly the New World Order envisaged by President Bush and others did not come forth, and some of the dangers of a Europe divided along economic lines have.

The demise of the Soviet Union and the dissolution of the Warsaw Pact and the associated "bloc" at the United Nations were probably two of the most significant changes to occur in international relations in the twentieth century, with considerable implications for diplomatic practice in the United Nations. One of the most important implications was the release of the peoples and countries of East and Central Europe, as well as of the Baltic region, from a tightly controlled system, to take their place in the international community as sovereign nation-states and to pursue independent foreign policies. Likewise, the emergence from Soviet domination of a group of Central Asian countries—Kazakhstan, Kyrgyzstan, Tajikistan,

Turkmenistan, and Uzbekistan—has altered the dynamics of diplomacy, presenting interesting prospects in terms of relationships within the UN. Indeed, there are significant geopolitical and strategic implications of these countries' geographical location and cultural-religious affinities with such countries as Pakistan, Iran, and Afghanistan.

Furthermore, all these countries could be classified as both developing countries and "economies in transition," causing a rather dramatic change in the distribution of development assistance and foreign direct investment (FDI). The redirection to these countries of the private investment and development assistance of Western countries and Western business interests has diminished the resources that the United Nations and other institutions, as well as private investors, had been making available to developing countries in other regions. This situation has intensified competition and rivalry between the governments of Eastern Europe and Central Asia and the governments of other developing countries in Africa, Asia, Latin America, and the Caribbean. It is also having an impact on the conduct of proceedings in the UN system and the multilateral financial institutions, generating tensions between the groups of countries concerned, a matter which requires careful approaches by diplomats on all sides.

Furthermore, the breakup of the Soviet Union has had an effect on other relationships and regional groupings of the international community. It has augmented the economic and political influence of the European Union (EU), now a powerful supranational entity, within the United Nations and in world affairs. The EU membership now stands at twenty-five countries, with more soon to be added, notably from Central Europe. Johan Kaufmann, writing in 1980, stated that "European communities have become a lobbying and caucusing group of considerable importance [in the UN], manifesting itself in two different incarnations." He pointed out that the Treaty of Rome requires the members to operate as a unit on virtually all economic matters. The second incarnation established was by way of "European Political Cooperation," a voluntary system of consultation among European Community members that coordinated positions in international organizations (Kaufmann 1980, 96–97). European coordination and cooperation have advanced over the years and have strengthened the position of the European Union in multilateral institutions. Other countries and their diplomats must more and more seek to deal with European countries as a group, through the European Union, in addition to the use of bilateral contacts and negotiations in the UN system and multilateral financial institutions.

Although some questioned whether the breakup of the USSR would result in the end of the North Atlantic Treaty Organization (NATO), which was designed to check the Soviet Union's expansion and influence, NATO succeeded in expanding its membership to include several Eastern European countries and in expanding its mission to include peacemaking in Kosovo and peacekeeping in Bosnia and Afghanistan. Another European multilateral institution that has had to adjust to the end of the Cold War is the Organization for Security and Cooperation in Europe (OSCE). Originally called the Conference on Security and Cooperation in Europe (CSCE), it was established in the mid-1970s as a rather loose forum for diplomatic deliberations, bringing together fifty-two countries of East and West by the early 1990s. By 1994 the CSCE had taken on a new mandate and a new name. The newly constituted Organization for Security and Cooperation in Europe is a fully fledged international organization with a secretary-general, a number of permanent institutions, and a growing interest in a number of issues, including human rights and the maintenance of peace and security.

Another important question, especially for many developing countries, is the future of the NAM. Some observers argue that the NAM has lost its purpose with the end of East-West confrontations, others that such a forum might still prove necessary, especially given the serious imbalance of power in the international political arena today. Indeed, the NAM continues to be relevant as a forum in which developing countries can examine and debate a broad range of issues and events, particularly in the international political sphere, and to seek, where possible, a common front.

For the countries of the Americas, in such close proximity to the United States, the breakup of the Soviet Union removed the "Soviet" or communist factor in regional relations. This had been a source of considerable tension between the United States and some of its neighbors to the south. But other problems that were muted by the East-West conflict continue to affect the diplomat in the Western Hemisphere. Regional concerns now focus on economic issues as well as the drug problem. Countries of the Caribbean, for example, benefit from the Caribbean Basin Initiative launched during the administration of US president Ronald Reagan in 1984 and revised in 1990, which provides opportunities for some access to US markets, investment funds, and some aid. But the relationship between the United States and the English-speaking Caribbean nations still encounters some thorny issues, in particular the problem of the movement of illicit drugs from or through the Caribbean region to the United States. The desire of US drug-control officials for free access to the territorial waters of these Caribbean countries has raised serious questions about sovereign rights, has caused considerable tension, and has required delicate diplomatic negotiations to resolve the differences.

But governments of the Americas, and their diplomats operating either at the bilateral or at the multilateral level, still encounter remnants of the

Cold War in the form of the US authorities' strong position against the Castro regime in Cuba. This situation originated with the revolution in that country, which was followed by the establishment of a communist regime and the development of very close relationships with the Soviet Union and the communist bloc. The presence in Cuba of Soviet military facilities brought the world close to a nuclear conflict in the early 1960s. Over the years the United States has attempted to isolate Cuba and to encourage similar action by other countries of the Americas. With the exception of a few countries, including the English-speaking Caribbean, relations with the island were cut off.

The Cuban embargo imposed by the US authorities some years ago, which remains in place, has been the subject of resolutions in the General Assembly over the past few years, with votes, in effect, censuring the US actions. The Helms/Burton Act, which seeks to penalize companies in other countries which deal with property or enterprises in Cuba formerly owned by US citizens and appropriated by the Cuban authorities, has further aggravated the situation and brought very strong protests, notably from Canada and the European countries. In recent years, Latin American countries' attitudes toward Cuba have thawed somewhat. But Cuba continues to attract unfavorable attention in regard to its human rights record, which has brought to a near halt the movement toward a more positive relationship between Cuba and the EU. The George W. Bush administration appears to be planning to reinforce the US embargo in the face of continuing moves inside and outside the US Congress to ease the restrictions. At the same time, the Caribbean/Caricom countries maintain cordial and cooperative relations with Cuba, despite the obvious displeasure of US authorities. Yet the political situation in the region today is more congenial than during the Cold War years, when some countries in the Caribbean (as well as some in Central America) were seen by the United States as coming increasingly under the influence of the communist states.

Other Post–Cold War Developments

Several developments that are now having an impact on relations between states, on diplomatic practice, and on the UN system were in train even before the post–Cold War period. One is the process of globalization, affecting, among other spheres of activity, finance, trade, production, technology, information systems, sports and entertainment, popular culture, and music, as well as criminal activity, the drug trade, terrorism, and the spread of diseases such as AIDS. Another development affecting the political sphere is the diminishing place of radical ideology, which was a potent force in national and world affairs for most of the twentieth century. However, the terrorist attacks of September 11 orchestrated by Osama bin Laden's Al Qaeda and the resurgence of militant Islam seem to have brought a new form of nonstate radicalism into world politics.

Still another development with late–Cold War roots is the wider acceptance of the free market system, although economists and nongovernmental organizations point out the possible dangers of an extreme approach in that direction.

And finally, there is the "democratic wave" that has washed across a number of continents, transforming the system of government in many countries, including the newly independent states of Eastern Europe. It is evident that this movement toward democracy and the growing emphasis on human rights in world affairs owes something to the waning of the Cold War itself. These developments are affecting the UN's agenda and changing the focus of diplomats in the organization.

The issues of economic development and international economic relations have occupied the UN system since its inception, and the organization has made a significant impact in those areas and has contributed to the improvement of the situation of developing countries. These countries mobilized their new majority in the United Nations in an effort to bring about institutional and other changes in the global economic system favorable to their interests. The North-South negotiations of the 1970s on the proposal for a NIEO formed the main expression of this movement. But the North-South summit held in Cancun, Mexico, in 1981 failed to overcome the objections of many industrialized countries to the holding of the proposed global round of negotiations in the United Nations on major economic issues, basically closing the door on such negotiations. Following that event the prospects for government-negotiated global resolutions in the United Nations with respect to such matters receded, to be replaced by a focus on the need for national policy reforms (Tessitore and Woolfson 1997, 108). This change of focus became known as the "Washington consensus," which was conceived and enforced by the World Bank, the International Monetary Fund, and the finance ministers of the Group of 7.

In the mid-1990s, the UN put together an "Agenda for Development" as a way to rekindle interest in the issue of economic development at the United Nations, but without the traditional North-South focus. It was referred to in some quarters as a "neutral agenda." As former UN Secretary-General Boutros Boutros-Ghali pointed out in his 1994 report on development and international economic cooperation, "The competition for influence during the Cold War stimulated interest in development. The motives were not always altruistic [presumably on both sides] but countries seeking to develop could benefit from that interest. Today the competition to bring development to the poorest countries has ended. Many of the poor are dispirited. Development is in crisis. The poorest nations fall further behind" (United Nations 1994, paras. 5 and 6).

More recently, Secretary-General Kofi Annan organized a Millennium Summit, preceding the fifty-fifth General Assembly, dedicated to reinvigorating the UN's role in economic and social development. The result was the UN Millennium Declaration (GA Resolution 55/2), which "outlined an ambitious set of priorities, including precise, time-bound development goals (or the Millennium Development Goals, MDGs) for future UN activities and reform. This list of priorities and goals is remarkable in that it reflects an important shift in attitude towards both the United Nations and how the United Nations should be restructured to meet the immense challenges of globalization" (Muldoon 2003, 201). Today, the gap in incomes between North and South has widened. The issue of development in the post–Cold War United Nations, in the multilateral financial institutions, and in programs of "donor" countries is increasingly focused on the problem of poverty. "We cannot forget that while the 'Iron Curtain' has been brought down, the poverty curtain still separates two parts of the world community," said Secretary-General Boutros-Ghali in his 1990 UN Day message. Clearly the situation has changed significantly since the Cold War in terms of the amount of pressure the developing countries are able to put on the UN system and the UN's responses to that pressure. But the North-South factor continues to surface in such contexts as the UN Conference on Environment and Development (the Earth Summit in Rio, 1992) and the debates over the Convention on Climate Change; the International Conference on Population and Development (Cairo, 1994); and the Summit for Social Development (Copenhagen, 1995).

Probably the best-known and most scrutinized facet of UN activity is peacekeeping, and there have been significant changes in that sphere since the end of the Cold War. The Secretary-General in a 1995 report noted that "there have been dramatic changes in both the volume and the nature of the United Nations activities in the field of peace and security" since the history-making Security Council Summit in January 1992, and he pointed out that "new and more comprehensive concepts to guide those activities and their links with development work are emerging." But all too often, the Secretary-General went on to say, media interest is "focused on only one or two of the many peace-keeping operations in which [the UN] is engaged, overshadowing other major operations and its vast effort in the economic and social and other fields" (United Nations 1995, para. 4). He compared the end of the Cold War to "a major movement of tectonic plates with the aftershocks still being felt."

Many of the UN's post–Cold War peacekeeping operations have been related to conflicts within member states. Sir Brian Urquhart, a distinguished
former UN Under Secretary-General with responsibility for peacekeeping,
called attention to the fact that the United Nations is not mandated to deal
with such situations (Urquhart 1995). In fact, Article 2, paragraph 7, of the
Charter specifically proscribes UN intervention in "matters which are essentially within the jurisdiction of any state." At the same time, Sir Brian
noted, the horrors of Bosnia, Somalia, and Rwanda evoked "a new sense of
human responsibility which have time and again forced the UN into action" (Urquhart 1995). The end of the Cold War has no doubt made it
more feasible for the Security Council to take action in such instances. But
as we saw in the divisive deliberations within the Council over the war on
Iraq, what may be feasible is not always possible. So, this is delicate ground
indeed. Perhaps more important is the fact that all diplomats—even those
whose countries are not on the Security Council or are not directly involved
in peace-related operations—must now devote attention to the growing
number of complex UN peace-related operations and other UN interventions to protect humanitarian missions or to monitor elections.

Matters relating to ethnic questions are increasingly prominent on the
UN's agenda and are likely to become more explicit in diplomats' consideration of substantive issues in the United Nations. The finding of effective
approaches to the management of issues of culture and ethnicity poses a
great challenge to the United Nations, other multilateral organizations, and
the diplomats who work in them, as well as to nation-states and peoples.

Environmental issues have risen to a particularly prominent position
on the UN's agenda over the past decade, especially in the light of the major threats to the global environment, such as global warming and the
erosion of the ozone layer which protects the planet from the sun's harmful rays. There is by now wide acceptance of the notion—as indicated in
Agenda 21, the agreement signed by the governments attending the UN's
Earth Summit—that to achieve sustainable development and an effective
system of environmental management will require new concepts and major changes in lifestyles, production methods, governance, and even relations among states, and this realization has had its echo in new
institutional developments at the United Nations. The Commission on
Sustainable Development and Inter-Agency Committee on Sustainable
Development at New York headquarters are among these new arrangements, as is the system of regular reporting by countries on their efforts to
implement Agenda 21 and the continuing General Assembly reviews of
progress on the matters involved, not to mention the entering into force
of the International Conventions on Climate Change, on Biodiversity, and
on the Law of the Sea, each with its own secretariat and regular confer-

ences. All of these developments widen the scope of the activities that have to be covered by governments and diplomats.

The issue of nongovernmental organizations (NGOs) at the United Nations is another area of dramatic change. The great increase in the presence and activities of NGOs of all sorts at the United Nations—spurred by a decision of the Preparatory Committee for the Earth Summit (and endorsed by the General Assembly) to widen considerably NGO access to the intergovernmental process—adds a dimension to the conduct of UN affairs and diplomacy. More and more NGOs are able to interact with the diplomatic process directly through their accreditation to conferences and meetings or their presence on individual country delegations, and indirectly through the NGO forums that parallel the UN's intergovernmental world conferences. The right of NGOs to a presence during UN deliberations rests originally on provisions in Article 71 of the Charter, but the new situation goes far beyond the founders' vision. Indeed, increasing NGO involvement in intergovernmental activities would have been resisted during the Cold War period by many countries. In the light of increasing numbers of NGOs wishing to participate in UN meetings, practical procedures must be fashioned to accommodate them as far as is feasible. All of this is in line with the great increase in the number of NGOs operating at the national level and their demands for a way to participate in international governance.

A variety of comments have been made about the general changes at the United Nations since the end of the Cold War. A report prepared in 1996 by Sir Brian Urquhart and another UN veteran, the late Erskine Childers—at a time when the organization was poised to elect a new Secretary-General—sums up the post–Cold War reality at the United Nations, which today's diplomats are facing:

> This is a testing time for the United Nations. It is a time when the urgent need for international action is confronted by coalitions of powerful special interests and potentially explosive restiveness in many parts of this fragile world, as well as outspoken ideological opposition to international organization. It is a time when the balance between national sovereignty and international responsibility has constantly to be adjusted. It is a time when wise transitional leadership is vital for human well-being, perhaps even for human survival. (Urquhart and Childers 1996, 35)

The United Nations and Other Multilateral Diplomatic Forums

Over the period of the UN's existence there has been a considerable growth of various types of multilateral forums—subregional, regional, and supraregional, many of them intergovernmental bodies. These are to be distinguished from the UN's own Regional Economic Commissions established early in its history and an important element in the organization's structure and functions. They must be distinguished as well from the groupings of UN member states based mainly on geography that perform a number of (primarily) procedural and organizational functions— electing the chairs and other officers of committees and selecting candidates for seats on UN bodies with limited membership, like the Security Council—the central aim being to achieve equitable geographical representation and to handle cases of competition between countries within a region for such opportunities. All of this requires the active interest and involvement of diplomats and governments and often entails sensitive negotiations.

The formation of multilateral organizations outside the UN was in response to particular circumstances and the perceived needs of countries in a particular region. In 1948, for example, sixteen countries of war-devastated Europe established the Organization for European Economic Cooperation (OEEC) to channel the Marshall Plan aid that the United States was providing for reconstruction. Later reborn as the Organization for European Cooperation and Development (OECD), its new purpose is to work toward the achievement of "the highest sustainable economic growth and employment and a rising standard of living in member countries [and] to contribute to the development of the world economy" (Article 1(a) of the OECD Convention). The OECD's membership has been extended over the years to include Japan, Australia, New Zealand, South Korea, Mexico, Finland, the Czech Republic, Hungary, Poland, and the Slovak Republic.

The Arab League, established in 1945, reflected the growth of nationalist sentiments at a time when many of its member countries were under European control.

The Organization of American States (OAS) was established in 1948 (succeeding the International Bureau of American Republics established in 1896) as a framework to deal with differences between the United States and other countries of the Western Hemisphere. The main tasks of the OAS are to ensure the peaceful settlement of disputes between members and to lay down procedures for mediation and arbitration. But the scope of its activities has widened over the years to involve, among other issues, human rights and economic matters. The Latin American Economic System was established as a multilateral framework to deal with economic development issues in the Latin American and Caribbean region. There are also a number of subregional organizations—among them the Central American Common Market, the Caribbean Community, and the Common Market of the South (MERCOSUR)—most with a focus on economic development and integration, although some have other interests. In the case of the Caribbean Community these interests include education and human resource development and a regional university. More recently, security has become a critical concern.

In Asia, the most developed regional organization is the Association of Southeast Asian Nations (ASEAN). It was established in 1967 and is meant to strengthen the bonds of regional solidarity and cooperation among member countries; to discourage external interference in the region; to accelerate economic growth, social progress, and cultural development; and to settle regional problems through peaceful means, according to the principles of the UN Charter. ASEAN plays a prominent role both inside and outside the United Nations on both economic issues and political and security matters affecting that region.

For the continent of Africa, there is the newly constituted African Union, which is the successor to the Organization of African Unity (OAU). The OAU was established in 1963, a time when the liberation of African countries was gaining momentum. It was long occupied with the movement for political independence and the struggle for liberation in southern Africa, especially the effort to end white minority rule in Rhodesia and overturn the system of apartheid in South Africa. Today, the African Union has gotten involved in the peaceful resolution of internal disputes and conflicts in a number of African countries—some of them triggered by ethnic rivalries—working cooperatively with the United Nations in addition to its focus on economic development and integration of the continent. Subregional organizations have also played a role in these areas, such as the efforts of the Economic Community of West African States (ECOWAS) to bring peace to warring sides in Liberia.

It is inevitable that the activities of regional multilateral organizations increasingly include matters in which the UN system has an active involvement and responsibility. Johan Kaufmann, in his book *United Nations Decision Making,* pointed out that even during the early years of the UN Economic and Social Council's existence, major economic issues of worldwide significance were dealt with, whether within or outside formal meetings, in other forums, some of them outside the United Nations. He included the OEEC, later the OECD, and the General Agreement on Tariffs and Trade (GATT) (succeeded by the WTO in 1995), as well as the World Bank and the IMF (Kaufmann 1980, 55). The Group of 10 major industrialized countries (later succeeded by the Group of 7) was also seen as making decisions on international monetary matters outside the IMF. More recently the UN's role has been in danger of being limited by the possibility of having the Bretton Woods institutions supersede it in the consideration of international economic issues. There appears to be a need to develop lines of communication and cooperation between the UN system and regional organizations. The fact that the

United Nations has had difficulty in coordinating its own multiplicity of agencies (some of them, such as the specialized agencies and the multilateral financial institutions, essentially autonomous) indicates the enormity of the task. One of the major challenges of the twenty-first century is for the UN system to work effectively with regional and other interests while also carrying out the responsibilities to which the global intergovernmental body is uniquely suited.

What are the UN's special or even unique advantages as a framework for multilateral diplomacy? First, at the annual sessions of the General Assembly and other UN-related gatherings, the United Nations brings together leaders of all member states, far more than does any other diplomatic forum. The United Nations is also the convener of global conferences on a range of critical subjects, such as the status of women, population and development, the environment, human settlements, and social development. These entail extensive preparations at the national, regional, and global levels and seek to fully involve NGOs and other civil society interests. These characteristics of world conferences, and the follow-up activities required to implement decisions made, have introduced new elements into diplomatic practice.

Second, the United Nations can focus the attention of the international community on particularly pressing problems, through its proclamation of International Decades, International Years, and "Days," each generating special activities and wide popular participation. Again, there is the UN's work in the preparation and negotiation of international conventions on such important subjects as the environment, international terrorism, human rights, labor, biodiversity, climate change, racial discrimination, and the law of the sea. It can also focus attention on, and elicit global support for, countries and peoples who are disadvantaged or facing special risks. The United Nations has established the machinery for a global response to emergencies, natural or caused by humans, assisting their victims and rebuilding national infrastructure. It is the only body able to marshal global forces to combat the international drug trade, terrorism, and cross-border crime. There are also the wide-ranging activities of the specialized agencies and other bodies of the UN system, with their expertise in a variety of important areas (such as health, natural resource management, population control, civil aviation, education, and agriculture) and their activities in developing countries toward the promotion of economic and social development.

Even this partial list of activities constitutes an enormous agenda. It is not possible to imagine a world without the UN system. For diplomats working at the UN as well as those posted to regional associations, it is important to have some understanding of relationships between regional and international organizations and the possibilities of successful cooperation between them. Such matters should be included in training programs. In addition it would seem that the vast network of intergovernmental bodies and institutions that exists today for the management of transnational problems poses a challenge to governments, especially with respect to the organization and operation of the foreign ministries and other government agencies with relevant responsibilities for international relations.

Some Requirements for the Multilateral Diplomat Today

The increasing use of telecommunications technology and the new developments in that field are likely to have a profound effect on the operations of multilateral organizations, on governments, and on diplomatic activities pursuant to the work of those organizations. The sheer volume, variety, and complexity of the operations of those organizations—the United Nations, in particular—and the vast quantity of information and documentation generated have made the task of diplomacy difficult for all concerned. The United Nations and its member states have been moving rapidly toward the greater use of the Internet in multilateral diplomacy. Indeed, it was anticipated that, by the end of the 1990s, diplomats would be able to search thousands of UN documents in any of the official languages, including any resolutions adopted by the General Assembly on the previous day, and then immediately forward this material to their capital, with comments (see United Nations 1996). The Internet should also help diplomats to overcome the situation in which a single country may take one position on a particular matter in a specialized agency and another in ECOSOC. It also should be of particular aid to small developing countries, given the limited resources of their national ministries. The prospect that diplomats and governments will be able to link up quickly and easily and to discuss related matters that are being dealt with in a variety of bodies is very encouraging.

What, then, is required of the individuals engaged in diplomatic work in multilateral organizations? Brian Urquhart argues, "The art of multilateral diplomacy . . . consists to a large degree in long and intricate negotiations, contacts and conversations. . . . Multilateral diplomacy is usually a laborious and nerve-racking process that requires great stamina as well as intuition, intellect, understanding and negotiating ability" (Urquhart 1972, xiii). And what type of person is best suited to this work? Perhaps it ought to be said at the outset that some persons discover, on being sent to the United Nations, that they have a natural aptitude for the multilateral environment, which is different in important respects from a bilateral one. Of course, some diplomats have worked in both, as well as in their national ministries, and this three-dimensional experience is useful, if not essential, particularly in the matter of coordinating the work on specific issues. This coordination is especially helpful to smaller countries, with their relatively limited resources. It is inevitable that some persons will be posted to work in multilateral organizations without having had much experience in diplomacy in any form. But experience, for example, in government agencies whose work has international dimensions can be an asset to the new diplomat as well as to the multilateral organization itself.

In the multilateral system, diplomats play multiple roles. First and foremost is their function as the representative and promoter of their country's interests. But the United Nations seeks to serve the interests of the global community, and its members must also contribute to that endeavor. In some instances regional interests are involved, and these also demand consideration. Not to be overlooked is the frequent possibility of some positive fallout for a country in this process. Johan Kaufmann notes, "A country can build up its influence in the United Nations to be used in pursuit of its own objectives in the future"—whether these are related to UN issues or to matters outside the organization (Kaufmann 1980, 11). Another part of the multilateral diplomat's role is to serve as political adviser to national authorities on particular issues, but it is also his or her role to be guided by the instructions of national authorities. On some issues where special knowledge is required, the diplomat has also to be both student (tutored by the appropriate national ministry on particular issues) and researcher (able to delve into the subject on his or her own).

The community in which the UN diplomat operates is composed of the representatives of other governments, UN staff at all levels, and representatives of the media and of NGOs. Within each group there is great diversity in nationality, culture, race, and interests. And the contacts between and among the members of this community can take place at any time, formally or informally, in committee rooms or lounges, at receptions, lunches, dinners, and other events.

It would be difficult to develop a profile of the typical diplomat at the United Nations or any other multilateral organization. In fact, diplomats present an infinite variety. But it is possible to list some of the most desirable characteristics for those who aspire to such work. Fluency in a second language, one of the six officially used in the organization, is an important asset for the multilateral diplomat. Even more important, perhaps, is a good education, along with a capacity to learn, for there is much to learn in such work. Today, some special knowledge of international economics (including trade matters) can be a very useful asset, as can a background in international law, since there is so much technical content related to these fields in the issues that diplomats have to address. Then, too, since many issues and relationships in the international sphere have roots in the past, a background in history can be useful. Of course, formal training in international relations offers a good basis for this work, too. In an increasingly complex and changing world, all training programs for diplomats must keep abreast of developments and of activities in the UN system. In this respect, training programs offered by the UN Institute for Training and Research have been of special value.

For work in the United Nations especially, it helps to have an outgoing personality and a capacity to establish good personal relationships—even with representatives of countries whose positions on important issues are opposed to one's own. These characteristics will also go a long way toward overcoming differences of culture and race and of interest and are especially helpful for diplomats who are new to a multicultural milieu. The ability to speak convincingly at meetings and to prepare statements for oneself or for one's seniors is essential for diplomats at the United Nations, as are negotiation and arbitration skills, since these are the dominant activity of multilateral diplomacy today. The UN's seemingly endless series of meetings, committees, working groups, regional caucuses, and other encounters are the venue in which these skills are in demand. Diplomats have extraordinary opportunities to practice their leadership skills at the highest level in the United Nations, because the presidents and chairpersons of the General Assembly, the Security Council, and other bodies, agencies, and committees are drawn from the ranks of government representatives. An effective president or chair of a UN body calls for a sound understanding of the structure, workings, and evolution of the organization, as well as a command of the procedures and rules of the body.

The increasing role and presence of NGOs at the United Nations require of diplomats and their governments an understanding of that dimension of multilateralism; the nature of the participation of these interests, at both the national and the global levels; their interaction with delegations; and the fact that in some instances individuals from such organizations are included in national delegations. Moreover, NGO-sponsored seminars and conferences outside the United Nations provide UN diplomats with opportunities to broaden their horizons—and with platforms for expressing their views on particular issues. This is also a venue for correcting some of the public's serious misperceptions of the United Nations and even, in some cases, of the diplomat's own country.

Notwithstanding the prominence of recent debates on the relevance of the United Nations for particular nations or problems, the United Nations and other multilateral organizations will continue to play an essential role in diplomacy. Diplomats today will find their work in such organizations just as demanding as did diplomats of yesterday, if not more so.

Notes

1. The United Nations' role was vital, but the colonial territories made a significant contribution by demanding, agitating for, and negotiating independence and in some cases fighting wars of liberation.

2. The records show that Bandung in 1955 was a meeting of twenty-nine heads of state of Africa and Asia and was followed six years later in Belgrade by the First Conference of Heads of State and Government. Therefore, the NAM was conceived at Bandung and born in Belgrade.

References

Bush, George H.W. (1990) "Address Before a Joint Session of the Congress on the Persian Gulf Crisis and the Federal Budget Deficit," September 11 [http://bushlibrary.tamu.edu/research/papers/1990/90091101.html].

Kaufmann, Johan. (1980) *United Nations Decision Making* (Alpen aan den Rijn, te Netherlands: Sijthoff & Noordhoff).

Muldoon, James P. (2003) *The Architecture of Global Governance: An Introduction to the Study of International Organizations* (Boulder: Westview Press).

Tessitore, John and Susan Woolfson, eds. (1997) *A Global Agenda: Issues Before the 52nd Session of the General Assembly of the United Nations* (New York: UNA-USA).

United Nations. (1994) "Development and International Cooperation: An Agenda for Development," UN Document A/48/935.

United Nations. (1995) "Supplement to an Agenda for Peace: Position Paper of the Secretary-General on the Occasion of the Fiftieth Anniversary of the United Nations," UN Document A/50/60.

United Nations. (1996) "Coordination Questions: International Cooperation in the Field of Informatics—Report of the Secretary-General," UN Document E/1996/81.

Urquhart, Brian. (1972) *Hammarskjold* (New York: Knopf).

_____. (1995) "The United Nations and Useful Intervention," *Development and Cooperation*, No. 1.

Urquhart, Brian and Erskine Childers. (1996) *A World in Need of Leadership: Tomorrow's United Nations* (Uppsala, Sweden: Dag Hammarskjold Foundation).

THE JOURNEY OF
AN IRAQI DIPLOMAT

*From Bilateral to Multilateral Diplomacy and
on to the United Nations Secretariat*

Amer Araim

My own diplomatic journey started with a childhood in Iraq and later involvement in Iraqi politics before entering into the Iraqi Foreign Service in 1964 and fourteen years later a new career with the United Nations Secretariat. I am now an academic and lecturer on Iraq and the United Nations as well as a Muslim imam (leader in congregational prayers) and actively involved in interfaith dialogue in Contra Costa County and the Bay Area of California. While engaged in bilateral diplomacy in the United States and India, I found it very important to get to know the people and the country. In spite of differences in policies between my country and the host country on specific issues, relations on a personal level could be quite amicable. As an Iraqi diplomat at the United Nations I had to represent my country's interests at the United Nations but was often given much freedom to act as I saw fit. As a United Nations official I no longer needed to obey instructions from any one government but found myself hampered by the conflicting demands of many. Now, as an academic teaching and writing about the United Nations, I continue to work for what I see to be the interests of the Iraqi people, my adopted country the United States of America, and peace and justice all over the world. I am able to take positions on issues without instructions from anyone as well as push for reform of the United Nations.

Prelude to Diplomacy

My career as a diplomat and a senior political affairs officer of the United Nations was influenced by my early involvement in Iraqi politics. I had been aware of and indulged in the politics of my country since I was eight years old. I recall that my father took me with him to bid farewell to the Iraqi troops, which went to Palestine in 1948. Then, after the cessation of military operations, I again accompanied him to greet them on their return. However, I noticed that the aura was different than before. I asked my father about the change in the mood of the people. He told me that the Arab governments had betrayed the Palestinian people because they were stooges of the colonial interests in the region, particularly Britain. He added, "When you grow up I would like to see you supporting the Palestinians." I wish to underline that my family had a very amicable relationship with the then Iraqi royal family, and my uncle was a member of parliament and of the party of Prime Minister Nouri El-Said, who was a staunch supporter of the West. Nevertheless my generation witnessed what is known in the Arab world as the catastrophe (referring to the plight of the Palestinians), which deeply influenced us and led to participation in politics whether in underground movements or political parties by many individuals of that generation.

As a matter of fact, Iraqis of my generation were involved in politics while they were young for a number of reasons. First, the regimes that emerged after World Wars I and II in the Middle East came into being in cooperation with Britain or France, the colonial powers, which occupied the region supposedly in the name of liberty but in reality were solely concerned with their own strategic and economic interests. The emerging regimes were weak, based on tribal loyalties and selfish interests, and were dominated by groups of politicians, who thought that the salvation of the region would be achieved only by following the diktat of London and Paris. The oil companies, which represented the international oil cartels, did not provide Iraq or other oil-producing countries in the region with enough revenues to satisfy the socioeconomic needs of the Iraqi and other peoples concerned. The British government considered the economic and strategic interests of their oil companies in Iraq and the Middle East paramount and not only totally ignored the welfare of the Iraqi and other peoples in the region but also imposed regimes that lost the confidence of their peoples. The British government even put pressure on the national Iraqi government to curb any criticism of the policies of either government, to maintain British military bases in Iraq, and to ensure that the policies of the Iraqi government on the question of Palestine would be consistent with Western strategic interests, including Israeli military superiority over the region. Iraqis have been known throughout their history for their involvement in politics and their attempts to assume a dominant role in the Middle East, and my generation of Iraqis was not different from the previous ones.

Entry into the Iraqi Foreign Service

The appointment of politicians in the foreign service as diplomats and the recruitment of the latter for international organizations have always raised discussion among students of diplomacy as well as others involved in government policies and public service. Appointment of politicians to the diplomatic service of their country sometimes brings people of political vision as well as deep commitment to major goals and political programs of the government. However, occasionally diplomatic political appointments are based on personal or political purposes. Furthermore, political appointments adversely affect the development of a career foreign service. In my case, the appointment to the Iraqi Foreign Service meant an end to my involvement in the internal politics of Iraq. In joining the Iraqi Foreign Service in 1964 I was determined to build my career as a diplomat and not a politician. Therefore I took seriously the foreign service exam. In fact, I prepared a book containing questions and answers in Arabic and English on all issues covered by the exam. Unfortunately I did not publish the book, but I gave it to other colleagues who were preparing for entry into the service or for the promotion exams.

As an Iraqi diplomat, I was in a very difficult and absurd position as a diplomat of a country that was under the most severe tyrannical rule ever witnessed by Iraq in its modern history, unable to publicly criticize that regime and in the meantime championing the causes of human rights and political freedoms in other countries. Iraqi career diplomats at the ministry headquarters were afraid to make any decisions for which they would be held responsible if the leadership disapproved of such a position. Therefore Iraqi diplomacy witnessed a continuous struggle to avoid making any decisions because of the deep fear of the consequences. As a matter of fact, Iraqi diplomacy had been paralyzed since the beginning of the Iraqi state in 1921, but under the rule of the Baath Arab Socialist Party, it witnessed not only paralysis but also tyranny and continuous struggle to justify the unjustifiable. Before 1958 the British Foreign Office in London had an influence on Iraqi diplomacy. From 1958 to 1968 there were so many changes in the Iraqi government and its policies that it was very difficult to discern a coherent Iraqi foreign policy. However, nothing could be compared to the last thirty-five years, which led Iraqi diplomats either to resign and take refuge abroad, seek a new career with international or regional organizations, or continue to live with constant fear not only for their jobs but also for their personal and family safety from the vengeance of the regime. In addition each Iraqi diplomatic mission abroad had one staff member or more of the Office of the General Intelligence. Although this practice is followed by many countries, in the case of my country, Iraqi diplomats often lived under the daily humiliation of being under surveillance.

First Assignment Abroad: Washington, D.C.

I began my career dealing with matters of bilateral diplomacy, such as technical assistance and consular matters. Because of my involvement in politics and being in opposition to the regime in power then, I was not expecting to be assigned to a first-class post such as Washington, D.C. However, the director general to whom I reported was appointed to a committee to decide on assignments abroad. That committee circulated forms to ascertain the wishes of staff on their assignments to different diplomatic missions. I indicated that I was willing to serve in a number of posts which were not highly favored by the staff. The director general returned my form and asked me to write a new form with Washington as my first choice. He told me, "You are a hard-working staff member, and I want you to serve in the best diplomatic mission abroad, Washington, D.C." I asked him whether he was certain that the Minister for Foreign Affairs would agree, taking into account that I was believed to be from the opposition. In the meantime, I restated what I had told him before, that I was interested in becoming a career diplomat and would serve in Washington with full energy and enthusiasm. He replied that I should submit a new form because assignments would solely depend on the qualifications. I did so and was assigned to Washington.

I was fascinated by Washington, not only by the beauty of its lofty buildings, including its museums and libraries, as well as surrounding green parks, but more important by the political freedoms which were enjoyed in this country even though the United States was passing through the most difficult time since the Civil War. The Civil Rights Movement was reaching its turning point. The opposition to the Vietnam War and to the military draft was dominating the academic and public life in America. I was dealing with consular matters and developed close relationships with many Iraqi students studying in American universities inside and near the Belt Parkway area. I decided to take courses for postgraduate studies at Virginia University and the Catholic University. Therefore I became more in touch with the American academic life. I traveled outside Washington and was able to witness the beauty of this country and its great achievements. Because we had not experienced democracy in Iraq, I was particularly impressed by democracy in this country, even though the Civil Rights Movement had not yet achieved its goals and the US government was refusing to heed the wide opposition to the Vietnam War.

Furthermore, I was disturbed by the lack of understanding of the plight of the Palestinian people, whether in the United States government or the media. In the spring of 1967 the State Department organized a seminar for young diplomats assigned to Washington, and I was invited to participate. I was pleased not only by this participation but also because I was given the opportunity to speak even though my statement was not about the relations between Iraq and the United States but dealt with the plight of the Palestinian people. I recall saying that Iraq and the Arab world as a whole were hoping to promote diplomatic, economic, technical, and cultural relations with the United States. However, it was expected that the US government would play a more active role in assisting the Palestinian people to attain its legitimate rights. To my surprise the organizers of the seminar were pleased by my statement.

In the meantime, the situation in the Middle East was rapidly deteriorating, and the region was speedily moving toward war. It was expected that the US government would intervene to stop the parties from engaging in combat, particularly since Egypt made an important decision on the eve of the war by sending its vice president to Washington to find a peaceful solution to the crisis. Despite all international efforts to halt the conflict from developing into a full-scale war, such efforts proved futile. The war began on June 5, 1967, and lasted for six days before a cease-fire. Egypt lost the whole of the Sinai as well as the Gaza Strip. Syria lost the Golan Heights, and Jordan lost control of the West Bank. Thus the entire territory of Palestine came under the control of Israel, with hundreds of thousands of new Palestinian refugees to be added to the millions of refugees who had lost their homes since 1948. My stay in Washington during this serious setback in modern Arab history provided me with an opportunity to study in depth the position of the United States on this major and serious issue impacting the relations between the United States and the Arab and Muslim worlds.

On American television stations, I was able to observe the war as it occurred. I was able to distinguish between the rhetoric and the truth, though the latter was very bitter. I realized that the Arab world (with its tyrannical and corrupt regimes) was no match for Israel with the massive support it received from the West and particularly the United States. But unfortunately despite its military superiority and the extensive support it received from the United States and other Western countries, Israel refused to deal with the Palestinian question on the basis of international legitimacy. The then Iraqi and other Arab governments accused the US government of siding with Israel in the war, and Iraq therefore decided to break off diplomatic relations with Washington and London.

Regardless of the rupture of diplomatic relations between Iraq and the United States, which led to the shortening of my stay in Washington, I returned to Iraq with an attachment to democracy and human rights in the United States, notwithstanding the plight of African-Americans. Upon my return to Iraq I informed many of my friends and comrades that the only way to progress in Iraq and the Middle East as a whole was (and still is) to observe the principles of democracy and to respect basic human rights. I was really impressed by the Civil Rights Movement in America even though I was surprised to see that the leadership of the movement did not speak out about the plight of the Palestinian people. As a matter of fact the Civil Rights Movement in America in the 1960s had not yet approached the issues of democracy and human rights from a global perspective, notwithstanding the support of Martin Luther King, Jr., of the struggle of the people of South Africa and other African causes. However, in the 1970s the Civil Rights Movement began to forcefully voice its concern about the issues of freedom and human rights in Africa, Palestine, and other parts of the world.

Return to the Headquarters in Baghdad and Later Assignment in New Delhi, India

After my short stay in Washington and my return to Baghdad, I began my work in the Foreign Ministry's legal office. Whereas my returning colleagues from London and Washington were assigned to European capitals, I remained for one year in the ministry headquarters. Then I was informed that there was a vacant post in New Delhi, India, which I accepted. I was assigned to the Iraqi embassy there in charge of political, cultural, and press matters. It was a great experience in diplomacy as well as in the educational, cultural, and informational fields. India is a subcontinent with diverse cultural, political, and educational orientations. Diplomatic service in

India was just like having a sabbatical leave or having an advanced course in diplomacy. Success in diplomacy depends on a knowledge of the issues, personal initiatives, and pursuits of each diplomat as well as appreciation of the traditions of the country. Some prefer to limit their relations to their contacts with the host government's Ministry of External Affairs as well as some embassies. Others, including me, sought to establish contacts not only with the Ministry of External Affairs and other diplomatic missions, but also with members of political parties, the media, and academic institutions. The Indian government, not like many other governments in the Third World, did not view such contacts with suspicion. On the contrary, having vast contacts with different segments of Indian society was considered an indication of appreciation of the country, its political system, and its culture. When I met ordinary Indian citizens, their curiosity about foreigners seemed very obvious. Talk with them would cover every matter from the weather to world politics.

The diplomatic, cultural, economic, and educational relations between Iraq and India were excellent. My major political assignment was to ensure that the support of India on the Palestinian question would not be shaken because of the defeat of the Arab states in the Six-Day War of 1967. Furthermore, the media in India, which are known to be vibrant, were generally supportive of the Palestinian cause. However, since the situation was so volatile and subject to intense campaigns to influence the hearts and minds of people everywhere, it was essential to maintain close contacts with the editors of different newspapers and the chiefs of the media bureaus covering the Middle East to continuously review developments in this regard.

The issue of Kashmir was also of major concern to me and to diplomats from Islamic countries as well as other countries. Therefore this issue was followed very closely. In the meantime, the Indian government and media considered the question of Kashmir an absolutely internal matter and not only did not appreciate intervention in this issue but considered any intervention an unfriendly gesture. Nevertheless, that position did not prevent me from raising the issue of the human rights of the Kashmiri people and referring occasionally to the resolution of the United Nations in this regard in my private discussions with journalists and academics. I visited Kashmir and met with Muslim scholars and community leaders there. It is worth mentioning that there is now a rule in international law saying that the plight of minorities in any country is a question of international concern. As far as the question of Kashmir, there is a resolution by the United Nation recognizing the right of the Kashmiri people to self-determination.

The other issue which impressed me in India was the work of the Asian African Legal Consultative Committee, which is an intergovernmental organization initiated by Mr. B. Sen, a brilliant Indian lawyer. He noticed in the early 1960s that even though the Asian and African states would be affected by the new developments in international law, particularly the laws of the sea, international rivers, the environment, and international trade, many of these states did not have the legal expertise to be actively involved in these matters or even to determine their interests. Therefore he pressed for the establishment of this organization and became its secretary-general with a nominal salary of one dollar a year. During my assignment in New Delhi, I became liaison officer with this organization, and it was a very important part of my work. I attended conferences of the organization in New Delhi and Colombo, Sri Lanka, where the laws of the sea, international rivers, and international trade were thoroughly debated. I continued to have contacts with that organization even after leaving New Delhi. I attended its annual meeting in Tokyo in 1975 and organized its annual meeting in Baghdad in 1977. As a matter of fact, diplomats and international legal experts from the United States and Europe attended the meetings of this organization because of the high level of its legal debates of issues before the United Nations.

Assignment to the Permanent Mission of Iraq to the United Nations

My assignment to the Permanent Mission of Iraq to the United Nations, which began in January 1973, represented a turning point in my career and a job that I sought because of my attachment to multilateral diplomacy. It also opened an opportunity for me to later have a new career as a staff member of the United Nations. During my assignment to the Permanent Mission, I was able to obtain my master's degree in government and politics from St. John's University in New York. I wrote a thesis on the legal aspects of decolonization. The same arguments used in my academic research I presented to the United Nations to underline the importance of the commitment of states to respect the right of people to self-determination. In that thesis, I argued that the adoption by the General Assembly of resolutions calling for the rights of colonial countries and people to self-determination, decolonization, and respect for human, civil, and political rights had created a new rule of international law. Under the Charter of the United Nations the resolutions of the General Assembly are recommendations, whereas the Charter states that the members of the United Nations agree to accept and carry out the resolutions of the Security Council. However, in the case of decolonization and apartheid, as well as human rights, the resolutions of the General Assembly have the force of law rather than mere recommendations, and all states are committed to respect them, particularly the right of people to self-determination, to be free from racial and colonial domination, and to live free from oppression, intimidation, and humiliation. When the rules of international law are violated, the world community is obliged to act rather than merely convey its moral indignation.

Because of my legal background, I was hoping to deal with legal matters. But since Iraq was an active member of the Special Committee on the Situation with Regard to the Implementation of the Declaration on the Granting of Independence to Colonial Countries and Peoples (the Decolonization Committee), I was assigned to that committee. I was elected chairman of its Subcommittee on Petitions and Information as well as vice chairman of the Fourth Committee of the General Assembly. It is appropriate to advise young diplomats that when they are assigned to any diplomatic function, they should fulfill their duties despite their personal desire or preference to work in a specific field of diplomacy. In addition to decolonization, I was assigned to work on the Law of the Sea as well as matters regarding the Asian African Legal Consultative Committee.

It is a reality that the major success of the United Nations has been in decolonization. During my assignment, the African territories under Portuguese colonial rule were able to obtain their independence. My delegation worked very hard on the questions of Namibia and Southern Rhodesia (now Zimbabwe), which took a longer time to obtain their independence, particularly the former. Many issues were considered by the Decolonization Committee, such as the Western Sahara, Puerto Rico, Gibraltar, the Falkland Islands, and East Timor, which created deep rifts within the members of the United Nations because they represented a different situation from traditional colonial rule. In the cases of Gibraltar and the Falklands the colonial power (Britain) had brought new people to the territories while they were claimed by Spain and Argentina, respectively. Argentina and Spain have occasionally engaged in separate negotiations with Britain on the Falkland Islands and Gibraltar. The United Nations has always advocated and repeatedly affirmed the position that in order to determine the future status of colonial territories, the free will and desire of the colonial peoples should be ascertained, and this is paramount in the decolonization process. In the meantime, all the parties concerned may engage in negotiations to agree on how to implement the process of decolonization.

Some states have indicated that the United Nations Declaration on Granting Independence to Colonial Countries and Peoples did not apply where part of the territory of the state was under colonial occupation. The Western Sahara and East Timor had been taken over by Morocco and Indonesia, respectively, which considered their actions a return of their own previously occupied territories rather than unlawful annexation of colonial territories.

Indonesia was able to control East Timor for more than a quarter century in the same manner as Morocco has been controlling the Western Sahara. However, Indonesia was forced to withdraw its forces and allow the people of East Timor to exercise their right to self-determination under the supervision of the United Nations. Currently East Timor is an independent state.

As for the Western Sahara, the United Nations has been deeply involved with all parties concerned for approximately thirty years. During my time as an Iraqi diplomat at the United Nations, the Iraqi Ministry of Foreign Affairs rarely instructed the delegation with the exception of very few cases, and one of them was the question of the Western Sahara. This territory was under the colonial rule of Spain and therefore included in the list prepared by the United Nations for Colonial Territories. In 1975 Spain decided to withdraw from the territory, and Morocco, which had an old claim and considered the Western Sahara part of its national homeland that was under colonial rule, decided to annex it. The Moroccan government decided to organize a popular march to implement its annexation decision. In the meantime, individuals and groups within and outside the territory were demanding the right to self-determination. Morocco stated that these groups and individuals were Moroccan citizens. Algeria was strongly in favor of the right of the people of the territory to self-determination. My instruction was very clear: to support Morocco in its claim because the territory was Moroccan under Spanish colonial occupation. That position made me differ with other delegations from the Third World countries, which were cooperating with my delegation on the issues of decolonization. King Hassan II of Morocco was asked why he was praising Iraq's support on the question of the Western Sahara, whereas all that Iraq had done was to issue a statement just as other countries had. The king replied that the support of the Iraqi delegate at the United Nations was more important than sending forty thousand troops to the Western Sahara. In the meantime, there were proposals to grant the territory self-rule and to remain under Moroccan sovereignty. These proposals are different from the normal process of decolonization in the United Nations and, so far, have not been approved by all the parties concerned. The modalities for ascertaining the wishes of the people of the territory, including the refugees and those who have settled in neighboring countries, are being constantly considered.

With regard to Puerto Rico, the US delegation has always believed that the people of that territory have already exercised their right to self-determination through their electoral process. Furthermore, the General Assembly removed Puerto Rico from the list of Non-Self Governing Territories in the 1950s. On the other hand, some other delegations, particularly Cuba, argued that when the General Assembly adopted the Declaration on Granting Independence to Colonial Countries and Peoples in 1960, Puerto

Rico was neither an independent state nor integrated into nor associated with the United States. Therefore, this territory should be considered within the list of colonial territories. When I joined the Iraqi delegation to the United Nations in New York in 1973, Cuba was not a member of the Decolonization Committee. However in the previous year the Iraqi delegation had pushed the issue of Puerto Rico in the committee in coordination with the delegation of Cuba. The US delegation put heavy pressure, through other delegations, to change the position of the Iraqi delegation as well as other delegations. I noticed that even the delegations of the Soviet Union and other members of the Eastern bloc were hesitant to make a statement or to sponsor the draft resolution on Puerto Rico, which was proposed by Iraq on behalf of Cuba. They also refused to be involved in discussion of the resolution. I thought then that the Soviet Union was reluctant because it felt vulnerable regarding the territories under its domination; as a consequence, it wanted to show solidarity with Cuba and embarrass the United States without the appearance of playing a role in this regard. Initially I received instruction from my ambassador to support the Cuban request and therefore prepared arguments in favor of consideration of the question by the Decolonization Committee. After failing to put pressure on me through the members of the committee, a US ambassador went to the Iraqi Mission and requested a meeting with the Iraqi ambassador. He asked him to instruct me to stop supporting the resolution, even though the two countries did not have diplomatic relations then. According to the Iraqi ambassador, he told the US ambassador, "We did not come to your mission to request you to restrain your delegates from supporting Israel; therefore we cannot accept this request." As a matter of fact I was given a hero's welcome that evening when I returned to the mission from the United Nations Headquarters. However, two days later I received a new instruction not to defend the resolution publicly, but not to withdraw it and to keep a low profile. I was convinced that the US delegation had pressured our delegation through other delegations, particularly those of Arab states friendly to the United States. Another piece of advice to diplomats in multilateral diplomacy, on controversial issues such as Puerto Rico one should implement the instructions very carefully and not attempt to read into them any more than their precise meaning.

The second major issue I worked on while an Iraqi diplomat at the United Nations was the Law of the Sea. This was really a new field because in the past the laws of the sea had been mainly related to freedom of navigation and regional or local fishery disputes. However, with the establishment of the exclusive economic zone, which extended to two hundred nautical miles, a new and expanding interest was shown in this subject by member states. New technologies also made it possible to explore and exploit the resources of the seabed and ocean floors beyond two hundred nautical miles. I attended the United Nations Conference on the Law of the Sea, which was convened in Caracas, Venezuela, in 1975. In addition to debating the issues of the Law of the Sea, I led efforts to invite to the conference the Palestine Liberation Organization and the African liberation movements recognized by the Organization of African Unity.

Three events are worth mentioning about my involvement in the law of the sea. As stated before, even though Iraq and the United States did not have diplomatic relations the two countries supported the freedom of navigation through international straits. Therefore the two delegations held meetings to exchange information. I explained in detail our concern to maintain the freedom of navigation through the Strait of Hormuz. In the same conference, the Iraqi delegation submitted a proposal to give special status to semienclosed seas. The delegation of the then Soviet Union was concerned that if there was a special regime for semienclosed seas their interests might be adversely affected. Therefore a member of the Soviet delegation met with me and requested that the proposal be withdrawn and referred to a special treaty concluded between Iraq and his country in 1972, which required coordination between both countries. My reply was that I had been a member of the delegation that prepared that treaty, but it did not oblige us not to defend Iraq's interests in international treaties. I added that the Soviet Union had not consulted our delegation on the issues of the Law of the Sea. The third event related to the cooperation between the states in the region. It had been difficult to cooperate in maritime matters because the Arab states called the Gulf the Arabian Gulf, while Iran called it the Persian Gulf. The United Nations Environment Program came with a proposal to solve this problem by extending the coverage of the proposed convention to the Gulf of Oman, which would be called the Maritime Area, and thus avoiding the political dispute regarding the name of the gulf. All the states in the region agreed to this proposal, and I sought instruction from my Foreign Minister in this regard. When we arrived in Kuwait the head of the Iraqi delegation was not with us and arrived later. On the first day of the conference I was elected rapporteur general of the conference. Immediately after the opening a senior member of the Iraqi delegation made a statement without consulting me, though I was representing the Iraqi Ministry of Foreign Affairs. He emphasized that the gulf should be called the Arabian Gulf and Iraq would defend the Arabian Gulf against all ambitions, foreign and local. I saw the Iranian delegate raising his hand to speak and realized that if he spoke he would insist on naming it the Persian Gulf and then the conference would collapse and the Iraqi delegation would be blamed. Therefore I called for a point of order and requested the adjournment of the conference for fifteen minutes. The delegations agreed. I informed the member of the Iraqi delegation, who was senior to me, that his statement was contrary to the instruction I had from the Minister of

Foreign Affairs and would lead to the collapse of the conference. He assured me that he would not repeat such a statement. I also spoke with the Iranian delegate, assuring him of our agreement not to raise the issue of naming the gulf and requested him not to insist on speaking on this issue after the resumption of the meeting.

Another issue that brought confrontation between the developing and developed countries was the question of the new international economic order. The developed countries preferred to limit the role of the United Nations in the economic field to distributing statistical information, organizing donor conferences, and spearheading relief efforts. The developing countries expected the United Nations to be deeply involved in the restructuring of the international economic system, which suffered from chronic imbalances due to the legacy of colonialism. The United Nations was not able to achieve progress despite the great work done by the United Nations Conference on Trade and Development. The situation remained static until the Arab-Israeli War of 1973 and the decisions of the Arab states to impose an oil embargo on the United States and other states for their support to Israel. The United States and other Western governments came to the United Nations to utilize it as a forum to put pressure on the Arab oil-producing states as well as other members of the Organization of Petroleum Exporting Countries (OPEC). The latter did not join the Arab states in their embargo but took advantage of the energy crisis to adjust the prices of oil, which had been very low for a long time because of the domination of the Western-based transnational oil companies over the international oil market. As a result of these unfolding events the developing countries insisted that in order to discuss the energy crisis the whole international economic system should be reconsidered. The developed countries acquiesced, though reluctantly. There were two special sessions of the General Assembly in 1974 and 1975 in which I participated. The academic communities in the United States and all over the world paid close attention to these developments. When I resumed my doctoral work after returning to the United States to begin my new career at the United Nations, I wrote my dissertation on this subject, which was later published by Praeger as a book entitled *Intergovernmental Commodity Organizations and the New International Economic Order* (1991).

Working for the United Nations Secretariat

On the question of international civil service there is a debate whether staff members should be recruited at entry levels (in the United Nations these positions are identified as P-1 or P-2 levels) or whether diplomats, politicians, or academics should be allowed to join the Secretariat at higher levels. There are arguments in favor of admitting diplomats and others to join the Secretariat at higher levels to benefit from their diplomatic skills and to bring new blood to international civil service. Currently famous actors or athletes are appointed as honorary representatives of the United Nations or other international organizations to promote public support for their noble causes. The argument against appointing diplomats to international organizations relates to the need to develop a career international civil service and to ensure that the new staff members are committed to the position of the organization rather than their own political ideology or their preconceived position on international issues, which they have developed while in the service of their own governments. In practice both approaches are followed now, though there is an emphasis on the creation of career diplomatic as well as international civil services.

Being involved in multilateral diplomacy saved me from entanglement in a very tense and suspicious relationship between my government and many other governments. It also motivated me to seriously consider applying for a job with the United Nations. I sought to join the United Nations Secretariat on a loan basis, since I was supposed to return to Iraq after three years. However, the approval of my government was withdrawn after I had begun my job, because of personal jealousy and differences among decision-making authorities in Iraq. That decision was a blessing in disguise because the Iraqi authorities had already informed the United Nations of their approval and did not inform the UN of their subsequent decision. Therefore I submitted my resignation from the Iraqi Foreign Service immediately after beginning my functions at the United Nations. I informed the United Nations Office of Personnel of my resignation by submitting the letter of the Iraqi authorities accepting my resignation, which later made it possible for me to get a permanent contract without a new approval by my government, which I was unlikely to obtain. Since at that time submitting a resignation was tantamount to an act of treason, I was not able to visit my country for twenty-five years except for one time when I entered with a United Nations *laissez passer*, was detained at the border while trying to leave the country, and departed only after the intervention of the United Nations. In addition, my resignation was motivated by multiple factors, including my attachment to working at the United Nations permanently because it represented an advanced forum for multilateral diplomacy. Furthermore, being in the Secretariat enables the staff member to be well aware of the positions of many member states, which I could not achieve while with the Iraqi Foreign Ministry dealing with bilateral matters. Even while in India dealing with bilateral matters, I was engaged in multilateral diplomacy because I was a liaison officer with the Asian African Legal Consultative Committee, which dealt with numerous issues of international law. Although working in the United Nations Secretariat involves negotiations, conducting missions and research, for me it was very much different from performing my diplomatic functions, particularly representing a state and always taking positions.

In August 1978, I began my work at the United Nations Centre Against Apartheid (CAA) in New York City. I was assigned responsibility for the issues on sanctions against the government of South Africa. These sanctions were imposed by the United Nations to force South Africa to abandon its policies of apartheid, including abolishing the laws, regulations, and practices which led to tremendous oppression of the black majority in South Africa. As a result of these policies and the mounting struggle of the people of South Africa, the authorities there began to escalate their aggression against neighboring African states. The South African government also refused to withdraw from Namibia in spite of numerous resolutions of the Security Council and the General Assembly, as well as a judgment of the International Court of Justice. There were also reports about the attempt of the South African government to develop nuclear weapons as well as to circumvent the voluntary arms embargo imposed by a Security Council resolution in 1963. A consensus was emerging in the United Nations that the then government of South Africa constituted a threat to international peace and security and that comprehensive and mandatory sanctions were the most appropriate measures to solve this crisis by peaceful means. As a result of the Soweto uprising of 1976, the reports on the attempts of South Africa to develop military nuclear technology, the death of South African political black leader Steve Biko while he was in police custody, and the continuous violations of human rights by the South African authorities, the Security Council adopted its Resolution 418 (1977), which imposed a mandatory arms embargo on South Africa. My work in the CAA was different from that of the Security Council committee to oversee the implementation of Resolution 418, though I was assigned as a liaison officer to that committee. My work in the CAA included, among other things, promoting comprehensive sanctions against South Africa, overseeing the implementation of the voluntary sanctions adopted by member states or regional organizations, and maintaining contacts with many nongovernmental organizations which were campaigning all over the world to ensure the effective implementation of voluntary sanctions placed by governments, groups, and individuals, as well as pursuing the issue of further sanctions. The United States and other Western governments were opposed to comprehensive and mandatory sanctions against South Africa because they asserted that such sanctions would harm the black majority. However, the majority of the member states of the United Nations had a counterargument emphasizing that the policies of apartheid were more harmful to the people of South Africa than the additional temporary burden they would suffer as a result of sanctions.

Although the Security Council was not able to adopt comprehensive and mandatory sanctions, the Special Committee Against Apartheid (SCAA), supported by a vast majority of UN member states, was successful in its requests to the General Assembly to adopt sanctions, including oil and trade embargos as well as measures to boycott South Africa in cultural, sports, scientific, and entertainment matters. Furthermore, the Secretariat, on the instruction of the General Assembly and the SCAA, began to monitor the sanctions. In reality these instructions expanded the role of the Secretariat, which conferred on me heavy and special responsibility. During my work at the CAA I established contacts with many sports, cultural, educational, and other organizations. One of the most active and effective antiapartheid groups in Europe was the Shipping Research Bureau (SRB) in Amsterdam, which was monitoring the illegal supply of oil and petroleum products to South Africa. After the liberation of South Africa, the SRB invited each of those who had worked on the oil embargo to contribute a chapter to a book, which was published under the title *Apartheid Oil Secrets Revealed* by Amsterdam University Press in 1995. I was honored to contribute to the book a chapter on "The United Nations and the Oil Embargo against South Africa." Nelson Mandela wrote the introduction to the book, in which he expressed appreciation for the role of the United Nations in assisting in the struggle against apartheid and in particular the role of the oil embargo and other sanctions in the elimination of apartheid in South Africa.

Upon the conclusion of the work of the Special Committee Against Apartheid, I was assigned to deal with West African states which were struggling to achieve democratic rule. It was another difficult assignment because many of these countries refused outside intervention. However, there was great momentum as a result of the dismantling of the Soviet Union and the collapse of the Berlin Wall. There were many tense and interesting developments. One event worth mentioning related to the Mission of the Secretary-General to Nigeria, to which I was assigned as rapporteur. While the members of the mission were concluding their meeting with an opposition group and bidding them farewell, the Nigerian police and security forces tried to arrest them. The members of the group demanded that I, as a representative of the United Nations Secretariat, provide them with protection. I was forced to confront the police and insisted that before our arrival we had received guarantees from the

Permanent Mission of Nigeria to the United Nations that our mission would have the freedom to meet any person without any intervention from the authorities. While I was arguing with the police, many journalists as well as many activists gathered. This confrontation was resolved after the intervention of government officials and the release of the members of the group.

The final functions that I performed with the United Nations were as Secretary of the Special Committee on Decolonization and related programs. The delegations of Britain and the United States were always skeptical about the work of that committee, which represented part of the differences between these two delegations and the delegations of the Third World countries and some European countries on many issues, including decolonization, Palestine, and international economic matters. Because of these differences the voting on a major draft resolution on the general question of decolonization had been deferred in the session of the General Assembly before I assumed my functions as secretary. There were negotiations between these delegations and members of the SCAA. I was able to assist in these negotiations, and for the first time in years the General Assembly adopted a resolution on this issue by consensus.

Conclusion

The journey I undertook in the diplomatic service of my country and later in the United Nations was both rewarding and arduous. Believing in democracy, living in two major democratic countries, and being deeply concerned about the lack of respect for basic human rights in many countries, particularly my own, have deeply influenced my careers both as a diplomat and as an international civil servant. I was able to contribute to noble causes such as the striving of the Palestinian, South African, Namibian, Zimbabwean, and many other peoples who were engaged in bitter struggles for their right to self-determination and liberty. The great achievements in advancing the cause of freedom and social justice advocated by the Third World delegations at the United Nations were consistent with principles pronounced by the American and French Revolutions, as well as the noble Fourteen Points of President Woodrow Wilson. The same principles were advocated by the Mahatma Gandhi, Martin Luther King, Jr., and Nelson Mandela, who championed the cause of the liberation of Africa, particularly to eradicate the vicious system of apartheid. Nevertheless, there are those in the West who still not only cast doubt on decolonization and the eradication of apartheid, as well as other issues relating to human rights and political freedoms, but also attempt to undermine the United Nations.

However, the United Nations is an instrument of multilateral diplomacy representing a historical process aimed at avoiding the scourge of wars and assisting in ending poverty and other socioeconomic problems. Although many of its critics think that the organization has gone beyond what the drafters of its Charter wanted it to be, others defend that as a progressive development in international organization. Many, including myself, have been advocating a more central role for the United Nations in the present crises in Iraq, Chechnya, Kashmir, and Palestine. During my career as a diplomat I also advocated a more active role for the United Nations in socioeconomic matters. Although I was involved in political issues while working for the Secretariat of the United Nations, I followed very closely its deliberations and research on environmental issues, the law of the sea, and international economic matters. However, less emphasis is placed now on these issues because the United States, which has become the only superpower in the world, is no longer interested in the involvement of the organization in these questions.

The United Nations is a vital and important instrument for international peace and security, particularly for the Third World. Many of these states cannot afford to have diplomatic missions in many countries and thus conduct their bilateral relations through their missions accredited to the United Nations. The multilateral diplomacy conducted through the United Nations, the background information, studies, and research provided by the Secretariat, and the determination of member states to reach consensus contribute to better understanding and mutual respect that upholds the causes of world peace and security. No doubt a lot of legitimate criticism can be directed against the United Nations, but the Secretariat, though it is not immune from mistakes, should not be blamed for the lack of the member states' will to make the organization a robust instrument of peace.

The present Secretary-General was criticized for his failure to warn the Security Council and world public opinion about the massacre in Rwanda. He read the negative mood among the Security Council's five permanent members and decided to ignore the imminent danger threatening the lives of millions of innocent people, who were killed in the most malevolent manner without any outside help. He did not take bold steps either, to prevent the US invasion of Iraq of 2003, which has so far led to the death of tens of thousands of Iraqis, mostly civilians, and a hundred thousand injured, as well as destruction amounting to tens of billions of dollars. Whereas the First Gulf War of 1990–1991 was considered by many a great achievement in international law because the organization worked through the agreement of the five permanent Security Council members, the Second Gulf War represented the total failure of the organization. Nevertheless, I regard the First Gulf War as inconsistent with the spirit of the Charter, which emphasizes the importance of the use of peaceful means to settle international disputes. Those who followed closely the statements of the Secretary-General on the Iraqi crisis since the beginning of 2003 would notice that he was trying to fend off criticism for his inaction. He may be hoping to have a third term, but the Asian group is demanding that the new Secretary-General should be from Asia. All depends on whether the United States will allow the election of a replacement. His predecessor was informed by the United States that it did not want to renew his term. Nevertheless he wasted the time of the organization for more than a year campaigning to force the United States to reverse its decision.

In view of my experience in the United Nations I suggest certain reforms. The office of the Secretary-General should be strengthened by being limited to one seven-year term in order to prevent wasting the time of the organization on electioneering. More efforts are needed to ensure that the next Secretary-General will be able to undertake the great task entrusted to him by the Charter and not to be the man of any member state. Reform of the UN Secretariat should not diminish its role, as suggested in some previous proposals, but should strengthen it. I won many cases against the Secretary-General in the Administrative Tribunal of the United Nations. These cases clearly demonstrated that there is a gap in the administration of justice in the organization. I tried also, through my membership in the leadership of the Staff Union of the United Nations, to push for reform, but to no avail. I suggest further that the Charter should be amended to abolish the division of the membership of the Security Council into permanent and nonpermanent members and to increase the membership to twenty-five, to be distributed on an equitable geographical basis, with a gentleman's agreement that the United States, China, Russia, and the European Union be always members of the Council.

THE UNITED NATIONS
THROUGH THE EYES OF
A RUSSIAN AMBASSADOR

Ambassador Sergey Lavrov

The United Nations, the most universal multilateral forum, has proven its viability and unique capacities but needs to be strengthened and adapted to meet the challenges of today. This is the consensus of the entire international community, expressed at the highest political level during the Millennium Summit of the General Assembly in the fall of 2000, as well as on a number of other occasions. A broad reform process is now under way, aimed at helping the UN system meet those challenges.

Numerous proposals for increasing the effectiveness and efficiency of UN activities have been put forward over the last several years by many countries, including the Russian Federation. Even with this lofty goal in common, many of the proposals differ on the specific methods of achieving it. It will take intense negotiations to reduce these various ideas to a common denominator and reach agreement on optimal approaches to strengthen the UN system. Such negotiations are the everyday work of the permanent representatives of member countries to the United Nations in

New York City. I would like to offer an insider's view of this work and of the diplomatic methods they employ.

The Security Council holds a special place among the principal organs of the United Nations, empowered as it is by the organization's Charter to make decisions binding on all UN members. (The General Assembly exercises such power in matters concerning the UN budget, but its other decisions are in the nature of recommendations.) This places a great responsibility on the fifteen member states of the Security Council, and especially on its five permanent members. The special status accorded the permanent members on the Council demands that they not only use their position in the interest of their respective countries (which is natural and necessary) but also in the interest of the international community and answer for their actions to all other UN member countries.

The Security Council has a number of time-tested mechanisms for making collective decisions. It carries out the bulk of its work through closed-door consultations of the whole that take the form of frank, often harsh, exchanges of opinion. Informal meetings of the five permanent members play a key role in the decisionmaking process, too, since many items on the Council's agenda are discussed among the five in a preliminary way. There is also an informal "nonaligned caucus" made up of Council members belonging to the Non-Aligned Movement. The Russian delegation and other permanent members hold regular and fruitful working consultations with the caucus. On specific issues that come before the Security Council—Georgia, Afghanistan, Western Sahara, and the former Yugoslavia, for instance—there are apt to be a "group of friends" or a "contact group" that hold their own consultations. After the groups have discussed drafts of would-be Security Council decisions or resolutions, these are submitted to other Council members for consideration.

Bilateral consultations between Security Council members are also quite important. We hold them with all the delegations represented on the Council. Personal relations and confidential contacts between the permanent representatives contribute in very important measure to the normal, efficient functioning of the Council. Most of the permanent representatives in the Security Council are very interesting personalities, with an original mind and wide experience in diplomatic work.

In associating with colleagues, the Council values good relations, erudition, a sense of humor, and flexibility. A joke, a well-chosen quip, or a story told by a permanent representative at the right moment can help to ease tension and channel discussion in an appropriate direction. Still, jokes and stories play only an auxiliary role. Solid arguments to defend and/or advance national interests are the more usual fare. If a country formulates its interests in precise and persuasive terms and according to the principles of international law, primarily the UN Charter, its consistency in defending or advancing them wins respect and support at the Security Council.

In the early 1990s, when Russian representatives on the Security Council were seeking UN support for peacekeeping operations of the Commonwealth of Independent States (CIS), they faced the task of overcoming the reluctance of some Council members even to discuss the possibility and the desire of others to attach unacceptable strings to such support. But perseverance and well-founded persuasion enabled us to win over the majority of Security Council members to the idea of taking modest but nonetheless real steps toward drawing the United Nations into peacekeeping efforts in the Republic of Georgia and in Tajikistan. The Security Council decisions on these subjects recognized the need for greater UN involvement in efforts to settle these two conflicts, including the dispatch of contingents of UN peacekeepers to both places, and they acknowledged the importance of co-operation between the UN peacekeepers and the CIS peacekeeping forces stationed in the two countries. Since then the conflict in Tajikistan has been successfully solved, and the UN now keeps a small political office there to promote peace building.

In the case of Iraq, now that the war is over, it is important to concentrate on implementing all relevant Security Council resolutions. True, sanctions were lifted, but there is an urgent need to make the life of the Iraqi people less miserable and to create conditions under which they themselves will determine their own political future and control their natural resources. That's what Resolution 1483, adopted unanimously in May 2003, is about. It also calls for international verification that Iraq has indeed stopped all its past programs for creating weapons of mass destruction. To bring this issue to a closure is important for the credibility of the Security Council and that of each of its members.

Needless to say, perseverance and even a rigid position must be combined with flexibility. Generally speaking, tactical flexibility in pursuing a fundamental position is even more important to diplomacy at the United Nations than in bilateral diplomacy. In what sort of lab are a nation's UN policies devised and analyzed? Indeed, how does a country's representative on the Security Council learn what sort of tactics to adopt? Capitals do a huge amount of work by analyzing and processing the diverse information the country receives from its many embassies, shaping a national position on this or that world event, and drawing up instructions for their representatives at the UN's New York City headquarters. These instructions lie at the basis of the work of any representative on the Security Council.

At the same time, information received through bilateral channels generally acquires important shadings at the United Nations. This is probably natural, for it is one thing to inform an ambassador to your country about your government's position on a particular issue and quite another thing to state your country's position publicly in a multilateral debate at the United Nations. What reaches the Council (and other UN bodies) as a rule is not a "maximalist" statement of the nation's position but a "moderate" version, adjusted for consideration by a body in which many diverse and often clashing points of view are represented and whose work is to search for compromise, concessions, "exchanges," and ways to untie a knot. All of this reflects the essence of the United Nations as a center for coordinating national positions and individual efforts to resolve global problems through a search for compromises based on a balance of interests.

Of course, the Security Council does not confine its contacts to representatives of Security Council member states. The Council considers questions relating to the peace and security of various regions, which may affect the interests of any number of states. Hence the special attention that Security Council members give to everyday contacts with the delegations of nonmembers. I would like to focus on Security Council relations with representatives of the CIS member countries. These relations are highly important to Russia, and not only because Russia had been presiding over the CIS for many years (until Ukraine took over the CIS chairmanship in 2003). It is important, too, because, in response to requests from the commonwealth countries themselves, the Security Council has started to concern itself directly with the task of supporting peacekeeping efforts in CIS conflict areas. The CIS, for its part, was granted observer status at the UN General Assembly and is an active participant in periodic meetings convened by the UN Secretary-General to consider issues of interaction between the United Nations and regional organizations in the fields of peacekeeping and conflict resolution. As of 2003, there were new participants in these meetings from the CIS and neighboring area: the Organization of the Collective Security Treaty and the Shanghai Co-operation Organization. Thus the cooperation of the Security Council with the delegations of CIS states reflects the Council members' stake in seeing the United Nations contribute more effectively to the promotion of peace and stability in these countries. Great attention is also being paid to the developing countries and to their groupings represented in the United Nations, among them the Non-Aligned Movement, the Group of 77, the African Union, the Organization of Islamic Conference, and the League of Arab States.

An important aspect of Security Council work is interaction with other UN bodies. The Council is indisputably the main UN organ responsible for the maintenance of international peace and security, but it cannot operate in isolation. Modern conflicts and crises often have humanitarian, socioeconomic, ethnic, and other "unconventional" factors as their primary causes, and thus it is necessary for the Council to seek the involvement of other UN bodies (with due regard to the jurisdiction of each). The Council is cooperating on a growing scale with the General Assembly, which makes an important contribution to such new efforts as assisting with democratic elections, monitoring respect for human rights, and postconflict peace building and reconstruction. The increasing significance of the humanitarian aspects of present-day crises (protection of refugees, alleviating suffering among civilians, delivering relief aid, and so)—and the realization of a majority of UN members that sanctions should be used in a more responsible manner—account for a visible interest in promoting interaction between the Security Council and the UN Economic and Social Council (ECOSOC) that was envisaged in the UN Charter.

Daily visits to UN Headquarters—be it in connection with Security Council consultations, official meetings, or informal discussions with various delegations—bring Security Council members into contact with the UN Secretary-General and the work of UN Secretariat staff. Most of them are highly competent international officials who are enthusiastic about their work and show flexibility in tackling their tasks. The Secretary-General is assisted in his daily activities by Under Secretaries-General, Assistant Secretaries-General, and his special envoys and representatives in various regions, seasoned diplomats all. They are integral to the functioning of the United Nations, and members of the Security Council work with them daily. The Secretariat units that help the Security Council carry out its work are staffed by experienced professionals. It is gratifying that Russian citizens are in this group. It goes without saying that the UN Secretariat has its problems, as does any bureaucratic entity. Therefore, member states generally support the efforts of Secretary-General Kofi Annan to bring about an effective reform in order to make the international civil service leaner, more efficient, and better prepared to respond to new threats and challenges.

The UN's work involves not only the delegations of member countries, the intergovernmental bodies under its aegis, and the Secretariat, but also the press, or what is known as the fourth estate. UN activities are covered by correspondents from many countries, and to a large extent they shape world opinion on many important issues on the UN agenda. It is anything but easy to cultivate good working relations with foreign, especially American, media. At the windup of every SC consultation (to say nothing of every formal Council meeting), diplomats are beset in the UN lobby by a crowd of reporters. TV camera operators take close-ups of the ambassadors, ask them to step nearer, thrust out their mikes. Of course, you can make a getaway through a side door, as some diplomats have done more than once. Or you can pause to answer the questions that are showered on you, each reporter trying to outshout the others in the hope of eliciting an answer to his or her question.

The very wording of the questions shows that the reporters who ask them want to hear something sensational. Well, it cannot be helped, because the media are business enterprises and need a bit of sensational stuff, a hint of scandal for the front page, to attract readers. I remember one occasion on which a reporter asked me what the Security Council had discussed that day. Upon learning that the Council had registered a successful completion of the UN operation in East Timor, he remarked disappointedly, "Successful? Then there's nothing to write about!" Be that as it may, ambassadors should not exit hastily through a side door unless they want the position of their country to be left to the guessers and speculators.

Many delegations attach great importance to working with the press. Some of them even rent premises at UN Headquarters where they can give representatives of leading media a closed briefing before an important meeting or right on its heels, offering a frank assessment of the problem or of the reefs on which a solution can founder. This "enlightenment" costs a pretty penny but is undertaken as a necessity. "Do you know why we do this?" asked the press attaché of a West European mission in a moment of frankness as he chatted with his Russian colleague. "You will remember Carl Kraus, a well-known Austrian publisher and journalist of the early twentieth century, . . . who said that diplomats lied to journalists but, on reading the press the following day, came to believe their own lies." Well, there is some truth in this joke, as in any other. And it is a fact that diplomats, UN Secretariat staff, and even journalists themselves rely to a large extent on what they read in the press or see on television.

What I have described and am most familiar with, of course, is the methods that the Russian Mission uses in its work—the diplomatic methods that are highly important in the fulfillment of our tasks. These tasks may be broadly defined as promoting Russia's national interests at the United Nations, just as other countries strive to promote their own. But the unique nature of the United Nations means that you succeed in promoting the interests of your country only when you harmonize them with the interests of others. This requires mutual concessions and compromises, but that's how multilateral diplomacy works. One cannot hope to introduce a national initiative in the United Nations and see it endorsed by all other 190 member states without a single change. There must be changes and modifications to accommodate the interests of others. But the hoped-for result—a consensus among the UN's members—would be worth much more than any unilateral action, since it promotes a global approach to the solution of the modern world's inescapably global problems.

Chapter TWO

THE DIPLOMACY OF INTERNATIONAL PEACE AND SECURITY

The Role of the United Nations

THE UNITED NATIONS

Dealing with Threats to the Peace in the Twenty-first Century

Earl Sullivan

What role should the United Nations play in the coming decades? For the Security Council, the answer to this question will depend on the kinds of issues brought before it and the resources, military and otherwise, made available to the organization by its members. For the most part, the Security Council deals with crisis situations that are determined to constitute a threat to the peace. The type of crises the global community will face in the future may differ substantially from those crises assumed to be most likely when the United Nations came into being.

Created in the aftermath of World War II, the UN was set up to counter challenges to peace similar to those that precipitated that war, a conflict so recent, and so searing, that it colored all aspects of organizing the postwar international order. It was assumed by the founders of the UN that future threats to world order would be similar to those of the past. At the head of the list of anticipated problems was naked aggression by one state against another. Furthermore, Great Power harmony was assumed as a precondition for successful collective action by the United Nations on behalf of peace and security.

The theory underlying the peacekeeping system authorized in the UN Charter is generally referred to as *collective security*. The essence of this concept is that the threat of collective force would deter aggression, or in the event that deterrence did not work, that the actual employment of collective measures would defeat an aggressor state. As a major theorist of international relations stated many years ago: "The principle of collective security requires that states identify their national interests so completely with the preservation of the total world order that they stand ready to join in collective action to put down any aggressive threat by any state, against any other state, anywhere" (Claude 1962, 194).

A brief review of how the UN Charter reflected the theory of collective security may shed light on how UN principles diverge from full implementation of this theory. The first paragraph of the first article of the Charter specifies that a principle purpose of the organization is "to maintain international peace and security." In order to accomplish this objective, the organization is authorized "to take effective collective measures for the prevention and removal of threats to the peace, and for the suppression of acts of aggression or other breaches of the peace, and to bring about by peaceful means, and in conformity with the principles of justice and international law, adjustment or settlement of international disputes or situations which might lead to a breach of the peace." Although the UN is prohibited (Article 1, para. 7) from intervening "in matters which are essentially within the domestic jurisdiction of any state," the same article states that "this principle shall not prejudice the application of enforcement measures under Chapter VII" of the Charter.

Chapter VII gives the UN Security Council wide-ranging authority to determine whether a threat to the peace exists and to authorize provisional measures (Article 40), sanctions (Article 41), or the use of force (Article 42) in order to deal with this threat. Members of the organization are expected to support decisions taken by the Security Council (Article 43). Some or all of them may be authorized to implement decisions of the Security Council "for the maintenance of international peace and security" (Article 48).

The Charter also outlines provisions for the establishment and operation of a Military Staff Committee (Article 47) that would "consist of the Chiefs of Staff of the permanent members of the Security Council or their representatives." The purpose of the Military Staff Committee was "to advise and assist the Security Council on all questions relating to the Security Council's military requirements for the maintenance of international peace and security, the employment and command of forces placed at its disposal, the regulation of armaments, and possible disarmament." In order to enable the UN to respond reasonably quickly to threats to the peace, Article 45 calls for member states to "hold immediately available national air-force contingents for combined international enforcement action." All of these provisions were made with the understanding that any of the permanent members could veto any action to be taken under Chapter VII. Thus, the UN version of collective security did not envisage that "collective action [would be used] to put down any aggressive threat by any state, against any other state, anywhere." Rather, "the veto provision was adopted with full awareness, and deliberate intent, that any of the major powers might use it to block collective action. Its insertion represented a declaration that the United Nations would not be drawn into any attempt—presumably foredoomed to futility and disaster—to implement the collective security principle in opposition to a great power" (Claude 1962, 159).

As a result of the veto or threat of the veto, the UN did nothing to restrain the Soviet Union when it invaded Hungary in 1956, had little or no role in ending the prolonged conflict in Vietnam between 1946 and 1975, and was inactive with regard to the conflict between China and Vietnam in 1979.

For a variety of reasons, the actual practice of the UN with regard to acting in response to threats to the peace did not fully conform to what was set out in the Charter. The Cold War, which began shortly after the United Nations was established, prevented the Military Staff Committee from doing what the Charter stipulated. The UN did not develop rapid response capabilities, and the Great Power unity assumed in 1945 was stillborn. The logic of the Cold War rather than the logic of the UN's truncated version of collective security prevailed, and the UN became a Cold War battleground. UN peacekeeping activities reflected this geopolitical reality. Furthermore, Cold War reasoning dictated that the UN be used to prevent the two superpowers from clashing on a Third World battlefield. Thus, for most of its first fifty years, "peace-keeping ... was given over primarily to the treatment of conflicts between nations [and] missions were deployed to separate antagonists, verify cease-fires, and promote accord" (Annan 1996, 175–176). Also, it is important to understand that "UN peacekeeping forces, in the form in which they have emerged, were not even envisaged in the UN Charter. As observer, interposition, or buffer forces, they simply grew in response to numerous crises within and between states" (Howard 1994, 77).

The UN engaged in several peacekeeping operations during the Cold War period. Between 1948, when the United Nations Truce Supervision Organization (UNTSO) was created to deal with the aftermath of the first Arab-Israeli war, and 1989, when the United Nations Observer Group in

Central America (ONUCA) was established, a total of eighteen UN peace-keeping or observer forces were deployed. In many ways, the most notable of UN operations in the first two decades of its history were those in Korea and the Congo. However, neither fit the definition of a conventional UN peacekeeping activity. The UN operation in Korea from 1950 to 1953 "is not generally regarded as a peacekeeping or observer force, especially as it was under national (American) rather than UN command, was not based on the consent of the parties to the conflict, and was fully engaged in active combat operations" (Roberts and Kingsbury 1994, 541).

Another aspect of the UN operation in Korea was that the Uniting for Peace Resolution, in which the General Assembly authorized UN action, was used for the first time. Security Council Resolution 84 first authorized the operation on July 7, 1950. However, authorization was possible only because the Soviet Union was boycotting the session in which the vote was taken. Once they returned to the sessions, the Soviets used their veto to block further UN action in Korea. The United States then resorted to the innovative idea of seeking General Assembly authorization to give legal color to its activity in Korea. The move succeeded, but the USSR refused to pay any of the costs associated with this operation.[1]

The UN Operation in the Congo (ONUC) began in 1960 soon after Belgian forces left the new state after granting it independence. Civil war followed independence. ONUC ended in 1964, when the civil war ended and some semblance of order was established. Although this was an intrastate rather than an interstate conflict, several major powers also became involved, at least indirectly, by providing support for one or more of the factions in the struggle. The UN became a partisan in the civil war after the death, apparently accidental, of the secretary-general, Dag Hammarskjold, in September 1961. Thus, although called a peacekeeping operation, ONUC became in actuality a peace enforcement operation. As such, it became enormously controversial. The UN did preserve the territorial integrity of the new state but it paid a high price. Countries that did not agree with what the organization and its dynamic Secretary-General were doing refused to pay for ONUC's activities, and the UN teetered on the edge of bankruptcy. In 1965, a deal was struck that returned the UN to solvency, thus permitting the organization to continue to function. It did so, however, on the understanding that it would stick to peacekeeping and refrain from peacemaking, and that all future peacekeeping operations would be authorized by the Security Council, not by the General Assembly (Howard 1994, 63–69; Morphet 1994, 197–200).

The propensity of the Security Council to authorize peacekeeping and other deployments escalated in the wake of the Cold War. Between 1990 and 1993, the Security Council authorized eleven UN peacekeeping or observer forces (Roberts and Kingsbury 1994, 538–542). More important, the type of event that goaded UN peacekeeping in the 1990s was often quite different from the kinds of threats to the peace that had roused UN action up to that time. Some of the most serious of these situations involved violence *within* rather than *between* states (such as in Somalia and Cambodia); others were occasioned by the disintegration of a state (such as Yugoslavia). As was the case in the Congo, crises such as these carried the potential for spilling over borders or for producing large numbers of refugees. They also shared with the Congo operation the potential for controversy and failure. Indeed, a critic of UN peacekeeping activities has argued that these programs were seldom, if ever, able to *resolve* conflicts and that the UN may be better suited to contribute to the peace *after* the basic conflict has been resolved (Diehl 1993, 98–106).

The situations in such places as Somalia and Yugoslavia to which UN peacekeepers were sent were correctly identified as threats to the peace, but it must be admitted that the threat in these cases differed from the clear act of aggression by Iraq against Kuwait that occasioned Security Council Resolution 678 (of November 29, 1990). This resolution authorized states to use "all necessary means" to free Kuwait and was cited as legal authority by the United States and its allies in the Gulf War of 1991. Like the UN operation in Korea, this was not a traditional UN peacekeeping or observer operation.[2] The allied forces that attacked Iraq were nominally under a joint command, but the operation was dominated, as in Korea, by the United States. Thus, it was not a UN force that liberated Kuwait, although multilateral diplomacy and UN resolutions were essential prerequisites to the multilateral military action that took place. Strictly speaking, the United Nations did not *act* in the Gulf War (Matthews 1993, 69–90). However, it did serve as the forum for much of the diplomacy related to the conflict, and it continued to do so for several years after the Gulf War ended.

The record of the United Nations in responding to threats to the peace has been uneven. However, the organization has acted to deal with such threats, or has been the forum for diplomacy on behalf of peace, on several occasions. In doing so, it has become a part of the institutional structure for dealing with international crises and threats to the peace.

An international crisis can be thought of in a number of different ways. One commonsense notion of an international crisis is that it represents a situation that threatens the vital interests of certain states; another is that it indicates an unanticipated event; a third concept of such a crisis is that it is a situation that is "out of control" or that could easily get out of control. Authorities on the subject of international crises note that these events are marked by unpredictability and high stakes (Schelling 1966, 97). The record suggests that the United Nations is most effective when it addresses crisis situations in which the interests of its leading members are at stake *and* when those interests are complementary rather than directly competitive. Historically, the UN has not been good at anticipating and thus preempting crisis situations. What the UN has often been asked to do, however, is to deal with conflicts that were already out of control. High stakes for states, individuals, and the institutions of civil society have certainly characterized the crises in Somalia, Cambodia, and the former Yugoslavia. "Success" in such situations is hard to define, let alone produce, as no outcome is likely to fully satisfy all interested parties to the dispute. Some degree of "failure," therefore, is virtually inevitable. Thus, the United Nations has often been blamed for failing to solve a problem that has no easy solution, perhaps no solution at all. This is like criticizing a physician for failing to heal a person who has only been brought to the hospital after he has already died.

In UN parlance, before the organization may take action, a crisis must be declared to be a "threat to the peace." The UN's procedures for engaging in an international crisis require that its operations be authorized by the Security Council.[3] In order for this to happen, the problem of the veto must be overcome: The five permanent members must either vote in favor of the authorizing resolution or abstain. The members of the UN, in particular the five permanent members of the Security Council, may decide that the United Nations is not the best forum for dealing with a particular crisis. For reasons of national interest, or because of the constraints of domestic politics in their home countries, one or more of the permanent members may conclude that unilateral action or even doing nothing is preferable to getting the UN involved.

The veto power of five states colors the politics of the Security Council and overshadows everything it does. Another all-encompassing issue is financing: Peacekeeping must not only be authorized, but it must also be paid for, and the diplomatic processes surrounding this aspect of UN operations are as vital as they are intricate. Also, peacekeeping operations must be staffed as well as financed, and all this requires an attention to detail that many diplomats lack. In addition, traditional peacekeeping requires the consent of the parties to the conflict, and securing such consent is often a daunting diplomatic task. Each of these substantive issues contributes to making the process of organizing UN peacekeeping missions unique in the annals of contemporary diplomacy. Finally, the UN Secretary-General plays a special role in crisis situations, adding a personal element to this complex process (De Cuéllar 1996, 122–142).

Several concepts are crucial to understanding UN peacekeeping and crisis management:

Peacekeeping occurs when the UN provides forces to monitor a cease-fire and to deploy between the contesting forces, separating them and thus reducing the risk of renewed engagement. Traditional UN peacekeeping requires that UN personnel be impartial and that UN troops not use force; the consent of the parties to the dispute is essential. Although the presence of a UN peacekeeping or observer operation may afford diplomats the opportunity to work out a permanent settlement to the dispute, many UN peacekeeping operations have been long-term activities, reflecting diplomatic stalemates. The first two UN operations, in the Middle East and in Kashmir, have been functioning since the late 1940s. Other long-term UN operations include those in Cyprus (since 1964) and the Golan Heights (since 1974).

Preventive diplomacy involves efforts to deal with potential conflict situations before they explode into crises. This can include programs to manage the underlying causes of a conflict (such as poverty) or mediation to resolve a dispute before it escalates. One of the most important ways the UN engages in this type of activity is through the "good offices" of UN personnel, especially the Secretary-General (Franck and Nolte 1994).

Peace enforcement is a complex process that attempts to create a peaceful situation rather than simply monitor a cease-fire as in a traditional UN peacekeeping operation. Coercion, in the form of military action, may be used to force a cease-fire. In this type of program, the UN is clearly a party to the conflict (as it was in Haiti and the Congo), and a military commander is in charge of the operation.

Humanitarian intervention operations are intended to alleviate the often terrible conditions that prevail in countries or regions characterized by ongoing violence and/or chaos stemming from the virtual collapse of authority. Examples include the first phase of UN activity in Somalia and the UN Protection Force (UNPROFOR) operations in Bosnia in 1992–1993.

Multidimensional peace operations are distinguished by having civilian officers rather than military personnel at the helm; they aim to settle internal conflicts (Durch 1996, 3–4 and 23–25). Examples include UN activity in Cambodia and some UN programs in Bosnia.

Peacekeeping and preventive diplomacy are largely traditional UN activities, whereas peace enforcement, humanitarian intervention, and multidimensional peace operations, which may include elements of all of these categories, are innovations of more recent times and have been prevalent especially in the wake of the Cold War.

In his essay later in this chapter, I. William Zartman discusses the vital issue of timely intervention in conflict situations to prevent them from becoming unmanageable crises. His basic argument is that preventive diplomacy can be an especially effective tool of multilateral diplomacy. As he states, we now live in a world in which "external intervention is required when populations need protection from their own rulers and from each other." He identifies the United Nations as the most appropriate locus for arranging such interventions.

Although military intervention is what most people think of in this regard, Zartman stresses the merits of such nonmilitary action as mediation
and convocation, "an extended form of mediation" in which all essential
actors in a dispute are brought together to address and hopefully resolve
the core elements of the dispute. As he correctly demonstrates, the United
Nations has unique capabilities and "enormous potential" for organizing
nonmilitary intervention, an avenue that could and should be put to much
better use by states and the United Nations than has been the case in the
past. In this regard, Zartman's views are similar to those of former UN Secretary-General Javier Pe'rez De Cuéllar, who argued that the UN could be
much more effective if conflict situations were not brought before the organization "too late for the Council to have any serious influence on their development" (De Cuéllar 1988, 181). We must learn to treat the patient
before the illness becomes fatal (Cahill 1996). The potential rewards of preventive diplomacy, like those of preventive medicine, are enormous. In this
era of increased globalization, a crisis anywhere may become a crisis everywhere, and a crisis prevented is a calamity avoided.

In his essay in this chapter, Ambassador Juan Somavia, former permanent representative of Chile to the United Nations and currently the director-general of the International Labor Organization, is concerned with the
way the United Nations deals with the kinds of threats to the peace that
seem to characterize the post–Cold War world. His special focus is on the
humanitarian dimensions of actions authorized by the Security Council. As
he notes, many UN actions in recent years have had major civilian aspects,
and workers associated with nongovernmental organizations (NGOs) were
sometimes more numerous in these activities than military personnel. Humanitarian intervention operations as well as multidimensional peace operations have become more the norm than the exception, and they require
new rules if they are to succeed. Also, sanctions are used more frequently,
often with deleterious consequences for the civilian population of the sanctioned country without having the desired effect on the behavior of the
leaders whose actions first occasioned the sanctions.

Ambassador Somavia's essay itemizes several suggestions for innovative
and forward-looking guidelines for the Security Council to follow *before*
authorizing such operations. These rules, if implemented, would require
that consideration of the humanitarian consequences of such actions be
paramount. Whereas the concept of preventive diplomacy is as old as the
UN Charter, Ambassador Somavia's proposals would take the UN and its
members into uncharted territory.

His essay implies that, in the post–Cold War era, the standard tools of
traditional diplomacy and geopolitics may not be effective in dealing with
threats to the peace and with crisis situations. He is not alone in this regard.

In response to this realization, the UN has expanded its existing structures and developed new methods for preparing the United Nations to do a better job of organizing and supervising its efforts to deal effectively with threats to the peace. For example, the Department of Peacekeeping Operations (DPKO) was created to deal specifically with peacekeeping, and it grew rapidly in the early 1990s. In 1993, Kofi Annan, in his capacity as under secretary-general of peacekeeping operations, created the UN Situation Center, giving the UN the capacity to monitor and support its peacekeeping operations around the clock. Furthermore, the Office for Research and Collection of Information (ORCI) was created to give the UN an independent ability to collect and evaluate data relevant to possible conflict situations around the world. The Situation Center has survived, but the DPKO's resources have declined considerably as the financial crisis at the UN has worsened. The ORCI was a victim of the budget crisis of the mid-1990s, and its reduced functions were transferred to the Department of Political Affairs.

In many crucial ways, the first several decades of the United Nations were marked by threats to the peace substantially different from those envisaged in San Francisco in 1945. With the end of the Cold War nearly a decade behind us, we have the luxury of not necessarily being blinded by hindsight. Can we reform the UN by looking forward rather than backward? Can we think about the kinds of crises the organization will have to respond to in the future and reorganize the Security Council accordingly? Or are we still prisoners of the ideas prevalent in 1945, particularly as they pertain to the role of multilateral diplomacy in the management of international crises?

The United Nations is in need of reform, and its ability to make the world a more peaceful place needs to be improved. The organization is a force for peace and not for war, and a stronger UN is likely to lead to a more peaceful and secure world (Doyle 1996, 54–86). As the world's principal venue for multilateral diplomacy, the United Nations can help states and people deal with threats to the peace, which will very likely continue to plague the planet. In order to ensure the UN's continuing role in this regard, its peacekeeping and peacemaking capacities will have to be strengthened. Not all threats to the peace have been brought to the attention of the United Nations in the past, and, as Zartman implies, not all should be in the future. However, in some cases, the UN is the only realistic avenue of conflict resolution. This is particularly true with regard to Africa, where ethnic and other tensions have sometimes erupted into unchecked genocidal violence. More emphasis should be placed on preventive diplomacy and on doing a much better job of managing humanitarian intervention and multidimensional peace operations. The UN needs adequate financing; it needs to be provided with the ability to monitor global trends so that it can anticipate (and thus possibly prevent) conflicts that could escalate into genuine threats to the peace; and it needs to be able to respond to peace-threatening events quickly.

In his 1997 report to the General Assembly, Secretary-General Kofi Annan proposed similar ideas to the member states (Annan 1997). A leading authority on UN peacekeeping has once again brought forward the suggestion inherent in the Charter that the UN needs a permanent force available for rapid deployment in order that UN intervention may be accomplished in a more timely fashion (Diehl 1993, 108–119). Furthermore, an eminent international lawyer has pointed out that the UN could be strengthened in a number of ways without revision of the Charter (Sohn 1997). It is not clear how these and other suggestions for improving the UN will fare in the global political arena. It is certain, however, that if the United Nations is not strengthened, genuine threats to world peace will fester and worsen because the organization will not have the resources necessary to enable it to respond rapidly and effectively. Although that result may please some ideologues opposed in principle to viable multilateral organizations, it will be to the detriment of humankind everywhere.

Some states may seek to reform the UN. Others may prefer to simply avoid it whenever possible. Not all states and statesmen prefer multilateral action to deal with crisis situations. Some leaders have a strong ideological preference for unilateral action, preferably of a military nature, whenever the interests of the state are threatened, and they doubt the wisdom of acting under the constraint of the need to seek UN authorization before acting. This is a particularly appealing stance for global (or regional) hegemons who have dominated diplomacy in the early years of the twenty-first century.

It is easy to argue that the United Nations is a necessity and that even a country as strong as the United States needs the United Nations in order to achieve its security and other vital objectives (Albright 2003; Tharoor 2003). If one follows this line of reasoning then it is easy to see that UN reform would strengthen the UN and therefore would also serve the interests of even its most powerful members. However, not all American leaders succumb to the logic of this argument. Some prefer to believe that the United States, as the sole surviving superpower, can and should act unilaterally or, at most, in a tight coalition it completely controls. This ideological preference for Unilateralism, as distinct from a pragmatic decision to act alone only in special and unusual circumstances, has profound consequences for the nature of global politics and the prospects for multilateral diplomacy in the early years of the twenty-first century. This theme will be developed further in the concluding chapter of this book.

Notes

1. The Uniting for Peace Resolution was also used in 1956 to create the first UN Emergency Force (UNEF 1), the peacekeeping force that served in Egypt after the Suez crisis. States that did not support this move refused to pay their share of the costs as determined by the UN General Assembly.

2. A useful source of information and documents related to the 1990–1991 Gulf War is Micah L. Sifry and Christopher Cerf, eds., *The Gulf War Reader: History, Documents, Opinions* (New York: Random House, 1991).

3. Although it is possible that the General Assembly could authorize action via a Uniting for Peace Resolution, this is exceptionally unlikely given political realities.

References

Albright, Madeleine. (2003) "United Nations," *Foreign Policy*, No. 138, September-October, pp. 16–24.

Annan, Kofi A. (1996) "The Peace-Keeping Prescription," in *Preventive Diplomacy: Stopping Wars Before They Start*, edited by Kevin M. Cahill (New York: Basic Books), pp. 174–190.

_____. (1997) "Renewing the United Nations: A Programme for Reform." UN Document A/51/950.

Boutros-Ghali, Boutros. (1995) *An Agenda for Peace* (New York: United Nations).

Cahill, Kevin M. (1996) *Preventive Diplomacy: Stopping Wars Before They Start* (New York: Basic Books).

Claude, Inis L., Jr. (1962) *Power and International Relations*. (New York: Random House).

De Cuéllar, Javier Pe'rez. (1988) "The United Nations and World Politics" in *The Global Agenda: Issues and Perspectives*, 2nd ed., edited by Charles W. Kegley, Jr., and Eugene R. Wittkopf (New York: Random House), pp. 178–185.

_____. (1996) "The Role of the UN Secretary-General," in *United Nations, Divided World: The UN's Role in International Relations*, edited by Adam Roberts and Benedict Kingsbury (Oxford: Oxford University Press), pp. 125–142.

Diehl, Paul F. (1993) *International Peacekeeping*. (Baltimore and London: Johns Hopkins University Press).

Doyle, Michael W. (1996) "Managing Global Security: The United Nations Not a War Maker, a Peace Maker," in *U.S. Foreign Policy and the United Nations System*, edited by Charles William Maynes and Richard S. Williamson (New York: W. W. Norton), pp. 54–86.

Durch, William J., ed. (1996) *UN Peacekeeping, American Politics, and the Uncivil Wars of the 1990s*. (New York: St. Martin's Press).

Franck, Thomas M. and Georg Nolte. (1994) "The Good Offices Function of the UN Secretary-General," in *United Nations, Divided World: The UN's Role in International Relations*, edited by Adam Roberts and Benedict Kingsbury (Oxford: Oxford University Press), pp. 63–80.

Howard, Michael. (1994) "The Historical Development of the UN's Role in International Security," in *United Nations, Divided World: The UN's Role in International Relations*, edited by Adam Roberts and Benedict Kingsbury (Oxford: Oxford University Press), pp. 63–80.

Matthews, Ken. (1993) *The Gulf Conflict and International Relations* (London and New York: Routledge).

Morphet, Sally. (1994) "UN Peacekeeping and Election-Monitoring," in *United Nations, Divided World: The UN's Role in International Relations*, edited By Adam Roberts and Benedict Kingsbury (Oxford: Oxford University Press), pp. 63–80.

Princen, Thomas. (1992) *Intermediaries in International Conflict.* (Princeton: Princeton University Press).

Roberts, Adam and Benedict Kingsbury, eds. (1994) *United Nations, Divided World: The UN's Role in International Relations* (Oxford: Oxford University Press).

Schelling, Thomas C. (1966) *Arms and Influence* (New Haven: Yale University Press).

Sifry, Micah L. and Christopher Cerf, eds. (1991) *The Gulf War Reader: History, Documents, Opinions.* (New York: Random House).

Sohn, Louis B. (1997) "Important Improvements in the Functioning of the Principal Organs of the United Nations That Can Be Made Without Charter Revision," *American Journal of International Law,* Vol. 91, No. 4, October, pp. 652–696.

Tharoor, Shashi. (2003) "Why America Still Needs the United Nations," *Foreign Affairs,* Vol. 82, No. 5, September-October, pp. 67–80.

THE HUMANITARIAN
RESPONSIBILITIES OF THE
UN SECURITY COUNCIL

Ensuring the Security of People

Ambassador Juan Somavia[1]

T he question of the humanitarian responsibilities of the UN Security
Council is a natural follow-up to the 1997 World Summit on Social
Development. It also represents an important and new focus of the Security Council for the post–Cold War United Nations. We are once again
addressing the challenge of putting people at the center of development
and international cooperation, this time in a different sphere of action
within the United Nations. In addition, the work that humanitarian
NGOs do is very much part and parcel of social advancement. Humanitarian tasks and development objectives are continually crisscrossing and
reinforcing each other. They are not sequential but are different dimensions of an integrated understanding of how to promote the security of
people.

Framework Definitions and Key Issues

The United Nations Charter confers on the Security Council primary responsibility for the maintenance of international peace and security. Until recently, this has been understood basically to mean resolving disputes among states with international consequences. That was the original intention of the Charter. Yet these two bedrock concepts—peace and security, the very conceptual foundations for the organization's mission—are undergoing a radical change of perception today. Peace, we agree by now, is much more than the mere absence of war. Peace has come to mean more than harmony among nations; it also means harmony within nations. Countries that are not actively "at war" with other countries are not necessarily at peace with themselves. In an era when individual people and communities struggle to hold their own against seemingly insuperable odds, peace increasingly means the absence of threats and discriminations. It means freedom from fear and want. For people everywhere, the heart of peace is peace within our own hearts, within our families, our schools, our workplaces, our communities. Peace has acquired a human and community dimension much greater than the original state-centered notion of the UN Charter, and we have learned that its absence at the local and national level can have multiple international implications.

The concept of security, in turn, is also evolving. Today, it means inclusion, cohesion, and integration—a sense of belonging to a society and a prevailing order within and among nations predicated on fairness and respect for differences and human dignity. The only legitimate (and lasting) security is security rooted in the well-being of people. We have all observed that you can have a secure state—in the traditional sense—full of insecure people facing poverty, destitution, and different dangers to their integrity. The security of people has thus emerged as a complementary and distinct notion from that of the security of the state.

Another important evolution has been the growing presence in the Security Council agenda of internal conflicts in which the "parties to a dispute" are not sovereign states but groups or factions within a state, sometimes even mere warlords, most of which do not represent an entity that has the attributes of a state as defined by the traditional norms of international law.

The first ten years of the Security Council's activities were marked by state conflicts arising out of Cold War situations, the initial tensions of the decolonization process, threats of external aggression, and traditional frontier disputes among countries. In all of these conflicts, the humanitarian dimension existed but was not a central feature of the dispute. In the last ten years, by contrast, the agenda of the Security Council has been filled with conflicts within states in which the humanitarian aspects of the crises are of major importance. The examples are too numerous to mention, but they include conflicts in Namibia, Cambodia, El Salvador, Guatemala, Afghanistan, Georgia, Angola, Mozambique, Liberia—and also Somalia, Rwanda, Burundi, and the former Yugoslavia. In these conflicts, it is civilians (unarmed and unprotected) who are the principal victims of civil strife. During World War I, 5 percent of all casualties were civilians; in Cambodia and Rwanda, almost 95 percent were.

Furthermore, it is understood that the Security Council is to operate under the aegis of the basic principles of international law, a central tenet of which is noninterference in the internal affairs of states. Yet, if the Council is to be effective in promoting solutions and agreements to end these conflicts, it inevitably ends up knee-deep in the internal affairs of that particular society. Moreover, if the humanitarian crisis is serious enough, there are, understandably, strong reactions from public opinion asking the Council to "do something" to stop the death and destruction. Over the past years, the Security Council has repeatedly been told, "Look at the horrible tragedies that are going on in the world. Do something about them!" But the entire tradition of diplomacy leads elsewhere. It is difficult to apply classical diplomacy to these new conflicts.

The evolution of the concepts of peace and security—against the backdrop of mainly internal conflicts with strong humanitarian dimensions and an international public opinion demanding action—raises new issues in which the Council must reexamine the appropriateness and effectiveness of the available instruments and traditional diplomatic courses of action. Under such conditions, a stronger link must evolve between the United Nations, the Security Council, and organizations like Oxfam—which are on the ground, doing humanitarian work, which are touching those societies, looking into the eyes of the people in danger, learning who they are and what is going on and who the factions are and what relations people have with their leaders. Much of this kind of information never gets to the table of the Security Council.

A Window Toward Civil Society

Some initial conclusions can be drawn with respect to the work of the Council. Maintaining peace and security must also take into consideration the underlying causes of conflict, which are often development-related, as well as expressions of obvious power struggles among leaders and factions. The nature of preventive diplomacy, conflict resolution, peacemaking, and peace building, however, is still too state-centric. Together, governments and civil society must evolve a more dynamic concept and praxis within which nongovernmental actors play a key role. The notion of what some of us call *preventive development* is crucial: Conflicts very often have development origins but are too often dealt with as if they were exclusively political problems. We need to link analysis of the development causes to the actual political processes under way. We can also build upon the lessons learned from experiences of conflict-resolution efforts at the interpersonal level and within divided communities, which are sometimes more relevant than classical dispute-resolution tools.

The tendency to speak of peace and security basically in state-centric and crisis terms fails to take into the account the multiple development and humanitarian factors that undergird the security of people, or the vital need to safeguard and support individual actors in civil society whose energy and mutual confidence are essential to maintaining peace and security in the long term within those societies.

A critical feature of the 1990s has been the development of a burgeoning global civil society movement. The impact of nongovernmental actors of innumerable variety—representatives of unions, churches, voluntary groups, and grass-roots organizations—has been tremendous. Together, they have helped shape our contemporary definitions of sustainable development, population, gender, and human rights, and in their characteristically practical style they have pushed governments to develop the concrete means to translate these concepts into action. This role in socioeconomic thinking and actions is well known and generally acknowledged.

But nongovernmental actors are also centrally involved in humanitarian relief, thus helping to increase the chances of conflict resolution. The profoundly internal dimensions of contemporary crises—and the increasingly central role nongovernmental actors play in forging a culture of sustainable peace—have brought actors much closer than before to the analysis and action of international political affairs. This is happening de facto, but in my view it is insufficiently recognized by the Security Council, and consequently the experience of humanitarian organizations is being underutilized.

The Council's mandate and method of work are sufficiently broad to incorporate, in an appropriate way, inputs coming from civil society organizations within its scope of operations. However, these elements are quite narrowly interpreted—and less than flexibly applied. Indeed, given the highly sensitive nature of the Council's work, more widespread consultation and transparent decisionmaking is necessary not only to enhance accountability vis-à-vis the General Assembly, member governments, and public opinion but also to have a broader basis of information, experience, and professional advice for the Council's decisionmaking.

Given that so many nongovernmental actors are increasingly involved in assisting, safeguarding, and enhancing the security of people threatened by active conflict, it is only logical that their role be fully acknowledged and that they be enabled (safely and successfully) to carry out their specific humanitarian contribution in the field. It is thus in practical terms that I wish to evaluate the role of the Security Council, because I am convinced that it could be better organized to this end. In this connection, I wish to call attention to several provocative suggestions set forth in an excellent 1996 report prepared by the Steering Committee of the Joint Evaluation of Emergency Assistance to Rwanda entitled "The International Response to Conflict and Genocide: Lessons from the Rwandan Experience."

The report contains a number of practical suggestions, highlighting a reinvigorated role for the Department of Humanitarian Affairs as well as for regional and nongovernmental organizations, the military, judiciary, and the media—which are all well worth considering.

I would add that what the Council truly needs is an additional mechanism to raise the political profile of humanitarian coordination—to put it on par with military coordination. Let me offer a practical example: Chile and other countries have advocated that countries contributing troops be directly privy to Security Council deliberations over where and how their soldiers will be deployed in peacekeeping operations. A special provision for consultation has been approved for this purpose.

Similarly, there should be a regular "consultative window" through which to engage outside actors who have a unique and often firsthand perspective on the specificity of a given conflict and on where and how humanitarian operations can most safely and productively be executed. Such background information and exchange would enhance the decision-making capacity of the Council. In this respect, I also wish to interject a note of caution in the sense that the autonomy and independence of humanitarian work have to be safeguarded in all circumstances. Such a "window" could evolve from the present contacts with humanitarian NGOs undertaken by the Department of Humanitarian Affairs and could have an informal character.

Security of Humanitarian Relief

What protections exist amid conflict and in complex humanitarian emergencies for other members of the nongovernmental community? As stated before, with the end of the Cold War, the United Nations has become increasingly involved in conflict resolution within states in crisis. Demands upon the UN to assume a proactive role in responding to complex humanitarian emergencies have increased apace. In this context, the safety on the ground of United Nations and non-UN personnel alike has become a pressing issue.

NGO staff members have increasingly fallen victim to brutal attacks and harassment while in the field. In recent years, an Oxfam worker was killed in Angola; three Red Cross workers were murdered in Burundi. The irony is that while their loss was mourned among many in the nongovernmental community, it provoked nowhere near the response that the loss of uniformed military personnel has elicited in connection with UN peace-building operations elsewhere. Indeed, sometimes governments appear more willing to sacrifice the lives of relief workers than those of their own troops: The former serve out of the conviction that their presence builds peace; the latter have accepted participation in the dangers of conflict as part of their terms of service. Yet, it is often nonuniformed relief and development workers who are on the front lines of conflicts to which some governments are reluctant to commit their own troops.

This is quite incredible: One group are the professionals of danger—they were instructed and trained to deal with it—and for a variety of domestic political reasons, governments don't want to put them in a place of danger. The other group are in conflict zones out of conviction, out of their beliefs and values, and are prepared to face the dangers and difficulties. Yet relief and development workers operate with far fewer resources or protections and stay long after the active fighting has ceased—remaining as long as possible, until security in its fullest sense is ensured or until it is patently impossible for them to stay.

Some would argue that relief and development workers have become de facto advance teams in conflicts where a state has no real political intent or practical means to guarantee their safety—let alone achieve peace. Others allege that the political and humanitarian dimensions of complex emergencies are poorly understood and that lack of coherent situation assessment, priority setting, and field operations on the part of the international community not only lengthens the agony of people living in countries in crisis but puts at risk those trying to help them.

The Security Council itself, in light of the tragedies which have unfolded since the early 1990s in Afghanistan, Angola, Bosnia, Burundi, Georgia, Haiti, Lebanon, Liberia, Rwanda, Somalia, and elsewhere, has begun to reference explicitly in its decisions the role of nongovernmental humanitarian actors in peace-building and emergency situations. A 1996 statement on Somalia by the president of the Security Council reflects this trend: "The Security Council considers the uninterrupted delivery of humanitarian assistance to be a crucial factor in the overall security and stability of Somalia" (UN Document S/PRST/1996/4). I consider this statement a very significant political recognition of the role that humanitarian agencies are playing in conflict situations.

Humanitarian concerns have indeed become central to the calculus of whether and how the UN's continued (official) presence in a country can advance the peace-building process. Statements on Liberia by the Security Council president have been equally direct, noting that, as of early April 1996, "factional fighting, the harassment and abuse of the civilian population and humanitarian and relief workers" had increased to the point where the country's political leaders "risk[ed] losing the support of the international community" (UN Document S/PRST/1996/16).

The challenge is to develop a series of interlocking legal and logistical safeguards—shored up by the international political will to enforce them and implemented through a coherent UN system that functions in tandem with regional, national, and local institutions. The ultimate responsibility for peace, however, rests with those in power in a country in crisis. I deliberately avoid the use of the word *government* for in many conflicts, those in power have not necessarily been elected, and they often do not conduct themselves with any sense of civic obligation toward majority rule or display the capacity to govern effectively. Their claim to legitimacy often rests on nothing more than having gained physical control of the capital city and seat of government through force. Pressure can nonetheless be brought to bear upon those in power—pressure not only to resolve a conflict but to respect the humanity of individuals engaged in building the foundations of a sustainable peace, whether formally in partnership with the United Nations or independent of it.

I also believe the Council should consider, in particular, the compelling issue of strengthened legal provisions for protection of humanitarian workers. This is an extremely complex issue, but we know that law is only as vigorous as its application. We must address the challenges of implementing international humanitarian law. It could be argued that discourse on this subject has occupied policymakers and academics for the better part of the past century; however, I raise the issue because of the compelling nature—indeed, the urgency—of the subject, given the proliferation of highly complex conflicts in which the principal disputants appear increasingly dismissive of these fundamental anchors of global order. Given, too, the multiplicity of agents involved in relief work, we must find new ways to strengthen the legal safeguards available.

There is a gap in international law today, where nongovernmental workers are acting more-or-less autonomously in a conflict situation, unprotected. At present, a UN convention safeguards those who perform humanitarian work done in agreement with and under the aegis of the framework of the United Nations—but no one else. Humanitarian NGOs could lead others in civil society to press for the creation of a separate convention that explicitly protects nongovernmental personnel and others in civil society affiliated with UN relief efforts—whether or not they fall directly under the umbrella of UN control.

I believe we should explore what kinds of protections and enforcement should be guaranteed by such a convention. Who would adjudicate it? And how could reporting and related enforcement be expeditiously and effectively ensured? What can be done to strengthen the mechanisms for the implementation of international humanitarian law? Signatory states are enjoined, under the Geneva Conventions, to respect core provisions concerning the protection of the sick and wounded, prisoners of war, and civilians. Through a mix of injunctions and prohibitions on contracting parties, the Geneva Conventions seek to protect "undefended localities" from attack, at the same time forbidding murder, torture, collective punishment, and hostage taking, all of which are woefully common in contemporary conflict.

However, as pointed out in Oxfam's September 1995 position paper prepared on the occasion of the UN's fiftieth anniversary (provocatively entitled "A Failed Opportunity?"), "international humanitarian law, including the Geneva Conventions, [is] upheld in very few modern conflicts. . . . The debate about addressing the problem concentrates more on limiting the rights of states, rather than seeking to enforce the rights of individuals." This is a very apt assessment.

The fact that sanctions on states in breach of the conventions are extremely problematic has led some to suggest that individual reprisals are preferable. The tribunals established to address war crimes in the former Yugoslavia and genocide in Rwanda offer a useful example of mechanisms for punishing individuals who violate the rules of international humanitarian law. It is encouraging to recognize that people in societies throughout the world are saying, "Enough—an end to impunity." Think about the difference in our collective consciousness from the days of Pol Pot—and the murder of millions in Cambodia, where there were no tribunals—to our efforts today.

However, the operative (and financial) challenges faced by these tribunals is sobering. And even if an individual approach is pursued, there are blank spots in the Geneva Conventions; for example, they do not cover "gender crimes," like mass rape as a method of torture and intimidation. Herein, states can and must exercise their responsibility to ensure that humanitarian law is respected and rights fulfilled. The difficulty in bringing to justice the Bosnian Serb leaders Radovan Karadzic and Ratko Mladic, together with less visible Croatian and Bosnian Muslim personnel indicted, is a clear example—a painful reminder—of the separation between the notion that becomes law and the capacity to make the law become reality.

Above all, the importance of international NGO contributions to humanitarian efforts cannot and should not be allowed to substitute for political will on the part of governments. Neither reforms in the organization of the Security Council and its consultative mechanisms nor the creation of additional juridical protections for humanitarian workers can substitute for what governments and governments alone can do.

Governments have the political responsibility to use their political clout, military capability, financial resources, and diplomatic capacity to help solve these conflicts. The increasing role of humanitarian agencies is no excuse for the inaction of governments. Highlighting the role of NGOs should serve to reinforce the responsibility of governments in solving conflicts.

Making Sanctions More Humane and Effective

Refugees and displaced persons; famines and shortages of food and water; prisoners of war and combatants missing in action; human rights violations; genocide and gross breaches of international humanitarian law; the effects of economic sanctions—these are among the central humanitarian consequences of conflict. With limitations, there are existing international mechanisms to address some of these consequences, among them the office of the UN High Commissioner on Refugees, the World Food Program, the Geneva Conventions, the human rights mechanisms of the UN system, the international criminal tribunals for the former Yugoslavia and Rwanda, and the commission of inquiry for Burundi.

By contrast, economic sanctions are a rough, blunt, and extremely unsophisticated measure. We need to develop policies and instruments to make sanctions more humane and at the same time more effective. Both the underlying concepts and the implementation mechanisms need to be reviewed, taking into account the fact that in some instances (such as in South Africa and Burundi) some of the local and regional actors themselves felt that sanctions were necessary.

Let me note at the outset that I am not asserting sanctions are a priori illegitimate. On the contrary, at the foundation of every national legal system is the notion that breaking the law comes with a sanction. So it should be for the international system. There is no quarrel on the principle; that is why the Security Council has the authority to apply sanctions. The problem lies in the effects of the practical application of these measures.

A close reading of the UN Charter reveals that sanctions essentially aim to condition the behavior of a state that poses a threat to international peace and security—not to punish or otherwise exact retribution from the state, and even less to contribute to a humanitarian crisis in the nation affected.

Sanctions must be based on fundamental respect for human dignity. Indeed, the aim is to bring a state that has violated justice into good working relations within the community of nations, to cite one thoughtful interpretation of the issue.

Chapter VII of the Charter thus empowers the Security Council to use both military and nonmilitary measures to maintain or restore international peace and security. Article 41 outlines the nature of nonmilitary sanctions—specifying that the Security Council may call upon the member states of the United Nations to apply "complete or partial interruption of economic relations and of rail, sea, air, postal, telegraphic, radio and other means of communications, and the severance of diplomatic relations" in order to give effect to the Council's decisions.

Yet the conceptual basis for sanctions is itself flawed in that sanctions are premised on implicitly democratic assumptions but are normally leveraged upon authoritarian regimes. It is assumed that the people in a targeted country who will first feel the negative impact of sanctions are sufficiently empowered to pressure the government to cease the aggression or offense that triggered the sanctions. This is not often the case in an undemocratic setting. Moreover, Johan Galtung and others have argued that sanctions can disempower and weaken a regime's opponents by offering the regime a common external enemy against which to rally collective opposition—thereby distracting attention from domestic problems.

Sanctions normally fail to affect the lives of the leaders of such regimes, instead hitting the target country's most vulnerable citizens hardest of all; in this sense, sanctions are highly disproportional. Although humanitarian exceptions can be made to allow the targeted country to receive or purchase medical or food supplies, for example, there are no set guidelines for regulating when and how humanitarian assistance is to be provided.

Iraq is a good case in point. In 1991, after the First Gulf War, the Security Council applied wide-ranging sanctions. Although the action included a humanitarian exception, a trade embargo was imposed at the same time. Iraq's means of making use of the exception became strongly limited, and it did not give priority to food and medicine in allocating the internal resources at its disposal. When data gathered by the Food and Agricultural Organization, the World Health Organization, and the United Nations Children's Fund (UNICEF), and private organizations began to reveal the terrible humanitarian consequences that ensued, the Security Council approved in 1995 the now well-known Resolution 986, which permitted the sale of oil for food and medicine. In 1996, an agreement was reached between the Secretary-General and the government of Iraq to implement this resolution.

This situation begs the obvious question: Did the Security Council have to wait until 1995 and Iraq postpone its response until 1996 to alleviate the suffering of the more destitute among the Iraqi people? Shouldn't the oil-for-food-and-medicine agreement have been a part of the initial sanctions resolution? Were all the deaths and infirmities necessary? What political purpose of the international community was served by them?

Furthermore, practice has shown that the targeted government will generally prefer to use the scarce resources available to prop up its own power through military spending and disbursements to the elites and the groups and factions that provide it with political support. The well-being of the general population (which, under authoritarian conditions, has little ability to react) has not proven to be a priority. Iraq is a textbook case. So is Yugoslavia (Serbia and Montenegro), which chose to use existing resources to wage regional wars and support its regime and its Serb allies in Bosnia and Croatia while downplaying the humanitarian impact of sanctions so as to avoid international pressure and scrutiny on the issue.

Ultimately, sanctions as currently applied produce large-scale human insecurity, the opposite of their intended effect. The Security Council needs to address the issue promptly. The principal objective would be to make sanctions regimes both more effective and more humane. Some ideas follow on practical ways of doing so.

As a first step, the Council should adopt a resolution approving a set of humanitarian standards and practices applicable to any sanctions regime to be established in the future. Such guidelines should acknowledge that humanitarian requirements may differ according to the stage of development, geography, natural resources, and other features of the affected society.

A clear position by the Council would have a number of advantages. It would avoid humanitarian double standards and would represent a practical response to a very real problem. The Council's position should be flexible enough to encompass different realities; its end result would be to ensure that the Council would act in such way as to avoid the potential humanitarian consequences of sanctions regimes. This approach goes much further than the manner in which the General Assembly has dealt with the matter (namely, by stating that "unintended adverse side effects on the civilian population should be minimized" by making appropriate humanitarian exceptions).

It is disingenuous to talk of "unintended side effects" when everybody knows that the sector most affected by sanctions, as now applied, are precisely civilian populations. There is nothing surprising or unintended about it. That's the way economic sanctions actually operate in practice. We are all perfectly aware of that.

Security Council action could include the following elements:

1. The Council should make clear that the purpose of sanctions is to modify the behavior of any party, not only governments, that is threatening international peace and security and not to punish or

otherwise exact retribution and even less to impose humanitarian hardships on the population at large. Sanctions regimes should be commensurate with these objectives and proportionality should be a guiding criterion.

2. Sanctions should be primarily addressed to the leaders in a conflict by targeting government bosses through the military and civilian structures that support their regime(s) and by targeting the factions, groups, and warlords that are parties to a civil war type of conflict. The Council needs to shift the impact of sanctions from the general population to the leaders responsible for the conflict through, for example, measures related to bank accounts, commercial interests, stocks and properties in foreign countries, residence status, and visas.

Indeed, the broader challenge is to develop effective sanctions that wholly prevent humanitarian costs. One example is sanctions on transit rights, along with selective air and sea boycotts (except for the transport of needed humanitarian goods). Another example involves limits to representation in intergovernmental forums. Also, military cooperation agreements, including training and representation abroad, should be canceled. Yet another example involves the refusal to provide arms to sanctioned regimes—this should include the shipment of arms already sold or promised. To date, the practical effect of arms embargoes has simply been to raise the price of arms. The Council must move toward commitment on the part of arms-producing countries to significantly improve monitoring of arms transfers—in effect, to engage in rigorous self-policing.

3. A provision for humanitarian exceptions should always be included in any sanctions regime, together with the means to make it effective. No exception will work if there are no national or international resources to draw upon. The processing of requests under the exception should be much more expeditious and should contain some elements of automaticity for UN agencies, the International Red Cross, and certain well-known humanitarian NGOs. A review and evaluation of the work of the Council's sanctions committees in relation to humanitarian impacts should be undertaken. In general, methods and procedures should be expedited.

4. A regular evaluation by the Council of the potential and actual humanitarian effects of sanctions on the target country should be undertaken. Rigorous criteria must be developed for judging their impact, particularly on the most marginalized and vulnerable

members of society. The Secretary-General should make available the following:

A. Prior to the imposition of the sanctions, an appraisal of their potential humanitarian effects and suggested measures to avoid them.

B. After the entry into force of the sanctions regime, a regular evaluation of its humanitarian impact and, if negative, mechanisms for making necessary changes to alleviate this impact.

C. To carry out such assessments and/or evaluations, the assistance of concerned international and financial institutions, relevant intergovernmental and regional organizations, and NGOs should be sought. To this end, appropriate systems must be developed for regular and unimpeded monitoring, evaluation, and dissemination of related data on the humanitarian impact of sanctions. When a humanitarian crisis is about to arise within a targeted country, it is critical that the crisis be brought to the immediate attention of the Security Council and that specific corrective steps be outlined; uniformity of assessment criteria and of sanctions rulings is critical.

5. In conflict-ridden societies, it is normal that humanitarian activities are already under way before sanctions are applied. The right of the general population to bodily integrity and access to subsistence goods should not be violated. Thus, authorities of the targeted country and of the different factions and parties to the conflict must commit themselves to ensuring a continuous, impartial, and expeditious delivery of humanitarian assistance. This includes:

A. Access to the necessary information required by United Nations and nongovernmental humanitarian agencies.

B. Assurance that the day-to-day activities of relief workers will not be hampered.

C. Guarantees of the security of humanitarian personnel, as well as of their offices, homes, and operational sites.

D. Unimpeded access to conflict areas and the use of ports, airfields, roads, and other infrastructure.

6. The sanctions regime should consider strict measures to ensure compliance with the above.

7. In more general terms, sanctions regimes should have clear objectives, provisions for regular review, and precise conditions for being lifted. This could entail warning countries in clear terms that sanctions are likely to be applied in consequence of specific actions; specifying an agreed-upon time frame for evaluating the extension, modification, or lifting of the sanctions; and outlining provisions for progressive, partial, or early lifting of sanctions (including the precise steps required from the target country).

Conclusions

Even with strengthened protections on paper for humanitarian workers (in the form of conventions for their protection), and even with active involvement in measures to ensure that sanctions themselves will not become the enemy of the good, the Security Council is, in the final analysis, a tool of governments. It can play a strong humanitarian role only at their behest.

Without the political will to truly avoid conflict, or to make the hard sacrifices necessary to preserve peace and promote long-lasting security, there is little guarantee that humanitarianism will not become deeply mired in its own inherent contradictions. For much of humanitarian "relief" today appears to even its most ardent supporters to be only a Band-Aid covering the scars of years of social and economic decay that confront us with the raw reality of women, children, and the elderly alike becoming snipers' targets—along with the persons seeking to assist them. What can we do to stem the tide of brutality and impunity? How can we heal the wounds of conflict that rend even societies that appear from the outside to be "at peace"? Taking notice and calling upon our governments to make human concerns central to statecraft is the first and most important step. Only when we are truly able to ensure the security of people will the Security Council itself have succeeded in its mission.

Well beyond the Council's immediate reach are the societies of its member states—indeed, all members of the family of nations. The challenge is to find ways to animate civil society with a renewed understanding of the contemporary means to pursuing peace and security—beyond the sometimes cynical and narrow political aims of "diplomacy" as traditionally practiced.

Among the most committed people working to achieve these aims are, in fact, individuals such as Jimmy Carter, Julius Nyerere, and Oscar Arias—all of whom have actively participated in politics at the highest level, and none of whom has lost sight of the humanism that must be at the heart of humanitarianism itself. If I end these words by referring to outstanding personalities, it is because there is no substitute for the commitment of individual human beings within government and civil society who want to make a difference and who are prepared to act on the basis of values and vision rooted in the belief that human beings can ultimately find solutions to seemingly insoluble problems.

Cynics would want us to believe that there is no space for values in the globalized world of today; in the words of Oscar Wilde, such people "know the price of everything and the value of nothing." We know from historical experience that humanitarian work has always entailed swimming against the current, in a never-ending struggle to promote and protect the dignity of people. We know that we will not give in to the moral indifference of our times and that our ethical convictions and political will to act are far from being exhausted. We are many, and of sufficient passion to make our world a better place in which to live.

Note

1. The essay is adapted from an address delivered on June 26, 1996, at Oxford, England. The ambassador's views are the result of having observed for many years the work of the Security Council from the outside—and, for six months, from the inside representing Chile (which was elected to sit on that body for the period 1996-1997).

Intervening to Prevent State Collapse

The Role of the United Nations

I. William Zartman[1]

In a world scarred by state collapse and murderous internal conflict (Zartman 1995a), external actors can no longer sit by and watch, mesmerized by the blood on their television screens. They can no longer hide behind the fear of their own nation's casualties or a disclaimer of national disinterest as an excuse for inaction. External involvement is required when populations need protection from their own rulers and from each other. Between two kinds of abuses—the actual misuse of sovereignty as a cover for a state's neglect and repression of its own citizens, and the potential danger of domination of a weaker state by a stronger one through interference in internal affairs—the real danger is paramount and requires a careful and appropriate response. The place to effectuate such a response is the United Nations.

Let me be unmistakably clear from the outset of this discussion that the UN is a place before it is a thing. The United Nations is rarely a corporate actor; it is merely a locus for the action of the members of its organs. Once the UN's missions become authorized, the representatives become actors strictly constrained by their mandate, defined by the UN as a place. It is meaningless—indeed, ignorant—to criticize the United Nations for either action or inaction (although it is relevant to evaluate the procedures within the UN system for carrying out authorized mandates). UN forces are a congeries of national forces operating under the UN flag; special representatives of the Secretary-General are individuals working under limited instructions; the Security Council is a nonsovereign meeting place for sovereign states.

Nonetheless, the flag of the United Nations—the legitimizing imprimatur of the meeting place—is crucial. The United Nations is the world security institution (as regional organizations are the security institutions of their regions), and action authorized and taken in its name carries a broad responsibility, the sum of the sovereignties that have sanctioned it. The members of the United Nations and of other international security organizations operating within specific regions have taken timely action in a number of cases, have eventually but belatedly responded in others, and on occasion have missed important opportunities (Zartman 1997). There are now and there will continue to be chances to reduce the last category and to respond appropriately.

Much has been written about the military aspects of diplomacy within the UN involving peacekeeping and peace-enforcing activities under Chapters VI (and "VI 1/2") and VII.[2] Many of the most striking missed opportunities—as well as some diplomatic highlights—in the 1990s have involved occasions on which military intervention was required in order to save literally hundreds of thousands of lives. The most prominent failure was in April 1993, when the United States and others voted in the UN Security Council against augmenting UN forces in Rwanda and expanding their mandate, as requested by the Canadian general in charge of those forces, a measure that in all likelihood would have significantly diminished the magnitude of the genocide that soon occurred in the country. The focus of this discussion, however, is on the nonmilitary diplomacy that necessarily accompanies such activities, but that can also operate independently. Even without military involvement, diplomatic intervention can have and indeed has had a major impact on the management of interstate and intrastate conflict. Although there are many types of diplomatic action, I will focus on mediation and convocation.

Mediation

Mediation is appropriate when there is a limited number of clear sides and when the interests of all need to be incorporated into any agreement that ends violence and restores a functioning political system (Touval and Zartman 1985; Rubin 1981; Mitchell and Webb 1988; Bercovitch and Rubin 1992; Bercovitch 1996; Kleiboer 1997). These conditions bear elaboration. Mediated negotiations are possible only when authorized representatives of a small number of parties (preferably two) are available to meet. If the parties are many or the representatives are not clearly authorized, the mediator may first have to convince the parties to form coalitions and to designate representatives for mediation purposes; this entails involvement in internal politics, from the inside or from the outside, and seriously complicates the mediator's task. The United States at Dayton did arrange for Serbian president Slobodan Milosevic to speak on behalf of the Bosnian Serbs, but not without complications in the process of negotiation and in the subsequent implementation of the Dayton Accord.

Like any negotiation, mediation also carries with it the implication that the parties are legitimate and equal in standing (even if not in power), that they have legitimate interests to be protected, and that none of them is seeking suicide. It also implies that no party is in charge and therefore that none is able to convene a hierarchical negotiation between sovereign government and aggrieved petitioner. These were the assumptions under which Sant' Egidio (with the United States, Russia, Portugal, Italy, Zimbabwe, Kenya, and Zambia sitting by) mediated in Rome in 1990–1992 on Mozambique between Resistência Nacional Moçambicana (RENAMO) and Frente de Libertação de Moçambicana (FRELIMO), and under which the United States and the United Nations mediated in Lusaka in 1994—before that Portugal in Estoril in 1991—on Angola between Uniao Nacional para a Independência Total de Angola (UNITA) and Movimento Popular de Liberação de Angola (MPLA). Although problems of numbers and representatives did not trouble these negotiations, contests over standing and legitimacy delayed them for years.

Mediation is standard activity in interstate relations, but it is more difficult to practice when the conflict is internal than when it involves two sovereign states. Mediation in an internal conflict is resisted by the central government, since it implies that the government cannot handle its own problems; it also inevitably works to strengthen the weaker party, the rebellion, by giving it recognition and equal standing before the mediator. Indeed, the need for mediation indicates that the conflict can no longer be handled hierarchically and that the only workable resolution will be a new political system that accords the rebellion a place in legitimate politics (Zartman 1995b).

Implementing mediation is also difficult in internal conflict because such conflicts tend to take the form of cultural (ethnic, religious, even ideological) clashes over selecting an appropriate form of government, and because the rebellion often entails active terrorism as well as manifesting a broader form of passive alienation. For example, it is hard to find an appropriate mediator in the Algerian or the Sri Lankan conflict. Some French and Algerian officials have called for mediation in the war that pits state terror against Islamicist terror in Algeria, but there is little to mediate between these two extremes and there are few mediators (and certainly not France or the United Nations) that would be acceptable to both sides. The diligent efforts of Sant' Egidio in 1994–1995 brought together dispersed opposition parties to form a political middle ground where none had previously existed, but these efforts were unable to overcome Algerian nationalist resistance to bring these parties (including the Islamic Salvation Front [FIS]) together with the government. Similarly, in Sri Lanka, India was able to mediate an agreement between the central government and the separatist Tamil Tigers in 1987 but soon found itself under attack by the very Tigers it had brought into the agreement (Wriggins 1995). In such cases, it is only when the terrorists are worn out and have become fully isolated from a population alienated by their tactics that they become amenable to a return to civil politics and the conflict becomes susceptible to mediation.

When the rebellion is asked to surrender or the government is asked to depart, these purposes must be clearly specified from the beginning, because they indicate a special type of mediation not to be confused with the more typical negotiations and their assumptions. Thus, until US Ambassador Bill Richardson clarified American aims at the end of April 1997, efforts to produce mediated negotiations in South Africa between ailing Zairean dictator Mobutu Sese Seko and rebel leader Laurent Kabila hung on the assumption that both parties were legitimate players with a legitimate interest in staying in the game and that a cease-fire would lead to cooperation between two territorial regimes; consequently, neither party had any interest in the mediation, since it would serve to legitimize the other. The only mediation that made sense in the situation was one that would declare Zaire's capital, Kinshasa, an open city and secure Mobutu's departure, much as the mediation of US Assistant Secretary of State Herman Cohen in May 1991 secured the departure of Mengistu Haile Mariam and the subsequent peaceful takeover of Addis Ababa by the forces of Meles Zenawi.

These various conditions mean that a UN mediatory role is often hard to achieve, largely because of the restraints on UN interference in internal affairs and the obligation of the United Nations to deal with sovereign states. Nonetheless, through special representatives of the secretary-general (SRSGs), the United Nations has been able to provide useful mediation on occasion, as indicated by the Congolese, Zairean, and Angolan examples. SRSGs have also headed larger operations authorized under Chapter VI, involving responsibility for large-scale government transitions as in Mozambique (ONUMOZ), Cambodia (UNTAC), Namibia

(UNTAG), Western Sahara (MINURSO), and elsewhere that have required an exercise of mediation among sovereign and nonsovereign parties. In such cases, the United Nations has proven to be the only agency capable of carrying out such activities.

Convocation

Convocation of a conference of the remaining political forces in the country—an extended form of mediation—is necessary when there are many parties and a need to fill a power vacuum in the collapsing state. Although one might think that an outside state or international organization would have little legitimacy in calling a national conference of internal political forces, this form of intervention has frequently been used. States of the Arab League led by Syria convened national conferences on Lebanon in Damascus in 1976, Geneva in 1983, Lausanne in 1984, Damascus in 1985, and Taif in 1989; members of the Economic Community of West African States (ECOWAS) convened conferences of the warring parties of Liberia at Yamoussoukro in 1991, Cotonou in 1993, Geneva in 1994, and Abuja in 1995; member states of the Intergovernmental Agency on Development (IGAD) in the Horn of Africa called conferences on Somalia in Djibouti in 1991 and Addis Ababa in 1992; the president of Gabon and the special representative of the secretary-general of the Organization of African Unity (OAU) called a conference in Libreville of warring parties to the Congolese elections in 1993; the United States mediated a conference of the Bosnian parties in Dayton in 1995, acting in coordination with NATO, and of the Haitian parties in New York in 1993, acting in coordination with the Organization of American States (OAS) and the United Nations.

Convocation also involves treating the parties as equals and therefore requires the government (if there is one) to accept participation along with other political forces on an equal footing. Generally, this can be accomplished by inviting the participation of the ruling party along with other parties, rather than of the government, as in the Lebanese (1976–1985), Brazzaville Congolese (1993), Rwandan (1992), and Haitian (1992) conferences. But convocation becomes particularly useful when there is no government but rather conflicting rebel factions fighting to fill the power vacuum, as in Liberia (1991–1995) and Somalia (1991–1993), where all parties need to be assured equal access, even if not equality in results; a complication in these cases, akin to the first set of cases, occurs when one (or more) of the warring factions claim(s) government status, without recognition by the others. Equality is the key to fruitful talks in all cases.

Although some of these examples of convocation represent successful interventions, many other convocations could have occurred much earlier or could have produced better results. For instance, conferences were proposed to bring together the Yugoslav parties in 1990 and 1991, the Zairean opposition in 1997, and the Somalian factions in 1988 and earlier in 1991. Even when conferences were called, most of them broke up with incomplete results. In wearying of their own initiative, the conveners neglected a number of elements that are necessary for a successful intervention. Conveners need to regard the parties to the conflict as parties to the solution and not negotiate exclusively among their own friends or the moderates. They need to keep the convoked parties at the table until an agreement has been reached on implementing details and not let them leave when deadlock, superficial agreement, or conference fatigue sets in. They need to mediate as communicators, formulators, and even manipulators and not leave outcomes to the devices of the conflicting parties. They need to create confidence-building measures during and after the intervention to build trust and enable the parties to check on their progress as they move from conflict to reconstruction. They need to extend the agreements to cover power allocation and institutional structuring and not be satisfied merely with a ceasefire. These five elements were missing in the failed convocations and made the difference in successful ones.

The situation in Zaire at the beginning of May 1997 was crying for a national conference, and instead diplomatic activities inside and outside the United Nations were monopolized by enormous efforts to bring winner and loser together for a handshake. In the process, other vital elements of the dismembered body politic—the nonviolent opposition (Union for Democracy and Social Progress [UDPS] of Etienne Tschisekedi), and the much more pluralistic civil society, including the churches as well as business and economic interests—waited for an occasion to join in establishing the rules and institutions of a new polity. Neither the members of the UN Security Council nor of the OAU, nor South Africa, the United States, or France produced efforts in that direction, which is where the future, not the past, of the country lay. Similarly, efforts by the Nyerere initiative of East African States, where the UN members have not dared to venture, to foster the much-vaunted dialogue in Burundi have been weak; the coordinated activities behind the economic sanctions have not produced a positive intervention that seeks to build a new political atmosphere.

Entry Points

Diplomatic intervention requires an entry point, a defined moment which, if passed by, becomes a missed opportunity (Sahnoun 1994; Lyons and Samatar 1995; Maresca 1996) and, if seized, becomes an occasion for effective action. Such moments are sometimes defined by events and sometimes only by context. Elections are scheduled events that require a response, whereas massacres, riots, coups, and rebellions are unscheduled events that require a response. Thus the August 1995 shelling of Sarajevo galvanized the NATO allies into intervention in Bosnia, whereas the 1988 massacre in Northern Somalia, the 1991 and 1993 riots in Kinshasa, the 1991 coup by Raoul Cedras in Haiti, and the unconstitutional installation of a new Haitian president in May 1994 triggered no decisive action. A response in these situations could have saved countless lives and made state restoration a less overwhelming task.

Without an event, scheduled or unexpected, to provide an entry point, diplomatic intervention needs to be justified by the context. The established model indicates that a ripe moment for intervention is composed of a mutually harmful stalemate, from which parties seek or respond to efforts to extricate themselves (Touval and Zartman 1985; Zartman 1989). Such a stalemate has occasionally been seized as an opportunity for intervention, by the United States when the South African and Cuban-Angolan armies checked each other at Cuíto Carnevale in 1987 (Zartman 1989; Crocker 1992), by Portugal when MPLA and UNITA forces repeated the exercise at Mavinga in 1990 (Rothchild and Hartzell in Zartman 1995b; Knudsen and Zartman 1995), by Sant' Egidio and friends when the drought brought the Mozambican civil war between RENAMO and FRELIMO to a deadlock in 1990 (Msabaha 1995), and by the All African Council of Churches when the Anyanya and the Sudanese army bogged down in armed conflict in 1972 (Assefa 1987). Stalemates were allowed to slip away in early 1984 when the parties to the Lebanese civil war met in Lausanne under Syrian auspices but failed to move to an agreement, and in 1991 and again in 1993 when the parties to the Liberian civil war had fought to temporary standstills and met in Yamoussoukro and then Cotonou under ECOWAS auspices but failed to negotiate a complete agreement to end their war (Adibe 1997, 471–488). In these instances, the intervention failed because the convener did not invest appropriate skill and energy in follow-through once the convocation had occurred. A UN special representative of the Secretary-General was present in the Liberian mediation, but the SRSG did not coordinate effectively with other diplomatic efforts and did not become deeply involved because of a desire to let the West Africans take the lead.

More often, particularly in cases of convocation, stalemates have not been permanent; they have entailed clearly, if unequally, worsening conditions for the parties, and therefore the diplomats needed to find their own opportunities to justify their action (Zartman 1995b, 18–20 and 334–335). This was the case in the subsequent conferences convoked by various West African states in the Liberian conflict, or the 1993 Governor's Island meeting convoked by the United States on Haiti, and the unsuccessful Damascus conferences convoked by Syria in 1976 and 1985 on

Lebanon and then finally the successful Taif conference convoked by Saudi Arabia in 1989.

The outcome promised by the intervention must be attractive to the parties in and of itself, carrying the prospect of a better future if implemented, along with the assurance of a worse future if not implemented. The combination is crucial. An intervention cannot be based on simple predictions of an end to the conflict it seeks to remedy, since such predictions are usually attractive only to the powerless populations; it must be backed by threats and warnings to the targeted incumbents, who have caused and benefited from the worsening situation, and it may also have to involve promises and inducements.[3]

Promises targeting the new political system usually involve aid, reconstruction, and recognition and entail the cancellation of previously activated threats: resumption of aid, revival of recognition, or lifting of sanctions. Special incentive plans need to be devised for rulers forced to step down from power, ranging from retirement homes to amnesties, but executive buyouts may be limited by resources or the need to impose justice, so that negative sanctions may also become necessary. Warnings that an unbearable situation will continue and even worsen if the initiative is rejected lie at the heart of intervention. They are most powerful when the moment is ripe and the stalemate is mutually harmful, but as seen, stalemates are often quite soft.

That leaves the matter of threats. Every intervention should carry a threat if met by nonacceptance. Sanctions involve a gamut of measures from unilateral trade and travel restrictions to consolidated international measures. Secretary Chester Crocker's threat in Angola-Namibia, like Sant' Egidio's threat in Mozambique, was to drop the intervention and let the war continue; Secretary Holbrooke's threat in Bosnia was to allow the sanctions against Yugoslavia and the Muslim-Croat advances against the Bosnia Serbs to continue. Sanctions were used in Haiti but were only gradually applied, with large leaks, and their disastrous effects weighed more heavily on the suffering population than on the junta and the supporting elite that they sought to remove from power. In Zaire, many sanctions were in place for quite some time—aid discontinuance, travel bans, credit cutoff—although not all countries applied them; but other threats—freezing of assets, detainment of Zairean officials abroad, recognition of the opposition—were not used or implemented. Although the UN per se has only some of these instruments of threat at its disposal, it can mandate their use by its members, as it imposed embargoes on Haiti and Yugoslavia.

Conclusions

In a world scarred by state collapse and murderous internal conflict, external actors can no longer sit by and watch, wringing their hands at the savagery on their TV screens. In the current era, foreign affairs has become a macabre sort of entertainment, having lost its sense of purposive action. Many standard measures can be taken to improve deteriorating situations, short of the body-bag bugaboo. Unfortunately, the United States as a responsible intervenor is frequently late and often absent. Yet its own actions, along with those of others, in the past provide illustrations for a handbook in intervention.

Behind such actions lies a new conceptualization of sovereignty that calls for careful debate, as Secretary-General Boutros Boutros-Ghali himself took the lead in recognizing when he called current notions of sovereignty "outmoded" (Boutros-Ghali 1992; Obasanjo 1991; Deng et al. 1996; Lyons and Mastanduno 1995). Instead of protection against external involvement in internal affairs and license for the mistreatment of one's own populations, sovereignty needs to be treated as a responsibility. A sovereign state needs to be held responsible for the minimal well-being of its population and, as a baseline, for refraining from their repression. Other states, in turn, have a responsibility to help a government carry out this responsibility, lending assistance when called upon, much as they would respond to an appeal for assistance in self-defense. However, when a state does not exercise its sovereign responsibility, other states also have a sovereign duty to give the same assistance to the oppressed populations and carry out effective intervention. The doctrine of sovereignty as responsibility should be accepted as the basis for responsible diplomacy.

At the same time, the enormous potential of the United Nations deserves to be recognized and utilized. For great powers reluctant to appear as "the world's gendarme," the United Nations provides an environment for collective responsibility and multilateral safeguards that dilute unilateral exposure. For small countries wary of Great Power domination, the United Nations provides the opportunity for both participation and protection in a forum that engages small as well as large in the multilateral exercise of conflict management. The specter of the UN goblin, expressed in the United States by the caricature of fear of a UN takeover of the country and in central Africa by emotional rejection of UN peace-keeping forces, needs to be exorcised by a realistic recognition of a UN operation's capabilities and responsibilities. Such honesty begins with a distinction between with United Nations as a place, where collective and individual responsibilities are exercised, and the United Nations as a thing, with the potential to overcome problems and carry out the orders that its members give it.

Notes

1. I am grateful to the Carnegie Corporation for their support of my project on this subject. For an earlier discussion of the subject, see I. William Zartman, "Intervening to Prevent State Collapse," *Brown Journal of International Affairs* (September 1997).

2. On distinctions between peacekeeping and peace-enforcing, the dispositions of the UN Charter and its interpretation, and the nonmilitary form of diplomacy termed peace building, see Boutros-Ghali 1992.

3. For distinctions between threats and warnings and promises and predictions, see Shelling 1960, 177; James Tedeschi, "Threats and Promises," in Swingle 1970, 162–180; Baldwin 1971, 19 note 38; and Zartman 1974, 385-399.

References

Adibe, Clement. (1997) "The Liberian Conflict and the ECOWAS-UN Partnership," *Third World Quarterly,* Vol. 18, No. 3, pp. 471–488.

Assefa, Hizkias. (1987) *Mediation of Civil Wars* (Boulder: Westview Press).

Baldwin, David. (1971) "The Power of Positive Sanctions," *World Politics,* Vol. 24, No. 1.

Bercovitch, Jacob, ed. (1996) *Resolving International Conflicts* (Boulder: Lynne Rienner).

Bercovitch, Jacob and Jeffrey Z. Rubin, eds. (1992) *Mediation in International Relations* (New York: St. Martin's Press).

Boutros-Ghali, Boutros. (1992) *Agenda for Peace* (New York: United Nations).

Crocker, Chester A. (1992) *High Noon in Southern Africa* (New York: Norton).

Deng, Francis et al. (1996) *Sovereignty as Responsibility* (Washington, D.C.: Brookings Institution).

Kleiboer, Maricke. (1997) *International Mediation* (Boulder: Lynne Reinner).

Knudsen, Christine with I. William Zartman. (1995) "The Large Small War in Angola," *Annals of the American Academy of Political and Social Sciences*, Vol. 541, September, pp. 130–143.

Lyons, Gene M. and Michael Mastanduno, eds. (1995) *Beyond Westphalia?* (Baltimore: Johns Hopkins University Press).

Lyons, Terrence and Ahmed I. Samatar. (1995) *Somalia: State Collapse, Multilateral Intervention and Strategies for Political Reconstruction* (Washington, D.C.: Brookings Institution).

Maresca, John J. (1996) "Lost Opportunities in Negotiating the Conflict over Nagorno Karabakh," *International Negotiation,* Vol. 13, pp. 471–499.

Mitchell, C. R. and Keith Webb, eds. (1988) *New Approaches to International Mediation* (New York: Greenwood).

Msabaha, Ibrahim. (1995) "Negotiating an End to Mozambique's Murderous Rebellion," in *Elusive Peace: Negotiating an End to Civil Wars,* edited by I. William Zartman (Washington, D.C.: Brookings Institution).

Obasanjo, Olesegun. (1991) *The Kampala Document* (New York: Africa Leadership Forum).

Rothchild, Donald and Caroline Hartzell. (1995) "Interstate and Intrastate Negotiations in Angola," in *Elusive Peace: Negotiating an End to Civil Wars,* edited by I. William Zartman (Washington, D.C.: Brookings Institution).

Rubin, Jeffrey Z., ed. (1981) *The Dynamics of Third Party Intervention* (New York: Praeger).

Sahnoun, Mohamed. (1994) *Somalia: The Missed Opportunities* (Washington, D.C.: US Institute of Peace).

Shelling, Thomas. (1960) *The Strategy of Conflict* (Cambridge: Harvard University Press).

Swingle, Paul, ed. (1970) *The Structure of Conflict* (New York: Academic Press, 1970).

Touval, Saadia and I. William Zartman, eds. (1985) *International Mediation in Theory and Practice* (Boulder: Westview Press).

Wriggins, Howard. (1995) "Sri Lanka: Negotiating in a Secessionist Conflict," in *Elusive Peace: Negotiating an End to Civil Wars,* edited by I. William Zartman (Washington, D.C.: Brookings Institution).

Zartman, I. William. (1974) "The Political Analysis of Negotiation: How Who Gets What When," *World Politics,* Vol. 26, No. 3, pp. 385–399.

_____. (1989) *Ripe for Resolution* (New York: Oxford University Press).

_____, ed. (1995a) *Collapsed States: The Disintegration and Restoration of Legitimate Authority* (Boulder: Lynne Rienner).

_____. (1995b) *Elusive Peace: Negotiating an End to Civil Wars* (Washington, D.C.: Brookings Institution).

_____. (1997) "Negotiating to Prevent State Collapse." Paper presented to the International Political Science Association, XVII World Congress, Seoul, Korea, August 19.

Chapter THREE

INTERNATIONAL ECONOMIC DIPLOMACY

Taming the Globalization Beast

THE CHALLENGES OF THE
GLOBAL ECONOMY FOR
MULTILATERAL DIPLOMACY

James P. Muldoon, Jr.

The preoccupation with economic globalization is one of the most striking aspects of international relations and multilateral diplomacy since
the end of the Cold War. The speed of "globalization" of the world economy since the early 1990s has been spurred on by the collapse of the Soviet
Union and the disintegration of centrally planned economies of the communist world. Many politicians and business leaders believed that the world
was entering a golden age of economic prosperity and peace—a "New
World Order" built upon a set of shared values (namely, democracy and
market economics) had emerged. But the champions of globalization and
unfettered global market capitalism in the 1990s were humbled by the outbreak of new and unexpected conflicts and problems. The "peace" that was
believed imminent after the defeat of Iraq in the First Gulf War never mate-
rialized; instead, religious, ethnic, and cultural conflicts erupted across the
planet. Economic globalization renewed tensions between developed and

developing countries, generating intense discussions and increasingly heated debates in the corridors, meeting rooms, and halls of the United Nations, and in national legislatures. Clearly, the world in the twenty-first century is more complex, confusing, and uncertain than had been expected.

The World Economy and Multilateral Diplomacy

In the early years following World War II, the Cold War splintered the world economy into two competing political-economic systems—one in the West, a liberal multilateral economic system with established rules and structures to manage financial and commercial relations among the major industrial states; and another in the East based on Soviet hegemony and its economic system of central planning (Spero 1981, 2). Each system established international and regional institutions: In the West, the Bretton Woods system (which includes the World Bank and the International Monetary Fund [IMF]), the Organization for Economic Cooperation and Development (OECD), the European Economic Community (EEC), and the General Agreement on Tariffs and Trade (GATT) were created; while the East established the Council for Mutual Economic Assistance (CMEA or the Comecon), the International Bank for Economic Cooperation (IBEC), and the International Investment Bank (IIB). The competition between these systems was an important part of the larger East-West confrontation of the Cold War, though it was of lesser consequence than the conflicts in the security arena.

As international economic issues grew in significance in foreign policy during the Cold War, the traditional national foreign policy establishment and its focus on strategic security and political issues began to change. The growing awareness of economic interdependence after World War II encouraged the domestic departments of most governments to put themselves in the foreign policy business, causing "diplomatic inflation" and eventually leading to internal disputes and problems among national ministries over the coordination of economic and security policies. In his book *The Diplomats*, Martin Mayer reports:

> "During the fifties and sixties, when economies grew," said Erik Holm of the Danish Foreign Ministry, "there was a feeling that the future lay with economics, and a number of economists came in. The new generation of ambassadors came from economics. . . . Now the economic side is politicized. We know it can't run as a well-oiled machine. And now a number of international economic questions are settled by the Prime Minister, not the Foreign Minister. It creates a great deal of unrest among the diplomats." . . . Somehow, responsibility for national decisions that have international implications

must be allocated among domestic experts, domestic politicians, home-office diplomats and diplomats *en poste*. This will never be easy. "You need someone," said P. W. Unwin of the British Foreign Office, "to keep the recognition that though the meeting may be about fish, it has a political purpose." Asked about this as a rule, Unwin's boss commented, "You also may have to remind the man that though the purpose of the meeting is political, he was chosen because of his expertise on fish." (Mayer 1983, 22–24)

In addition, as countries in Africa and Asia gained independence in the 1960s and 1970s a new dimension was introduced into international economic relations. Although these newly independent and underdeveloped countries were considered part of and quick to join the international economic system of the West, the asymmetry in the level of industrialization between these countries and the countries in Western Europe and North America ultimately led to the North-South conflict, which pitted the developed countries against the developing countries (or the Third World) in a contentious debate over how the multilateral economic system should be managed.

As more and more developing countries joined the international community, the economic divisions between three groups of countries—the "market economies" of the industrialized countries (often referred to as the First World), the "centrally planned economies" of the socialist/communist countries (the so-called Second World), and the developing economies (many of them preindustrial) of over one hundred countries in Africa, Asia, and Latin America—became more pronounced. The North-South conflict developed into a serious challenge of the major industrial states' dominance in multilateral economic affairs. As Miles Kahler points out:

The organization of international economic relations frequently demonstrated the same mixture of a multilateralism supported by great power collaboration and diluted by bilateralism [that occurred in international security relations]. . . . The minilateral system of governance through great power collaboration that developed in international economic affairs after 1945 came under increasing attack as the number of independent developing countries grew during the 1960s. In the 1970s, a developing country "bloc" view of governance was proposed. This view had found its expression in the UN Conference on Trade and Development (UNCTAD), which was formalized in 1964, and later in other institutions, existing and proposed. The attempt by developing countries to bring the weight of their numbers and the leverage of their commodity power to bear on governance was subsequently expressed in demands for a new international economic order (NIEO), demands that foundered on worsening economic conditions in the 1980s and heightened ideological resistance by the industrialized countries. (Ruggie 1993, 301–304)

The North-South conflict was a major factor in the development of "group diplomacy" and the emergence of blocs and interest groups, particularly the formation of the Group of 77 (G-77) of developing countries, at the United Nations. According to Keith Hamilton and Richard Langhorne, this was an important development in multilateral diplomacy:

> It is the methods by which [the G-77] has tried to achieve consensus amongst its members, firstly at a regional sub-group level, and then amongst these sub-groups, and its mode of negotiations with other blocs and groups, which make G-77 interesting from the point of view of the evolution of diplomatic practice. . . . This form of international collective bargaining has helped to overcome some of the problems faced by the more highly industrialized powers in participating in those assemblies and conferences where, despite their size and strength, they have had to reckon with majorities made up of representatives of micro-states and the remainder of the less developed world. At the same time it has allowed smaller countries with limited diplomatic resources to have at least some say in the framing of accords on global matters. (Hamilton and Langhorne 1995, 198–199)

The practice of "group diplomacy" and "associative diplomacy" (a technique developed by the European Union with the seventy-seven African, Caribbean, and Pacific [ACP] countries through the Lomé Agreements that governed the ACP countries' access to EC markets) came to typify international economic relations and is still practiced at the United Nations and in other multilateral economic institutions (Hamilton and Langhorne 1995, 207–209). However, it did not iron out the complexities or give order to an inherently messy process. The rift between developed and developing countries clearly widened as the end of the Cold War approached. The terms of trade for the South deteriorated and the income disparities between North and South grew, the result being the so-called lost decade of development in the 1980s as economic development assistance came to a standstill.

The End of the Cold War: Adjusting to Rapid Global Change and Contending with Globalization

After the Cold War, the world economy divided into two camps: the industrialized countries (some even argue that this group is subdivided into industrial and postindustrial countries) in the North and the industrializing

countries of the South. Unlike the Cold War economic divisions of nation-states, the post–Cold War divide is less between competing political-
economic systems and more over the stage of economic development of
countries within basically one economic system. With the "market" taking
center stage in world affairs, countries, as well as nonstate actors such as
multinational corporations (MNCs) and nongovernmental organizations
(NGOs), began to viciously compete with each other for access to financing
and advanced technology.

The end of the Cold War unleashed a veritable flood of global economic
activity, sweeping up the world—East and West, North and South—in a
frantic race for money and profits, technology, and market share.[1] And the
growth in the world economy is nothing less than spectacular, at least for
some. Clearly, the real winners in and beneficiaries of the globalized economy have been the leading industrialized economies or the "triad" of the
US-Japan-European Union, closely followed by the newly industrialized
countries (NICs) of Asia, the so-called Asian tigers or dragons—Singapore,
South Korea, Hong Kong, and Taiwan—and by the incredible economic
rise of the People's Republic of China since the mid-1980s. However, the
world's poor in Africa, Latin America, and Asia haven't seen much benefit
from globalization. In fact, the economic liberalization and rapid integration of, and into, financial markets advocated by the Bretton Woods institutions during the 1980s and early 1990s under the erstwhile "Washington
consensus" have disadvantaged most developing countries, which have neither the assets nor the capabilities to enter global markets, and plunged the
world into a series of economic and financial crises (see Stiglitz 2002).

Henk-Jan Brinkman points out later in this chapter that three factors
emerged near the end of the 1990s—"policy convergence, troubling aspects
of globalization, and unfolding, and at that time poorly understood, financial crises"—that enabled serious global economic negotiations to resume
at the United Nations, but in a different way from the UN's "standard economic negotiations." This led to the 2002 UN Conference on Financing for
Development (FfD), which

for the first time discussed systemic global economic issues at the United Nations. Until FfD, they were discussed mostly at the Bretton Woods and other
forums. Perhaps they were not discussed at the United Nations because the
developing countries have such a large voice at the United Nations. These issues were eventually discussed at the United Nations, perhaps because developing countries have such a large voice at the United Nations. They wanted
to discuss these issues at the UN and they pushed for it. A convergence of factors helped them. As a result, ministers of finance, trade and development cooperation are now a regular sight at the United Nations. They discuss issues
like investment, finance, debt, trade, ODA, debt and systemic aspects of the

global financial structure in a holistic way. There is no other forum where all these issues are discussed at the same time with their interlinkages.

Economic issues have risen rapidly from their subordinate position in international politics during the Cold War era to their status as *the* politics of post–Cold War international relations. According to Isaac Cohen, states are struggling to stay abreast of an expanding economic agenda and searching for mechanisms to manage a world "characterized by the primacy of economics amid increasing globalization." He points out that economic globalization contributes to the expansion of traditional agendas, adding "many more issues, previously reserved for the domestic realm," but "this formidable expansion of the international economic agenda has yet to lead to the emergence of a new institutional framework, comparable to the institutions designed half a century ago."[2]

Globalization dramatically affects the international political economy, reducing the scope of states' autonomy and limiting their power. As James Mittelman points out:

> Just as globalization gives impetus to cultural homogenization (e.g., the diffusion of standard consumer goods throughout the world), so too does a global thrust undermine state power and unleash subterranean cultural pluralism. This contradictory process merges with a dialectic of subnationalism and supranationalism. Many polities are disrupted by substate actors and simultaneously seek advantage in global competition through regionalization. ... Thus, the state is being reformed from below by the tugs of subnationalism and from above by the pull of economic globalization. (Mittelman 1996, 7–8)

Furthermore, nonstate actors, especially MNCs, are more prominent players in the global economy, adding another layer of complexity to international economic relations and challenging the intergovernmental machinery that structures international economic diplomacy. Because of the internationalization of capital markets that occurred in the 1980s and of progress in information and transportation technologies, MNCs have come to occupy a pivotal position within the global economy, commanding incredibly large financial resources (some corporations have more money than many of the developing countries combined) and an ever-widening "global reach" (Akbar and Mueller 1997, 60–61). In recent years, corporate executives have become more involved in activities that are strikingly "diplomatic." Criss-crossing the globe in hot pursuit of new markets, cheaper labor, and greater production values, CEOs are received by presidents and prime ministers and negotiate deals with national and provincial officials. The influence of these "private-sector diplomats" now extends into the highest reaches of national governments and of regional and international organizations. Through international business associations such as the International Chamber of Commerce (ICC) and the World Economic Forum (WEF), the private sector has been able to break into the multilateral diplomatic game, bringing resources and financial and technical expertise that were lacking in the international public sector to key environmental and economic issues on the global agenda (Hocking and Kelly 2002).

This is, however, nothing new, as Jeremy Taylor reminds us later in this chapter. He points out that merchants were among the first diplomats and that "leaders in the private sector have been for hundreds of years and remain essential participants in economic and public policy arenas." Globalization has given business a more pronounced role in international economic relations, pushing corporate executives to become private-sector diplomats. What executives of major MNCs say or do can cause financial chaos in markets around the world or determine the future of entire countries. Taylor argues that

> the globalization of economies, business enterprises, and financial markets is bringing about a convergence of interests between government, business, and civil society in many parts of the world, and new and evolving forms of partnership are on the rise. This trend deepens the business community's participation in the diplomatic process of international economic affairs, particularly as governments rely more and more on markets to "regulate" the global economy and look to the private sector to strengthen the economic relationships between countries. With increasing stakeholder pressure on international business to assume broader social, development, and environmental responsibilities, business executives are discovering that to successfully manage the diversity of stakeholder relationships they must have strong diplomatic skills.

Therefore, it is likely business executives will continue to play an important role in international economic relations and essential that private-sector leaders be more skilled in the art of diplomacy.

The complex web of extensive bilateral relationships, regional frameworks, and global regimes that has managed the international economic system since the end of World War II is not able to do so in this era of globalization. The incredible pace of global economic activity is outstripping the rate at which national and international institutions can adapt to these changes. According to Ambassador S. Azmat Hassan, writing later in this chapter, globalization is creating a "crisis in governance" and defining the role of the United Nations in the new century. He points out that the "United Nations has struggled with the challenges of globalization for several years, especially since the 1997–1998 Asian financial crisis served as a wakeup call for the international community" and has been exploring "the different dimensions of globalization and the appropriate policy approaches by which the UN system can help better manage the risks and secure the benefits of globalization." Over the course of his tenure as UN Secretary-General, Kofi Annan has made economic and social development the primary focus of the UN system and has backed innovative initiatives, such as the Global Compact, that make the system more flexible and effective in meeting the challenges of globalization.

Clearly the extensive unstructured array of multilateral arrangements and institutions that have been created since 1945 is in need of reform and is the most difficult challenge we face at present. But it remains to be seen if multilateral diplomacy and the United Nations system are up to the task of meeting the complex challenges of globalization and the global economy in the years ahead.

Notes

1. For an excellent discussion of "globalization," especially the many ways it is manifested in the post–Cold War world, see James Mittelman's book, *Globalization: Critical Reflections*. Also see *Governing Globalization: Issues and Institutions*, edited by Deepak Nayyar, and *Taming Globalization: Frontiers of Governance*, edited by David Held and Mathias Koenig-Archibugi.

2. See Isaac Cohen, "International Economic Diplomacy and International Organizations," in the first edition of *Multilateral Diplomacy and the United Nations Today*, edited by James P. Muldoon, Jr., JoAnn Fagot Aviel, Richard Reitano, and Earl Sullivan (Boulder: Westview Press, 1998), pp. 87–101.

References

Akbar, Yusef H. and Bernard Mueller. (1997) "Global Competition Policy: Issues and Perspectives," *Global Governance*, Vol. 3, No. 1, January-April, pp. 59–82.

Hamilton, Keith and Richard Langhorne. (1995) *The Practice of Diplomacy* (London: Routledge).

Held, David and Mathias Koenig-Archibugi, eds. (2003) *Taming Globalization: Frontiers of Governance* (Cambridge, UK: Polity Press).

Hocking, Brian and Dominic Kelly. (2002) "Doing the Business? The International Chamber of Commerce, the United Nations, and the Global Compact," in *Enhancing Global Governance: Towards a New Diplomacy?* edited by Andrew F.

Cooper, John English, and Ramesh Thakur (Tokyo: United Nations University Press), pp. 203–228.

Mayer, Martin. (1983) *The Diplomats* (New York: Doubleday).

Mittelman, James H., ed. (1996) *Globalization: Critical Reflections* (Boulder: Lynne Rienner).

Nayyar, Deepak, ed. (2002) *Governing Globalization: Issues and Institutions* (Oxford: Oxford University Press).

Ruggie, John Gerard, ed. (1993) *Multilateralism Matters: The Theory and Praxis of an Institutional Form* (New York: Columbia University Press).

Spero, Joan Edelman. (1981) *The Politics of International Economic Relations*, 2nd ed. (New York: St. Martin's Press).

Stiglitz, Joseph. (2002) *Globalization and Its Discontents* (London: Penguin Books).

INTERNATIONAL ECONOMIC DIPLOMACY AT THE UNITED NATIONS

Henk-Jan Brinkman[1]

People would in general not associate the United Nations with economic diplomacy. The United Nations is typically known for its work in matters of peace and security. And the Security Council is probably the most widely recognized image of the United Nations. Yet the Charter of the United Nations pays equal attention to development and to peace and security. The preamble and Article 1 mention "better standards of life" and "international cooperation in solving international problems of an economic, social, cultural, or humanitarian character." Article 55 is more explicit. It states, "The United Nations shall promote:

- higher standards of living, full employment, and conditions of economic and social progress and development;

- solutions of international economic, social health, and related problems; . . . and

- universal respect for, and observance of, human rights and fundamental freedoms for all without distinction as to race, sex, language, or religion."[2]

Economic Diplomacy at the United Nations

What is economic diplomacy like at the United Nations? If diplomacy is understood as the art and practice of conducting negotiations between nations (as my dictionary says), *economic diplomacy* refers to negotiations on economic issues. Economic issues have been on the agenda of the United Nations from the very beginning. In fact, "no other international body has discussed so many world economic issues for so long or proclaimed the case for international cooperation so vigorously." (Rahman 2002, xii).

Inside Baseball Inside the United Nations

Economic diplomacy at the UN is not always exciting. It is sometimes a little like making sausages: You do not want to see the process up close. But in contrast to the end product of sausages, the result of economic diplomacy does not always look good either. Often the resolutions are not easy reading, because of the inevitable compromises among the member states.

An agenda item usually starts with a general debate. Unfortunately, there is very little debate. Representatives mostly read statements, one after another, which have been prepared and/or approved in capital cities. Only insiders with a trained ear for nuances, such as the ears diplomats have, can hear subtle shifts in positions. This used to be different. In the 1950s and 1960s, great orators, like Abba Eban of Israel, and ad hoc interventions enriched the discussions at the UN. Of late, debates are rarely exciting, and if that is the case, it is lamentably the result of politically sensitive issues, like the situation in the occupied Palestinian territories.

Part of the problem in the debates is that positions are often predictable and repetitive. During the Cold War, this was even worse because of ideological bias and geopolitics. Debates, particularly before the 1990s, often got stuck in a blame game: the North blaming the South for their own troubles, and the South blaming the North for a hostile international economic environment that prevents development.

The first draft of a resolution on economic issues is usually tabled in a formal meeting by the Group of 77 (G-77), as the group of developing countries is named at the UN. (The group originally had 77 members, but it now has 134.) Other countries or groups of countries, such as the European Union, might give a first reaction to the draft in the formal meeting. The real work of negotiation, however, is done in "informal" meetings, where the protocol of running a meeting is less strict and no record is kept of what is said, and particularly in "informal informals," where representatives no longer sit behind the nameplates of their countries (and most sit next to the chair of their groups, i.e., the European Union or the G-77) and call each other by their first names. At "informal informals" there is also no simultaneous translation, and discussions in New York City all take place in English.

Nowadays, these negotiations sometimes use a big screen that projects the text of the draft. Member states are at this stage deeply engaged in the negotiations. Often during these negotiations, developing countries try to extract commitments from developed countries regarding aid, technology transfers, access to their markets, commodity prices, and debt relief. Developed countries, on the other hand, try to avoid "giving" away anything or much and, in addition, demand economic reforms in developing countries as well as reforms regarding human rights and governance (although the latter term became fashionable only in the 1990s).

Sometimes, these negotiations might appear to be haggling over words. The participants might, for example, deeply disagree over whether governments should be "urged" or "encouraged," or whether the phrase "as appropriate" should be added and, if so, where, giving countries the opportunity to ignore the resolution by arguing that it is not appropriate in their situation. Suggestions are included between square brackets until agreement is reached. Sometimes, one member state can push a pet project or hobbyhorse or a particular issue relevant only to it. For example, in one set of negotiations, one member state wanted to delete any reference to subregional integration because it was not on friendly terms with its direct neighbors and felt that subregional integration was not something it wanted to pursue.

At times, member states select a "facilitator," a well-respected representative among them, to reach a compromise. The facilitator might decide just to listen to the different positions and redraft a compromise text himself or herself, which he or she will present at the next meeting. He or she might try a few iterations of redrafting, but the horse-trading over words can seldom be avoided.

One aspect in particular makes these negotiations in informal settings more interesting than the formal meetings at the United Nations: They are not scripted. Even if the negotiation positions are determined in capitals, the actual negotiations are done without prior prepared statements. Thus the personalities of the diplomats often shine through their diplomatic politeness and rituals. And because these diplomats come from around the world, there is a wide range of colorful people, who are at times quite entertaining.

Resolutions in the economic area are almost always adopted by consensus. One consequence of this process is that the resolution often reflects the lowest common denominator, so it is rather bland. It also has not contributed to the clarity and relevance of the resolutions for governments, let alone for common people in the street. The fact that resolutions adopted by the Economic and Social Council (ECOSOC) or the General Assembly are not legally binding does also not help to increase their relevance and does not put pressure on the negotiators to make resolutions intelligible.

These negotiations can be very time-consuming. Sometimes hours are spent on a few sentences. Deadlines help in that regard, although they often mean that meetings go deep into the night or the wee hours of the morning. Nothing puts more pressure on compromise than a deadline, sleepiness, and hunger, with the regular cafeteria closed and nothing left except snacks from vending machines!

In recent years, several efforts have been made to make the discussions at the UN more interactive and interesting. One common method is the use of "roundtables." Member states are divided up in smaller groups and sit across from each other instead of behind each other. These are also informal meetings, although the chair or cochairs might issue a summary of the discussions. Another innovation has been panel discussions, where a number of experts from the outside (for example, academics) are invited to give a presentation, and a question-and-answer period with the delegations follows.

These roundtables and panels have been somewhat successful in breaking the mold. Perhaps the most promising way to keep economic diplomacy at the UN interesting to outsiders is to include those outsiders. Interactions with nonstate actors[3] are often the most interesting segments of the debates. Representatives of nongovernmental organizations (NGOs) and the private sector have often been given a seat at the table.

The United Nations has a long history of inviting NGOs. They were, for example, present at the signing of the treaty that founded the UN in San Francisco in 1945, and the Charter allows for consultations between the Economic and Social Council and NGOs (in Article 71). But the involvement has become more structured and official in recent years. Their presence has played a particularly important role at the major conferences that the United Nations organized in the 1990s and in 2002, not in the least by raising the visibility of the conferences and awareness of the issues and promoting certain actions. For example, eighty-two hundred representatives of civil society attended the World Summit on Sustainable Development in

2002, compared to ninety-one hundred diplomats. As a matter of fact, the conferences played a major role in the mobilization and internationalization of and creation of several networks among NGOs.

Yet the participation of nonstate actors in an intergovernmental organization like the United Nations remains somewhat controversial. Ultimately, governments take decisions at the UN. Their attitude is a bit like opening the door and closing it. To find a more structural solution to the ambivalence of the member states and practical ways to give a voice to civil society, as it is not able to give a seat to each of the more than thirty-seven thousand international NGOs that currently exist, the Secretary-General appointed a panel under the chairmanship of the former president of Brazil, Fernando Enrique Cardoso, which will report its recommendations in 2004.

Significant moments often highlight the unique and important functions of the UN. For example, during the World Summit on Sustainable Development, at one of the roundtables, the president of the Maldives made a passionate plea about the exorbitant consumption of fossil fuels in developed countries. This was not just the South blaming the North. For this country it is literally a matter of life and death, because if predictions about climate change as a result of greenhouse-gas emissions come true, the Maldives will be totally submerged by rising seawater. For small countries like the Maldives, the United Nations provides a unique, and often the only, opportunity to voice these concerns directly to other member states and the world community at large.

The Financing for Development (FfD) process has also made an attempt to change the nature of the negotiations. But that will be discussed below.

A Short History of Economic Diplomacy at the United Nations[4]

Immediately after World War II, discussions at the UN were focused on the reconstruction of the war-devastated economies, particularly in Europe. But since the early 1950s, development issues have dominated the debates under economic and social agenda items at the United Nations. This can partly be explained by the changing composition of the membership of the United Nations. In 1945, 33 were developing countries, out of 51 original members. But large numbers of newly independent states joined the United Nations after that, especially in the 1960s and 1970s. By 2003, of the 191 members, 136 were developing countries.

The key development issues that have been debated and negotiated at the United Nations are poverty, aid, commodities and international trade, debt (since the 1980s), transnational corporations (particularly in the 1970s), and the environment.

In the 1950s and 1960s, debates at the United Nations were dominated by a focus on growth, with industrialization as its main driving force. Initially, domestic determinants of development played a significant role in the debates. Since the 1950s, however, the debates at the United Nations have increasingly pointed to external factors as important constraints.

Already in the late 1950s, there was talk at the United Nations about international cooperation for development, which culminated in declaring the 1960s the First UN Development Decade. Subsequent Development Decades were backed by an International Development Strategy, which were "the most quoted and referred to documents in economic dialogues at the organization" (Rahman 2002, 107), at least up to the end of the 1990s. And the first International Development Strategy (for the Second Development Decade) included the number that has probably been the most quoted number at the United Nations: Developed countries should devote at least 0.7 percent of their national income to official development assistance (ODA).

This number was based on the calculation that in order to reach the 6 percent growth rate of GDP that the Second Development Decade aimed for, developing countries needed foreign resources equal to 1 percent of the national income of the developed countries. About 30 percent of this 1 percent would come from private sources. Hence, the remainder had to come from official sources.

During the 1970s, demands for a more favorable international economic environment for developing countries surged. These were partly fueled by rising oil (and other commodity) prices, which gave the developing countries a sense of power and unity. The culmination was discussions at the United Nations about a new international economic order (NIEO). These discussions took place at several forums. The first was the Sixth Special Session of the General Assembly of the United Nations in 1974, which adopted a Declaration on the Establishment of a New International Economic Order and the Programme of Action on the Establishment of a New International Economic Order. The second forum was the negotiations within UNCTAD on the Charter of Economic Rights and Duties of States, which was also adopted by the General Assembly in 1974. The third forum was the Conference on International Economic Cooperation, hosted by France in Paris in 1975, with subsequent meetings in 1976 and 1977, which by then were reporting to the General Assembly.

These forums were supposed to merge into the "global negotiations" to establish an NIEO. But these negotiations never actually took place, as there was no agreement on the issues to be discussed. The two thorniest issues were energy and the international monetary system. (This was just after two oil price shocks in 1973 and 1979 and after the collapse of the

Bretton Woods system of fixed exchange rates in 1971.) The developing countries did not want to discuss energy and the developed countries did not want to discuss the international monetary system at the United Nations. The stalemate was never resolved and the consultations to launch the global consultations petered out in the mid-1980s.

By then the state of affairs was drastically different from that in the 1970s. The oil price increases of the 1970s had at first united the developing countries but, by the early 1980s, had divided the developing countries as oil-importing countries suffered from high import costs. The higher oil prices contributed to the debt crisis of the 1980s, which erupted with a vengeance in 1982 with Mexico's default on its national debt. The 1980s was for many developing countries "a lost decade," particularly in Africa and Latin America, with significantly lower growth rates than in the 1960s and 1970s.

The attempt to launch global negotiations was similar to what would be tried—and succeed—two decades later by the Conference on Financing for Development. By then, energy issues had faded into the background, but the international monetary system was still (or again) on the agenda, although for different reasons. But it was then also difficult to get agreement even to place this issue on the agenda.

Recent Developments in Economic Diplomacy at the United Nations

Two major events in recent years have significantly changed the nature of economic diplomacy at the United Nations. The first was the Millennium Summit, and the second was the International Conference on Financing for Development.

The Millennium Development Goals

In September 2000, a record number of 147 heads of state or government (always a measure of success for a conference) assembled in New York City for the Millennium Summit. They came to discuss the Millennium Report, *We the Peoples: The Role of the United Nations in the Twenty-first Century,* one of the truly readable, visionary, and inspiring reports of the Secretary-General. They also came to adopt a resolution, called the Millennium Declaration, which covers a range of issues from peace and security to human rights.

The Millennium Declaration is also very readable and more interesting than the usual UN resolutions, partly because the resolution was not negotiated in the way that is common in the economic area. It was based on the

Millennium Report. That report contains a chapter which could be considered the first draft of the Millennium Declaration. The president of the General Assembly presented subsequent drafts to an informal meeting of the General Assembly. Member states provided their comments but did not negotiate the text directly. On the basis of the comments, the president, with the help of others, including the Office of the Secretary-General and a number of ambassadors, would redraft and present the next version. When heads of state were already arriving and the pressure of time started to kick in, the final text was agreed on.

The Millennium Declaration contains a development chapter with a number of concrete numerical targets with deadlines, foremost among them the goal to halve poverty by 2015. These goals became known as the Millennium Development Goals (MDGs) (see Table 3.1). They were based on the goals that were agreed on in the different conferences that the United Nations organized in the 1990s, such as the World Summit for Children in New York City (1990), the UN Conference of Environment and Development in Rio de Janeiro (1992), the International Conference on Population and Development in Cairo (1994), the Fourth World Conference on Women in Beijing (1995), and the World Summit for Social Development in Copenhagen (1995).

In just three years since the adoption of the Millennium Declaration, the Millennium Development Goals have transformed the global development agenda. How have they been able to do that? What is so new and exciting about the MDGs?

First, rarely, if ever, have there been goals that are so widely accepted across countries and across segments within societies. In fact, there never has been such a broadly accepted set of goals in the area of development, even if they are not everywhere accepted (to the same extent). Second, the MDGs focus on ends, rather than means, representing a marked shift from previous discussions at the UN. Third, the MDGs are people-centered, partly following the advances made by the focus on human development, initiated by the UN Development Programme and its Human Development Report. Fourth, the MDGs form a whole with an important synergy between the different goals, for example, between the health and the education goals. The MDGs also reflect the multidimensional nature of poverty by giving equal attention to, for example, education and health in relation to poverty (i.e., the number of people earning less than $1 a day). Fifth, the MDGs are simple and everybody can understand them, including laypeople in the streets of Cairo, Canberra, Caracas, Colombo, and Copenhagen. Sixth, the MDGs are time-bound, providing a sense of urgency. Most of the target dates are 2015. Seventh, the MDGs reflect a balanced compact with equally important actions required from the North and the South. This is a very important aspect of the MDGs, which is also very much reflected in Financing

Table 3.1 The Millennium Development Goals

	GOALS	TARGETS
Goal 1	**Eradicate extreme poverty and hunger**	• Halve, between 1990 and 2015, the proportion of people whose income is less than one dollar a day • Halve, between 1990 and 2015, the proportion of people who suffer from hunger
Goal 2	**Achieve universal primary education**	Ensure that, by 2015, children everywhere, boys and girls alike, will be able to complete a full course of primary schooling
Goal 3	**Promote gender equality and empower women**	Eliminate gender disparity in primary and secondary education, preferably by 2005, and to all levels of education no later than 2015
Goal 4	**Reduce child mortality**	Reduce by two thirds, between 1990 and 2015, the under-five mortality rate
Goal 5	**Improve maternal health**	Reduce by three quarters, between 1990 and 2015, the maternal mortality ratio
Goal 6	**Combat HIV/AIDS, malaria, and other diseases**	• Have halted by 2015 and begun to reverse the spread of HIV/AIDS • Have halted by 2015 and begun to reverse the incidence of malaria and other major diseases
Goal 7	**Ensure environmental sustainability**	• Integrate the principles of sustainable development into country policies and programmes and reverse the loss of environmental resources • Halve by 2015 the proportion of people without sustainable access to safe drinking water • By 2020 to have achieved a significant improvement in the lives of at least 100 million slum dwellers
Goal 8	**Develop a global partnership for development**	• Develop further an open, rule-based, predictable, non-discriminatory trading and financial system • Address the special needs of the least developed countries • Address the special needs of landlocked countries and small island developing States • Deal comprehensively with the debt problems of developing countries through national and international measures in order to make debt sustainable in the long term • In cooperation with developing countries, develop and implement strategies for decent and productive work for youth • In cooperation with pharmaceutical companies, provide access to affordable essential drugs in developing countries • In cooperation with the private sector, make available the benefits of new technologies, especially information and communications

for Development (FfD) and forms an important departure from the previous discussions at the UN, in which the North and the South blamed each other. Finally, the MDGs are important tools for awareness raising and advocacy to trigger policy reforms, budget reallocations, and institutional change. The MDGs have been agreed to by governments and they can be held accountable against benchmarks. The MDGs are their commitments.

As a set of measurable, shared objectives endorsed by all UN member states, the MDGs have changed not only the international development agenda but also the actions on the ground. They have been embraced by such diverse institutions, as the African Union and the Group of 8 (the seven largest industrialized countries and Russia). They have provided an unprecedented focus for the work of the development agencies within the UN system, including the Bretton Woods institutions. Thus they have led to improvements in the coherence and the effectiveness of the work of these agencies at the country level. Beyond these actors, the MDGs have also mobilized many other actors, from civil society to parliamentarians.

The MDGs have also given more focus to the economic deliberations at the United Nations. For example, they have provided an overall framework for the discussions on operational activities, mostly in the Economic and Social Council, of the United Nations. Yet in this area progress is slowest. The MDGs are often still referred to as "internationally agreed development goals, including those contained in the Millennium Declaration" because the acronym itself does not appear in the Millennium Declaration and thus, as is argued by some, were not officially adopted by the General Assembly.[5]

Financing for Development

The International Conference on Financing for Development, held in March 2002 in Monterrey, Mexico, was another watershed event. Given the history of the discussions on economic issues at the United Nations, it was just short of a miracle that it ever took place. In fact, up to a few months before the conference, it could easily have fallen apart. The achievements of this conference are also quite remarkable. To give just one example, ever since Monterrey, the agenda of the Bretton Woods institutions has been dominated by items that came straight out of the Monterrey Consensus. Thus, the Communiqué of the Development Committee of September 2003 had a number of references to the Monterrey Consensus and several of the agenda items of that meeting were derived from the Monterrey Consensus (or from the Millennium Summit).

As discussed above, previous attempts to hold a conference along these lines had failed in the 1970s and 1980s. But this time a number of converging factors allowed it to become a reality. FfD has its origins in the second half of the 1990s, a period when the world economy was changing rapidly and showed a number of (financial) crises and other troubling phenomena. An additional factor that contributed to the decision to organize the FfD conference was evolvement in the policy area, leading to a narrowing of the divide between the North and the South and the East and the West.

To set the stage, in the 1950s and 1960s, the growth of national income per capita was considered the main objective of development. It was thought that growth of GDP would, at least at one point, benefit everybody ("trickle down"). State interventions were regarded as imperative to kick off economic growth.

By the 1970s, however, doubts were increasingly raised about the effectiveness of this strategy, but the definite verdict was reached by the early 1980s, when many developing countries faced a severe decline in economic performance. The desperate need for external finance prepared the way for increased lending by the World Bank and the IMF, conditioned on neoliberal policy prescriptions known as *structural adjustment*.

Thus, during the 1980s, a convergence at a rather general level emerged between the IMF and the World Bank, both based in Washington, D.C., about what kind of policy conditions should be attached to their loans. This convergence of opinion became known as the *Washington Consensus*, which basically meant expanding the role of markets and reducing the role of governments in economies. At the end of the 1980s, the breakdown of central planning in Eastern Europe and the USSR further expedited the convergence on a larger reliance on markets. At this point, the ideological pendulum had swung to the other end: If in the 1950s governments could do everything, in the 1980s they could do hardly anything.

Even if the convergence was never complete[6]—and hence the word *consensus* was inappropriate—this still constituted a remarkable shift from the disagreements that existed up to the 1990s. By the late 1990s, ideological differences had largely disappeared or at least had been significantly reduced. This general convergence did not mean that opinions were static. During the 1990s, the pendulum swung back a little. Increasingly, the importance of the role of governments in market economies was recognized. This role, however, was markedly different from the role of governments in the 1950s. Governments, for example, were not to engage in the production of such goods as steel but were critical in the provision of social services and safety nets and in creating and maintaining the institutions that are necessary for markets to operate (such as the protection of property rights, enforcement of contracts, and supervision and regulation of financial markets). The important but different role of governments and the emphasis on governance and institutions were partly a result of doubts that were raised about the Washington Consensus and particularly its meager results in Africa and in a number of economies that were in transition from a centrally planned to a market economy.

The neoliberal economic policies that had come so vigorously to the fore in the 1980s, captured in the Washington Consensus, were still prevalent in the early 1990s. Foreign trade liberalization and the liberalization of domestic financial markets played dominantly in this agenda. Yet liberalization of international financial flows had not been part of the original formulation of the Washington Consensus. This only became part of the prevailing consensus in the mid-1990s, when private capital flows to developing countries surged. The IMF started to push for convertibility of the capital account of the balance of payments, which—in contrast to currency convertibility—is not part of the IMF's Articles of Agreement.[7]

The push for a greater role for liberalized markets has been a main determinant of globalization. Globalization is a process which started decades, if not centuries, ago. The process has accelerated recently to such an extent that one can perhaps speak of a new paradigm. *Globalization*, in economic terms, refers to the increasing economic integration of the markets of goods, services, capital, technology, and labor at a global level. The two major driving forces behind this process have been the liberalization of markets and information and communications technology. Telecommunication, for example, has allowed the instantaneous transfer of information, ideology, images, and money and has increased transportation capabilities to move more goods and people quicker and at lower costs. Even if not all indicators imply that the world economy has reached unprecedented levels of globalization, the changes that have taken place in recent decades are profound. The present wave of globalization "is not only different in degree [but] also different in kind. [It goes] farther, faster, cheaper and deeper," as Thomas L. Friedman writes in his popular book on globalization, *The Lexus and the Olive Tree*.

Globalization has created enormous opportunities, but many developing countries are not able to take advantage of them. The capacity of the poorest countries to benefit from the opportunities is limited by such factors as low educational attainments, skill levels, and technological capabilities and poorly developed institutions. Thus, although many countries have experienced rising incomes per capita, particularly in East Asia, there is a large group of countries, largely in Africa, that remain marginalized and that have even suffered falling per capita incomes.

One essential element of globalization was the rapid increase in the flows of private finance to developing countries in the 1990s. This was partly a result of the liberalization of financial markets. For example, from 1986 through 1990, the net-debtor developing countries lost about $10 billion per year in net financial transfers.[8] In contrast, these countries received in net transfers more than $86 billion per year from 1991 through 1996, a turnaround of net financial transfers of nearly $100 billion per year!

But globalization and the increase of private financial flows have not been without problems. Troubles first emerged with the Mexican financial crisis at the end of 1994. But they really came to the fore with the financial crises that started in Thailand in July 1997 and subsequently affected other Asian countries, such as Indonesia, Malaysia, and the Republic of Korea. Here was a group of countries that was generally admired for their enormous success in development. Some had moved from being poor developing countries in the 1950s to near developed-country status in about four decades. This movement was unprecedented in the history of the world.

Economists, not the least, were very puzzled by the sudden crises that affected these countries. (Indeed, there were only one or two who, prior to the crises, publicly warned of the severe imbalances that were emerging.) Disagreements still exist about the real causes. Yet most economists agree that the premature liberalization of the capital account and financial markets without proper financial regulation and supervision in place, along with excessive (short-term) borrowing, was among the root causes.

During this time, the Bretton Woods institutions, particularly the IMF, were severely criticized. Several prominent economists argued that the IMF had attached too severe and sometimes irrelevant conditions to the loans it was giving to the crisis countries in Asia. Others maintained that the world does not need an IMF in the first place. As a consequence, the financial crises during the 1990s raised questions about the "international financial architecture."

The negative effects of globalization and financial crises did not go unnoticed. Alternative-globalization activists[9] rose prominently to the scene, starting in the streets of Seattle during the Third Ministerial Meeting of the WTO in December 1999 ("the battle of Seattle"). Protests have focused on multilateral economic institutions like the IMF, the World Bank, and the WTO, as they are perceived as the main drivers of globalization.

The growing backlash against globalization coincided with an increasing concern about poverty reduction by the general public, social movements, and international organizations, including the Bretton Woods institutions. Within the United Nations, poverty had since the 1970s been an explicit concern with the Second United Nations Development Decade. UNICEF had already pointed out in 1985 that structural adjustment was often accompanied by a decline in the living standards of the more vulnerable segments of society. Poor people have been affected by reductions in output, real wages, employment, and government expenditures, as well as by changes in relative prices. UNICEF argued that social dimensions should be an integrated part of the adjustment programs ("adjustment with a human face").

Then came the preparations for the conference. Given these three phenomena (policy convergence, troubling aspects of globalization, and unfolding and at that time poorly understood, financial crises around the world), it is perhaps not surprising that the chances of organizing a conference on financing for development at the UN had increased at the end of the 1990s.

Even during its darkest periods, it is generally acknowledged that the UN has enormous power to convene meetings and more legitimacy and acceptance, certainly among the public at large and civil society, than any other international organization. The United Nations had proven itself in that regard by organizing a string of conferences during the 1990s. The Conference on Financing for Development fit into that sequence.

From the very beginning it was realized that FfD had to be different from the standard economic negotiations at the United Nations. Hence several informal meetings in formats different from the usual UN meetings were organized to create trust among the member states and some consensus on the issues that might be on the agenda of the high-level event, as the conference was first hesitantly called.

It is hard to imagine that building trust was so important. But given the sometimes acrimonious discussions on economic issues and the failures of the past, it was a critical step. Even if there was convergence in the policy area and the Cold War was over, old arguments were not buried very deep. Thus, sometimes negotiations did not really advance because countries suspected a hidden agenda. Convincing each other that there were no secret plans was critical.

The meetings were kept as informal as possible, with no formally negotiated outcome, as it was feared that if negotiations began, the member states would fall into old patterns, with the risk of losing the whole process. This approach was largely successful. A different way of reaching an agreement was practiced by FfD. Until the very last session of the preparatory process, there were broad exchanges of views but no negotiations on texts. After the meeting, the facilitator, who was appointed by the Preparatory Committee, would draft or redraft. In that way, three different drafts were produced, but only the last draft was word-for-word negotiated.

Another facet that was innovative in FfD was the early decision not to have a lengthy plan of action, which had become so typical of the series of conferences that the UN had organized in the 1990s—often reaching seventy pages. It was determined that the final report of the conference was to be short. It aimed at twelve pages and it largely succeeded, as the Monterrey Consensus is only sixteen pages long.

A third critical element was the involvement of the Bretton Woods institutions (BWIs), which created a certain comfort level among the developed countries. The extent of the involvement of the BWIs was not only critical but also unprecedented. Collaboration occurred at several levels: at the management level, as contacts between the heads of the institutions became more frequent; at the intergovernmental level, as meetings took place between the executive boards of the BWIs and government representatives at the UN; and at the intersecretariat levels, as the BWIs seconded staff to the UN Secretariat in preparation for the conference, working, for example, very closely on the recommendations of the Secretary-General to the Preparatory Committee.

The involvement of the BWIs made it possible to put issues like the international monetary system on the agenda. Yet the argument that certain aspects of that agenda item should be discussed in the intergovernmental bodies of the BWIs was raised continually, especially by the United States. As a result, the BWIs were "encouraged" in the Monterrey Consensus, rather than "asked," to take actions in certain areas. Despite these subtleties, the Monterrey Consensus has already made a real difference. To name just two areas, for the first time in years, official development assistance increased in 2002 (by $4.6 billion). This increase partly reflects the commitments made at Monterrey. The OECD estimates that ODA would increase by $16 billion per year by 2006, when all commitments made in Monterrey have come on full steam. In the second area, a serious discussion has been started in the BWIs about giving more voice to the developing countries in the BWIs' governing bodies. (It is rather anachronistic that a country like Belgium has more voting power in the BWIs than, for example, Brazil.)

Perhaps even more important than these concrete results, is the change in the tone of the debate, not only at the United Nations, but also throughout the development community and forums. One now speaks of a global partnership or global compact based on mutual responsibilities and mutual accountability.

The International Conference on Financing for Development discussed for the first time systemic global economic issues at the United Nations. Until FfD, they had been discussed mostly at the Bretton Woods and other forums. Perhaps they were not discussed at the United Nations because the developing countries have such a large voice at the United Nations. These issues were eventually discussed at the United Nations, perhaps because developing countries have such a large voice at the United Nations. They wanted to discuss these issues at the UN and they pushed for it. A convergence of factors helped them.

As a result, ministers of finance, trade, and development cooperation are now a regular sight at the United Nations. They discuss issues like investment, finance, debt, trade, ODA, debt, and systemic aspects of the global financial structure in a holistic way. There is no other forum where all these issues are discussed at the same time with their interlinkages.

The name for the outcome document of the conference, the Monterrey Consensus, was, of course, not a coincidence. It sought to replace the Washington Consensus, even if that was never explicitly stated. Not without success. Ian Goldin, a World Bank vice president, declared at the High-Level Dialogue on FfD in the General Assembly in October 2003 that the Washington consensus is dead. One consensus, which never really was a consensus but came out of powerful international financial institutions dominated by economists educated in the Anglo-Saxon world, was replaced by a much broader consensus.[10]

Conclusion

Change at the United Nations mostly occurs incrementally. The nature of international economic diplomacy at the United Nations has definitely changed over the decades. But sometimes one realizes that a few small steps in a relatively short period of time amount to something significant. The Millennium Development Goals and the Monterrey Consensus appear to have triggered some important changes. Do they amount to a dramatic shift? It is perhaps too early to tell,[11] but there certainly are important changes.

The adoption of the Millennium Development Goals and the Monterrey Consensus has shown the advantages of the United Nations as a forum for international economic diplomacy with its universality, legitimacy, ability to set global norms, convening power, and participatory approach. The FfD process was initiated before even the idea of the Millennium Summit existed, but the MDGs were born before the Monterrey Consensus was adopted. Thus, the MDGs were inserted, under pressure by the European Union, as an important goal of FfD, although not the only one. It appears that the MDGs (the goals) and FfD (the means) are inseparably intertwined and have changed the nature of international economic diplomacy at the United Nations for some time to come.

Notes

1. The views expressed are those of the author and do not necessarily reflect those of the United Nations. Comments from Barry Herman, Moncef Khane, and James P. Muldoon, Jr., were much appreciated.

2. In fact, the Charter (Article 55) explicitly links the goals for peace and development by arguing that "the creation of conditions of stability and well-being . . . are necessary for peaceful and friendly relations among nations."

3. Definitions of nonstate actors, civil society, and nongovernmental organizations (NGOs) are not always crystal clear. Generally, one can think of them as Russian dolls, with NGOs being a subset of civil society and civil society a subset of nonstate actors. The most significant difference among them is that nonstate actors include the private for-profit sector (business firms), organized crime, and religious organizations, such as churches and mosques, and that civil society includes also informal institutions, networks, and loosely organized movements.

4. This section benefited from Emmerij et al. (2001) and particularly Rahman (2002).

5. In a report of the Secretary-General to the General Assembly in 2001, they were named MDGs. That report also included the indicators that specified how to measure them. The General Assembly resolution, however, "noted" the report and did not "endorse" the report. Another reason for that phrase is that especially the United States had problems with the way the eighth MDG is measured, particularly with the inclusion of an indicator for aid. Hence the persistent usage of "internationally agreed development goals, including those contained in the Millennium Declaration."

6. Disagreements continued over, among other things, the proper speed, scope, and sequencing of reform measures. Moreover, it left to the political process decisions regarding the trade-off between efficiency and equity. In addition, the Washington Consensus was criticized by a number of dissenting economists and several influential international NGOs. The financial crises at the end of the 1990s have put this goal, however, on hold.

7. The financial crises at the end of the 1990s have put this goal, however, on hold.

8. The watershed year was 1982, when Mexico was the first country to default on its foreign debt. Net-creditor developing countries are all developing countries except Brunei Darussalam, Kuwait, Libyan Arab Jamahiriya, Oman, Qatar, Saudi Arabia, Singapore, Taiwan POC, and United Arab Emirates.

9. They are often called antiglobalization activists, but that is largely a misnomer as most activists are not really against globalization, just mostly arguing passionately for a different kind of globalization, one that is more just and more equitable, benefits more people, and has fewer risks and uncertainties associated with it.

10. Truth begs me to add that several NGOs that did participate in the FfD process did not accept the Monterrey Consensus as they viewed it as still too much like a neoliberal document. Moreover, Cuba denounced the Monterrey Consensus, even as it officially adopted it. President Fidel Castro said in Monterrey that "the Consensus draft, which the masters of the world are imposing on this conference, intends that we accept humiliating, conditioned and interfering alms."

11. Certainly by the standard of Zhou En-lai who replied to Henry Kissinger's question whether he thought the French Revolution was a success, "It's too soon to tell."

References

Emmerij, Louis, Richard Jolly, and Thomas G. Weiss. (2001) *Ahead of the Curve? UN Ideas and Global Challenges* (Bloomington and Indianapolis: Indiana University Press).

Herman, Barry. (2002) "Civil Society and the Financing for Development Initiative at the United Nations," in *Civil Society and Global Finance*, edited by Jan Aart Scholte and Albrecht Schnabel (London: Routledge), pp. 162—177.

Herman, Barry and Krishnan Sharma, eds. (1998) *International Finance and Developing Countries in a Year of Crisis* (Tokyo: UNU).

Rahman, Mahfuzur. (2002) *World Economic Issues at the United Nations: Half a Century of Debate* (Boston: Kluwer).

PRIVATE-SECTOR DIPLOMACY: THE ROLE OF BUSINESS IN INTERNATIONAL ECONOMIC AFFAIRS

Jeremy S. Taylor

Even after twenty-five years of experience with international business—first as a student of international affairs; then as a banker in global corporate finance; then as a partner in a data, research, and reporting firm in the leveraged markets; and finally as both the president of an executive search firm specializing in international financial markets and a consultant in an international practice—I still find the intricate and evolving relationship between business and society fascinating as well as challenging to master. Ascertaining the role of business in today's globalized, wired, networked society has become one of the most hotly debated issues of our time. Business leaders, policymakers, and civil society groups are engaged in a complex process of redrawing the boundaries of the public and private sectors and redefining relationships. The international political economy is in the midst of an incredible transition, and international business is a key player in the process.

Although the role of business in society has been a subject of much debate since the creation of joint-stock companies in the eighteenth century, the intense scrutiny of global capitalism and transnational corporations in this era of globalization indicates a significant qualitative difference in the status of business in the global system. The "soft power" of the private sector in the world economy and world politics has clearly expanded. Globalization, in the broadest sense of the term, has elevated the profile and clout of international business within the burgeoning constellation of nonstate actors in contemporary international relations. International business can no longer downplay its political influence, ignore the social and ecological consequences of its activities, nor dismiss as irrelevant the responsibilities that naturally emanate from power.

The growing influence of businesspeople in international economic relations is reflected by the greater participation of private-sector leaders in international forums, private and public, that address regulatory or legal issues of market creation, international trade and finance, employment, and intellectual property and other global issues with broad environmental, social, and distributive implications. Since the mid-1990s, a whole new generation of international public policy forums, industry associations, and consultative bodies has been created that enable the private sector to advance their interests and increase influence in the international arena. Through international business associations such as the International Chamber of Commerce (ICC) and the World Business Council for Sustainable Development, international business has been able to "affect the outcomes of issues on the international agenda by inserting themselves at critical points in policy processes," to preempt "national and international legislation and regulation through adoption of self-regulation and standards-setting," and to deepen "already close relationships with national governments and regional and global institutions" (Hocking and Kelly 2002, 205 and 218). The conventional view of the role and responsibilities of business in society—simply to produce goods and services and to sell them for a profit—doesn't really fit the new global reality as national and local economies further integrate with the global market economy.

Ambrose Bierce once defined politics as the "strife of interests masquerading as a contest of principles"; so, might I add, is much of what appears as the global agenda for corporate citizenship and social responsibility. It is only in forums where these conflicting agendas and interests can be realistically addressed that progress, however incremental, is made. My purpose here is not to defend or justify the role that business plays in multilateral economic diplomacy and public policy. Leaders in the private sector have for hundreds of years been and still remain essential participants in economic and public policy arenas. My purpose is to demonstrate how private-sector diplomats play vital roles in the economic, financial, political, legal, social, and strategic agendas of both the state and the international community.

It should be remembered that merchants were among the first diplomats, connecting peoples and economies as they ventured across frontiers in the pursuit of spices, gold, and other profitable commodities. Since the beginnings of civilization, merchants have traveled far and wide, plying their trade and often acting as emissaries of their rulers to foreign heads of state. It was an arrangement of convenience, as well as of mutual benefit. From the earliest times, merchants have been adept at coopting governments to act in their interest. Mercantilism was just such a partnership. Although mercantilism flourished in the seventeenth, eighteenth, and nineteenth centuries, there were earlier examples of mercantile policies. Venetians were seafaring commercial brokers who, in 1380, gained mastery of the seas by defeating the Genoese, the only other major European sea power. It was the commercial aspiration of the Venetian merchants to control the lucrative trade of the Adriatic that drove their government to war.

Likewise, centuries later the British and other Western merchants drove expansion of markets in China. They used their economic power and the seduction of expanding commercial opportunity to influence their governments to take military action against the Chinese in order to force open markets. The Opium Wars of 1839–1842 and 1856–1860 were the result. The first was a consequence of China's decision to outlaw the importation of opium by the merchants. The Chinese lost, and Western merchants won an expanded entree to China's markets. The second war furthered the interests of the West, legalized its highly profitable trade in opium, and expanded both its rights and its access. Indeed, there are many examples throughout history of merchants' convincing their governments to take military action on their behalf, thereby redefining both domestic and international economy in what has become known as *gunboat diplomacy*.

But to influence today's global economy is a much more complex enterprise for business. The infrastructure of trade policy, governmental and multilateral bureaucracy, and the complexity of international financial markets, not to mention the proliferation of interested parties (stakeholders), require leaders of international business to marshal more information utilizing more sophisticated skills than ever before. Indeed, the very survival of companies, industries, and countries depends on the abilities of their leaders to grasp today's global political and socioeconomic realities and to influence events in the world marketplace. Economic globalization has elevated the significance of decisions made and strategies formulated in corporate boardrooms and executive suites. The prosperity and stability of sovereign states and of the international economic system are increasingly tied to the fortunes of and actions taken by private commercial and financial institutions.

Some of the largest international financial service institutions are spending more and more of their resources on evaluating and attempting to mitigate the risks associated with doing business, whether domestic or international. Credit risk, market risk, foreign exchange risk, counterparty risk, sovereign risk, and portfolio risk, to name just a few areas of potential exposure, require familiarity with a very broad range of issues. Business, like government, depends upon professionals with numerate capacity and the capability to compile and analyze information, which in itself requires sophisticated system interfaces, programming, and database management. The challenges facing those analysts in sourcing and analyzing that information, in an increasingly interdependent world, can be monumental. We have had some very sobering examples of the global repercussions that poor management and lax oversight can have on the global economy in the very recent past, for example, the 1997–1998 Asian financial crisis and the WorldCom and Enron scandals. Faulty accounting, specious reporting, and fraud by a number of major multinational corporations have severely effected global markets, eroded trust in accounting standards and management, and, as a result, diminished public confidence in business leadership, corporate governance, and social responsibility.

The fallout from corporate malfeasance of late has renewed the mistrust of big business among social justice, environmental, and community activists and development-oriented nongovernmental organizations, representing a diplomatic setback for those business leaders who have embraced the social responsibility agenda and have been at the forefront in building a new relationship with international organizations and erstwhile critics from the NGO community. "Many development organizations are deeply skeptical of the apparent conversion of business [to the development agenda], and fear that the fast-emerging fields of corporate social responsibility, public-private partnerships and the like is little more than a public relations exercise. Many still believe the only way to bring business into line is through the establishment of global rules, such as are being discussed in Geneva" (Turner 2004a, 2). Nevertheless, the globalization of economies, business enterprises, and financial markets is bringing about a convergence of the interests of government, business, and civil society in many parts of the world, and new and evolving forms of partnership are on the rise. This trend deepens the business community's participation in the diplomatic process of international economic affairs, particularly as governments rely more and more on markets to "regulate" the global economy and look to the private sector to strengthen the economic relationships between countries. With increasing stakeholder pressure on international business to assume broader social, development, and environmental responsibilities, business executives are discovering that to successfully manage the diversity of stakeholder relationships they must have strong diplomatic skills.

Profile of Private-Sector Diplomacy

Diplomacy is the practice of building relationships. Businesspeople are often so goal-oriented and agenda-specific that they fail to respect the process of culturally specific relationship building, particularly with their business counterparts and the government officials of other countries, not to mention NGOs and social activists. They seem to have forgotten or simply don't know that relationship building in an international context often requires a very different set of sensitivities and skills, not to mention an understanding of the unique practices of the culture they are attempting to build relationships in. They need a diplomatic architecture, a framework of standard practices, to function effectively in international forums and meetings. So, what are the skills, talents and sensitivities that produce an effective private-sector diplomat?

The description of the qualifications of a nineteenth-century diplomat in an excerpt from *Embassies and Foreign Courts: A History of Diplomacy*, published in 1855, entitled "Roving English Gentlemen," is both amusing and instructive.

> They tell us with a grave and enchanting simplicity that the representatives of a great nation should know something more than how to dine and dance—to bow with becoming reverence, and to modulate his voice in such a manner that it may be heard without offence within the precincts of the court. They very justly set a proper value on the qualifications above mentioned; for a diplomatist can scarcely be useful in his office if he is not also a polished and genial gentleman—a happy mixture of the scholar, the philosopher, and the man of the world. They do not, however, subscribe to an opinion which has been of late years rather too prevalent in Britain—that accomplishment and the graces are alone sufficient recommendations for entrusting to any gentleman the most vital interests—the peace and honor of nations. They do not churlishly reject the popular, and, in the main, useful theory as most popular theories are when we examine them fairly that an ambassador should be something of a beau-cavalier—agreeable, witty, gentle-mannered, a clubbable man, indeed; only they think that he should also possess some other qualities and attainments, and that the outward glitter should be the mere setting of the gem within. (Embassies and Foreign Courts 1855, 38–39)

This description reflects how the homogeneity of social etiquette and tradition provided the architecture of diplomacy at the time, reminding us that diplomacy is an art that requires a broad international perspective and a foundation of commonality. But today's realities demand a very different set of rules and requirements for the practice of diplomacy.

A "diplomat" in this era of globalization needs to be what Professor Donald G. Tewksbury, a former professor with Teacher's College at Columbia University, called a "mature international person." According to Tewksbury, a mature international person is:

- One who has examined objectively the strengths and weaknesses of his own culture.

- One who is eager to consider seriously what other peoples think of his culture.

- One who is not too sensitive about criticism of his own culture.

- One who is able in traveling, to identify with other peoples and to listen and learn from them.

- One who has experienced and passed beyond the stage of "cultural shock" in relation to cultures that differ sharply from his own.

- One who has personal and friendly relations with a number of persons from other countries on a long-term basis.

- One who has international friends in one's own specialized profession or occupation.

- One with whom persons from other countries can be frank and in whom they may have confidence.

- One who can discuss other cultures without bringing in name-calling, stereotyping and extreme categorization.

- One who does not wish to make over other peoples and cultures in his own image.

- One who is actively concerned with promoting the exchange of contributions between one's own and other countries.

- One who has at least an elementary familiarity with the family of languages and sees his own language as one member of this family.[1]

In my opinion, these characteristics of a mature international person are part of the constitution of an effective diplomat today, whether in politics or business, and essential for building relationships of trust. But it is hard to find business leaders who have all or even some of these qualities, not to mention an awareness of their strengths or weaknesses in this regard. Most business school programs are not structured to develop the qualities of a "mature international person" within their students or to instruct business executives on how to handle the growing complexity of relationships in the global economy. As Jeffrey Garten, Dean of the Yale School of Management, points out:

> As companies face challenges for which there are no consistent global laws or concrete standards—challenges relating to the environment, labor, business practices, corporate roles in education, and human rights—they must balance their fiduciary responsibility to shareholders in a highly competitive marketplace with considerations that include their own corporate and moral values, their roles in strengthening the society around them, and the rewards and risks to their reputation. The issues are horrendously complex, and virtually no CEO is trained to handle them. But one thing is certain: To make the best judgements, companies must develop cooperative strategies with home and host governments, international institutions, and nongovernmental organizations. . . . A new paradigm for business leadership requires rethinking the basics of business education. We must equip CEOs to manage their companies for short-term profitability but also for long-term value. They must learn to focus not only on the internal efficiencies of their companies but also on the external relationships and policies—including interaction with governments, international institutions, and nongovernmental organizations. Business executives must understand better their overall responsibilities when it comes to the system, values, and culture that drive their global enterprises. (Garten 2002, 15–16)

Emblematic of the changing notions of what constitutes the architecture of diplomacy is two private "diplomacy organizations": Diplomacy International and Diplomats Without Borders/Diplomates sans Frontières (DSF). The premise behind these organizations is the belief that "it is impossible to be a good political leader without having substantive economic and diplomacy skills. It is impossible to be a good business leader without sufficiently understanding international politics and being a good diplomat.

And it is equally impossible to be a good diplomat without understanding the world economy and international business."[2] Diplomacy International offers a range of practical "diplomatic" services to businesses, international organizations, and nongovernmental organizations, including information gathering, analysis and evaluation, negotiation and mediation assistance, protocol and advice on intercultural relations, and image building and public diplomacy. Likewise, Diplomats Without Borders, which was founded by a group of professionals from the fields of international trade and investment, corporate business, government diplomacy, banking and finance, and the military, defines private diplomacy as "the art and practice of negotiating, mediating, and managing relations between people in a private, nongovernmental capacity" and seeks "to broaden the practice of private diplomacy as a means of building bridges between governments, businesses, and non-governmental organizations (NGOs)."[3] These organizations simply illustrate the growing importance of diplomatic skills for meeting the challenges of doing business.

Business and the Diplomacy of Sustainability

The concept of sustainable development has been in one form or another with us for three or four decades.[4] In 1962, Rachel Carson published *Silent Spring*, which is regarded by many as the first significant cry for attention to the reckless human assault on the harmony of nature. This was followed by Paul Erlich's book *The Population Bomb*, published in 1968, which addressed the relationship between population, resource allocation, and the environment and the 1968 UNESCO Conference on the Biosphere. Both of these books were the first stirrings of what has become a much more integrated and comprehensive discussion of human survival and the human fiduciary responsibility to the planet and to other people. Then came Earth Day in 1970—the first significant large-scale call to action on the global threat to the environment—when some 20 million Americans participated in a nationwide teach-in on the problems confronting the natural environment. This awareness-raising event coupled with the books by Carson and Erlich and the biosphere conference made ecological and environmental issues and concerns the original pillars of the sustainable development movement and the first components of the movement to be addressed and acted upon globally. As John Muir, the naturalist, explorer, and writer, once mused, "When one tugs at a single thing in nature, he finds it attached to the rest of the world."

From the outset, the business community was an obvious target of environmentalists and development activists, who make up the base of the sustainable development movement. The International Institute for Environment and Development (IIE), established in 1971, was among the first institutions to bring research to bear on the problem of making economic progress without denigrating the natural resource base and to present the case for holding commercial interests responsible for their conduct. Over the next twenty years, the pressure on business over its impact on the environment and role in economic and social development intensified, spawning a new cottage industry of governmental and nongovernmental groups that were focused on corporate accountability and corporate social responsibility (CSR).

The business response to the pressure was initially combative and querulous. But as the sustainable development movement gained momentum in the 1980s, particularly after the report of the World Commission on Environment and Development, *Our Common Future* (the Brundtland Report), was released in 1987, the business community started to change its approach, seeking cooperation rather than confrontation. In a way, the sustainable development movement can be credited with shaping private-sector diplomacy and altering the perspectives within the international business community on the value of CSR. The breakthrough moment came in 1992 at the UN Conference on Environment and Development when the World Business Council on Sustainable Development (WBCSD) was formed to coordinate business input at this landmark event.

The WBCSD's vision of the business community's role in sustainable development was outlined in *Changing Course: A Global Business Perspective on Development and the Environment*, which was published by the WBCSD in 1992 in time for the Earth Summit in Rio. Now, a dozen years later, the WBCSD has grown significantly from its original 50 business leaders to an international organization with "170 international companies drawn from 35 countries and more than 20 major industrial sectors, involving some 1,000 business leaders globally," and the "vision of business contributions to sustainable development are now well-established within the WBCSD, and spread through extensive member involvement, stakeholder consultations and research reports tackling the most pressing sustainability issues affecting today's corporate world."[5] The sustainability issue has become a focal point for the more prominent international business associations like the International Chamber of Commerce and the World Economic Forum and has a permanent place on the international business agenda. The International Institute for Sustainable Development (IISD) argues that "by adopting sustainable practices, companies can gain an edge, increase their market share, and boost shareholder value" and that "business has entered into a new phase in which sustainable business performance is regarded as a global competitive advantage; a catalyst for innovation; a way to capture new market and financing opportunities."[6] This view is supported by other influential research organizations such as the International Business Leadership Forum (IBLF) and Business for Social Responsibility (BSR). This outlook within the international business community is gaining some traction (though it is still a minority who have truly embraced the sustainability agenda), compelling many business leaders to become involved in public policy discussions on the international level.

Over the 1990s, the part played by business in the diplomacy of sustainability grew. This is evidenced by the proliferation of public-private partnerships and international initiatives. One example of this trend is the UN's Global Compact:

> Kofi Annan, UN Secretary General, launched in 2000 the Global Compact, acknowledging the power of global enterprise, but inviting it to enter into a partnership to promote nine core human rights, environmental and labor goals. . . . Over the intervening period it has attracted more than 1,400 participants, making it the largest such grouping in the world. In essence, the compact is a forum for business leaders and civil society groups to discuss how to promote its standards, and asks companies to assess their impact in their annual reports. It is a voluntary organization which does not attempt to set rules, make judgments, or promote its members. (Turner 2004c, 4)

Likewise, the Global Policy Dialogues on issues related to globalization convened under UN auspices have brought together business interests, with UN agencies, labor, NGOs, and other interests to produce solutions.

Of course there are myriad international initiatives—for example, public-private partnerships, global public policy networks, and corporate citizenship and corporate social responsibility programs—that promote both opportunity and communication between business and other societal actors. Some of the more prominent proponents of business leadership in such initiatives include the World Economic Forum, the International Chamber of Commerce, the World Business Council for Sustainable Development, the United Nations Global Compact, the International Institute for Sustainable Development, and the International Business Leaders Forum. However, it must be recognized that only those companies that find that their financial survival depends on playing the citizenship and the sustainability cards will actually play them. Profit, after all, is what companies owe their investors. The highest-profile industries, such as the oil companies and the pharmaceuticals, tend to be among the most scrutinized for their citizenship roles given the important public policy challenges we face today, and therefore, they have been forced to take corporate social responsibility and sustainable development seriously. Other industries and firms are involved more for PR than for reasons of substantive concern. So, in the final analysis, the success of corporate social responsibility and citizenship will only come on the back of enforced legal sanctions or its irrefutable link to profitability. Signing on to international initiatives accomplishes nothing on its own, so all the lip service to CSR remains largely that.

Nonetheless, business participation in so-called multisector partnerships side by side with international agencies, governments, and NGOs to overcome poverty, disease, inequality, and environmental degradation around the world is growing. These partnerships are "'catalytic' strategies in which [both governmental and nongovernmental] actors bring to a policy milieu a differing mix of resources without which neither can their objectives be sustained nor a diplomatic conflict resolved. In turn, this demands the development of appropriate strategies and structures—formal, informal, or a hybrid mix—through which communications can be maintained and successful outcomes pursued" (Hocking and Kelly 2002, 208). It is exposure to and participation in these organizations and the interaction with other organizations involved in international initiatives that produces the private-sector diplomat.

Conclusion

Private-sector diplomacy dictates that business executives play an active role in world affairs. Indeed, all leaders in business must now by definition act on a global stage and practice the art of diplomacy. Diplomacy is the vehicle through which the private sector's role in the emerging global society will be defined and private-sector interests articulated. It is no longer an option for corporate leaders to ignore or deny the importance of social and environmental issues to their companies' bottom line and shareholder value. "If companies do not take account of emerging social, environmental and other trends, they are taking on big risks and could also be missing out on opportunities for growth" (Turner 2004b, 3). Just as commercial interests drove the diplomatic functions of the early European states, those in commercial practice today must develop the awareness, skills, and commitment to the institutions and visions of our time, as well as actively participate in the great questions of the day in helping to drive focus on our commonality of purpose. It is good business, good diplomacy, and, most important, good global citizenship.

Notes

1. This list is from a handout for one of Professor Tewksbury's courses in the 1960s.

2. From the website of Diplomacy International at [www.diplomacyinternational.com].

3. From the website of Diplomats Without Borders [www.diplomatswithoutborders.org].

4. See the "Sustainable Development Timeline" compiled by the International Institute for Sustainable Development [www.iisd.org/timeline].

5. From the history section of the WBCSD website [www.wbcsd.ch].

6. From the IISD website [www.iisd.org].

References

Embassies and Foreign Courts: A History of Diplomacy (1855) (London: G. Routledge).

Garten, Jeffrey. (2002) *The Politics of Fortune* (Boston: Harvard Business School Press).

Hocking, Brian and Dominic Kelly. (2002) "Doing the Business? The International Chamber of Commerce, the United Nations, and the Global Compact," in *Enhancing Global Governance: Towards a New Diplomacy?* edited by Andrew F. Cooper, John English, and Ramesh Thakur (Tokyo: United Nations University Press), pp. 203–228.

Turner, Mark. (2004a) "Seeds of a New Understanding," Special Report: Business and Development, *Financial Times*, June 24, p. 2.

_____. (2004b) "Appealing to Money Men," Special Report: Business and Development, *Financial Times*, June 24, p. 3.

_____. (2004c) "The Global Compact—Effort to Bury Mistrust," Special Report: Business and Development, *Financial Times*, June 24, p. 4.

THE UNITED NATIONS IN
AN ERA OF GLOBALIZATION

Ambassador S. Azmat Hassan

The United Nations Charter affirms, "We the Peoples of the United Nations [are] determined ... to employ international machinery for the economic and social advancement of all peoples." Furthermore, Article 55 of the Charter requires that the organization promote higher standards of living, full employment, and conditions conducive to economic and social development. The Charter, therefore, makes explicit provision for an active UN role in fostering economic and social development among all its member states.

Sixty years after the UN Charter was signed by 51 states in San Francisco, membership in the organization has expanded to over 190 nations. Countries with different histories, cultures, populations, and levels of industrial and technological development give expression to the principle of universality by being members of the only truly global organization in the world today. Are the actions of the United Nations today consistent with the Charter, especially in a new era of economic globalization?

The Challenges of Globalization

A new era of interaction among national economies and people is being shaped by globalization. The transnational movement of capital, goods, and people and the emergence of new communication technologies are creating an unprecedented integration of markets, capital, technology, and culture, and they are creating new problems. Technological advancement and economic integration are compelling countries to "share" their sovereignty with regional and global institutions as well as international business and nongovernmental organizations.

Globalization is increasingly becoming an unavoidable component in governmental decisionmaking. The increased flow of capital, the rapid growth of international trade, the expanded role of multinational companies, and their growing integration into the global economy have created enormous opportunities for sustainable human development. Many developing countries have adopted economic policies of economic liberalization and privatization in the hope that integration with the world economy will assist them in promoting their own development and thereby reduce poverty and its human, political, and social consequences. Unfortunately, while generating wealth and choices for a few, globalization has more often than not widened the gap between rich and poor, both among and within nations. In many countries, the number of people living below the poverty line has increased. In other countries, social inequality has sharply increased. A new digital divide has aggravated the traditional gaps between the haves and have-nots by eliminating low-level jobs, depressing wages, and weakening workers' rights.

A crisis in governance has also been generated by globalization, when the concerns of those excluded, bypassed, or impoverished by the globalization process are not adequately addressed. In essence, the rules governing the international economy are perceived by many people as benefiting the few rather than the vast majority of people living in developing or even developed nations. This perception and the reality of global inequality have produced a growing backlash against globalization.

There is also broad consensus that the benefits of globalization cannot be acquired nor the risks contained without a firm commitment by governments to reform and to create good governance institutions in order to take advantage of globalization's emerging opportunities. Whereas some governments recognize the need to eliminate corruption and to create, reorganize and retool institutions to effectively deal with the impacts and opportunities of globalization, many do not. In short, globalization has democratized information, deconcentrated power, empowered citizens, and generated political openness. The synergy of the free market, democracy, and civil society can make the process of globalization and the concept of good governance mutually reinforcing. National governments are facing growing demands on their governing capacity as national and global governance become inextricably interconnected. Governments must now seize this unprecedented opportunity to change the lives of so many of the world's people for the better.

In summary, the international market economy, the information technology, a broad consensus on democratization, the globalization of social values, and the emergence of global civil society organizations are impacting all nations. An assertive civil society has become an important player at the global and national levels. The revolution in communication technologies and the Internet are enabling citizens to become more engaged in the management of public affairs. The participation of civil society organizations in the recent global conferences relating to social development, women, population, and environment has increased their influence in shaping not only world public opinion but also governmental policies in the economic and social fields. Furthermore, as national boundaries are overrun by economic forces, environmental change, and technology, governments are being forced to deal with the clout of multinational corporations. Many sectors of economic activity are not as firmly within the control of governments as in the past, since integration of the international economy is breaking down the financial and trade barriers. The result has been the pooling of national sovereignty between governments and multinational corporations.

The UN's Role in Globalization

UN Secretary-General Kofi Annan has observed that "arguing against globalization is like arguing against the laws of gravity." He noted that "we cannot wait for governments to do it all. Globalization operates on Internet time. Governments tend to be slow moving by nature, because they have to build political support for every step." Annan also suggested that open markets "offer the only realistic hope of pulling billions of people in developing countries out of abject poverty, while sustaining prosperity in the industrialized world," but he warned, "we must ensure that the global market is embedded in broadly shared values and practices that reflect global social needs, and that all the world's people share the benefits of globalization." As for the UN's role in globalization, he said that if the organization "does not attempt to chart a course for the world's people in the first decades of the new millennium, who will?"[1]

John Ruggie, who has served as a key adviser to the Secretary-General, has concluded that the growing backlash against globalization is due to persistent world poverty, pronounced income inequalities within and among countries, and environmental practices that threaten the life support systems that nature provides. These are clear signals, therefore, that globalization, as we now know it, may not be sustainable.

As Ruggie notes, there are two major problems with globalization. First, the developing countries cannot buffer themselves from the "rapidly expanding and unfettered market forces." These forces often produce economic instability and social dislocation at an accelerating pace. Second, even in the most powerful countries, people worry about their jobs being eliminated because they are being moved to a developing nation where wages are low, working conditions are bad, environmental hazards are serious, and governments are corrupt. Ruggie believes that multilateral collaboration can and must play a central role in bridging the gap between global markets and national communities. Ruggie reminds us of the speech that Secretary-General Kofi Annan was supposed to deliver but could not at the tumultuous December 1999 WTO ministerial in Seattle: "What is needed is not new shackles for world trade, but greater determination by governments to tackle social and political issues directly—and to give the institutions that exist for that purpose the funds and the authority they need. The United Nations and its specialized agencies are charged with advancing the causes of development, the environment, human rights and labor. We can be part of the solution."[2]

The United Nations has struggled with the challenges of globalization for several years, especially since the 1997–1998 Asian financial crisis served as a wakeup call for the international community. Since 1998, a series of discussions have been under way in the UN's Administrative Committee on Coordination (ACC)—an institutional mechanism (renamed the Chief Executives Board [CEB] in 2000) that brings together the heads of all parts of the extended UN family including the specialized agencies, the Bretton Woods institutions, and the World Trade Organization to oversee and help in the implementation of the multifaceted activities of the UN system—that have explored the different dimensions of globalization and the appropriate policy approaches by which the UN system can help better manage the risks and secure the benefits of globalization. These discussions laid the groundwork for a range of new initiatives that were "aimed at enhancing the United Nations system's flexibility and effectiveness in operating within a changed environment."[3]

The outcomes of these discussions within the ACC has been the development of new relationships between the United Nations system, the private sector, and civil society organizations arranged in what has been called *global public policy networks.* For example, the United Nations identified the "digital divide" as a major challenge after CEB discussions increased awareness of the significant gaps in information and communication technologies (ICT) that exist between the industrialized and developing countries. UN experts recognize that bridging the digital divide is not so much an issue of transfer of technology as of capacity building in developing countries—capacity not only in terms of physical infrastructure, but, more important, of knowledge and learning. The UN convened an expert working group, which led to a ministerial declaration on the issue in 2000. This led to the creation of the ICT task force in 2001 and the International Telecommunication Union taking the lead in organizing the World Summit on the Information Society. The ICT task force is the first body ever created by a UN intergovernmental decision in which governments, the private sector, civil society organizations, and UN agencies participate on an equal footing.

Another example of considerable importance is the formation of the UN Global Compact. Secretary-General Annan first proposed the Global Compact in an address to the World Economic Forum on January 31, 1999. The Global Compact's initial phase was launched at UN Headquarters in New York in July 26, 2000. The Secretary-General challenged business leaders to join an international initiative—the Global Compact—that would bring companies together with UN agencies, labor, and civil society to support nine principles in the areas of human rights, labor standards, and the environment:

Human Rights

Principle 1: Businesses should support and respect the protection of internationally proclaimed human rights within their sphere of influence.

Principle 2: They should make sure that they are not complicit in human rights abuses.

Labor Standards

Principle 3: Businesses should uphold the freedom of association and the effective recognition of the right to collective bargaining.

Principle 4: They should eliminate all forms of forced and compulsory labor.

Principle 5: They should abolish child labor.

Principle 6: They should eliminate discrimination in employment and occupation.

Environment

Principle 7: Businesses should support a precautionary approach to environmental challenges.

Principle 8: They should undertake initiatives to promote greater environmental responsibility.

Principle 9: They should encourage the development and diffusion of environmentally friendly technologies.

Through the power of collective action, the Global Compact seeks to advance responsible corporate citizenship so that business can be a part of the solution to the challenges of globalization. In this way the private sector—in partnership with other societal actors—can help realize the Secretary-General's vision: a more sustainable and inclusive global economy.

Today, hundreds of companies from all regions of the world, as well as international labor and civil society organizations are engaged in the Global Compact. A direct initiative of the Secretary-General, its staff and operations are lean and flexible. The Global Compact is a voluntary corporate citizenship initiative with two objectives—making the Global Compact and its principles part of business strategy and operations and facilitating cooperation among key stakeholders and promoting partnerships in support of UN goals. To achieve these objectives the Global Compact offers facilitation and engagement through several mechanisms: policy dialogues, learning, local structures, and projects. The Global Compact is not a regulatory instrument—it does not "police," enforce, or measure the behavior or actions of companies. Rather the Global Compact relies on public accountability, transparency, and the enlightened self-interest of companies, labor, and civil society to initiate and share substantive action in pursuing the principles upon which the Global Compact is based.

The Global Compact is a network. At its core are the Global Compact Office and five UN agencies: the Office of the High Commissioner for Human Rights, the United Nations Environment Program, the International Labor Organization, the United Nations Development Program, and the United Nations Industrial Development Organization. The Global Compact involves all the relevant societal actors: governments, which define the principles on which the initiative is based; companies, whose actions it seeks to influence; labor, in whose hands the concrete process of global production takes place; civil society organizations, representing the wider community of stakeholders; and the United Nations, the world's only global forum, as an authoritative convener and facilitator. Approximately 30 percent of the companies that have joined in the Global Compact are classified as small and medium enterprises (SMEs). While the other UN agencies focus on advocacy and operational roles in respect to their mandates, the United Nations Industrial Development Organization (UNIDO) will help realize the objectives of the Global Compact at the field level in UNIDO's client countries.

In April 2003, some of the major NGOs, including Amnesty International, Oxfam International, Human Rights Watch, and the Lawyers Committee for Human Rights, addressed a letter to Louise Frechette, Deputy Secretary-General of the UN, seeking clarification of the role of NGOs in the compact. These NGOs feared that their role in the Global Compact was not properly defined. The Deputy Secretary-General responded on June 3, 2003, in a letter aimed at allaying their concerns. Frechette concluded, among other things, that "the Global Compact remains an ambitious experiment in cooperation. As a voluntary initiative which is meant to complement regulatory approaches, the success of the initiative depends largely on the active involvement of its participants."

On the eve of the UN's Millennium Summit, convened in September 2000 and attended by a majority of the world's leaders, Secretary-General Kofi Annan issued an important report—"*We the Peoples*": *The Role of the United Nations in the Twenty-first Century* (A/54/2000)—in which he reminded the heads of state and government that the founding members of the United Nations in 1945 set up an open and cooperative system for the international community. The system "worked and made it possible for globalization [eventually] to emerge." Responding to the challenges posed by globalization is a major problem confronting all nations today. Crime, narcotics, terrorism, pollution, disease, weapons, refugees, and unrestricted immigration all move across frontiers more easily than ever before in history. New technologies have also created opportunities for mutual understanding and common action. Annan referred, however, to the disparities in wealth, the "miserable conditions in which well over a billion people live, the prevalence of endemic conflict in some regions," and environmental degradation. These factors combined to make the present model of development unsustainable unless remedial measures are forthcoming.

Annan listed six shared values reflecting the spirit of the Charter, which are of particular relevance to the new century. They are freedom, equity and solidarity, tolerance, nonviolence, respect for nature, and shared responsibility. The Secretary-General also pleaded for help from all member states to strengthen the United Nations. He noted that without a strong

UN, it will be much more difficult to meet all the challenges confronting the international community. The Secretary-General's comprehensive and lucid report evoked a positive response from the leaders who had assembled in New York City. They pledged to work for and implement the millennium development goals (MDGs)[4] outlined in the Millennium Declaration (A/RES/55/2), in particular the eighth goal, to "develop a global partnership for development" that would

- further expand an open trading and financial system that is rule-based, predictable, and nondiscriminatory, including a commitment to good governance, development, and poverty reduction—nationally and internationally;

- address the least-developed nations' special needs, including tariff- and quota-free access for their exports; enhanced debt relief for heavily indebted countries; cancellation of official bilateral debt; and more generous official development assistance for countries committed to poverty reduction;

- address the special needs of landlocked and small-island developing states;

- deal comprehensively with developing nations' debt problems through national and international measures to make debts sustainable in the long term;

- in cooperation with the developing countries, develop decent and productive work for youth; and

- in cooperation with pharmaceutical companies, provide access to affordable drugs in developing nations.

Kofi Annan has been widely praised for his direction, commitment to, and advocacy of the steps required at the national and international levels to achieve a more harmonious and equitable world economic and social system, sensitive and receptive to the needs of the least-developed countries. But there are limits to what the United Nations can and should do in the development field in an era of rapid and bewildering globalization. The fundamental (and ultimate) responsibility for implementing the policy recommendations of the United Nations resides with national governments, which are frequently jealous of their sovereign right to determine their economic and social future. Some of these governments oppose the

UN's recommendations on national and global economic issues, which while economically sound, may not be politically palatable to their leaders or politically sustainable at home. The United Nations must tread carefully and delicately to juggle often competing and clashing interests.

Nevertheless, the Secretary-General reminds us all that the

> key challenge that must be met . . . is to place development at the center in considering how globalization is managed, and not to view it as a by-product of globalization. Development goals should shape the framework of globalization rather than allowing the blind forces of globalization to define the development outcome. This implies not only ensuring greater policy coherence at the global and national levels, but also making the international trade, finance and technology regimes much more responsive to development.[5]

Notes

1. Annan's comments are from various public statements on globalization that he made in 1999 and 2000, which were collated by the on-line magazine *The Globalist* in 2001 [www.theglobalist.com].

2. UN Press Release SG/SM/7237/Rev. 1, November 26, 1999.

3. ACC/1999/2/Add. 1, para. 4, p. 2.

4. See the full list of MDGs on-line at www.un.org/millenniumgoals.

5. "Role of the United Nations in promoting development in the context of globalization and interdependence, a Report of the Secretary-General," A/56/445 (5 October 2001), paragraph 64, p.11.

References

United Nations. (1999) "Summary of Conclusions of the Organizational Committee of ACC at Its Second Regular Session" (Parts I and II), ACC/1999/2/Add. 1, December 9.

United Nations. (2001) "Summary of the Conclusions of the Administrative Committee on Coordination at Its First Regular Session of 2001," ACC/2001/4, June 6.

United Nations. (2001) "Role of the United Nations in Promoting Development in the Context of Globalization and Interdependence," A/56/445, October 5.

Chapter FOUR

NONGOVERNMENTAL DIPLOMACY

Revitalizing Multilateral Diplomacy

NGOs and
International Affairs

JoAnn Fagot Aviel

As discussed in earlier chapters, since the end of the Cold War, diplomacy has expanded from the narrow dictionary definition limiting it to the peaceful conduct of relations between nation-states. Because of the globalization of actors, issues, and problems, the international system today cannot be understood or international relations effectively managed without taking into account nonstate actors such as nongovernmental organizations (NGOs). The need for global action on transnational problems and the increasing ease of instant communication have helped to expand the number of NGOs at the global level as well as their role in multilateral diplomacy. In contrast to 1947, when the member states were virtually the sole actors in the international process, UN Secretary-General Kofi Annan noted that "non-governmental organizations are now seen as essential partners of the United Nations, not only in mobilizing public opinion, but also in the process of deliberation and policy formulation and—even more important—in the execution of policies, in work on the ground" (Annan 1997).

Key Features of NGO Influence:
Diversity, Commitment, Expertise, and Networking

Even though estimated numbers of NGOs vary widely as do definitions of what constitutes an NGO, all agree that, no matter how defined, their numbers and influence have increased tremendously in recent years. In 1949, the UN Economic and Social Council (ECOSOC) under Article 71 of the UN Charter—the only specific mention of NGOs in the Charter— had granted only ninety NGOs consultative status, whereas by 2003, there were over twenty-three hundred NGOs with consultative status with ECOSOC.[1] Although not giving a specific definition of an NGO, the ECOSOC has endeavored to regulate the type of organization which is to be given consultative status. ECOSOC Resolution 1996/31 states that the organization shall have an established headquarters, a democratically adopted constitution, and a representative structure with appropriate mechanisms of accountability to its members as well as other requirements.

Diversity

NGOs vary tremendously in their size, organizational dimensions, range of concerns, and mechanisms for ensuring accountability to both members and funding. Their diversity is a source of both strength and weakness. They can be created quickly and expand or reduce their size and programs in response to perceived demand and needs. Some are small and local; others are global in scope. Some rely principally on volunteers for their personnel; others have large paid staffs. Some are supported primarily by financial contributions from their members or are supported by private foundations. Others, including some of the largest NGOS such as the International Committee of the Red Cross and CARE, rely on contributions from governments for most of their operating funds.

The range of concerns of NGOs is also quite diverse. Some are concerned with single issues—International Rivers Network, Rainforest Action Network, or Indigenous World Association are among these—and attempt to set norms and influence policy on them. Others—such as the Women's Environment and Development Organization (WEDO) and Human Rights Advocates—have broader concerns. Still others—for example, the many "operational NGOs" involved in refugee relief or development aid—are primarily concerned with executing policy and administering programs.

Commitment

NGOs focus on single issues or sets of issues to the exclusion of others. They are intensely committed to causes that states often give lower priority, and they can apply their resources in a manner that is more focused than the attention and resources that states, especially smaller states, or international organizations may be able to devote to the same issue. Some NGOs now have more resources than those of multilateral organizations. The head of the UN Center for Human Rights in Geneva commented, "We have less money and less resources than Amnesty International, and we are the arm of the United Nations for human rights" (Clark 1995, 512–517). Since the end of the Cold War, operational NGOs have become key players in multilateral humanitarian relief efforts and have experienced sizable increases in their resources—reaching some $8 billion annually from various funding sources (*Liaison News,* May 1996)—as governments cut back. As their involvement has increased, so has the loss of lives of NGO workers, at least ninety-one having been killed in regional conflicts since 1988. The president of Oxfam-America stated, "No country wants to see its soldiers die on CNN. But when an aid worker gets killed, there's no political heat" (Nickerson 1997).

Commitment to an issue can at times be a weakness. NGOs are sometimes labeled as representing special interests or a small elite, or they may be so blinded by their commitment to an issue not to see any possibility of compromise. In the debate over core labor standards at the December 1996 World Trade Organization (WTO) meetings, for example, some NGOs, such as Oxfam, joined with labor confederations in supporting the inclusion of core labor standards in the purview of the WTO. However, other NGOs, led by the Third World Network, joined with employers' organizations in opposing the link (O'Brien and Williams 1997, 16). Consensus among such varied interests can be hard to reach, and too strong a commitment sometimes prevents acceptance of an incremental or partial approach to solving a problem, which is often needed to reach agreement in multilateral negotiations.

Expertise

NGOs have acquired an expertise on the history and substance of many issues that is often greater than that of government agencies or international organizations. For international organizations, NGOs are often the only source of information apart from official government reports. Their reporting function is described by Pamela Chasek later in this chapter in her case study of the *Earth Negotiations Bulletin*. They can be instrumental in preparing the ground for future intergovernmental agreements as described in the essay by Gayle Meyers, Megan McIlwain, and Stephanie Hertz later in this chapter. NGOs are often consulted on the drafting of texts formally advanced by states in intergovernmental discussions and have even been asked to draft particular texts (Clark 1995, 516–517). For example Greenpeace, which had been attending meetings of the contracting parties of the London Dumping Convention (LDC) as an observer, was allocated the task of drafting an improved procedure for ocean dumping permits (Stairs and Taylor 1992, 123).

Expertise gained by being on the front lines in providing refugee relief or development aid enhances the credibility of operational NGOs when they speak out on related public policy issues or convey their information privately to government delegates in an effort to influence decisions. Their presence in the field provides them with information on local conditions that can be invaluable to international organizations. The later essay by Meyers, McIlwain, and Hertz emphasizes the importance of NGO involvement in mediation and transformation activities that can prevent violence.

Networking

NGO participation in networks—involving not only other NGOs but also international organization officials and government representatives—is today necessary and increasingly indispensable. Because of the overwhelming number of NGOs wanting to take part in UN conferences, the United Nations has encouraged all but the largest NGOs to participate through some form of representation by networks as many already do. Clearly, networking enables NGOs to combine their expertise and resources and to maximize their strengths and minimize their weaknesses, and thus to increase their influence at multilateral conferences as well as in the field.

NGO networks exist not just to influence national governments and intergovernmental organizations, but also to make policy among themselves. For example, the NGO Global Forum at the 1992 UN Conference on Environment and Development (UNCED or the Earth Summit)—the largest gathering (up to that date) of nongovernmental groups in history, attracting approximately nine thousand organizations—adopted by consensus more than forty-six "citizen treaties" on the environment and development. These treaties had been developed through an electronic conference on EcoNet by citizens worldwide, most of whom had been unable to attend the Earth Summit (Preston 1994). NGOs have organized global conferences of their own, such as one focused on the development of effective NGO strategies for engagement in the UN system and another on the role of NGOs in the twenty-first century, and have made their own agreements on the actions that NGOs themselves would undertake. Alicia Bárcena argues that the Earth Summit was "a defining moment in the dialogue among global citizens because, in an unprecedented gathering, some 18,000 private citizens of every race, religion, social class, and nationality convened together to draft more than forty-six citizens' treaties agreed by consensus, setting agendas for cooperative voluntary action" (Bárcena 1998, 195–196). Another example on a much smaller scale at the regional level was the September 1993 meeting in Hong Kong of ten NGOs from eight Asian countries that reached agreements on human rights information exchange and networking (Guzman 1995).

Informal networking is more widespread and has proved more successful in coordinating NGO action than formal arrangements, which usually limit the number of organizations that can be involved. However, the very nature of networking makes authority and accountability more vague than is the case with the more hierarchical structure of nation-states and international organizations. It is thus more difficult to ascertain whether a network has the authority to make an agreement or can be held accountable if an agreement should fail to be implemented.

NGO Influence: Before, During, and After UN Conferences

NGO commitment to and expertise on a subject can be a potent tool in the negotiation of agreements where one word or phrase can make a difference. NGOs are usually committed to pursuing a clear set of goals related to a particular issue or set of issues and thus, at multilateral conferences, often have an advantage over governments, which may have more difficulty in developing a clear set of goals because of competing national interests. Because the expertise of many NGOs is either very specialized or limited to local conditions, some lack personnel with the breadth of knowledge needed in some multi-issue multilateral conferences or the sometimes special knowledge of diplomacy. However, this is changing as NGO participation in multilateral conferences and negotiations grows, and thus their knowledge of multilateral diplomacy increases and their expertise in conference tactics is refined. The Johannesburg conference was the most participatory with nonstate actors in the same venue and interacting directly rather than in parallel forms and able to present critical comments on the outcomes at plenary. (United Nations 2003)

However NGO success at conferences has resulted in a backlash. NGO success at the Ottawa conference on banning landmines prompted states at the subsequent conference on curtailing small-arms traffic to limit the participation and access of NGOs along more traditional lines with no access during negotiating sessions and only one morning to make presentations to delegates (Krause 2002).

Being There at the Beginning

NGOs have learned over the past few years that for multilateral negotiations to succeed, ideas must be tested and a public consensus formed on the existence of a problem and possible solutions well before a conference begins. They have found that the best time to influence a world conference is during the preparatory process—at least 60 percent of the final outcome of a UN world conference is determined during the preparatory process (UNIFEM 1995, 13)—often through expert-group meetings, which are most open to NGO participation. The women's movement has achieved notable success by mounting global campaigns, building coalitions and consensus, and drafting their own policy documents to influence the composition of official delegations before conferences have even begun (Weiss and Gordenker 1996, 151). Much time in the PrepComs has been consumed in discussion of NGO participation, mostly focusing on issues of accreditation and expressing differences between member states over political priorities and cultural values, resentment being expressed that "NGOs were 'taking over' the conferences." However for the first time at the United Nations the World Summit on Information Society created a Civil Society Bureau to facilitate the contribution and participation of civil society in the process (United Nations 2003). In addition, NGOs have ensured their being in at the beginning by joining with governments and international organizations to sponsor conferences as well as by calling conferences on their own. For example the heads of four agencies (UN Development Program; UN Educational, Scientific and Cultural Organization; UNICEF; and the World Bank) invited governments, intergovernmental organizations (IGOs), and NGOs to participate in the preparatory process and in the World Conference on Education for All in 1990 on the basis of complete equality of status and decisionmaking among all participants (Weiss and Gordenker 1996, 184).

During the Conference

Inside and outside tactics . . . Some NGOs work on the outside of multilateral conferences, staging protests and demonstrations to influence the conference proceedings; some work on the inside of a conference, joining national delegations or as official observers; and still others do both. One example of working on the outside was a noisy protest staged at the 1995 UN Women's Conference in Beijing by some two hundred women from Latin American NGOs on the main escalators in the convention center to demand more aid and funding for Third World nations (Reuters, September 13, 1995, in Lexus-Nexus). Other NGOs on the outside choose to work with sympathetic official delegates on the inside to achieve their goals. For example, at the Cairo Population Conference, the prime minister of Norway cooperated with the NGO forum outside the official conference in planning initiatives that ended by being accepted in the official proceedings (Toulmin 1997).

One of the most effective ways to work from the inside is by becoming part of a national delegation. At the Earth Summit at least fourteen countries had environmental NGO representatives in their national delegations (Weiss and Gordenker 1996, 111). At the Cairo Population Conference in 1994 NGO representatives constituted a large part of many official delegations—half in the case of the US delegation (Weiss and Gordenker 1996, 149; Higer 1996, 34). NGOs gave one third of the plenary speeches at the Beijing Conference on Women (United Nations 2003).

Effective work from the outside can lead to working inside. For example, NGOs from Latin America agreed on a strong declaration urging their governments to include community participation in environmental policy-making during an NGO forum held parallel to the ninth meeting of regional environment ministers (Inter Press Service, September 28, 1995, in Lexus-Nexus). This led to the ministers' taking the unprecedented step at their tenth regional meeting the following year of merging with the NGOs gathered in a parallel meeting of the Latin American Participation Forum (Inter Press Service, November 12, 1996, in Lexus-Nexus).

Bringing together in caucuses those on the inside and outside who share a common expertise or perspective can help to facilitate success at a conference. At several world conferences, women who felt they shared a common perspective as women joined together to form a women's caucus. For example, the women's caucus at the Vienna Conference on Human Rights was sponsored by UN Fund for Women (UNIFEM) to promote dialogue between women who were members of UN agencies, official government delegations, the press, and NGOs attending the conference. The dialogue between NGOs and official delegates was crucial to ensuring that the recommendations made by women's groups were incorporated into the final document, since the drafting committee was closed to NGOs (UNIFEM 1995, 31).

NGOs continue to debate whether it is better to work from inside or outside. For example there were five "counterconferences" taking place during the official meetings of the Asia-Pacific Economic Cooperation (APEC) forum, all of which opposed its goal of free trade by the year 2020.

A spokesperson for one coalition of NGOs—the Asia-Pacific Sustainable Development Initiative (APSDI), which had succeeded in getting language on sustainable development into the Philippine plan for tariff reduction and was lobbying for similar language from APEC—stated, "We are trying to change things from within." However, other NGOs attacked APSDI for negotiating with the government (Son 1996). Some NGOs fear being coopted by governments and their goals' being compromised if they work too closely with government representatives.

Formal and informal tactics: . . . NGOs working from the inside are better able to take advantage of formal conference tactics, but all NGOs have learned to utilize informal conference settings. In the last UN conferences, NGOs were allowed to participate formally by requesting a place on the speaker's list to make statements (UNIFEM 1995, 33). The 1996 UN Conference on Human Settlements (Habitat II) was the first major global UN conference to permit NGOs to make interventions from the floor during working-group and committee negotiations, and to give official recognition to NGO amendments (WEDO June-July 1996, 13–14). However as NGO representatives have increasingly gained the right to observe and even address formal meetings, there have been some attempts by government delegates to resort to informal groups closed to them. This occurred at meetings of the Ad Hoc Group on the Berlin Mandate (AGBM) attempting to negotiate a binding climate treaty in Geneva in 1996. NGOs attending protested, because being excluded from informal settings can mean exclusion from where the real negotiation takes place (*ECO*, July 19, 1996). As one experienced US delegate stated, "The real business of negotiations takes place in the small groups, in ad hoc constellations of delegations and in informal contacts among individuals in the corridors or at meals. It is in these behind-the-scenes restricted groups that the hardest (and most interesting) bargaining takes place" (Preston 1994, 3).

The women's movement has gained a mastery of both formal and informal tactics. For example, at the Vienna Conference on Human Rights in 1993 "women's organizations lobbied governmental delegates at every possible minute and in every possible place of the conference, the halls, the cafeteria, and even the bathrooms" (Joachim 1996, 44). At the 1994 International Conference on Population and Development in Cairo, the women's movement demonstrated that it was the first among the citizen movements to truly master the official negotiations (Bárcena 1998). Later in this chapter Carolyn M. Stephenson describes the critical role of NGOs at the four global conferences on women, and Pamela Chasek describes how NGOs have changed the nature of international environmental policymaking.

Follow-Up After the Conference

NGOs also play an important role after conferences—building public support for the agreements, monitoring commitments made, and coordinating activities through networking. For example, the Women's Environment and Development Organization (WEDO) has compiled progress reports from information provided by governments and other NGOs on implementation of the Beijing Platform for Action. (WEDO June-July 1996, 3) To mark the first anniversary of the Beijing conference, WEDO organized a workshop in New York in September 1996 on "Holding Governments and International Agencies Accountable to Their Promises: Monitoring and Advocacy Strategies for Advancing Women's Agendas"(WEDO November-December 1996, 70). Habitat II broke new ground in recognizing the role of NGOs in the follow-up of a UN Conference (UNCHS Press Release 98/03, January 16, 1998). Based on a recommendation of the Earth Summit plus 5, the Commission on Sustainable Development initiated in 1998 multistakeholder dialogues. These allow major groups, including NGOs and governments, to interact on equal footing on a specific agenda issue, with parliamentary rules put aside in favor of interactive discussion, and have had considerable influence on decisionmaking (United Nations 2003).

NGOs and Policymaking

Traditionally NGOs were not involved in multilateral policymaking, but their increasing role, especially in the area of human rights and humanitarian relief efforts, has brought NGOs closer to internal United Nations decisionmaking. From the beginning NGOs have been accredited to ECOSOC, which gives them access to observing UN meetings and conferences. However, the increase in applications has outpaced the UN's capacity to deal with them, thus creating a backlog which stood at eight hundred applications in 2003. NGOs first addressed a General Assembly committee in 1993 and since then have spoken at a number of plenary meetings of GA special sessions (United Nations 2003). The International Committee of the Red Cross was the first NGO to gain permanent status as an observer in the General Assembly, followed by the Order of Malta and the international Federation of Red Cross and Red Crescent Societies in 1994, after which further NGOs were blocked (Foster and Anand 1999, 273–274). Since 1994 the New York representative of the International Committee of the Red Cross (ICRC) has met monthly with the serving president of the Security Council in an informal and confidential atmosphere that allows both sides to exchange information and concerns (Weiss and Gordenker 1996,

86). In 1996 the presidents of the Security Council began to meet informally with representatives of the NGO Working Group on the Security Council, which had been formed in 1995 by a number of NGOs interested in the Security Council (Alger 2002). Sadako Ogata, the former UN High Commissioner for Refugees, had regular meetings with humanitarian and other NGOs that work on the problems of refugees in war-torn and starving regions (Toulmin 1997). The heads of prominent NGOs have had much more frequent meetings with the Secretary-General.

The UN Secretariat and agencies have chosen to take NGOs on as partners. The UN Department for Humanitarian Affairs hosts regular meetings every four to six weeks with the main operational NGOs in the humanitarian area (Weiss and Gordenker 1996, 87). The Inter-Agency Standing Committee attempts to coordinate the work of UN agencies and NGOs involved in complex humanitarian emergencies, but it does not include the donor aid agencies, which fund most of the work nor have the power to force integration of UN agencies (Weiss and Gordenker 1996, 63 and 77–78). To improve coordination and increase effectiveness in responding to humanitarian emergencies, a number of new initiatives have been proposed. The International Federation of Red Cross Societies has called for developing a code of conduct for NGOs involved in operational and humanitarian activities (Annan 1997). The UN High Commission for Refugees (UNHCR) and the International Council on Voluntary Agencies (ICVA) initiated Partners in Action (PARINAC), which opened a year-long series of consultations culminating in a conference in Oslo in June 1994 attended by more than 450 NGOs. The resulting Oslo Plan of Action made a commitment to create new mechanisms for responding to humanitarian emergencies. When serving as UN High Commissioner for Human Rights, Jose Ayala Lasso in October 1995 called for a Human Rights Council, an intergovernmental body for policymaking and coordination that would include NGOs (Tessitore and Woolfson 1996, 248). Although this council has not been established yet, at the 2003 session of the Commission on Human Rights NGOs used one third of the general debating time (United Nations 2003).

The UN Office for the Coordination of Humanitarian Affairs cochairs with InterAction, an NGO network, regular monthly meetings between Secretariat officials and NGOs. There is also NGO representation on the Inter-Agency Standing Committee for Emergency Relief (Alger 2002). Mohamed Sahnoun, former special representative of the UN Secretary-General in Somalia, has proposed the creation of a new international institution for conflict management that would coordinate humanitarian action and foster ties between organizations and agencies from the international down to the local levels (Aall 1996). The new agency, UNAIDS, is the first UN agency to have nongovernmental organizations as part of its governing structure, which includes twenty-two governments, eight UN agencies, and five NGOs (see www.un.org/reform). New coalitions on global issues have emerged based on equality among the partners involved. An example is the Global Alliance for Vaccines and Immunization (GAVI), which involves, in addition to NGOs, multinational and bilateral agencies, international development banks, foundations, the pharmaceutical industry, and national government health programs (United Nations 2003).

Although NGO participation in UN policymaking has been most important in the area of human rights and humanitarian relief, it exists in other areas as well. For example the World Bank has established an NGO committee and included NGOs in the design, execution, and evaluation of Bank-financed projects (O'Brien and Williams 1997, 12–13; Nelson 2000, 413–419) About half of Bank-financed projects now involve NGOs (United Nations 2003). The Bank publishes an annual report on cooperation with NGOs—*Cooperation with NGOs: 1997 Progress Report*. The UN Nongovernmental Liason Service in Geneva facilitates the work of the many NGOs working with the United Nations on development projects and is helping the UN's Chief Executive Board to review the state of collaboration between the UN and NGOs (United Nations 2003). The Earth Council and a NGO Steering Committee link NGOs with the UN Commission on Sustainable Development in order to help implement the agreements reached at the Earth Summit (Bigg and Mucke 1996).

Clearly, NGO influence and participation in the work of the United Nations are changing the process of multilateral diplomacy. Scholars recognize that NGOs have been instrumental in changing traditional conceptualizations of sovereignty and diplomacy. They have helped to make governments, international organizations, and private firms more accountable even as their own authority and accountability are at times questioned. Diplomats and international organization officials now realize they must include NGOs in the coalitions that are essential to any successful multilateral diplomacy or peace-building process. NGO representatives have successfully practiced multilateral diplomacy by participating in these coalitions and often helping to build them. The later essay by Meyers, McIlwain, and Hertz shows how an NGO can act as a third-party facilitator in conflict situations through grassroots capacity-building initiatives as well as through dialogue of mid-level and prominent elites to prepare for more traditional diplomacy.

The president of the fifty-first session of the United Nations General Assembly, Ambassador Razali Ismail, praised as a milestone event the participation of NGOs in the General Assembly's 1997 special session (Earth Summit plus 5) dedicated to an overall review and appraisal of the implementation of Agenda 21. However he expressed disappointment that the wider issue of NGO participation in the work of the United Nations remains unresolved. . . . While some are concerned about the logistical aspects of dealing with NGOs . . . some in fact fear the prospects of greater transparency, accountability and public participation in the intergovernmental decision-making process, using any manner of legal arguments to prevent this from happening. (Razali 1997, 2)

Although he did not name the member states opposed to a greater role for NGOs, there is no doubt that fears have been aroused by the growing influence of NGOs in multilateral diplomacy. Nevertheless, in October 1997, the UN General Assembly approved the first phase of Secretary-General Annan's reform plan, which expanded the role of NGOs in UN activities (Turner 1997). NGOs accepted Secretary-General Annan's invitation to hold a People's Millennium Assembly alongside a Millennium Assembly of the United Nations (Annan 1997). Many NGOs would like to see a People's Assembly become a permanent feature of the United Nations system. Whether this should occur or not, NGOs have already added an important new dimension to diplomacy. In June 2003 the Secretary-General's Panel of Eminent Persons on Civil Society and UN Relationships, chaired by former Brazilian President Fernando Enrique Cardoso, held its first meeting. It is to make its final report on how to make the relationship between the United Nations and civil society more meaningful in 2004 (see, www.un.org/reform/panel). A background paper prepared for the panel outlines different views on this relationship both within and between nongovernmental organizations, governments, and United Nations agencies. It contains a list of sometimes contradictory recommendations for improving the relationship (United Nations 2003). Whatever the panel may recommend, NGO engagement in multilateral diplomacy will continue.

Notes

1. The number of NGOs with official consultative status is much smaller than the number with some relationship to the United Nations. There are over sixteen hundred organizations currently associated with the UN Department of Public Information, and the list continues to expand each year; and several thousand more have established a relationship with the United Nations through the series of UN-sponsored global conferences during the 1990s. For a list of NGOs in consultative status with the ECOSOC and more information on the relationship between the United Nations and NGOs see the United Nations website [http://www.un.org].

References

Aall, Pamela. (1996) "Reframing the Issues: A Report of a Conference, Arranged by the U.S. Institute of Peace, on the Roles of NGOs," *Journal of Humanitarian Assistance.* [http://www-jha.sps.cam.ac.uk/CONF/Cr006.htm]

Alger, Chadwick. (2002) "The Emerging Roles of NGOs in the UN System: From Article 71 to a People's Millennium Assembly," *Global Governance,* Vol. 8, No. 1, January-March, p. 93.

Annan, Kofi. (1997) "Opening Address to the Fiftieth Annual Department of Public Information/Non-Governmental Organization (DPI/NGO) Conference." United Nations Press Release, SG/SM/6320, PI/1027, September 10.

Bárcena, Alicia (1998) "The Role of Civil Society in Twenty-first Century Diplomacy," in *Multilateral Diplomacy and the United Nations Today,* edited by James P. Muldoon, Jr., JoAnn Fagot Aviel, Richard Reitano, and Earl Sullivan (Boulder: Westview Press), pp. 190–200.

Bigg, Tom and Peter Mucke. (1996) "Synthesis Paper on NGO Priorities and Concerns for the 1997 General Assembly Special Session" [www.igc.apc.org/habitat/csd.97/synthes.htm].

Clark, Ann Marie. (1995) "Non-Governmental Organizations and Their Influence on International Society," *Journal of International Affairs,* Vol. 48, No. 2, Winter.

Foster, John W. and Anita Anand, eds. (1999) *Whose World Is It Anyway?* (Ottawa: United Nations Association in Canada).

Guzman, Manuel. (1995) "Asia." Paper presented at the Second Annual Meeting of the Canada-US Human Rights Information and Documentation Network (CUSHRID Net)— November 3–5, University of Maryland. [http://www.aaas.org/spp/dspp/shr/panel2.htm]

Higer, Amy J. (1996) "International Women's Activism and Change: Understanding Feminist Influence at UN Population Conferences." Paper presented at the American Political Science Association meeting in San Francisco, August.

Joachim, Jutta. (1996) "How Women's Issues Get on the UN's Agenda: International Women's Organizations and Violence Against Women." Paper presented at International Studies Association San Diego meeting.

Krause, Keith. (2002) "Multilateral Diplomacy, Norm Building, and UN Conferences: The Case of Small Arms and Light Weapons," *Global Governance,* Vol. 8, No. 2, April-June, p. 247.

Liaison News, May 1996. [www.oneworld.org/liason//n17e.htm#europe]

Nelson, Paul. (2000) "Whose Civil Society? Whose Governance? Decisionmaking and Practice in the New Agenda at the Inter-American Development Bank and the World Bank," *Global Governance,* Vol. 6, No. 4, October-December, pp. 405–432.

Nickerson, Collin. (1997) "Aid Workers in the Cross-Hairs," *San Francisco Chronicle*, August 9, 1997.

O'Brien, Robert and Marc Williams. (1997) "Global Economic Institutions and Global Social Movements Project." Paper presented at International Studies Association Toronto meeting, March.

Preston, Shelley. (1994) "Electronic Global Networking and the NGO Movement: The 1992 Rio Summit and Beyond," *Swords and Ploughshares: A Chronicle of International Affairs*, Vol. 3, No. 2, Spring, pp. 1–9. [www.sas.upenn.edu/African_Studies/Comp_Articles/Electronic_Global_19411]

Razali, Ismail. (1997) "Blind Unilateralism Will Be Undoing of United Nations, Assembly President Tells Closing Meeting of Fifty-first Session." United Nations Press Release, GA/9293, September 14.

Son, Johanna. (1996) "Philippines: NGOs Split over How to Tackle APEC." *Inter Press Service*, November 20, in Lexus-Nexus.

Stairs, Kevin and Peter Taylor. (1992) "Non-Governmental Organizations and the Legal Protection of the Oceans: A Case Study," in *The International Politics of the Environment*, edited by Andrew Hurrell and Benedict Kingsbury (Oxford: Clarendon Press).

Tessitore, John and Susan Woolfson, eds. (1996) *A Global Agenda: Issues Before the 51st General Assembly of the United Nations*. (Lanham, Md.: Rowman & Littlefield).

Toulmin, Stephen. (1997) "The UN and Japan in an Age of Globalization: The Role of Transnational NGOs in Global Affairs". [http://www.usc.edu/dept/LAS/CMTS/ngos.html]

Turner, Craig. "U.N. Embraces 1st Phase of Annan Reforms," *San Francisco Chronicle*, October 13, 1997.

United Nations. (2003) "UN System and Civil Society—An Inventory and Analysis of Practices." Background paper for the Secretary-General's Panel of Eminent Persons on United Nations Relations with Civil Society, May. [www.un.org]

United Nations Center for Human Settlements (UNCHS) Press Release 98/03, "Partnership, Informatics and Participation Workshops in Bangkok and London," January 16.

United Nations Development Fund for Women (UNIFEM). (1995) *Putting Gender on the Agenda, A Guide to Participating in UN World Conferences*. (New York: UNIFEM).

Weiss, Thomas G. and Leon Gordenker. (1996) *NGOs, the UN, and Global Governance*. (Boulder: Lynne Rienner).

Women's Environment and Development Organization (WEDO). (1996) *News & Views*, Vol. 9, Nos. 1–2, June-July, and Vol. 9, Nos. 3–4, November-December.

THE COMMON GROUND APPROACH

A Case Study of an NGO

Gayle Meyers, Megan McIlwain,
and Stephanie Hertz[1]

Since the mid-1990s, policymaking circles have recognized the value of a nongovernmental role on what has traditionally been considered diplomatic turf. The dramatic successes are well known. In South Africa, the transformation of the country was and still is motivated by grassroots efforts and commitment to rebuild society. The activism of individuals in the country and worldwide forced the government to grapple with the realities of apartheid and made its perpetuation impossible.

The Oslo Agreement, as the 1993 breakthrough in the Israeli-Palestinian impasse came to be called, was formulated first as exploratory discussions at an academic, nongovernmental level. Even after government negotiators replaced the scholars, the confidentiality, informality, and camaraderie of the talks remained. Unfortunately, the peace process broke down in 2000 before resolving the most contentious issues, and scholars continue to analyze the pros and cons of the Oslo method. However, NGOs are once again playing a critical role in maintaining communication between the two societies and supporting the search for peace.

In Rwanda, a major actor was the media. Within the country, "hate media" dominated the scene, distorting facts on the ground and inflaming ethnic and political passions. Meanwhile, the daily atrocities were broadcast via international media to the world. That provided an imperative in the international community to act and led to a huge outpouring of support through the United Nations and a myriad of private organizations. Although unsuccessful in preventing much of the violence, this was an early instance of the power of television and the media in general in exposing the horrors of interethnic conflict, paving the way to international reconciliation efforts.

Search for Common Ground (SFCG), like other organizations, learned from these and other experiences in various parts of the world. With its beginnings in the 1980s working with US-Soviet relations, SFCG developed a variety of approaches to deal with conflict. As a third-party facilitator, Search for Common Ground brought innovation, flexibility, and creativity to conflict situations and successfully developed programs that resonate at both the governmental and grassroots levels, demonstrating that third-party intervention and Track II diplomacy can occur through grassroots capacity-building initiatives as well as through dialogue of mid-level and prominent elites. Over the course of two decades of experience, the organization refined its core principles and operating methods—collectively called the *common ground approach*—and is employing them in fourteen locations around the globe. This chapter will describe the common ground approach and illustrate how it was applied in two diverse conflict areas: Burundi and the Middle East.

The Common Ground Approach

The mission of Search for Common Ground is to facilitate social change that transforms a community's approach to conflict from destructive adversarial strategies toward cooperative processes and solutions. Through a wide range of domestic and international experiences, the organization has identified five core principles that are essential for working with conflict constructively:

Conflict is natural: Conflict is neither positive nor negative; it is merely a natural result of natural differences. The global community boasts a wealth of diversity, and it is indeed these differences——in ideology, belief systems, ethnicity, and/or social and cultural values—that enrich our lives. Differences and conflict are completely natural; therefore, what is important is how people deal with these differences and the natural conflicts they produce. One fundamental distinction SFCG makes is that conflict and violence are not synonymous. Human beings have an instinctive, emotional response to conflict that is often based on fear of differences. This emotional response can often overwhelm people's ability to reason and can subsequently lead to violence. Conversely, when differences are acknowledged and approached in nonadversarial ways, such as looking for common interests, conflict can be constructive and lead to progress.

Conflict can be transformed: In understanding that conflict is a natural phenomenon, Search for Common Ground's objective is not to attempt to prevent, manage, stop, or even ameliorate conflict. Instead, the organization is attempting to transform the way communities and societies view and deal with their differences—so that conflict is no longer perceived as a source of violence and discord but is instead used as a catalyst for progress. Conflict transformation can be as simple as reframing a situation or refocusing the energy on the issue rather than defeating the opposition.

Peace building is a process: Conflict transformation is not instantaneous; it is a long-term process and not a short-term event. For a third party to have an effective impact in a conflict situation, sustained involvement is necessary. Extended engagement is important in overcoming local skepticism about an organization's long-term interests and commitment and in enabling local groups progressively to build relationships of trust that allow them to focus on the issue rather than each other.

Finding common ground: Popular perception almost invariably associates finding "common ground" with compromise—which is often attached to a negative connotation that everyone must sacrifice something to meet in the middle. Search for Common Ground challenges this perception by not advocating that two sides meet in the middle on one issue, rather that they identify something to which they both can aspire and toward which they are willing to work. People's underlying interests, concerns, and values tend to be much broader and less polarizing than their negotiating positions. From this perspective, the truth of each competing point of view can be appreciated and creative options that benefit all parties can be created.

Relationship and interdependence: The concepts of interdependence and interconnectedness are gaining awareness and acceptance throughout the world. The fundamental tenet of the globalization phenomenon is that everything and everyone throughout the world is interconnected, and that a seemingly insignificant action or nonaction in one area of the global system can have a profound impact on another community on the other side of the globe. Therefore, SFCG focuses its conflict transformation efforts on developing and strengthening relationships and building levels of mutual respect between groups of divergent opinions.

SFCG's extensive experiences have fortified its belief in these foundational principles and have guided the development of a working methodology, which is articulated through several operating principles:

1. *Having respect for all voices and for everyone's humanity*: The inclusion and representation of all parties involved in the conflict is essential to facilitating transformation.

2. *Becoming immersed in the local culture*: Immersion in the local culture enhances a third party's cultural and contextual sensitivity, making it possible to recognize opportunities and expeditiously cope with challenges. In addition, in places where political situations and the nuances of relationships are ever-changing, both a presence on the ground and regular consultations with local partners can greatly enhance one's effectiveness and legitimacy within the targeted community.

3. *Building relationships over time*: Building and strengthening relationships are vital to the process of conflict transformation, and building relationships of increasing trust is important to both facilitators and stakeholders. Third parties should allow sufficient time to enlist the knowledge and wisdom of local partners in shaping their own programs.

4. *Engaging and empowering the local community:* A lasting settlement has never been imposed from the outside; it must come from within. Sometimes the most useful role a third party can play is to provide opportunities for the parties to interact and develop a dialogue and then allow them the prerogative of shaping the parameters of their relationship and the activities in which they are involved.

5. *Engaging in the situation:* Always assess the context and the situation before becoming actively involved to determine what exactly is needed and where your involvement would be most constructive. There is no "one size fits all" blueprint—

every situation is different and requires the design of a unique strategy and set of activities.

6. *Being a social entrepreneur:* Use creativity and vision to develop innovative ways of bringing people together, and look for the opportunities in every situation to strengthen social cohesion.

7. *Developing an integrated, multifaceted approach:* Conflict is multidimensional and often requires a range of interventions on a variety of levels to effectively shift the conflict from destructive to constructive tendencies. An integrated approach requires working on multiple levels, including people in the process from the public sector, grassroots groups, and international agencies. An integrated, multifaceted approach also involves developing and implementing programs that operate on several fronts simultaneously in a coordinated manner to increase the overall impact.

These values, core principles, and collection of operating methodologies constitute the philosophical and applied essence of the common ground approach. The common ground approach attempts to serve as a paradigm of conflict transformation, within which people of different backgrounds and perspectives can develop an interactive dialogue and agree to come together over time to build relationships of increasing trust. The common ground approach is a model for facilitating social transformation as a means of working with conflict and transforming destructive tendencies into constructive opportunities for cooperation and change.

Burundi

In 1994, ethnically motivated political violence and genocide erupted in the densely populated Central African country of Rwanda. The ethnic tensions and violence spilled over to affect the Hutu and Tutsi populations in Rwanda's neighboring state of Burundi. In recognizing the increased potential for genocide in Burundi, Search for Common Ground began to consider how it might intervene in Burundi as a way of preventing Burundian Hutus and Tutsis from succumbing to the same fate as their Rwandan neighbors. The animosity between Burundian Hutus and Tutsis is primarily a legacy of colonialism, which institutionalized socioeconomic inequities and deeply polarized society. This type of polarization often mandates the intervention of an impartial third party to facilitate reconciliation, providing an opportunity for an NGO like Search for Common Ground. NGOs are often ideal candidates to facilitate reconciliation at the grassroots level, because their lack of affiliation with a particular government or international organization allows them to project a sense of impartiality in both their appearance and practices.

In late 1994, a delegation cosponsored by Refugees International and Search for Common Ground visited Burundi to confer with local leaders and organizations about establishing conflict resolution and reconciliation projects throughout the country. The field assessment, an essential first step in any successful field operation, was invaluable in determining how, where, and what type of services Search for Common Ground could provide to help alleviate the ethnic tensions and foster reconciliation. To avoid duplication of efforts, the members of the delegation coordinated their inquiry as much as possible with other NGOs, international organizations, and governments. The assessment process revealed that despite the overwhelming need, very few projects that emphasized reconciliation existed in Burundi. By analyzing the conclusions of the Burundi assessment, Search for Common Ground identified several areas in which it could make a unique contribution to interethnic reconciliation, most notably by creating an independent studio to produce radio programs and establishing a women's peace center.

Before Search for Common Ground could implement its prospective program in Burundi, the organization needed to gain support from the local and international communities for SFCG's intervention. During the assessment trip, consultations were held with both grassroots leaders and high-level political figures representing both Hutus and Tutsis, all of whom were supportive of the proposed intervention. Significant among these were meetings with the widow of Melchior Ndadaye, the Hutu president whose assassination in 1994 sparked a wave of mass killings and violence, and with a former president of Burundi, Pierre Buyoya, a Tutsi. Dialogue was also initiated with the heads of both major political parties in parliament, each generally representing the Tutsi and Hutu ethnic groups. Another key element in gaining entry into Burundi was international community support through the UN Secretary-General's special representative, who not only provided the auspices for the projects but also recommended immediate funding from the US Agency for International Development (USAID). In 1995, Search for Common Ground—Burundi (SFCG-B) was established in the capital city of Bujumbura. The combined team of expatriate and local staff set out immediately to implement its first project, the creation of the first independent radio studio in Burundi, Studio Ijambo (meaning "wise words" in Kirundi, the local language).

The overarching mission of Search for Common Ground—Burundi is to develop an integrated, multifaceted approach that seeks to promote reconciliation at and between all levels of society through engaging and empowering the local community. Since 1995, SFCG-B has launched a series of media and community projects in Burundi aimed at reducing ethnic violence and supporting peacemaking efforts. SFCG-B works toward this goal through three distinct yet complementary projects—Studio Ijambo, the Women's Peace Center, and the Youth Project—each of which serves as an organizational and operational unit that brings a different area of expertise to the overall program and reflects the values embodied in the common ground approach.

Radio (Studio Ijambo)

Limited accessibility to television sets combined with high rates of illiteracy makes radio an important source of information in Burundi and the surrounding Great Lakes Region. An estimated 85 percent of the population has access to radios, so radio is a remarkably cost-effective means of delivering information to the majority of Burundians. Unfortunately, radio has also been used effectively by national governments throughout the region for propaganda purposes, an important factor in inciting the Rwandan genocide. Studio Ijambo was established in Burundi in March 1995 as a balance to the wide dissemination of inflammatory "hate radio" broadcasting in the Great Lakes Region. Studio Ijambo is staffed by an ethnically balanced team of journalists and produces radio programs that promote dialogue, peace, and reconciliation. Its programs examine all sides of the conflict and highlight the points that can unite, rather than divide, Burundians. The Studio Ijambo slogan, "Dialogue is the future," captures the essence of this mission.

Studio Ijambo has proven to be a very effective method of promoting dialogue and peace building, especially given Burundians' reliance on radio as the primary source of information. Studio Ijambo's interethnic team of journalists are trained in common ground journalism techniques, and as a result, Studio Ijambo has earned a reputation for credible, unbiased reporting. In addition to its current affairs and news programs, Studio Ijambo produces a wide mix of documentaries, soap operas, discussions, and youth programs.

Over the years, Studio Ijambo has produced numerous high-quality radio programs with positive themes. Some of our most successful programs are *Heroes*, a documentary highlighting stories of cross-ethnic solidarity among Hutu, Tutsi, Batwa, and Ganwa people; *Iteka N'Ijambo*, a current-affairs program focusing on human rights issues; and *Our Neighbors, Our Family*, a soap opera depicting the complexities of conflict through the relationship of two neighboring families of different ethnic backgrounds.

The advancement of the Burundian peace process and the reduction of political violence have enabled many of the over one million Burundians displaced by the fighting to return to their homes. Unfortunately the return of hundreds of thousands of internally displaced persons (IDPs) and refugees presents a daunting challenge to Burundians on a variety of levels, ranging from resource and land allocation to the reintegration of ex-combatants into civilian society. The SFCG-B team, aided by their immersion in the local culture and their social entrepreneurial skills, recognized these new dynamics and engaged in the situation by immediately developing new programming that would address the issues of repatriation and reintegration. In 2002, Studio Ijambo launched two new radio series with support from the British Foreign and Commonwealth Office Human Rights Fund: one dealing with the complex land issues related to the repatriation of hundreds of thousands of refugees; the other exploring themes of justice and the quest for reconciliation. The studio produced *Ramutswa iwanyu* (Kirundi for "Welcome Back to Where You Belong"), a twenty-six-episode series, to inform the Burundian public and promote dialogue around the challenges of repatriation and land ownership. To address issues related to truth, justice, and reconciliation during the current transitional period, the studio produced a second series, *Inama n'ingingo* (Kirundi for "Let's Talk and Decide Together"). This program examined a number of themes related to transitional justice, including the relative merits of justice and reconciliation, the role of the death penalty, and the effects of trauma on the nation. Studio journalists traveled to South Africa, Cambodia, and Guatemala, and they included material on other countries' experiences with similar issues in each broadcast.

Also in 2002, a new independent national radio station, Radio Isanganiro (Crossroads Radio), was launched in partnership with Studio Ijambo to promote dialogue, peace, and reconciliation in Burundi and the Great Lakes Region, with a wide range of programming in Kirundi, French, and Swahili. The station broadcasts to much of Burundi and parts of Tanzania and Rwanda, and it reaches the Burundian diaspora around the world by broadcasting on the Internet at www.ijambo.net.

Women's Peace Center

The Women's Peace Center was established in 1996 to support Burundian women's efforts at becoming key players in the peace-building and reconciliation process, regardless of their ethnic, regional, religious, and generational differences. The center was the first organization to provide a space for Burundian women affected by the violence—from both communities— to share their experiences and plan joint actions to address their needs. Since then, the center has played a key role in developing and supporting a network of hundreds of women's associations that are involved in rebuilding the country, exemplifying positive interethnic solidarity, and mobilizing their constituencies for peace.

The Women's Peace Center provides meeting space and support to women's associations, offering training in conflict resolution skills, hosting roundtables and exchanges, and advocating on behalf of women and children affected by the conflict. In 2002, the Women's Peace Center began working in conjunction with the Friends' Peace Teams to alleviate social and personal problems associated with postconflict trauma. The center now offers information about and training in trauma healing, and listening sessions for trauma victims.

Youth Project

The Youth Project, established in 1999, works with at-risk populations that often take part in violent conflicts as a result of political manipulation. The Youth Project brings together youth from different ethnic and geographical backgrounds for recreational and solidarity-building activities. The Youth Project organizes conflict resolution trainings, retreats and exchanges for diverse youth groups, sports events and tournaments, and concerts where popular musicians bring a message of peace and reconciliation.

Also in 2001, the Youth Project collaborated with JAMAA, a local youth association, to produce a cartoon book called *Le Meilleur Choix* ("The Best Choice"). The book describes the real-life experiences of two young men who participated in the violence of the mid-1990s and their efforts to reconcile with the families of their victims. Through drama and humor, it encourages youth to avoid being manipulated by political interests that would pitch them against one another. The project oversaw the production of a two-hour movie based on the same story, which debuted on Burundian national television in August 2002. In March 2003, the book was awarded an honorable mention by UNESCO for excellence in peace literature.

In 2001, when ethnic tension threatened to turn violent at the University of Burundi, staff from Studio Ijambo and the Youth Project worked with student leaders to open channels of communication on the campus. At this time, troops had been installed on the university campus following a coup attempt in the country. Hutu students fled, fearing a repeat of the 1995 violence aimed at driving Hutu students off the majority-Tutsi campus. By airing student opinions on the radio and facilitating dialogue between different campus factions, the Youth Project and Studio Ijambo were able to help bring the students back to the campus in a matter of weeks. This work also led to the establishment of interethnic student groups and an ongoing constructive dialogue on the campus. Studio Ijambo and the Youth Project each used their strengths and expertise in a coordinated effort to intervene in this crisis, an excellent example of Common Ground's integrated, multifaceted approach in action.

Recent Activities

SFCG-B has recently launched an integration initiative to maximize the synergies among SFCG-B projects as they expand both geographically and in scope. The most significant manifestation of the integration initiative has been the opening of new "antenna" offices in Kamenge, Ngozi, Ruyigi, and Makamba provinces. In addition, SFCG-B has also taken the lead in forming a coordination structure for all local and international efforts in reconstruction and peace building.

Search for Common Ground's long-term engagement in Burundi has proven through regular independent evaluations to have had a tremendous positive impact on Burundian society and has been able to successfully facilitate conflict transformation throughout Burundi. Evaluations have revealed that Burundians now exhibit an increased ability to express themselves on a "variety of political, social, ethnic and health related issues, and increased awareness and application of conflict resolution and reconciliation methods."[2] SFCG-B's integrated, multifaceted approach has allowed it to link grassroots efforts with national campaigns, and its radio programs have helped to create a national dialogue around critical conflicts and issues that affect the peace process. Community outreach initiatives, including workshops, trainings, and facilitated dialogues, have helped communities to examine conflict and search for solutions at the grassroots and personal levels. Community outreach work often feeds into media programs, and vice versa, building momentum for peace building at all levels of society. The tools of high flexibility and immersion in the local cultures have allowed SFCG-B to respond rapidly to immediate conflicts while establishing more long-term programs to address the needs for dialogue, reconciling divided communities, and restoring relationships damaged by violence. Search for Common Ground in Burundi serves as an excellent example of an effective grassroots capacity-building third-party intervention dedicated to transforming a community's approach to conflict.

The Middle East

Since its inception in 1991, Search for Common Ground in the Middle East (SFCGME) has approached conflict transformation as grounds for opportunity and education outreach. With a history of experience working on regional security issues in the Middle East, SFCGME has developed to become a substantial branch in the larger organization Search for Common Ground. SFCGME networks with relevant actors on unofficial and official levels. It then capitalizes on their expertise by providing a safe space for knowledge exchange, and ultimately, by implementing cooperative action projects that they suggest.

A brief history of the program demonstrates how SFCGME has adapted its programming to allow for changes in the complex web of regional relationships and the ebb and flow of official peace processes. The project began as part of a US-Soviet dialogue with concerns about the ongoing conflicts in Lebanon. Lebanon was considered a theater of the Cold War and a potential home to terrorist activity. However, participants decided that the issue of Lebanon could only be dealt with in a regional context. Thus, SFCGME sought to design a multilateral process to address the whole of the Middle East and decided to model it conceptually on the Conference on Security and Cooperation in Europe (CSCE, now the Organization for Security and Cooperation in Europe, or OSCE). However, instead of operating solely on an official level, as the CSCE largely had done, SFCGME would work unofficially on a nongovernmental level as well.

SFCGME has realized that in order to contribute effectively to a conflict transformation process it is necessary to effect communication within and among multiple levels of society. This effort began in 1991 with the formation of the Security Program and its Security Working Group (SWG). The SWG enables well-connected but unofficial strategic experts, former government officials, and retired senior officers from across the Middle East to discuss sensitive issues on an informal, deniable basis. Its topical forums seek to complement the official processes in the region in several ways, by dealing with issues that are not currently addressed in official negotiations, opening alternative channels of communication, and providing a means by which participants can informally explore approaches to security issues in ways that could be useful to official policymakers. Among its noteworthy accomplishments are the following:

1. Sponsoring unofficial talks between Israelis and Syrians, which established mutually acceptable principles for a settlement on the Golan Heights.

2. Publishing a series of jointly authored Arab-Israeli monographs on security issues and a book on arms control. The
product of private dialogues, these papers can serve as a basis
for official negotiations.

3. Providing an opportunity for Israeli and Jordanian security
experts to work together on developing language that became
part of the 1994 Jordan-Israel peace treaty.

SCGME has conducted many successful projects outside the security
realm as well. As publisher of the quarterly *Bulletin of Regional Cooperation in the Middle East,* which moved from paper to Internet publishing in
the summer of 2003 and will be available in English, Arabic, and Hebrew
at www.sfcg.org, it stands at the heart of a web of relations among nongovernmental actors in the region. Other aspects of the multifaceted program include the following:

1. Providing training for the local practice and institutionaliza-
tion of conflict resolution in Gaza, the West Bank, Lebanon,
Egypt, and Jordan.

2. Establishing peer mediation programs in UN Relief and
Works Agency (UNRWA) primary schools in Gaza.

3. Establishing a regional campaign against torture linking medical rehabilitation centers with human rights activists and international organizations worldwide.

4. Creating the Common Ground News Service (CGNews).
Every week, CGNews sends out—in English, Arabic, and Hebrew—a selection of articles to about one hundred media
outlets across the Middle East that support the building of
bridges and finding peaceful solutions to contentious problems. To date, several hundred CGNews articles have been
reprinted in such publications as *Al-Hayat* (London),
Ha'aretz (Tel Aviv), *Al Quds* (Jerusalem), *The International
Herald Tribune* (Paris), *The Daily Star* (Beirut), and *Al-
Ahram* (Cairo).

In the last two years, the Security Working Group has made a shift and
augmented its policy-centered dialogue with functional cooperation. The
events of September 11, 2001, and the subsequent anthrax attacks in the

United States catalyzed a dramatic change in a subgroup on weapons of mass destruction (WMDs) that had been meeting since 1995. For several years, the group had focused on whether it would be desirable and feasible to create a WMD-Free Zone in the Middle East. Although they had found several important areas of common ground, it became evident that there was little possibility that agreements would be reached to limit or eliminate WMDs in the absence of an official arms control process in the region. In November 2001, however, group participants suggested that Middle Eastern states, despite their obvious differences, shared a common interest and could cooperate on being prepared to respond to a terrorist's use of such weapons.

As a result, SFCGME conducted a set of intensive consultations in the region and ultimately created two subject-specific working groups—the Middle East Consortium on Infectious Disease Surveillance (MECIDS) and the Middle East Chemical Risks Consortium (CRC)—to focus more closely on the region's technical preparedness for nuclear, biological, and chemical (NBC) attacks.

An examination of these two consortiums lends a solid understanding of SFCGME's evolving approach to conflict transformation. MECIDS is composed of governmental and nongovernmental specialists in public health and biological defense from Egypt, Israel, Jordan, and the Palestinian Authority, including the heads of the Centers for Disease Control of both Jordan and Israel. The aims of MECIDS are to reduce the region's vulnerability to disease outbreaks, whether natural or caused by a biological weapon, and to provide ways for health professionals to build trust and confidence across national lines.

Through providing forums within which MECIDS participants can privately and comfortably convene, Search for Common Ground has implemented its vision, which calls for individuals, organizations, governments, and societies to respond to their differences in nonadversarial ways, so that these differences stimulate social progress rather than precipitate violence. When MECIDS met for the third time in June 2003, participants made strides toward a future of regional cooperation. With plans to establish a surveillance system for food-borne disease outbreaks, participants have highlighted SFCG's principle of interdependence. This principle has developed out of the challenges facing today's highly globalized, interdependent world, in which there is a critical need to recognize most issues in terms of their effects across nation-states. With the creation of this food-borne disease surveillance system, SFCGME is positively affecting security systems both within and between states, lending a sense of regional security. The system will not only quickly and efficiently share information about suspected disease outbreaks between the participating organizations in the region but will also address a common health concern, build the capacity to detect disease outbreaks, and exercise the systems that would be used to respond to an outbreak caused by a biological weapon. All in all, SFCGME's implementation of the surveillance system will address interdependence as an opportunity to exchange and share information in mutually beneficial ways.

MECIDS also highlights SFCG's use of social entrepreneurship to develop innovative ways to strengthen social cohesion. As mentioned earlier, MECIDS grew out of a concern about biological weapons. After some time focusing on the traditional notion of security in the form of WMD prevention, SFCGME adjusted its vision to include doctors and hospitals on the front of a biological attack. Regional experts advised SFCG that it should build capabilities that meet both civilian health and military defense needs. For example, properly organized disease-reporting systems; trained doctors, nurses, and technicians; and efficient laboratories—all are essential components in responding to a biological attack, and states that enhance these capabilities also would be better equipped to prevent natural outbreaks such as influenza or West Nile virus.

Moreover, diseases are easier to discuss than biological weapons. Health professionals share a public-service orientation, and in the Middle East, they recognize that diseases can easily pass from one country to another. MECIDS participants often repeat the slogan "The virus doesn't stop at the checkpoint." According to an Al Quds University study, there were 148 Israeli-Palestinian cooperative health projects documented from 1994 to 1998. Groups like the Middle East Cancer Consortium and the Middle East Association for Managing Hearing Loss also have been founded in the last decade. Like MECIDS' own cooperative action projects, these examples reflect the understanding that conflict can be transformed through the cooperation among professionals with shared interests and expertise. They also suggest that changing its primary orientation from security to public health was an essential factor in the success of MECIDS.

SFCGME also attempts to develop an integrated approach in its projects. More specifically, SFCGME works on several fronts simultaneously, conducting programs in coordination with government workers, grassroots groups, and international agencies. In a parallel to the development of MECIDS, in January 2003 SFCGME convened several NGOs from Egypt, Jordan, Israel, and the Palestinian Authority and established a similar long-term commitment to regional security through the formation of a Chemical Risks Consortium. The NGOs will work collaboratively to build confidence, to develop closer regional ties, and to improve preparedness against chemical incidents, ranging from chronic pollution to chemical weapons attacks. As with MECIDS, the CRC transcends participants' differences in nationality and focuses instead on their similarities in the professional arena. In order to find a common ground on chemical risks assessment, participants in recent months have written case studies of a particular chemical incident from their respective states, from which new lessons for the region can be derived and shared. During the most recent CRC meeting in June 2003, participants presented and encouraged discussion on their findings. In this education process, not only will CRC participants expand their knowledge base of regional chemical incidents but they will also be able to see their case studies published in a single book as a tangible reminder of regional cooperation.

Conclusion

By putting the common ground approach into action, in the Middle East and Burundi, SFCG has developed programs that can easily identify and respond to the changing needs of the societies in which they work. As an NGO—unlike international organizations with many member states and governments with extensive deliberative and oversight mechanisms—the organization has the time to develop deep relationships and the flexibility to change its priorities. Because Search for Common Ground's mission focuses on transforming the process through which parties deal with difficult issues, rather than on particular outcomes, it creates a space for them to find their own sustainable ways to manage conflict.

Notes

1. Based on an earlier version by Richard Eisendorf and Timothy Werner.
2. Amr K. Abdalla, Noa Davenport, Leslie McTyre, and Steven A. Smith, *Independent Program Evaluation: Search for Common Ground in Burundi* (April 2002), p. 16.

ENVIRONMENTAL ORGANIZATIONS AND MULTILATERAL DIPLOMACY

A *Case Study of the* Earth Negotiations Bulletin

Pamela Chasek

Since the mid-1980s, there has been an increase in multilateral environmental diplomacy within the United Nations system as scientific and political understanding of global environmental issues has improved. The realization that environmental threats can have serious socioeconomic and human costs, and that these problems cannot be solved by unilateral decisions of states, has given impetus to increased international cooperation on a wide variety of issues from global warming to biodiversity conservation to international chemicals management.[1]

The emergence of global environmental issues within the UN system has also coincided with the rise of nongovernmental organizations and other nongovernmental actors, such as business organizations, local authorities, scientists, and indigenous peoples, as major forces in environmental diplomacy. NGO influence on global environmental politics is based on one or more of three factors. First, NGOs have expert knowledge and innovative thinking about global environmental issues, acquired from specializing in issues under negotiation. Second, they are dedicated to the goals that transcend narrow national or sectoral interests. Third, they represent constituencies within their own countries that command attention and that sometimes influence policies and even tight electoral contests (Porter, Brown, and Chasek 2000, 61).

This chapter will focus on the role that environmental NGOs can play within the UN system, including global conferences and within the conferences of the parties of a large number of international environmental treaties. After examining the different types of activities that NGOs engage in, this chapter will focus on the reporting function of NGOs—an activity that is often overlooked in other examinations of NGOs within the UN system. I will particularly focus on the role of one NGO, the International Institute for Sustainable Development (IISD) and its UN reporting service known as the *Earth Negotiations Bulletin*.

Roles of NGOs in Multilateral Diplomacy

Environmental NGOs, as well as those NGOs and major groups[2] involved in the larger context of sustainable development negotiations, have changed the nature of international environmental policymaking, especially since the 1992 United Nations Conference on Environment and Development (UNCED), also known as the Earth Summit. The international community now recognizes that effective global action requires meaningful stakeholder involvement in both international policymaking and implementation (Wapner, 2000; Gemmill and Bamidele-Izu 2002, 83). Many have categorized and analyzed the different roles of NGOs in multilateral environmental diplomacy (Charnowitz 1997; Esty 1998, 2002; Raustiala 1997; Porter, Brown, and Chasek 2000; Breitmeier and Rittberger 2000). There is general agreement that NGOs contribute in the following areas: advocacy, policy research and development, mobilizing public opinion, monitoring and assessing state commitments, and negotiations reporting.

Advocacy

Advocacy organizations can be understood as influencing the process of political agenda setting. NGOs educate the public, mobilize and organize citizens to show their concern about the issue(s) in question, and create pressure on, and lobby for, their goals with decisionmakers (Breitmeier and Rittberger 2000, 142–143)

Both domestically and at international negotiations, environmental NGOs influence state action primarily by pressuring government officials to support environmental protection efforts (Wapner 2000, 94). At the international level, NGOs try to insert themselves into the negotiating process and manipulate the dynamics of multilateral diplomacy and compliance with international agreements. During negotiations, NGOs have found several ways to influence the process. They actively lobby delegates in the hallways outside conference rooms. NGOs, such as the Women's Environment and Development Organization (WEDO), often go through draft texts of agreements and highlight sections that they believe should be amended. They "shop" these recommended amendments to friendly delegates, who then introduce the changes into the text during the negotiations.

NGOs also influence the negotiations as part of government delegations. Although this was the exception rather than the rule prior to the Earth Summit, the practice of having NGO representatives on government delegations to conferences and other multilateral negotiations has become more commonplace. During the preparatory process for the Earth Summit in Rio de Janeiro, Brazil, Canada was the first country to put NGO representatives on its national delegation. Canada also set another precedent by letting the NGO representative speak in plenary. Norway, Sweden, the United Kingdom, Denmark, Finland, Canada, New Zealand, the United States, Australia, the Netherlands, the Commonwealth of Independent States, India, Switzerland, and France all had NGOs on their official delegations in Rio (Finger 1994, 208). As part of the delegation, NGOs usually participate in the daily delegation briefing, are often privy to the negotiating strategies of their government, and are occasionally permitted to speak on their government's behalf. Although some NGOs admit that they felt more like window dressing than "official" delegation members, their participation on the delegation sends an important message that NGOs are to be considered part of the diplomatic process, not merely on the sidelines.

Policy Research and Development

Another major activity that NGOs undertake in multilateral environmental negotiations is to provide information about policy options. Some NGOs with large professional staffs are often able to devote more time researching and writing policy briefs on specific environmental issues than many governments, especially developing countries, which often lack the resources and expertise to allow adequate policy evaluation and creation. Many governments recognize that the quality and subjectivity of these policy briefs vary, depending on the source, yet still have come to rely on their work, especially when it is provided free of charge. The chief result of the large number of NGOs providing policy information and evaluation is that states can maximize policy information and research while minimizing expenditures (Raustiala 1997, 727). According to Raustiala (1997, 727–728), "By providing extensive information, evaluations, and legal opinions, NGO policy research permits governments to redirect scarce resources elsewhere, and provides perspectives and ideas that may not have emerged from a bureaucratic review process." For example, Greenpeace International provided government delegates with information about the extent of hazardous waste dumping in developing countries, which influenced the negotiation and adoption of the 1989 Basel Convention on the Transboundary Movements of Hazardous Wastes and Their Disposal. Greenpeace alerted importing states about shipments, published a newsletter on the waste trade, and raised the issue with national governments and international organizations (Wapner 2000, 95). FIELD, a London-based NGO, has been providing advice and legal expertise to the Alliance of Small Island States (AOSIS) during climate change negotiations. In fact, the early drafts of what became the 1997 Kyoto Protocol were developed by AOSIS with assistance from FIELD. In some cases, FIELD experts were included on government delegations to climate change negotiating sessions, representing such countries as Micronesia.

Mobilizing Public Opinion

In the field of environmental policymaking, advocacy-type NGOs provide the public with information about the state of the environment gleaned from reports produced by research institutes, international organizations, or state agencies, thus generally operating as transmission belts for and interpreters of scientific knowledge (Breitmeier and Rittberger 2000, 144). NGOs also have the ability to influence the public through campaigns and broad outreach. Environmental NGOs were among the first transnational actors adapting to changes in global telecommunications. They use communications media such as the Internet to create information networks and disseminate reports, press releases, and newsletters. This has strengthened their impact on agenda-setting processes, for early warning on environmental problems, and for shortening the time span between problem identification and eliciting a policy response (Breitmeier and Rittberger 2000, 145).

During global conferences, such as the 1992 Earth Summit and the 2002 World Summit on Sustainable Development, many NGOs increased citizen

awareness of the conference and sustainable development. Although many
of these groups did not actively participate in the negotiations, their impact
on conferences is still felt, particularly in the realm of public relations.
Most of these NGOs see their role as one of awareness raising. They appeal
to national governments and world leaders to listen to them, and they distribute statements and press releases to the world media. These mobilizing
efforts increase the visibility of the conference as well as the visibility of the
NGOs themselves (Finger 1994, 206).

Environmental NGOs were also successful in mobilizing worldwide
public opinion in opposition to the proposed multilateral agreement on investment (MAI). The MAI was a free-standing investment treaty being negotiated at the Organization for Economic Cooperation and Development
(OECD). The MAI was to be a comprehensive, high-standards agreement
establishing a legally binding multilateral framework for investment liberalization and investor protection. Negotiations on the treaty began in 1995.
In 1998, after the draft MAI was leaked to the public by a Canadian NGO
and disseminated over the Internet, there was an upsurge of activities by a
broad coalition of consumer, environmental, development, and public citizen groups in Europe, the United States, Canada, and Australia, challenging the rationale and effects of the MAI in their own countries as well as on
developing nations.

The draft MAI soon attracted widespread public opposition due to concerns about its implications for sustainable development (particularly
poverty eradication and environmental sustainability goals) and national
sovereignty. "The MAI would give foreign corporations unprecedented
power to directly challenge Governments' environmental, health, worker
and other laws, or circumvent them entirely," said a circular letter sponsored by an international coalition of NGOs (Khor 1998). NGOs managed
to mobilize thousands of people in more than half of all OECD countries
and numerous developing countries. Opponents ranged from environment
and development NGOs, to consumer organizations, human rights bodies,
trade unions, local governments, parliamentarians, and church groups.
Public campaigns, street protests, outraged parliamentarians, and interagency fights within governments erupted. On December 3, 1998, the
OECD announced that "Negotiations on the MAI are no longer taking
place" (Oxfam 1998), and the NGOs declared victory.

Monitoring and Assessing State Commitments

Most multilateral environmental treaties rely on states to report on their
own progress and compliance. However, many states lack the capacity to

gather the needed information, and others just do not make the effort (Raustiala 1997, 728). The lack of adequate and timely reporting by governments causes problems in any treaty compliance and verification system. Environmental NGOs provide an alternate route, however, since they are well positioned to provide independent assessments of individual states' compliance. Numerous national environmental groups, such as the Natural Resources Defense Council and Environmental Defense in the United States monitor their own country's compliance with environmental treaties. At the international level, Greenpeace and the Worldwide Fund for Nature have monitored the work of the International Whaling Commission.

TRAFFIC (Trade Records Analysis of Flora and Fauna in Commerce) tracks illegal wildlife trade that is in violation of the CITES agreement (Convention on International Trade in Endangered Species of Flora and Fauna). CITES covers more than thirty thousand species of plants and animals and has been endorsed by over 150 countries. However, the diversity of the species covered, which range from medicinal herbs to exotic pets, requires a level of international on-the-ground coordination that the CITES secretariat cannot do on its own. TRAFFIC, which is a partnership between the World Wide Fund for Nature and the IUCN—World Conservation Union, is a key component in the implementation of CITES. TRAFFIC works in twenty-two offices around the world to collect data on, investigate, and research trade in endangered species. It has become a key resource for governments and NGOs to use to monitor compliance with the treaty (Gemmill and Bamidele-Izu 2002, 88–89).

Negotiations Reporting

In addition to the highly analyzed roles that NGOs play in multilateral environmental diplomacy, one role has not gotten as much attention: reporting. According to Raustiala (1997, 730),

> Environmental regimes are marked by a high degree of institutionalized, long-term negotiation and adjustment. During the course of large-scale multilateral negotiations there is a numbing array of detail to be followed. Delegates often cannot keep track of everything that is going on, particularly if the negotiations occur through multiple working groups. NGOs have alleviated this problem of information overload by supplying daily bulletins.

One of the oldest NGO publications is *Eco*, which was first produced at the 1972 UN Conference on the Human Environment in Stockholm. *Eco* published daily commentaries and analyses of the proceedings during the

Stockholm Conference, as a joint publication of Friends of the Earth and the *Ecologist*. During the meeting, *Eco* came up with a copy of the Chinese proposal for a redrafted Declaration on the Human Environment and published it in its Saturday issue. "Delegates and journalists circled warily around this item; not one other paper picked it up, presumably because the other journalists were reluctant to accept it as genuine. Forty-eight hours later it became evident that the *Eco* scoop was entirely valid; and from then on *Eco* was required reading" (Stockholm Conference Eco 1972, 153). Since the Second World Climate Conference in 1990, *Eco* has also been produced at the international climate talks. Other editions of *Eco* have been produced by groups of NGOs at the Montreal protocol meetings (ozone depletion), the negotiations on the Convention to Combat Desertification, and other meetings.

Outside the environmental sector, other NGOs have provided reporting services over the years, trying to balance advocacy pieces, editorials, and conference reports. The Washington, D.C.–based Advocacy Project has provided online coverage of several conferences from the perspective of civil society, starting with the 1998 Rome conference to draft the statute of a new International Criminal Court. In 2001, the Advocacy Project reported on two preparatory meetings of the UN General Assembly for the NGO Committee on UNICEF. Both series were produced in printed as well as electronic versions. Their report is called "On the Record."[3] The International Committee to Ban Landmines has provided conference reporting on meetings dealing with the Landmine Treaty and the meetings of the parties.[4] Human Rights Internet, a Canadian-based NGO, provided daily reports from the World Conference Against Racism.[5] The Landmine Survivors Network and a group of related NGOs have been providing daily reports at meetings of the UN Ad Hoc Committee on a Comprehensive and Integral Convention on Protection and Promotion of the Rights and Dignity of Persons with Disabilities.[6]

At meetings related to the environment and sustainable development, there have been numerous NGO publications as well as conference newspapers published by other organizations. During the Earth Summit in Rio, Inter Press Service published *Terra Viva,* which incorporated numerous news stories and conference-related reports. The International Media Foundation published the *Earth Times,* beginning at the Earth Summit in 1992 and continuing at major UN conferences before it folded in 2002. The *Earth Times* combined conference news stories, editorials, and human interest stories in a tabloid publication.

Coalitions of NGOs have published several different newsletters at meetings of the UN Commission on Sustainable Development as well as at the 2002 World Summit on Sustainable Development (WSSD). The Stakeholder

Forum for Our Common Future (formerly UNED-UK) has published *Outreach*, a daily newsletter, at meetings of the Commission on Sustainable Development since 1997, combining conference reports and editorials.[7] Another coalition of NGOs, the Sustainable Development Issues Network (SDIN),[8] started publishing its own newsletter during the preparatory process for the WSSD. Their publication, *Taking Issue*, provided some conference reporting along with commentary on the proceedings.

Traditionally, NGO reporting services have consisted of a mixture of conference reporting and editorializing. This provides an avenue for NGOs to service the needs of delegates and other NGOs for a source of information about the meeting they are attending (or may not be able to attend), and at the same time advocating the position and views of the NGOs producing the report. This mixture of advocacy and reporting has served NGO interests for over twenty years. Yet, until 1992, there had not been any source of neutral, real-time conference reporting provided by NGOs, governments, or the UN system, until the *Earth Negotiations Bulletin* entered the scene.

The *Earth Negotiations Bulletin*

In spite of the millions of documents, press releases, and meeting summaries that the United Nations system produces each year, there was historically a lack of timely information that covered the intricacies of multilateral negotiation. "The reporting of ongoing negotiations is something countries cannot do easily or effectively on their own. If any one government were to attempt to provide such reporting, the reports would be derided as biased. If the UN or formal secretariat published daily reports, they would have the status of official documents and member governments would have difficulty agreeing on content, style, tone and so forth" (Porter, Brown, and Chasek 2000, 67). Although the UN press summaries of meetings are useful, their "correspondents" often have little knowledge of the politics underlying certain statements, and they only cover formal meetings, not the informal sessions where most of the actual negotiations take place.

Since 1992, delegates, NGOs, the media, and academics who follow UN environment and development negotiations have had another resource at their disposal, which has proven to be an indispensable record of a number of negotiating processes—the *Earth Negotiations Bulletin (ENB)*. The *Bulletin*, which is published by the International Institute for Sustainable Development (IISD), based in Winnipeg, Canada, provides objective daily and summary reports of UN negotiations on environmental and development issues. Beginning with coverage of the UNCED preparatory process in

Table 4.1 List of Negotiations Covered by the *Earth Negotiations Bulletin*

UN Conference on Environment and Development (PrepCom IV and Conference)	1992
UN General Assembly (discussion of sustainable development issues)	1992–1994
UN Convention to Combat Desertification	1993–present
UN Commission on Sustainable Development	1993–present
International Conference on Population and Development	1993–1999
UN Conference on Straddling Fish Stocks and Highly Migratory Fish Stocks	1993–1995
UN Conference on the Sustainable Development of Small Island Developing States	1993–1999
Biological Diversity and Plant Genetic Resources	1993–present
World Summit on Social Development	1994–2000
UN Conference on Human Settlements (Habitat II)	1994–2001
UN Framework Convention on Climate Change	1995–present
International Forest Policy (IPF, IFF, UNFF, FAO)	1995–present
Commission on the Status of Women and Fourth World Conference on Women	1995–2000
Chemicals Management (PIC/POPs/IFCS)	1997–present
UNEP Governing Council	1999–present
Ramsar Convention on Wetlands	1999–present
Convention on Migratory Species	1999–present
Montreal Protocol	1999–present
Basel Convention	1999–present
CITES	2000–present
World Summit on Sustainable Development	2001–2002
Financing for Development	2001
International Tropical Timber Council	2002–present
Intergovernmental Consultative Process on Oceans and Law of the Sea	2003–present

1992 (under the name *Earth Summit Bulletin*), the *Bulletin* has also provided coverage of more than twenty environment- and development-related
negotiations (see Table 4.1).

The *Bulletin* is the collective brainchild of three individuals who met
during the UNCED preparatory process in 1991. Langston James Goree IV
("Kimo") was working for a Brazilian Amazon-based NGO, Johannah
Bernstein was the coordinator of the Canadian Participatory Committee
for UNCED, and I was doing my doctoral research on multilateral environmental negotiations. During the third meeting of the UNCED Preparatory
Committee (PrepCom-3) in Geneva in August 1991, the three of us, with
assistance from other NGOs, started preparing weekly summaries of the
negotiation of Agenda 21, the program of action that was to be adopted at
the conference in Rio in June 1992. The original purpose of these summaries was to give NGOs a source of reliable information about the proceedings. Numerous NGOs around the world were unable to attend the
meeting, and others were arriving late. Thus, the reports were uploaded
onto an electronic mail and conferencing bulletin-board system called
Econet, part of the Association of Progressive Communications network,
and a few copies were printed out to distribute to newly arriving NGO representatives.

However, within a day of the distribution of the first weekly summary
report, government delegates heard about it and began asking for copies.
By the following Monday, delegates were already asking for the next
weekly summary, and as the meeting was drawing to a close, they started
asking if there was going to be a summary of the entire meeting. At that
point, we realized that we were onto something. During the next few
months, we prepared a funding proposal and started looking for support to
publish a daily report during UNCED PrepCom-4, which was to take place
in March 1992 in New York. Island Press, with Ford Foundation funding,
decided to support us, and on Monday, March 2, 1992, the first issue of the
Earth Summit Bulletin was put on the tables outside meeting rooms at UN
Headquarters in New York City.

The *Bulletin*, a two-sided, double-column, single sheet of paper that
summarizes the previous day's proceedings and lists the current day's
events, quickly became the one piece of paper delegates and NGOs looked
for each morning. Although many delegates were skeptical of an "NGO
publication" at first, they soon realized that the *Bulletin* was "devoid of
any NGO politicking," made a reasonable attempt at providing objective
and accurate information, and, perhaps most important, helped them to do
their jobs.[9] With numerous negotiating sessions going on at any given time,
the *Bulletin* provided a quick summary of what had happened in each one
of them. The length of morning delegation meetings decreased because delegates read the *Bulletin* and no longer had to give lengthy reports of the

previous day's events in their working group. Small delegations found that they could still keep up to date on what was happening in working-group meetings that they were not able to attend. If they read in the *Bulletin* that text was proposed that was not to their delegation's liking, they made sure they attended the next session of the working group in order to rectify the situation. Finally, when the meeting was over, many delegates relied heavily on the *Bulletin* to write their reports back to their capitals on what had happened at this five-week marathon meeting.

The success of the *Bulletin* in New York enabled the team to raise $60,000 in six weeks to go to Rio and produce ten thousand copies a day (only one thousand copies a day had been printed in New York) at the Earth Summit. After Rio, we thought we were finished, and we all went on with our lives. But during the summer of 1992, IISD contacted us and asked us if we wanted to continue the publication of the *Bulletin* at the forty-seventh session of the UN General Assembly that was to discuss UNCED follow-up. During the coming months we reached an agreement with IISD that established the Institute as the *Bulletin*'s publisher, changed the name to *Earth Negotiations Bulletin*, and set us off on a path that would hire Goree as the full-time managing editor of the *Bulletin*, develop a staff of twenty to thirty freelance writers (primarily Ph.D. students), cover twenty to thirty meetings a year, publish daily and summary reports (sometimes in French and Spanish as well), and raise US$1.5 million a year to keep the entire operation going.

The daily issues of the *Bulletin* are currently distributed at conference sites and in PDF and ASCII format to electronic mailing lists. They are also available on our Internet site, "Linkages" [http://www.iisd.ca/linkages/], which was one of the first two thousand sites on the World Wide Web when it was established in 1994. It is not known how many people receive the *Bulletin* through secondary and tertiary distribution and on the Internet, although approximately 61,582 subscribers are on the electronic mailing lists and the Internet site averaged 117,244 page views per week for the 2002–2003 fiscal year. People from over 130 countries have accessed the Internet site during this period and have downloaded 676,446 reports in PDF format.

The success of the *Bulletin* also gave rise to several additional publications, which currently comprise IISD-Reporting Services. *Sustainable Developments* is a reporting service that expands the services provided by the *Bulletin* to other meetings, such as government-sponsored conferences, workshops, symposia, or regional meetings. Sponsors and hosts of these meetings pay for daily and/or summary reports as well as a web page with photos and audio clips. *ENB on the Side* was developed to cover side events at major meetings, such as conferences of the parties to the UN

Framework Convention on Climate Change and the World Summit on Sustainable Development. *ENB on the Side* provides synopses of side events and photographs and is available on site as well as through list serves and on the Internet site. *Linkages Update* gathers the latest events in the multilateral environment and development policymaking world into a single publication, which is distributed through e-mail. News and information about upcoming and recent meetings, workshops, and other events are available, as are notices about recent publications, job vacancies, job changes of prominent people in the field, and information that links these various processes together. There are also several moderated e-mail lists that focus on specific topics, including climate change, forests, and water.

The Impact of the *Bulletin* on UN Negotiations

There is no definitive way to state how the *Earth Negotiations Bulletin* has affected UN environment and development negotiations. However, over the years, numerous people have testified to the usefulness of the *ENB*. For example, Dr. Charles McNeill, of UNDP's Environmentally Sustainable Development Group, stated in an address to the Tata Energy and Resources Institute, "The *Earth Negotiations Bulletin. . .* has helped transform the way global decisions are made and has broken down barriers between stakeholder groups around the world. Thanks to the *ENB*, now the whole world can squeeze (virtually) into the basement of the UN buildings to participate in dialogue and decision-making around critical global sustainable development issues" (McNeill 2002, 5). To gain a greater understanding of how readers use the *Bulletin* and other IISD-RS materials, and to see if these goals have been achieved, I asked our readers to respond to a three-question survey asking respondents who they are, how they use the *Bulletin,* and how they think the *Bulletin* has affected multilateral environmental diplomacy. Nearly 250 readers responded to the survey, and although this is not a comprehensive study of the use of the *Bulletin,* it does give some insights into how the publication has been used and regarded over time.

Some readers, including Sabrina Shaw, Secretary to the World Trade Organization Committee on Trade and Environment, believe that the *Bulletin* has "revolutionized" environmental negotiations in three main ways. It has provided instant transparency for delegates and the general public: "Small land-locked and island states can no longer claim they don't know what is going on." Furthermore, delegates as well as secretariats who were initially fearful that the *Bulletin* would "invade their space" came to depend on its services. Second, the *Bulletin* has provided accountability. It is a public record of the negotiations and meetings that otherwise took place without much transparency. UN reports of the meetings would only come out months later, when "nobody has the inclination or patience to read them." Third, the *Bulletin* has provided continuity and linkages between otherwise disparate multilateral environmental negotiations (Shaw 2003).

Government delegates at negotiating sessions credit the *Bulletin* with not only providing transparency but also allowing them to see the big picture. "The *Bulletin* is a very useful tool when someone is attending a meeting, because as part of an official delegation sometimes participants cannot attend several simultaneous groups or are more involved in dealing with their position and their interests, and they do not get a complete view of the meeting, side events or what is going on the corridors. So first thing in the morning they can consult the *Bulletin* and have a complete overview of what happened the day before," states María Teresa del Carmen Bandala Medina, Director of Environment and Natural Resources in the Ministry of Foreign Affairs of Mexico (Bandala Medina 2003). James Phiri, the former executive director of the Environmental Council of Zambia, a government agency, stressed the importance of the *Bulletin* for developing-country delegations. When finances are tight and delegations are small and often arrive late, it is not always possible to follow and attend critical "real deal making and breaking" meetings. "Under such circumstances, the only reliable means available is the *ENB*." The *ENB* not only provides transparency but is "the quickest means for bringing one up to speed with the negotiations jargon and the many acronyms used." The *ENB* also allows officials to provide the most up-to-date information to their ministers and help inform their decisions (Phiri 2003).

Government officials in industrialized countries also find the *ENB* a useful tool. Anne Franklin from the Royal Belgian Institute of Natural Sciences states that as the secretariat for the Belgian national focal point for the Convention on Biological Diversity (CBD), she "uses the *Earth Negotiations Bulletin* and the *Linkages* web site for its information on the CBD and other meetings (especially biodiversity-related conventions, and climate- and forest-related processes)." She adds, "It is very useful to keep actors in one multilateral environmental agreement (MEA) informed on what is happening under other MEAs. This is essential to avoid duplication of work between the different MEAs (even if they still need to work on this!). The *ENB* and web site are also extremely useful to keep the reports we have to write after international MEA meetings as short as possible, as we can provide references to them for a detailed account of what has happened" (Franklin 2003).

Claire Findlay at the Australian Department of Environment and Heritage finds the *Bulletin* a "very important means of keeping up with developments on particular issues." On a number of occasions she has incorporated information from the *Bulletin* in advice to her supervisor and through briefs to the Environment Minister. She adds, "I believe the *Bulletin* plays a significant role in the development of policies and briefs within this Department" (Findlay 2003).

The original idea behind the *ENB* was to help NGOs in their advocacy work, and it continues to perform this service. The Canadian Arctic Indigenous Peoples Against POPs (persistent organic pollutants) have not had the resources to send a sufficient number of representatives to the Intergovernmental Negotiating Committee meetings to monitor all of the working groups and contact groups at the negotiations. "We could review the *Bulletins* each morning and strategize where our lobbying efforts should be," notes technical adviser Stephanie Meakin. "I continue to use the *Bulletin* to get an overview of the international activities that affect the Inuit as we cannot possibly be involved in everything due to lack of resources. They allow us to remain informed on the current progress of negotiations and activities at the various conferences of the parties (COPs) and other meetings" (Meakin 2003). As Simone Lovera, Friends of the Earth International, points out, "The daily reports during meetings allow people to follow the meeting without having to spend hours listening to the actual meeting itself. This time can be effectively used for advocacy work (or bilateral negotiations) in the corridors. In short, it has changed the nature of these intergovernmental meetings" (Lovera 2003).

The Whale and Dolphin Conservation Society (WDCS) used the *Bulletin* in a unique way in the spring of 2003. The advocacy group sent out its own press release, "Japan and Norway Oppose Independent Reporting of the IWC Meeting," when the Governments of Japan and Norway refused to allow the *Earth Negotiations Bulletin* to have secretariat status at the fifty-fifth meeting of the International Whaling Commission in June 2003. Secretariats usually grant *Bulletin* writers secretariat or affiliate status at meetings, rather than NGO status, to allow us greater access. The Whale and Dolphin Conservation Society stated in its release, "*ENB* has provided a high quality and invaluable service at CITES, CMS [Convention on Migratory Species] and other international meetings where, incidentally, Japan and Norway have never objected to it. WDCS regrets the refusal by the whaling nations to permit *ENB* to report from the IWC meeting which, we believe, would have benefited from a neutral, authoritative and up to the minute account of their often disruptive activities" (WDCS 2003).

Nonprofit advocacy organizations are not the only ones who rely on the *ENB* to keep them informed. Trade associations and other business and industry representatives have found the *Bulletin* a useful tool in their international activities. Barney Chan, the general manager of the Sarawak Timber

Association in Malaysia, distributes the *Bulletin* and links to the Internet site to his three-hundred-member association e-list. Also, as the coordinator of the International Tropical Timber Organization (ITTO) trade advisory group, he distributes the same information to his six-hundred-member e-list covering many of the ITTO's fifty-six member countries. He adds, "Each May, I chair the Annual Market discussions at the ITTO meetings and I find your reporting of this event useful to our trade associates around the world. The audio file is particularly impressive for those who did not attend sessions but still like to hear 'the action.' Most people find the accompanying photos put a 'human face' on what used to be faceless meetings held half way around the world!" (Chan 2003).

Academics have also found the *ENB* to be indispensable in research and as a teaching tool. The *Bulletin* is used in courses on international public and NGO management, offered at Syracuse University, international environmental politics at the University of Oregon, environmental policy and institutions at Rutgers University, renewable energy and the environment at the University of Reading in the UK, the social issues surrounding climate change at the University of Leeds in the UK, and global environmental politics at Colorado State University, to name a few. Professors also report using the *Bulletin* in environmental law classes at Hebrew University in Jerusalem and La Republica University in Santiago, Chile; in agroecology courses at Ferdowsi University in Mashad, Iran; in architecture and urban design at Liverpool John Moores University in the UK and at the College of Economics and Management at Southwest Agricultural University in Chongqing Municipality in the People's Republic of China; in town and country planning at University Putra in Malaysia; in a city planning program at Dicle University, Diyarbakür, Turkey; in the Resource and Environmental Planning Programme at Massey University, Palmerston North, New Zealand; in the Department of Political Science at the University of Toronto; and in the Development Studies Institute at the London School of Economics. High school teachers have also used the *Bulletin* in such diverse ways as teaching about sustainability issues in a physics class in Swaziland and preparing students for model United Nations simulations in Tennessee.

Journalists use the *ENB* and other IISD-RS products to provide background information for their articles. Ehsan Masood, a former journalist for *Nature*, writes, "I first came across the Bulletin in 1995 while following the post-Rio follow up to the climate change and biodiversity convention negotiations. It basically meant that I could keep up-to-speed on negotiations from any part of the world on a daily basis without leaving my desk in London! It is fair to say that without the *Bulletin*, *Nature* magazine—for whom I worked for between 1995 and 1999—would have reported fewer news and feature stories on global environmental issues" (Masood 2003).

Karl J. Bondeson, the environmental editor for the *Goteborgs-Posten*, the morning daily in Goteborg, Sweden, concurs: "When the *Bulletin* first came it was like a small revolution. Suddenly there was detailed—almost instant—reporting about negotiations around the world that (for economical or practical reasons) were impossible for me to cover. Before *ENB*, the way to work was to call up single negotiators or NGOs by phone, who of course, gave their very biased picture of what was going on (if they answered the call at all). Having the *ENB* in my hand I now could ask more relevant questions, and put the actions of my own government (and others) in perspective." Bondeson further notes that not only does he think the media reporting has improved due to the *ENB*, but "efforts by governments improved as they realized that what is said and done during the negotiations is observed and reported by people that couldn't be dismissed as biased NGOs or government representatives. The *ENB* has thus pushed environmental negotiations to be more professional and has made the process a bit more transparent to the public" (Bondeson 2003).

Finally, the *Bulletin* has contributed to raising the global profile of international sustainable development policymaking. Jan McAlpine, a senior official with the US Department of State says, "I firmly believe that the *ENB* has raised attention to the importance of negotiations on environment/sustainable development issues over the last decade to the broad attention of not only the environment-related government and non-governmental community, but significantly also to industry and non-environmental related policy interests" (McAlpine 2003). Clive Stannard, at the Food and Agriculture Organization's Commission on Genetic Resources for Food and Agriculture believes that "the very presence of the *ENB* in negotiations ensures that they are seen to be important. The publication has helped open the frontiers of the various communities involved so that one group of specialists sees the relevance of what another group is doing" (Stannard 2003).

Conclusion

NGOs have been a part of multilateral environmental diplomacy for over twenty years by lobbying and advocacy work, providing scientific and technical information, monitoring government compliance with environmental agreements, mobilizing public opinion, and reporting on conferences and negotiations. Although all of these roles have been crucial in the development and implementation of international environmental policy, the reporting function has had a number of unforeseen beneficial results.

One of the most useful aspects to the *Earth Negotiations Bulletin* has been that it has provided transparency to multilateral environment and development negotiations. Governments and international organizations can now be held accountable for what they say and do in multilateral conferences and meetings. NGOs, academics, scientists, civil society, and even high-level government officials can now receive real-time information about what their government delegates are doing and saying at multilateral negotiating sessions.

The *Bulletin* has also contributed to leveling the playing field between the governments and NGOs of developed and developing countries. Delegates from developing countries can no longer claim ignorance of these negotiating processes. As a result, they have been able to enhance their own ability to participate, represent their country's interests, and influence international environmental policy.

Since the *ENB* is available free of charge and can be reprinted, as long as proper academic citation is used, we have found that many other organizations and governmental agencies have distributed the *Bulletin* to their own members or staff. For example, links to the *Bulletin* can be found on many Internet sites around the world, including those for convention secretariats, the United Nations Environment Program, Green Cross International, the World Bank, the United Nations Development Program, the US Global Change Research Information Office, the German Heinrich Böll Foundation, the Sustainable Development Networking Program in Bangladesh, the Congressional Research Service, the Austrian Council on Climate Change, the American Society of International Law, the Lawyers Environmental Action Team in Tanzania, and Réseau-Action-Climat-France. It has been translated into many languages, including French, Japanese, Korean, Farsi, Afrikaans, Xhosa, Spanish, and Portuguese.

Through primary, secondary, and even tertiary distribution, information about multilateral environmental diplomacy is now reaching people from local city planners to high-level ministers, providing useful information to policymakers and those interested in contributing to the policy development process. The *ENB* also serves to maintain an information flow to policymakers on the activities of other parallel negotiating processes, thus creating linkages between processes.

By developing a unique model using new and emerging communication technologies, running a virtual operation by keeping operational costs to a minimum, and hiring freelance writers (primarily Ph.D. students and environmental lawyers), IISD-Reporting Services has carved out an important niche in the world of multilateral environmental diplomacy. The work of the *Bulletin* illustrates the effectiveness of NGOs in the diplomatic arena and demonstrates the partnerships between governments (through their funding), the United Nations (through funding and access), and NGOs (through the provision of information) in opening up multilateral diplomacy for the world to see.

Notes

1. For more information about global environmental politics, see Gareth Porter, Janet Welsh Brown and Pamela S. Chasek, *Global Environmental Politics*, third edition. Boulder: Westview, 2000.

2. Major groups are defined by *Agenda 21* as NGOs, women, youth, farmers, scientists, business and industry, indigenous peoples, local authorities and trade unions.

3. See http://www.advocacynet.org/what_we_offer.html

4. See http://www.icbl.org

5. See http://www.hri.ca/racism/dailyupdates/index.shtml

6. See http://www.rightsforall.org/library.php

7. See http://csdngo.igc.org/outreach/index.htm and http://www.earthsummit2002.org/es/preparations/global/csd11.htm

8. SDIN consists of Northern Alliance for Sustainability, the Environment Liaison Centre International (ELCI) and Third World Network.

9. See F. McConnell, *The Biodiversity Convention: A Negotiating History*. (Kluwer, 1996); S. P. Johnson, *The Earth Summit* (Graham and Trotman/Martinus Nijhoff, 1993).

References

Bandala Medina, María Teresa del Carmen. (2003) E-mail correspondence, June 13.

Bondeson, Karl J. (2003) E-mail correspondence, June 14.

Breitmeier, Helmut and Voker Rittberger. (2000) "Environmental NGOs in an Emerging Global Civil Society," in *The Global Environment in the Twenty-first Century: Prospects for International Cooperation*, edited by Pamela S. Chasek (Tokyo: UNU Press).

Chan, Barney. (2003) E-mail correspondence, June 15.

Charnowitz, Steve. (1997) "Two Centuries of Participation: NGOs and International Governance," *Michigan Journal of International Law*, Vol. 18, No. 2, pp. 183–286.

Esty, Daniel C. (1998) "Non-Governmental Organizations at the World Trade Organization: Cooperation, Competition or Exclusion," *Journal of International Economic Law*, No. 1, pp. 123–148.

———. (2002) "The World Trade Organization's Legitimacy Crisis," *World Trade Review*, Vol. 1, No. 1, pp. 7–22.

Findlay, Claire. (2003) E-mail correspondence, June 15.

Finger, Matthias. (1994) "Environmental NGOs in the UNCED Process," in *Environmental NGOs in World Politics*, edited By Thomas Princen and Matthias Finger (London: Routledge).

Francis, Yvonne. (2003) E-mail correspondence, June 12.

Franklin, Anne. (2003) E-mail correspondence, June 16.

Gemmill, Barbara and Bamidele-Izu, Abimbola. (2002) "The Role of NGOs and Civil Society in Global Environmental Governance," in *Global Environmental Governance: Options and Opportunities*, edited by Daniel C. Esty and Maria H. Ivanova. (New Haven: Yale School of Forestry and Environmental Studies).

Khor, Martin. (1998) "NGOs in OECD countries protest against MAI," *Third World Resurgence*, Vol. 90–91, February-March.[http://www.twnside.org.sg/title/oecd-cn.htm]

Lovera, Simone. (2003) E-mail correspondence, June 13.

Mahsood, Ehsan. (2003) E-mail correspondence, June 12.

McAlpine, Jan L. (2003) E-mail correspondence, June 18.

McNeill, Charles I. (2002) "Inaugural Address to the Colloquium on Global Partnerships for Sustainable Development: Harnessing Action for the 21st Century." Tata Energy and Resources Institute, New York City, March 24.

Meakin, Stephanie. (2003) E-mail correspondence, June 13.

Oxfam. (1998) "MAI: Multilateral Agreement on Investment." Oxfam UK Briefing Paper, December. [http://www.oxfam.org.uk/policy/papers/mai_update/mai_update.htm]

Phiri, James S. (2003) E-mail correspondence, June 16.

Porter, Gareth, Janet Welsh Brown, and Pamela S. Chasek. (2000) *Global Environmental Politics*, 3rd ed. (Boulder: Westview Press).

Raustiala, Kal. (1997) "States, NGOs, and International Environmental Institutions," *International Studies Quarterly* Vol. 41, pp. 719–740.

Shaw, Sabrina. (2003) E-mail correspondence, June 13.

Stannard, Clive. (2003) E-mail correspondence, June 23.

Stockholm Conference Eco. (1972) *Your Environment*, Vol. 3, No. 3, Autumn, p. 153.

Wapner, Paul. (2000) "The Transnational Politics of Environmental NGOs: Governmental, Economic and Social Activism," in *The Global Environment in the Twenty-first Century: Prospects for International Cooperation*, Edited by Pamela S. Chasek (Tokyo: UNU Press).

Whale and Dolphin Conservation Society. (2003) "Japan and Norway Oppose Independent Reporting of the IWC Meeting." Press release. [http://www.adoptadolphin.com/dan/publishing.nsf/webnews/5FBF1B3D7BCA5B3680256D2E00682BB2]

WOMEN'S ORGANIZATIONS AND THE UNITED NATIONS

Carolyn M. Stephenson[1]

W"omen's rights are human rights!" The furthering of women's rights as human rights, and the official recognition that violence against women is a violation of those rights, in the Program of Action at the Vienna UN Conference on Human Rights in 1993, galvanized the international women's movement in the lead-up to the UN's Fourth World Conference on Women in Beijing in 1995. The UN Commission on Human Rights appointed a Special Rapporteur on Violence Against Women in 1994. These successes were due to several years of strategic planning by women's organizations, especially the International Campaign for Women's Human Rights, a project of the Center for Women's Global Leadership, headed by Charlotte Bunche at Rutgers University. Petitions with half a million signatures were presented at Vienna, and a million at Beijing were presented to the High Commissioner for Human Rights. The center had launched sixteen Days of Activism Against Gender Violence in 1991 and 1992 (from November 25, International Day Against Violence Against Women, to December 10, Human Rights Day, including December 1, World AIDS Day), an International Hearings Campaign to Document Violations of Women's Human Rights in

1992, and a Tribunal on Violence Against Women at the Vienna Conference in 1993 (www.cwgl.rutgers.edu/globalcenter; Pietila 2002, 52–54).

Although women's organizations have always been a part of the multi-lateral diplomacy at the United Nations, both their numbers and the centrality of their role increased with the advent of the UN International Women's Year conference in 1975 and the subsequent conferences in 1980, 1985, and 1995. The women's movement, reinvigorated by the feminist revolution of the early 1970s, became internationalized with the UN Decade for Women 1976–1985. The inclusion of the other half of civil society, which had been largely left out of traditional diplomacy, led both to new official UN organizations relating to women, such as UNIFEM (UN Development Fund for Women) and INSTRAW (International Research and Training Institute for the Advancement of Women), and to the increasing involvement of women's nongovernmental organizations (NGOs) in the wide variety of UN activities. Women's NGOs now focus their attention not only on the UN Commission on the Status of Women (CSW), created in 1946, but also on the relationship of women to development, environment, population, food, technology, and security activities, throughout the UN.

The Early Period 1945–1974

At the time of the formation of the UN, five US women's organizations were among the forty-two included in the US delegation to the San Francisco conference. The inclusion of civil society and demands by women's and other NGOs for continued inclusion in the UN led the conference to add Article 71 to the UN Charter. It read:

> The Economic and Social Council [ECOSOC] may make suitable arrangements for consultation with non-governmental organizations which are concerned with matters within its competence. Such arrangements may be made with international organizations and, where appropriate, with national organizations after consultation with the Member of the United Nations concerned.

Access to the UN through consultative status with ECOSOC is particularly important in the area of women, because the work of the Commission on the Status of Women falls within the purview of ECOSOC. It is ECOSOC status that determines access to the basic work of the UN, including General Assembly conferences. Each of the UN women's conferences was a General Assembly conference.

The women's movement, which began as early as the 1830s, had produced, by the late nineteenth century, international women's organizations such as the General Federation of Women's Clubs, the International Council of Nurses, the International Council of Women, the World Young Women's Christian Association, and the World Women's Christian Temperance Union.

Elise Boulding identified forty-seven women's NGOs just prior to the start of the Decade for Women. Boulding argued that women's NGOs are "an elite of the powerless" which can help to redistribute global power. Although her data show that less than 10 percent of headquarters were in the developing countries, later data show that over half of those thirty women's NGOs formed between 1980 and 1989 were based there (Boulding 1977, 165–218).

At its March 19, 1947, session, the ECOSOC Committee on Arrangements for Consultation with nongovernmental organizations had admitted thirteen women's organizations to consultative status. A total of thirty-three women's NGOs had some form of intergovernmental consultative status at the start of the decade, a smaller number having this status with ECOSOC itself. By 1989 there were fifty women's NGOs in consultative status with ECOSOC.

Many of the NGOs admitted formed the Conference of Non-Governmental Organizations in Consultative Status with ECOSOC (CONGO, now the Conference of Non-Governmental Organizations in Consultative Status with the UN) by the late 1940s. CONGO has run many successful forums at UN conferences, beginning when Rosalind Harris, as president of CONGO, persuaded its board to run the "Tribune," a nongovernmental gathering organized at the World Population Conference in 1974. One of the earliest committees of CONGO was its Committee on the Status of Women.

In the early 1970s, a new feminist movement generated new theories of power and social change. Sisterhood was powerful, but this conception of power was power *with* rather than power *over*, *con*structive power rather than *de*structive power. The new feminist *movement* of the 1970s set the stage for worldwide attention on women, and the older women's *NGOs* pushed for an International Women's Year.

Introduced by Romania, the actual idea for an International Women's Year in 1975 was conceived by a group of women's NGOs with long-standing consultative status with ECOSOC. The Women's International Democratic Federation (WIDF), in particular, had used its consultative status to introduce the idea in the CSW. WIDF, an Eastern -bloc-headquartered organization which had been among the first group of women's organizations granted consultative status, lost that status in 1954 in the midst of Cold

War politics and regained it in 1967, with strong support from other women's NGOs. It was the work of women's NGOs, particularly the International Council of Women and WIDF, consistently lobbying governments on the subject which ensured that the proposal did not get dropped at any stage (Foster 1989, 76).

Women's organizations contributed significantly to the series of large ad hoc or megaconferences which characterized UN politics during the 1970s, beginning with the UN Conference on the Human Environment (UNCHE) in Stockholm in 1972. These conferences differed from other UN conferences in that their purpose was primarily to raise issues in the international system which had been previously neglected. The official UN conferences, to which only NGOs in consultative status could come, were accompanied by unofficial NGO forums, for which anyone could register. The Mexico City International Women's Year Conference was one of these. The pattern of the world conferences established in the 1970s was largely repeated in the 1980s and 1990s.

Mexico City, International Women's Year, 1975[2]

The World Conference of the International Women's Year took place in Mexico City from June 19 to July 2, 1975. The "equality, development, and peace" subtheme linkage had been articulated as early as 1926 by the International Alliance of Women (Fraser 1995, 81). Nongovernmental organizations played a role at both the UN conference and the parallel nongovernmental Tribune. ECOSOC, on April 28, 1975, had authorized the UN Secretary-General to invite as observers NGOs in consultative status, which could make oral and written statements. In Mexico City, 133 states and 114 NGOs participated in the formal conference, while 7,200 individuals from 82 countries participated in the Tribune. NGOs both lobbied governments on amendments to the Plan of Action at the Conference and set up their own discussions at the Tribune at the Centro Medico.

Of the 154 organizations invited to participate, 114 sent a total of 192 individual observers to the conference. Some organized well in advance of the conference and submitted statements on various agendas to the UN in New York City, which were sent to Mexico City for distribution. NGO statements were submitted, some by individual NGOs and some by as many as thirty-six NGOs together, on topics ranging from justice for rural women to women's participation in strengthening international peace, from family planning as a human right to greater precision in provisions for review and appraisal of activities, including yearly reporting. The lateness of the opportunity to speak in the general debate meant less impact, as many delegates had gone on to working meetings or simply did not bother to attend for NGO statements. This pattern has been typical of subsequent UN conferences as well.

The Tribune

The Tribune operated with very different rules and practices. Either Tribune registration or International Women's Year (IWY) Conference identification was required for admission to sessions. No formal statement was allowed to come forth as a Tribune position, although groups could make and request signatures for statements. Tribune sessions were designed so that at least half the time was available for audience discussion.

The Tribune Organizing Committee, cochaired by Rosalind Harris, president of CONGO, and Mildred Persinger of the World YWCA, with representatives of thirteen other NGOs (four women's, nine others) appointed by CONGO, along with Tribune director Marcia Bravo, had in three months organized a program of 20 panels with simultaneous interpretation in English, French, and Spanish from June 20 to June 27, with an additional 191 panels from June 30 to July 2 planned in Mexico City.

The Tribune's opening plenary at 6 P.M. on June 19 began with the sound of the marimba—by an all-male band—and a speech by Señora Maria Esther Zuno Echeverria, first lady of Mexico, before the twenty-four hundred participants, who filled the auditorium to capacity. Panels covered building human community, women across cultures, Third World craftswomen and development, attitude formation and socialization processes, law and the status of women, agriculture and rural development, health and nutrition, education, women at work, women and the environment; urbanization, population and planned parenthood, women in public life, the family, and peace and disarmament.

Every morning at 8 A.M. the Tribune Organizing Committee met to assign additional rooms for the next day and deal with emergencies. At 9 A.M. there was a briefing on the proceedings of the United Nations World Conference. Beginning on June 24 the Tribune also held an informal press briefing every day at 1:30 P.M. This became an important source of information on changes in the Tribune program, which by that time had "grown like Topsy." The Tribune Press Information Office also put out mimeographed summaries of each of the panels and published *Xilonen,* a daily newspaper which reported, partly in English and partly in Spanish, on the events at both the conference and the Tribune.

Although there were formal panels at the Tribune, there was an air of informality and festivity to it as well. It is almost impossible to capture the fullness of the additional events scheduled by the Tribune committee, let alone the unscheduled happenings, exhibits, dancing, singing, praying, and talking. Several events organized by others are of special import, however.

An "Encounter for Journalists," sponsored by the UN Centre for Economic and Social Information, ran from June 16 to June 18 to acquaint journalists with the themes of the conference prior to its opening. Some of those attending, including Gloria Steinem, calling themselves the Feminist Caucus of International Women's Year, drew up a working document of a feminist manifesto, which became the nucleus for the statement issued by the "United Women of the Tribune" (see below).

The American Association for the Advancement of Science, together with the UN Institute for Training and Research and the UN Development Program, organized a seminar on women and development from June 16 to June 18. One important outcome of this seminar and discussions on women and development that continued throughout the Tribune was the eventual advent of Women's World Banking, which later became an NGO in consultative status with ECOSOC.

Each night at 6:30 P.M. the NGO Committee ran a special briefing and strategy meeting for NGOs in consultative status. The high level of sophistication and knowledge of some of these women long involved in the traditionally "volunteer" sort of organizations was aptly demonstrated at these briefings. The gap between these women (primarily American) and American feminists was even greater than that between American and Latin American feminists. Yet these women were the ones who set up the Tribune and provided opportunities or information to women trying to affect the international political process. Because of differences in age and approach, each group regarded the other warily, yet one NGO briefing session (June 23) was the source of much information on the UN process for the feminist group, which included Betty Friedan, author of *The Feminine Mystique*. NGOs overturned much of their own program to satisfy the need of these new groups to learn how to be effective in the context of different cultures and of multilateral diplomacy at the UN.

At the briefings, much discussion focused on the role of women in development and the effects of development on the status of women. Women's organizations spoke of the Singer sewing machines sent to Africa and used by men while women worked in the fields, the agricultural development courses given to men in countries where women do the agricultural work, the changeover of the market economy from women to men in Asia.

Many of the women who came to the Tribune had no conception of what the procedures of an international conference were, yet they expected to have an effect on the conference, and to be heard by the world as well as to talk to each other. Attempts at the Tribune to influence the conference resulted in two additional documents. On June 26, a Call to Action on Women, Food, and Population within a Development Strategy, signed by over six hundred women from eighty-three countries, was presented to the conference's secretary-general, Helvi Sipila, who had become the first female UN Assistant Secretary-General in 1972. The Call, initiated by the Washington-based Population Crisis Committee, was presented by Justice Annie Ruth Jiagge, head of the Ghana delegation to the conference and chairman of the Ghana National Council of Women and Development, on behalf of women leaders in agriculture, nutrition, women's rights, civic affairs, labor, and religion, to ask governments to take action to solve the interrelated problems.

Perhaps the most interesting, and certainly the most controversial, document that came out of the Tribune was the unauthorized thirty-four pages of suggested revisions to the World Plan of Action. Drafted in informal working groups, and eventually by a group of twelve to thirty-one women working late into the night, and somewhat ambiguously approved in a June 25 meeting of the roughly eighteen hundred "women of the Tribune" (that is, anyone who happened to come to the Plenary meeting at 1 P.M.), the document was presented to Helvi Sipila in her office on June 26. The main document proposed paragraph-by-paragraph changes to the World Plan, including a woman's right to control her own body and a UN office for women's concerns at the Under Secretary level. Some of these appeared in the Declaration of Mexico, an official conference document hammered out by a drafting committee chaired by Leticia Shahani, later to become a leader of the Nairobi conference.

The level of frustration over the lack of communication between the Tribune and the conference was noted at the beginning of the document itself. Betty Friedan, a prominent participant, had threatened to lead a demonstration of five hundred women at the conference but was persuaded not to do so.

On June 29 Mrs. Sipila came to the Tribune to explain that there was no channel for the presentation of the proposals of the "United Women of the Tribune" to the official conference. The next day a press conference called by the group to publicize the proposals broke up in the face of what many thought were deliberate outside attempts at disruption. Conflict broke out over the claims of some Latin American women that their ideas had not been incorporated. This roughly one hour of conflict over the microphone was well covered by the news media as an example of infighting among women. It was one of two short instances of such conflict.

In 1975 in Mexico City, peace, the third theme of International Women's Year, was conspicuously absent from the discussion. Not only did the themes of equality, development, and peace receive unequal attention, but they were also not related to the degree that they could have been. Some NGO preconference activities did focus on peace. In May 1975 the Women's International League for Peace and Freedom (WILPF) and the Women's International Democratic Federation cosponsored a seminar in New York City. Entitled Women of the World United for Peace and Disarmament and Its Social Consequences, it brought together 250 women from twenty-seven countries. The seminar marked the first time that an official Cuban representative was allowed to attend a nondiplomatic function in the United States since 1959 (Foster 1989, 76). Although WILPF and WIDF did continue to cooperate across Cold War lines at the Mexico City conferences, their ability to raise the issue of peace was only barely visible.

The Tribune forced the issue of women and development into the minds and feelings of many women, who, if they listened, realized that it was not a spurious issue, not a political move of governments, but a valid issue to be faced. Individual Third World women at the Tribune expressed with substantial emotion their interest in dealing with issues of adequate food, education, and medical care before issues of rape, abortion, or equal pay for work of equal value.

Differences in perspective between First and Third World feminism eventually led to synthesis into an international movement. Each brand of feminism was affected by the other. Women went home from Mexico City with an awareness that there was more to this business of feminism than they had experienced in their own country.

Perhaps the most important outcome of the Mexico City Tribune was the continuation of the organizational infrastructure which had set up the Tribune and the international communication which continued as a result. The International Women's Tribune Centre, Inc. (IWTC) was initiated by Mildred Persinger, chairperson of the IWY Tribune in Mexico City, who became its president, and other Tribune organizers, to respond to the requests for information and technical assistance from women around the world involved in developmental projects. Located near the UN in New York City, the center provided a resource center, technical assistance, and quarterly newsletters, the *IWTC Newsletter* (later *The Tribune*). Building on the list of registrants from the IWY Tribune, the IWTC facilitated the development of communication and networking among women worldwide and provided programs at later Forums.

Copenhagen, Mid-Decade Review Conference, 1980

At Copenhagen, as at Mexico City, the official Mid-Decade Review Conference of the UN Decade for Women was held at a different location, the Bella Centre, from the NGO Forum, which was centered at the Amager

University Centre. This time the forum ran only for the first part of the conference, July 14–24; the conference itself ran from July 14 to July 30. One hundred thirty-four NGOs registered for observer status at the conference. Twenty women's and thirty-three other NGOs submitted written statements, roughly five times the number submitted in Mexico City, on topics ranging from a report of an organization's own regional seminars, to the condition of Palestinian Arab women in the administered territories, to the status of older women, women and community development, education for peace against the arms race, refugee women, "the heroic women of Namibia and South Africa," indigenous women, and equal employment at the UN. The Programme of Action, paragraphs 100–105, included recognition of the role of NGOs in development.

Central to the Mid-Decade Review Conference was the Convention on the Elimination of All Forms of Discrimination Against Women (CEDAW), which fifty-seven states signed during the opening ceremony. CEDAW received the necessary twenty ratifications to come into force September 3, 1980, and by December 10, 2003, it had 175 states parties. Its forerunner is the Declaration on the Elimination of Discrimination Against Women, adopted by the CSW in 1967. The convention is monitored by the Committee on the Elimination of Discrimination Against Women, with constant attention by women's NGOs. The optional protocol to CEDAW, which provides for inspection and allows individual complaints to be made, came into force December 22, 2000, and counted fifty-eight states parties by December 22, 2003.

By the time of Copenhagen much of the NGO leadership had shifted to Europe. Edith Ballantyne of the Women's International League for Peace and Freedom, headquartered in Geneva, was president of the Conference of Non-Governmental Organizations in Consultative Status with the UN. Elizabeth Palmer, a former general secretary of the World YWCA, also based in Geneva, was the convenor of the CONGO Planning Committee of the Mid-Decade Forum itself. Ballantyne had been in charge of the international office of WILPF from the early 1970s and in 1976 became the first representative of a peace organization to head CONGO. Her role meant an increased presence for WILPF and for peace issues—ranging from issues of colonialism and apartheid through those of war—at the Copenhagen forum (Foster 1989, 60 and 77–79). Although the official UN conference added subthemes of employment, health, and education to the main decade themes of equality, development, and peace, all of these themes had already become the subject of discussion and panels at the forums.

The NGO forum began with an opening ceremony at 10 A.M. on July 14 and included eighteen substantive panels on the themes of equality, development, peace, education, health, and employment, as well as racism (including apartheid), sexism, the family, refugees, and migrants.

The logistics of the Copenhagen conferences were again significant. Not only was the conference at some distance from the forum, but this time the forum itself was spread out. The lack of any central gathering place, coupled with political conflict over issues such as Palestine and South Africa, contributed to a sense of fragmentation at this meeting.

Vivencia! was the centerpiece for most participants. Based on the Spanish word that means "an experience that becomes part of life," Vivencia! was a more informal program of over 370 events, displays, exhibits, meetings, and performances; over 130 films and slide shows; and workshops on project design, funding, mass media, and feminism that took place around the formal program. It was a colorful and noisy place, in which one could easily get lost, and in which there was constant meeting, organizing, and networking activity. Angry groups of men, women, and children from liberation movements paraded through the halls periodically with music and speeches. A march led by Domitila, a woman trade union leader from Bolivia who had been brought by Tribune leaders for the formal panels, left from here for the Bella Centre.

Feminist writers have noted that the issue of the equality of women, supposedly the main focus of the decade, had received short shrift in the Mexico City conference and was treated only marginally better at the Copenhagen conference. However, in both nongovernmental forums, equality was a main focus. By 1980 there was realization that equality was broader than just the Western feminist conception of women's rights. National liberation (or national development) and women's liberation were seen to be related, but national liberation and development were by no means seen as sufficient for women's liberation. Forum panels focused on the effects of multinational corporations on women's lives, on child care, on foreign aid, and on women and technology, as well as on a woman's rights related to her own body, and on women's studies, banking systems, and research institutes. Many panels focused on the achievement of equality for women in the areas of health, education, and employment, the three subthemes of the 1980 conference.

A heavy emphasis on development continued in the Copenhagen forum. The highly visible leaders of the women's rights movement in the United States, who pushed a Western brand of feminism at the World Conference in Mexico City, had by Copenhagen become both more sophisticated in international politics and more cognizant of the needs and demands of women in other parts of the world and, together with many others, participated in workshops on development, providing a real dialogue between the First and Third Worlds on issues related to women. These panels were a concrete illustration of the cross-fertilization and synthesis which had begun in Mexico City between First and Third World feminism.

Peace, the third theme of the decade, also began to be considered in 1980, both in discussion at the forum and at the conference, and in the Programme of Action, largely through the actions of NGOs. At the opening of the conference, Lucille Mair of Jamaica, and secretary-general of the conference, spoke of the problem of the use of scarce resources for war. A delegation of Nordic Women for Peace presented to United Nations Secretary-General Kurt Waldheim petitions signed by 500,000 women demanding an end to the arms race.

The joint statement made to the UN conference plenary on July 24, 1980 by Edith Ballantyne, head of CONGO, on behalf of the forty-five NGOs which had asked to speak, reaffirmed the goals of the Decade for Women, and urged governments to recognize that military expenditures were incompatible with these goals. The NGOs urged that peace be restored to equal emphasis with the other two goals of the decade.

The forum also dealt with the theme of peace, with two of the main panels held each day in the large auditorium, plus one summary panel, on peace. In addition, the World Peace Council, the Women's International Democratic Federation, the Women's International League for Peace and Freedom, and the newly formed Scandinavian action group, Women for Peace, ran ongoing series of panels on strategies for ending the arms race; the relationship between women, peace, and the mass media; the problem that national heroes have more often been heroes of war than of peace; the relationship between nuclear power and nuclear weapons; and disarmament education.

In the discussion of all issues at either the forum or the conference, the debate itself was far from peaceful. Attempts to achieve consensus at the conference were unsuccessful. Although there was increased emphasis on peace, the *process* itself was not peaceful. Many women were critical of the process on the basis that the politicization of issues of national policy precluded adequate consideration of issues specifically related to women. It was suggested that a successful consensus process, at the forum and the conference, would have increased the likelihood of successful implementation of the Programme of Action.

Nairobi, Conference to Review and Appraise the UN Decade for Women, 1985

Consensus was more in evidence at the July 15–26, 1985, Nairobi Conference to Review and Appraise the UN Decade for Women. During the February-March 1984 session of the Committee on the Status of Women, which was acting as the preparatory body for the world conference, seventeen

NGOs submitted a statement commending the preparatory body on its use of consensus and urged delegates to continue that same spirit of consensus. They emphasized implementation of the subthemes of education, employment, and health, urging the highest priority for rural women's health and food and water supply, as well as for the elimination of illiteracy, the needs of refugees and migrant women and children, older women, and children and youth, and for accelerating the participation of women in public life.

NGOs had been an active part of the process for 1985 from the beginning. The Spring 1983 Session of ECOSOC requested the UN Secretary-General to invite the active participation of NGOs in preparations for and in the next world conference. At the May 2–3, 1983, board meeting of CONGO, the president noted that CONGO's Geneva, Vienna, and New York committees would work together on NGO activities for Nairobi. She invited all interested CONGO member organizations to form a planning committee for NGO activities. At the Nairobi conference, 157 governments plus 163 NGOs were represented. The conference not only reviewed the decade but also agreed to the Forward-Looking Strategies (FLS) for the Advancement of Women to the Year 2000.

The Nairobi Forum '85 was again organized by CONGO, with a planning committee of sixty international NGOs, along with a Kenyan NGO Committee. Dame Nita Barrow served as convenor, and Virginia Hazard as coordinator of Forum '85. The CONGO planning committee sponsored NGO meetings before the regional UN preparatory meetings in Tokyo in March, Arusha in October, Havana in November, and Baghdad in December of 1984, where they authored recommendations to bring to the attention of the meetings. At the NGO Pre-Conference Consultation in Vienna in October 1984, ninety-one NGOs attended two series of workshops on equality, development, peace, health, education, employment, elderly women, refugees and migrants, women in emergency situations, and the media, plus a panel on young women and girls.

Forum '85 was the largest international meeting of women held to date, with over 13,500 in attendance, far more than had been expected. The forum opened at 10 A.M. on July 10, 1985, at the Kenyatta International Conference Centre, where the United Nations conference would be held beginning July 15. The next day it moved to the University of Nairobi and ran through July 19. This time the two sites were accessible to each other by means of a Kenyan-government-provided bus service at seventy-five cents per ride. This time translation in Arabic, English, French, Spanish, and Swahili was provided for the main forum sessions. Once again the NGO planning committee published a daily newspaper which provided a link between the conference and Forum '85.

The majority of forum activities took place at the University of Nairobi, where the planning committee coordinated plenary sessions in the areas of equality, development, peace, health, education, employment, youth, aging, migrants, refugees, women in emergency situations, and media, and where hundreds of other sessions were organized by nongovernmental organizations and women's groups from around the world. There were other activities, like craft demonstrations and music of all kinds, in the grassy area in the center of the university. A crafts marketplace was organized by Maendeleo ya Wanawake, the Women's Bureau of Kenya, and the Kenya External Trade Authority. Child care and development activities were coordinated by the Kenya NGO Organizing Committee, as were field trips to village projects. A ten-day International Women's Film Festival at the Kenya National Theater took place with only one major incident over the Kenyan government's requirement that it be able to censor each film. A five-day seminar for Third World women, the "Third World Forum on Women, Law, and Development," was sponsored by the Overseas Education Fund of Washington, D.C. The International Women's Studies Institute in Kenya provided training and support for twenty-six women, half Western, half African, over four weeks, to report on the sessions of the forum. Karibu, a Women's Centre for Women of All Faiths, was organized by the World Council of Churches, Church Women United, and the All-Africa Council of Churches, in a nearby church.

The fact that the final conference of the decade was held in Africa further helped to highlight the relationship between women and development. Similarly, the holding of the conference in Nairobi, site of the UN Environment Program (UNEP), shortly after the UN Environment and Development Conference of 1982, brought to the agenda the triple relationship among women, environment, and development. The Environment Liaison Centre in Nairobi, with 231 members in sixty-six countries, put on a "Women, Environment, and Development" program July 15–19, including plenaries and four workshops on women and water management, forests, energy, and sustainable agriculture. NGOs and environmental movements put on a "Tech and Tools" exhibit, coordinated by the International Women's Tribune Centre, which included a variety of practical technologies, such as solar cookstoves, which could benefit women. Their workshops and exhibits ranged from computers, to building low-cost duplicating machines, to the jam and jelly business, to building energy and environment networks. African NGOs took participants on trips to the countryside to witness tree-planting farms and multiple cropping techniques developed and carried out by women. All of this brought an air of practical reality to the panels and lectures sponsored by NGOs and others. One new NGO in particular, DAWN (Development Alternatives for

Women in a New Era), which had only been formed in 1984, put on a large number of outstanding panels which questioned many of the traditional assumptions of development theory. This was also true of the Trickle Up Program, a New York–based program that was oriented to small-scale development aid, and that particularly focused on women, which had grown from almost nothing to a major endeavor from its birth in 1979. The focus on women and development had come of age.

In the Nairobi forum, peace as an issue became equal to the other two themes of the decade. The result was visible and concrete. A blue-and-white-striped tent stood at the corner of the grassy courtyard inside the entrance to the University of Nairobi campus, where Forum '85 was held. Under the bright blue banner proclaiming "Peace Tent," women congregated from morning to evening. At one side was a hand-made globe, the height of a human being, that became completely covered with signatures and comments. When the nongovernmental forum was over, the globe was carried to the site of the official UN conference.

Forum panels and workshops on the peace theme ranged from strategies for ending the arms race, to peace education, disarmament education, the relationship between disarmament and development, a Palestinian-Israeli dialogue, a US-Soviet dialogue, to race issues, to more theoretical discussions on the relationship of women to peace, and whether women's view of peace is distinctly different from men's. In the peace tent, operated primarily by the newly formed Feminist International for Peace and Food and the Women's International League for Peace and Freedom, one of the oldest women's peace organizations (1815), the dialogues continued daily on all of these issues, with the tent almost always hot and packed, and the scene of stimulating discussions. Organizers, though they faced disagreements among themselves, as well as between themselves and other individuals and groups that had different visions of peace, managed to preserve an atmosphere of open debate and a spirit of reconciliation. This was also true of most of the panels on peace at the forum, in noticeable contrast to Mexico City and Copenhagen, where much of the debate on peace issues had broken down into serious disagreement and vitriolic misunderstandings. The underlying sense was that the women's movement had matured over the course of the decade.

One hundred sixty-three NGO representatives went on to the UN conference itself as observers, with delegations ranging in size from one to twelve members. Fifty-nine written statements were offered by NGOs, of which twenty were authored in whole or in part by women's organizations. Their subjects ranged from the effects of racism and militarism on women to women entrepreneurs in India, to African traditional practices, and to women and the household.

NGOs monitored and lobbied the conference, distributing their observers between the two committees and conversations with government delegates in the halls, some NGOs cooperating and sharing information with each other. Although it is almost impossible to trace direct impact, one example is notable. The International Wages for Housework Campaign, launched in Britain in 1972 by Selma James, was credited by an unsigned article in *Forum '85* with an amendment to paragraph 120 of the Forward-Looking Strategies, which said both remunerated and unremunerated contributions of women, including those in "agriculture, food production, reproduction and household activities" should be reflected in the GDP. In 1980 the Copenhagen conference had produced the more limited Resolution 103 on the subject, and the Campaign continued its work to expand Resolution 103 over the five years. The Campaign, which included organizations from Argentina, Australia, Barbados, Canada, Italy, Trinidad and Tobago, the UK, the United States, and West Germany, had a table outside the peace tent at the Nairobi forum for a petition on the subject. Its associated group, Housewives in Dialogue, which has consultative status with ECOSOC, began the forum with twelve thousand members but was said to have grown considerably since then.

There were references to NGOs in at least forty-three paragraphs of the Forward-Looking Strategies adopted by the conference. In the Summary of the General Debate, paragraph 97 noted that many countries referred to the valuable contribution of NGOs, stressing their contributions to community activities such as maternal and child care, vocational training for the disabled, and social services for the aged, and emphasized the need for strengthened cooperation (UN 1985, 112).

When the General Assembly took note of the Report of the Conference and endorsed the Forward-Looking Strategies on December 13, 1985, it urged not only governments and intergovernmental organizations but also NGOs to give high priority to the FLS. NGOs mattered, even to governments, in the area of women's issues at the United Nations.

Beijing, UN Fourth World Conference on Women, 1995

The Beijing Women's Conference, with almost fifty thousand participants hosted by China, September 4–15, 1995, is reputed to be the largest UN conference ever held. Like the conferences of the Decade for Women, it was actually two conferences. In addition to the official UN Fourth World Conference on Women in Beijing, which included 189 governments and more than 4,035 representatives of 2,602 NGOs plus press and UN staff, there was also the NGO Forum '95 in Huairou, roughly thirty-five miles northeast of Beijing, which had roughly twenty-seven thousand representatives of NGOs and individuals (Freeman 1996).

The UN conference was organized by the UN Commission on the Status of Women, with the UN Division on the Advancement of Women (DAW) serving as secretariat, and Gertrude Mongella, UN Assistant Secretary-General, as secretary-general of the conference. On its last day, the conference adopted by consensus the Beijing Declaration and the Platform for Action (PFA), which committed governments and others to a five-year plan of time-specific targets for the advancement of women and to the mainstreaming of a gender perspective. It identified twelve critical areas of concern (poverty, education, health care, violence against women, armed conflict, economic inequality, inequality in power and decisionmaking, institutional mechanisms, human rights, stereotyping and inequality in communications, inequalities in environmental management, and the girl child) (UN 1996, PFA para. 44). It reiterated the 1994 Cairo commitments to women's reproductive rights and the 1992 Vienna commitments that women's rights are human rights and that violence against women violates these rights.

The PFA specifically recognized that "non-governmental organizations have played an important advocacy role in advancing legislation or mechanisms to ensure the promotion of women", becoming "catalysts for new approaches to development" (UN 1996, PFA para. 26). An organized lobby, "Equipo," and the UN Secretariat briefed NGOs every morning at 8 A.M., and over twenty issues caucuses met and fanned out to work with delegates. The Linkage Caucus of over thirteen hundred women from seventy-three countries coordinated. Women's NGOs' conceptualization and lobbying over the course of years and at Beijing were largely responsible for the strength of these documents.

NGO Forum '95 was organized by the NGO Forum Facilitating Committee, with Irene Santiago as the executive director of the forum, in conjunction with the China Organizing Committee, which also provided bus transportation from Beijing hotels to Huairou, and between Huairou and the Beijing International Conference Center for those who were accredited to go to both conferences. The convener of the NGO forum was Khunying Supatra Masdit, president of CAPWIP, the Center for Asia-Pacific Women in Politics, which had organized the first Congress of Asia-Pacific Women in Politics in Manila for 155 NGOs from twenty-three countries in June 1994 (Freeman, 1996).

At Huairou there were rain and mud and confusion and unfinished buildings and the difficulty of getting on the bus to Beijing. But at Huairou there was every sort of women's organization: religious, political, environmental, professional, academic, human rights, and artistic. There were theme tents, regional tents, a peace tent similar to that in Nairobi, a grassroots tent, a lesbian tent, an older women's tent, a youth tent, a healing tent, and a quiet tent. There was singing, and a parade of quilts, and protest marches, and government surveillance, and a security entrance. There were panels organized by UN agencies, by governments, and by NGOs, on electoral systems, women's invisible work, health, sports, peace education, violence against women, sexual slavery, and the resumption of French nuclear testing in the Pacific, though many of the panels scheduled didn't happen, at least where scheduled. There was Hillary Clinton's address centering on women's rights as human rights, for those who could get into the auditorium after waiting for an hour in the rain. And there were daily newspapers, almost all in English, both at the conference and at the forum, some somewhat official, like *World Women* published by the English language *China Daily*, others that appeared regularly at UN conferences, like *Earth Times* and *Earth Negotiations Bulletin*, which had begun at the 1992 Rio Earth Summit, and others just for this conference, like *Forum '95*.

Among the wide variety of international women's organizations and networks formed from the time of the UN Decade for Women (1976–1985) are ISIS International (1974), strengthening feminist analysis; the International Women's Tribune Centre (IWTC) (1975); the International Women's Health Coalition (1980), which promotes women's reproductive health rights; Development Alternatives with Women for a New Era (DAWN) (1984); International Women's Rights Action Watch (IWRAW) (1986), which monitors the implementation of CEDAW; the Center for Women's Global Leadership (CWGL) (1989), which focuses on women's human rights and violence against women; and the Women's Environment and Development Organization (WEDO) (1990) (Pietila 2002, 70–72). All played central roles in Beijing and have continued to be central players since, including at the discouraging Beijing plus 5 meeting at UN Headquarters in New York City, June 5–9, 2000. Here the goal was simply not to go backward, and many women's NGOs nicknamed the conference "Beijing minus 5." But groups like WEDO held governments' feet to the fire. A total of 110 of the 189 governments at Beijing reported back to WEDO in 1997 that they now had national action plans to implement the Beijing Platform for Action. WEDO worked closely with UN agencies to monitor the implementation of commitments and reported this in the publication *Promise Kept, Promise Broken?* (WEDO 1997). WEDO's 50/50 Campaign was launched June 8, 2000, during Beijing plus 5, to work toward balancing the participation of women and men in local and national politics [www.ngo-congo.org/ngomeet/beijing5.htm]. The IWTC continued to facilitate international communication with the biweekly listserve Women's Globalnet. In March 1999, during PrepCom 1, a group of NGO women in communications discussed setting up a global information network for Beijing plus 5;

the result was the creation of WomenAction 2000 (Walker 1999). In other forums, like the Non Proliferation Review and the Conference on Disarmament, the Women's International League for Peace and Freedom and the NGO Committee on the Status of Women, part of CONGO, coordinate an annual joint NGO Statement on Disarmament. The work of WILPF and other women's NGOs was significant in getting the Security Council in October 2000 to pass Resolution 1325 on Women, Peace and Security (text at www.PeaceWomen.org/1325inTranslation/index.html), the first time the Council had taken up this linkage. CONGO's NGO Committees on the Status of Women in New York, Geneva, and Vienna do training for women's NGOs at the Commission on the Status of Women.

Conclusions

Women's organizations have been a significant factor primarily in the furthering of women's rights at and through the UN, but also in the increasing importance of NGOs, and in the linkages now being made between the wide variety of issues confronting multilateral diplomacy at the UN today. As diplomacy has moved from traditional bilateral diplomacy to the multilateral diplomacy of intergovernmental organizations, it has also moved to include nongovernmental organizations. Women's organizations have been important influences on this opening up of multilateral diplomacy at the UN. Drawing on their experiences at the League of Nations, women's organizations, during the construction of the UN Charter, helped both to ensure language guaranteeing "the equal rights of men and women" (Preamble; see also Article 1.3) and to ensure the future consultative role of NGOs at the UN (Article 71).

International social and political change can be described as having three general phases. First, a new idea is brought to the world stage. Second, it is accepted and becomes institutionalized in IGO and state organizations and treaties. Third, the norms and rules in these institutions are implemented to provide for actual change. Women's organizations brought women's equal rights issues to the UN Charter; were the initiators of International Women's Year and the UN Decade for Women, which produced the various institutions and treaties within the UN system and among states; and formed international networks to nurture and implement these achievements. As a result, women's organizations worked in coalition with women on state delegations and in the UN Secretariat.

Among the institutional achievements in which women's organizations have played a role are the creation of the independent Commission on the Status of Women under ECOSOC in 1947, the World Conference of the International Women's Year in 1975, the UN Decade for Women 1976–1985, and the specific documents that came out of the four UN conferences on women in 1975, 1980, 1985, and 1995. In addition to the CSW, the institutions created in the UN system include INSTRAW and UNIFEM (from the IWY Conference) and the Division for the Advancement of Women (DAW) in the UN Secretariat. In states, national plans of action and women's departments were created. The Convention on the Elimination of All Forms of Discrimination Against Women (CEDAW), prepared for signing at the Copenhagen conference in 1980, was the most important treaty, supplemented by its 1999 Optional Protocol.

Among the changes in norms and rules included in these and other documents and institutions are the equality of men and women, the recognition of women's rights as human rights, the recognition that violence against women is a violation of women's human rights (Vienna Human Rights Conference 1993 and Beijing Conference 1995), the idea that women have a right to reproductive health and to control their own bodies (Cairo Population Conference 1994 and Beijing Conference 1995), and the idea that the implications of all public policy should be scrutinized through the lens of gender and that gender mainstreaming should be implemented in the UN system (Beijing Conference 1995 and ECOSOC Agreed Conclusions 1997). WIDF and WILPF worked as early as 1975 to link women's issues to armed conflict and security, the eventual result in October 2000 being Security Council Resolution 1325. DAWN and others worked to advance the notion of gender and development. WEDO worked to demonstrate the linkage between women and environment at the 1992 Rio Earth Summit and in Beijing. Many women's organizations have worked not only for the rights of women, but to humanize the politics of states and IGOs, taking into account the implications not only for states, but also for individuals.

Although the UN Decade for Women Conferences and the Beijing Conference a decade later gave an enormous boost to women's rights, it was not only at the conferences that women's organizations had an impact. Probably the most significant impact of the UN Decade for Women was cross-fertilization between women's NGOs and social movements, the founding of new women's NGOs, and the development of international networks of women, which began to coalesce by the end of the decade into an international movement. The networks of women's NGOs have worked constantly at yearly meetings of the CSW and other UN bodies to bring in new ideas, get them introduced by states, and get them implemented.

It is said that a woman's work is never done. Nowhere are women yet equal. Among the tasks that remain are furthering the legal equality of women in states where that has not been done (e.g., on land and inheritance rights), furthering the economic equality of women everywhere, implementing the rights gained in UN documents, and making the entire international system more responsive to issues of discrimination and inequality wherever they appear. When there is a period of backlash, as at the UN General Assembly Special Session in 2000, the task is simply to hold onto the gains made. Although it is unlikely that there will be another UN women's conference anytime soon, given states' economic objections to more huge UN conferences of any kind, women's organizations will continue to work in the context of day-to-day multilateral diplomacy at the United Nations.

Notes

1. The author acknowledges with thanks the aid of a Research and Writing Grant from the John D. and Catherine T. MacArthur Foundation.
2. For fuller discussion of NGOs at the three Decade for Women Conferences, see Stephenson and other articles in Winslow 1995. Except where specific references are cited, reports of the conferences come from the direct observations of the author and UN documents referred to in the text.

References

Boulding, Elise. (1977) *Women in the Twentieth Century World* (New York: John Wiley).

Center for Women's Global Leadership. (1993) *International Campaign for Women's Human Rights 1992–1993 Report.* [www.cwgl.rutgers.edu/globalcenter/publications/92–93report.html]

ECOSOC. (1997) *Report of the Economic and Social Council for 1997.* UN Document A/52/3, pp. 27–35.

Foster, Catherine. (1989) *Women for All Seasons: The Story of the Women's International League for Peace and Freedom.* (Athens: University of Georgia Press).

Fraser, Arvonne S. (1995) "The Convention of the Elimination of All Forms of Discrimination Against Women (The Women's Convention)," in *Women, Politics, and the United Nations,* edited by Anne Winslow (Westport, Conn.: Greenwood Press).

Freeman, Jo. (1996) "The Real Story of Beijing," *Off Our Backs,* Vol. 26, No. 3, March, pp. 1, 8–11, 22–27. Available as "Beijing Report: The Fourth World Conference on Women." [www.jofreeman.com/womenyear/beijingreport.htm]

Pietila, Hilkka. (2002) *Development Dossier: Engendering the Global Agenda: the Story of Women and the United Nations* (Geneva: United Nations Non-Governmental Liaison Service).

Stephenson, Carolyn M. (1995) "Women's International Nongovernmental Organizations at the United Nations," in *Women, Politics, and the United Nations*, edited by Anne Winslow (Westport, Conn.: Greenwood Press).

_____. (2000) "NGOs and the Principal Organs of the United Nations," in *The United Nations at the Millennium: The Principal Organs*, edited by Paul Taylor and A.J.R. Groom. (London: Continuum), pp. 271–294.

United Nations. (1985) *Report of the World Conference to Review and Appraise the Achievements of the United Nations Decade for Women*. (UN Document A/CONF.116/28/Rev.1).

United Nations, Fourth World Conference on Women. (1996) *Platform for Action and the Beijing Declaration* (New York: United Nations).

Walker, Anne S. (1999) "Women's Initiatives and Activities Worldwide." IWTC Women's Globalnet #127, August 6. [www.jca.apc.org/fem/news/women2000/11.html]

Winslow, Anne, ed. (1995) *Women, Politics, and the United Nations* (Westport, Conn.: Greenwood Press).

Women's Environment and Development Organization. (1997) "More Beijing Action Plan Promises Are Kept," *News and Views*, September. [www.wedo.org/news/Sept97/more.htm]

Chapter FIVE

MULTILATERALISM AND THE UNITED NATIONS

Successes and Failures

MULTILATERAL DIPLOMACY, SUMMITS, AND THE UNITED NATIONS

Richard Reitano

Since our discussion concerning law will have been undertaken in vain if there is no law, in order to open the way for favourable reception of our work and at the same time to fortify it against attacks, this very serious error must be briefly refuted. In order that we may not be obliged to deal with a crowd of opponents, let us assign to them a pleader. And whom should we chose . . . ? (Grotius 1925)

Diplomacy is one of the oldest forms of human intercourse. The need for "pleaders" to negotiate for states predates the city-states of ancient Greece and Rome, and although multilateral diplomacy is nothing new, it clearly came into its own as a major diplomatic tool in the twentieth century. The two Hague Conferences in 1899 and 1907 and particularly the advent of the League of Nations in 1920 also symbolize the transition from the reliance on bilateral diplomacy to modern-day multilateral diplomacy.[1]

In 1945, as Hans Morgenthau and Kenneth Thompson noted in *Politics Among Nations*, the United Nations was built on "three political assumptions." The first involved the unity of the great powers after World War II, which would enable the organization to react to any "threat to peace and security, regardless of the source." The second factor was that their combined strength would be sufficient to respond to any international crisis. Finally, as the guarantors of world peace and stability, the great powers would never be the cause of international conflict (Morgenthau and Thompson 1985, 505–506).

The inability of the United Nations to respond to major conflicts in the Cold War, from the American intervention in Vietnam (1959–1973) to the Soviet intervention in Afghanistan (1979–1985) is well known. The "unity" principle dissolved rather quickly after World War II, and the UN was less effective as an instrument of peace than the Charter originally intended, from the advent of the Truman Doctrine in 1947 to the collapse of the Soviet Union in 1991. During the Cold War, summit-level diplomacy, which began in 1955 in Geneva, was essentially bilateral (Moscow in 1972; Vladivostok in 1974; Iceland in 1986) or multilateral (Paris in 1960[2]; Camp David in 1978) with little or no reference to the United Nations. As John Stoessinger points out:

> The modern phenomenon that combines all the weaknesses of the "new diplomacy" most dramatically is the "Summit Conference." . . . The participants found themselves in the role of gladiators, with the rest of humanity as their audience. While most of the onlookers desperately hoped for peace, few were willing to tolerate the kind of compromise that attainment of real peace would have required. (Stoessinger 1965, 222)

Professionals in the employ of foreign ministries often disdain summit meetings because of the "dangers" they pose for the diplomatic process, for example, unprepared heads of state (Reagan at the Reykjavik summit with Gorbachev in 1986), inexperienced presidents and prime ministers (Kennedy at the Vienna summit with Khrushchev in 1961), and the exclusion of the professionals at key points in the summit (Nixon and Brezhnev at the Moscow summit in 1972). Before he became US Secretary of State, Dean Rusk expressed concerns about other serious obstacles: no guarantee of results when the stakes are high and a simplistic view that understanding each other's positions is a sure guarantee of progress and accommodation. In a 1960 *Foreign Affairs* article, Rusk wrote:

> Picture two men sitting down together to talk about matters affecting the very survival of the systems they represent, each in a position to unleash unbelievable destructive power. . . . Is it wise to gamble so heavily? Are not these two men who should be kept apart until others have found a sure meeting ground of accommodation between them? (Beschloss 1991, 77)

In fact, Rusk's fears were realized during the Vienna summit of 1961, where Khrushchev bullied and attempted to intimidate a young and inexperienced president who had recently suffered a major foreign policy disaster at the Bay of Pigs. Kennedy's efforts to "sit down with him (Khrushchev) and let him see who he's dealing with (Kennedy)" proved to be a failure (Beschloss 1991, 77), and the Vienna summit is generally considered one of the major factors leading up to the Cuban Missile Crisis of 1962.

Even when the leaders are more secure, leader-to-leader negotiations, especially when the professionals are excluded, can create problems and achieve few worthwhile results. Thus, Henry Kissinger complained about the 1972 summit in Moscow between Nixon and Brezhnev by noting, "Neither of the leaders having achieved high office through their mastery of detail, the only agreement they could reach . . . (in face to face encounters) was on the untrustworthiness and inadequacies of their bureaucracies . . . in practice . . . the discussions between Nixon and the Soviet leaders lacked a central theme" (Kissinger 1979, 1208–1210). It was when the professionals were allowed to do their jobs, Kissinger maintained, that real progress and tangible results occurred.

Multilateral diplomacy in the form of "summit meetings" between and among heads of state is still employed although on a more infrequent basis than during the Cold War. Today, critics charge that summits have become "photo ops" for heads of state, meetings of friendly states rather than the meetings of adversaries which took place until the demise of the Soviet Union. Although UN-sponsored conferences have occurred frequently in the post–Cold War era, the entire concept of multilateral diplomacy and multilateral action, with or without the involvement of the UN, is increasingly under attack, as evidenced by the essentially unilateral intervention by the United States in Iraq in 2003.[3] Consider the following:

First, the Cold War has ended, thus creating fewer power centers in the world. In other words, since the end of the bilateral balance of power system between the United States and the USSR and especially after 9/11, a shift has occurred away from multilateral diplomacy and actions to a new doctrine of preemption and to unilateral actions, espoused by the United States. In this chapter, Shelton L. Williams, in "Citizen Diplomacy," notes that "unless the Bush administration does a radical about-face on its approach to multilateral arms control," the prospects for a successful 2005 multinational review of the Nuclear Non-Proliferation Treaty (NPT) are "unlikely." Williams also notes that the United States now believes that its previous positions on international arms control agreements do not reflect the "strategic realities in the era of a War on Terrorism."[4]

Second, many people around the world and diplomats, such as Rienk Terpstra (later in this chapter), however, continue to argue that many current global problems from the environment to Iraq do require multilateral action and the involvement of the UN. Although it is understood that the United States is the only remaining superpower (and given the lessons of postwar reconstruction in Iraq), it must continue to rely on international and regional organizations, such as the UN and NATO, when military force is applied to a conflict situation.[5]

Third, smaller countries continue to recognize that their influence is greater only when it is combined with that of other member states of the UN. Terpstra suggests that "except for the Security Council, the one-state, one-vote principle of the UN ... gives the majority of otherwise economically or politically inconsequential member states a significant voice that is substantially greater than their individual voices outside the organization."[6]

Fourth, even with all of their limitations, as Kofi Annan suggests "[UN-sponsored] conferences provide Governments and civil society with an opportunity to rethink development policies and development cooperation" (Annan 1997, v), particularly as those policies relate to new definitions of human security.

Finally, as Jacques Fomerand writes in this chapter, "Like the General Assembly, which can make only recommendations, UN global conferences are not instruments of authoritative decisionmaking. At best, they are incubators of ideas and approximate a global version of the general will of the international community." According to Fomerand, the action plans, which are offered at the conclusion of these conferences, have no "coercive value" because this is not their "business." Nevertheless, Fomerand reminds us that the 2002 Monterrey Conference (like other UN-sponsored summits) was "a consensus less about substance than about a process on general policy principles [and] the follow-up ... calls for the involvement of a whole range of actors extending beyond states."

Since 1947, the United Nations has held numerous special sessions on issues ranging from Palestine to economic development. The UN has also sponsored many world conferences, especially since 1990, sometimes referred to as summits, on a wide variety of issues, including the most recent Monterrey Conference on Financing for Development.[7] As James Rosenau notes, the UN can be "an agent of change" in many nonpolitical and military areas (Rosenau 1992). As a change agent, UN summit diplomacy can have a positive impact in the global arena because these "summits" focus the world's attention on the quality of people's lives throughout the world.

In his essay, "North-South Issues at the 2002 Monterrey Conference," Jacques Fomerand observes,

Global conferences are a long-standing characteristic of multilateral diplomacy, the origins of which may be traced back to the economic conferences organized in the early 1930s by the League of Nations. From its inception, the United Nations further broadened this practice, culminating in a series of major conferences taking place in the 1990s on a variety of development issues, including gender, population, the environment, social development, human settlements, natural disaster prevention, and human rights.

In fact, UN conferences serve a variety of purposes, including knowledge sharing, monitoring, early warning, and agenda building. The use of "summit"-level diplomacy sponsored by the UN has, therefore, achieved several goals: It focuses the world's attention on issues of controversy, such as the need to protect human rights; it brings the moral force of the UN to bear on societal abusers, for example, of human rights and the environment[8]; it opens a dialogue of governments with representatives of "civil society"; and it reinforces the activities of NGOs that derive their moral authority from the actions of the UN.[9]

In evaluating the role of the UN in multilateral summits or conferences, Secretary-General Kofi Annan has stated that the organization has played the "harmonizing role envisaged in its founding Charter, [serving] as an indispensable forum where diverse points of view were aired, where proposals were debated and where, most importantly, political consensus was achieved. As a result, the international community—Governments, nongovernmental organizations, representatives of civil society—has been able to set a new course for a new era in global affairs" (Annan 1997, v). There are several other factors in traditional summit diplomacy, which should be noted because they are relevant today to modern UN diplomacy on global issues. Keith Eubank suggests in his analysis of summit conferences from 1916 to 1960 that "theoretically the process of negotiating at the summit ought to be quiet, cut off from the world without diverting influences," but he concludes, "This has never occurred in the history of summit conferences" (Eubank 1966, 199). Although the media's attention can be useful in publicizing global problems, the "CNN effect" can also produce posturing, pandering, and ultimately flawed agreements. In addition, as Rienk Terpstra notes, "Teleconferencing, Internet, and news broadcast 24/7 have also given the public instant access to political decisionmaking and the unprecedented means to pressure national policymakers, foreign offices, and related institutions as well as regional and international organizations." Short of a retreat to a monastery, however, media and public attention have become a permanent fixture of summit diplomacy.

In his essay in this chapter, Shelton Williams explicitly acknowledges the hegemonic influence of the United States in multilateral diplomacy and conferences. In fact, Williams is pessimistic about the future of arms control agreements because of US objections and opposition. Unlike the Clinton administration, the Bush administration, Williams maintains, has no commitment to multilateral institutions, organizations, and agreements. He believes that the "2004 US presidential election may itself in part be a referendum" on the administration's lack of "support for and commitment to multilateralism."

There is another significant factor, which must be addressed when one evaluates the various uses and the value of diplomacy, including diplomacy conducted under UN auspices. Jessica Mathews concludes that national governments "are not simply losing autonomy in a globalizing economy. They are sharing powers—including political, social, and security roles at the *core of sovereignty* [italics added]—with businesses, with international organizations, and with a multitude of citizens groups, known as non-governmental organizations (NGOs)" (Mathews 1997, 50). Her general view is that most conflicts these days are "intrastate" in nature because security threats between states have decreased since the end of the Cold War. In her judgment, the issue of "human security" has become so significant a factor in global politics that it rivals (and in some cases displaces) the older preoccupation with national security. Many believe that human security issues may be what are behind much of the support which terrorists receive from passive populations and may be the recruiter for active participants, such as suicide bombers.

One of the basic reasons for the decline of the nation-state as the principal actor in the international arena has been the increasingly activist role played by thousands of NGOs worldwide. There are some, for example, in Amnesty International who even claim that the organization is "the arm of the U.N. for human rights" (Mathews 1997, 53). Clearly, NGOs have influenced national governments, and they do play a very serious and important role in the UN system. It is the focus on human rights by NGOs which has led the UN Security Council to broaden the definition of "international peace and security" to include what traditionally would be defined as intrastate conflict outside the purview of the Charter.[10]

Finally, George Kennan addressed the fundamental issues of UN-sponsored diplomacy fifty years ago. He noted that the "concept of nationality and national sovereignty" had been elevated by the UN to "an absolute value it did not have before." He criticized the "one government, one vote" principle as a "glorification" of national sovereignty by making it the "exclusive form of participation in international life." (Kennan 1951, 95–96) The UN has always operated on a contradictory basis. It reasserts national sovereignty through its voting practices in the General Assembly while it recognizes, evaluates, and offers solutions to problems caused by nationalism or reinforced by state sovereignty. This contradiction has never been adequately resolved. But as Rienk Terpstra suggests, "The importance of the UN to small countries goes beyond the abstract issues of sovereignty. The United Nations is a practical solution to the political, financial, and/or human resources that are required in order to participate effectively in the international arena."

What ultimately needs to be done is for the UN to help inspire the creation of a true coalition of the willing, of citizens, individually or as members of groups (NGOs), to act as Hedley Bull suggests, as "local agents of the common good" (Bull 1991). Perhaps, the real alternative, then, to Kenneth Waltz's anarchic structure of world politics is to foster what Ken Booth calls a global "community of communities." However indirectly, the UN can assist in the process of global community building through its diplomatic sponsorship, even when these meetings involve "citizen-diplomats" as major players.

Robert Kagan maintains that the "United States must sometimes play by the rules of a Hobbesian world. . . . It must refuse to abide by certain international conventions that may constrain its ability to fight effectively. . . . It must live by a double standard. And it must sometimes act unilaterally, not out of a passion for unilateralism but . . . because the United States has no choice *but* to act unilaterally" (Kagan 2002, 1). The record on unilateral American action, however, is decidedly mixed. The United States has won a war, but it has alienated its allies, it has diminished the effectiveness of post–World War II institutions it was instrumental in creating, and it has not won the peace. Multilateral diplomacy and UN diplomacy are not perfect, but they can bring together nation-states, NGOs, members of civil society, and other nonstate actors in effective alliances to confront and perhaps to resolve vexing global issues, which continue to make this world a difficult and dangerous place for all of its inhabitants.

Notes

1. World War I obviously did not signal the end to bilateral diplomacy, but it did usher in a new era based on the creation of more nation-states, the beginning of the end of Eurocentric global politics, the increasing use of multilateral diplomacy through international organizations, and the frequent reliance on summit-level conferences between and among world leaders.

2. See Michael Beschloss's excellent account of the failed 1960 Paris Summit in *May-Day/Eisenhower, Khrushchev and the U-2 Affair* (New York: Harper & Row, 1986).

3. In fact, summit diplomacy at the UN rarely occurs involving heads of state. It is more appropriate to evaluate the UN in this regard when the organization, through special conferences or summits, becomes a diplomatic forum for a discus-

sion and possible resolution of a major global problem. The issue today, however, is not UN-sponsored conferences; it is whether or not multilateral diplomacy at any level, as opposed to unilateral action, still has any relevance.

4. The NPT was negotiated at the UN in 1968 and went into effect in 1970 for a twenty-five-year period, thus requiring the convening of a review and extension conference at the United Nations in 1995.

5. As Immanuel Wallerstein has warned, "Today, the United States is a superpower that lacks true power, a world leader that nobody follows and few respect, and a nation drifting dangerously amidst a global chaos it cannot control" (Wallerstein 2002, 63).

6. Margaret Doxey notes, for example, in "Constructive Internationalism: A Continuing Theme in Canadian Foreign Policy" (1989), that only through "coalitions" can nations such as Canada "exercise an influence on (global) policy-making." This was a paper presented at the International Studies Association convention in London.

7. From 1990 to 2003, the UN has sponsored major conferences dealing with the issues of human security, from the World Summit on Children in 1990 to the International Conference on Finance for Development in 2003. The number of conferences has increased because it is clear that many problems are so universal that the older forms of diplomacy are inadequate and often inappropriate, especially in implementing proposed solutions.

8. Fomerand has noted that the "outcome" of these conferences "can lead to the creation of new sources on international law." He has cited Conventions on Discrimination Against Women (1975) and the Climate Change and Desertification and the Biodiversity Treaty (1992) as examples.

9. Michael Posner noted in "Rally Round Human Rights," *Foreign Policy* (Winter 1994–1995), "Human Rights advocates, such as Amnesty International and hundreds of national rights advocacy groups around the world, rely on international human rights standards that set minimum requirements for governments."

10. The decision by one hundred governments to ban landmines in September 1997, over the objections of the United States and without the participation of Russia and China, is ample evidence of how important NGOs can be on major global issues. It is the first time in seventy years that an active weapons system has been banned. Many observers credit NGOs, including Human Rights Watch, the Vietnam Veterans of America, Handicap International of France, and the Landmines Advisory Group of England, with the successful conclusion of the treaty negotiated in Oslo. The 1997 Nobel Peace Prize was awarded to Jody Williams and to the International Campaign to Ban Landmines (ICBL), the umbrella NGO responsible for coordinating the global antilandmines effort. The late Diana, Princess of Wales, also contributed to the antilandmines effort in 1997 in well-publicized trips to Bosnia and Angola.

References

Annan, Kofi. (1997) "Preface," *UN Briefing Papers/The World Conferences* (New York: United Nations Department of Public Information).

Bull, Hedley. (1991) Bull is quoted by Ken Booth in "Security in Anarchy: Utopian Realism in Theory and Practice," in *International Affairs*, Vol. 67, No. 3, July, p. 539.

Eubank, Keith. (1966) *The Summit Conferences/1919–1960* (Norman: University of Oklahoma Press).

Grotius, Hugo. (1925) *The Law of War and Peace* (1625), translated by Francis W. Kelsey, Vol. 2 of *The Classics of International Law*, edited by James Brown Scott (Oxford: Clarendon Press).

Kagan, Robert. (2002) "Power and Weakness," *Policy Review*, June-July, pp. 1–23. [www.ceip.org/files/Publications/2002-06-02-Policy]

Kennan, George F. (1951) *American Diplomacy, 1900–1950* (Chicago: University of Chicago Press).

Kennedy, John F. (1991) Kennedy's remark to Kenneth O'Donnell, an aide, is quoted by Michael Beschloss, *The Crisis Years* (New York: HarperCollins), 77.

Kissinger, Henry. (1979) *White House Years* (Boston: Little, Brown).

Mathews, Jessica T. (1997) "Power Shift," *Foreign Affairs*, January-February, pp. 50–66.

Morgenthau, Hans J. and Kenneth W. Thompson. (1985) *Politics Among Nations* (New York: Knopf).

Rosenau, James. (1992) *The United Nations in a Turbulent World* (Boulder: Lynne Rienner).

Rusk, Dean. (1991) Quoted by Michael Beschloss, *The Crisis Years* (New York: HarperCollins).

Stoessinger, John. (1965) *The Might of Nations* (New York: Random House).

Wallerstein, Immanuel. (2002) "The End of Pax Americana," *Foreign Policy*, July-August, pp. 60–68.

Multilateral Diplomacy: A View from the UN

Rienk W. Terpstra

Multilateral diplomacy in the early years of the twenty-first century reflects the challenges and stresses in the global political system. The profound changes in global politics with the end of the Cold War, although offering vast possibilities for more constructive international cooperation, have created disarray among the Western powers, which were only recently allies in various bilateral and multilateral organizations, forums, and anti-Soviet alliances. The war with Iraq clearly demonstrates that the United States, the only remaining superpower, now often bypasses allies and multilateral institutions, including the UN. The nation-state itself, the cornerstone of the international system, is also yielding influence and authority, increasingly to nonstate actors, such as nongovernmental organizations (NGOs), and even to terrorist organizations. These incongruities are key elements of an evolving global political system, and they are especially evident in multilateral diplomacy and its most significant institutional framework, the UN.

Since the end of the Cold War, the United Nations and its diplomats have struggled to adjust to a significant and rapid change of content and context. The breakup of the Soviet Union and Yugoslavia has swelled the

UN's membership and altered the composition of blocs and alliances. Since the early 1990s, in response to civil conflicts there has been an unprecedented increase in UN-sponsored or -sanctioned peacekeeping operations. There has also been a substantial increase in UN-sponsored megaconferences on global socioeconomic and human rights problems. The expansion of the diplomatic agenda has caused a significant increase in the number of those engaged in diplomatic activities, which today include multiple government departments and agencies, the private sector, and NGOs.

Career diplomats, therefore, now have to consider the views of military, intelligence, agriculture, and economic or cultural officials in the deliberations within their own UN missions. Teleconferencing, Internet, and news broadcast 24/7 have also given the public instant access to political decisionmaking and the unprecedented means to pressure national policymakers, foreign offices, and related institutions as well as regional and international organizations.

In response, the United Nations and multilateral diplomacy, in general, appear to be experiencing a serious identity crisis. The (perceived) lack of success of UN peace operations, the disappointing results, particularly the lack of follow-up to the UN's global conferences dealing with socioeconomic issues and human rights, the continuing financial crisis of the organization, and its most important member often ignoring it have undermined confidence both in the United Nations and in the credibility of multilateral diplomacy.

Sovereignty and Nation-States

The single most important principle in UN diplomacy is sovereignty. In theory, sovereignty is exclusively related to the nation-state and enables an independent nation-state within recognized borders to establish its own rule of law without interference from other nation-states. The concept of sovereignty has been especially important in the balance of power throughout the centuries, particularly in the survival of smaller states within the anarchic, conflict-ridden Westphalian state system. Jaap de Wilde maintains that since 1945, and even more since the end of the Cold War, many sovereign states have become more involved in international organizations (De Wilde 1996), as they voluntarily limit their autonomy by engaging in this form of cooperative behavior.

Nation-states join the United Nations because it is synonymous with their unequivocal recognition as sovereign entities within the community of nations. Johan Kaufmann, a veteran UN diplomat and leading authority on UN diplomacy, points out, however, that the United Nations also has been a vehicle for sovereign nation-states to further their national interests while providing a framework for international cooperation for peacefully settling disputes, promoting economic development, safeguarding human rights, encouraging self-determination, expanding international law, and collecting and disseminating information (Kaufmann 1980).

The UN and Small States

The importance of the UN to small countries goes beyond the abstract issues of sovereignty. The United Nations is a practical solution to the political, financial, and/or human resources that are required to participate effectively in the international arena. Developing nations also lack the resources to be represented in capitals around the world. Therefore, having a permanent mission to the UN in New York City, even if it is very small, provides them with an "affordable means of maintaining diplomatic contact with the rest of the world" (Hamilton and Langhorne 1995, 233). In addition, and perhaps more important, developing countries recognize that their numerical majority in the UN General Assembly is a source of considerable political power when they are united as a "bloc" in the United Nations. Developing nations created, for example, the Group of 77 (G-77), a loosely organized forum for political consultation among developing countries in the 1960s.

In contrast, even small industrialized countries in Western Europe have sufficient resources to sustain their participation in a wide variety of international forums. They maintain large permanent missions to the UN in order to take an active part in all of the organization's activities. But individually, they lack the political weight in the international community to make a difference on their own, and so even for these states, the United Nations is a practical solution to a lack of global political clout.

Except for the Security Council, the one-state, one-vote principle of the UN, consequently, gives the majority of otherwise economically or politically inconsequential member states a significant voice in world affairs that is substantially greater than their individual voices outside the organization. Clearly, sovereignty remains the ultimate condition for participation in the international arena on an equal basis, but once inside, sovereignty becomes a bargaining chip in intraorganizational negotiations.

The principle outcomes of conference diplomacy are resolutions and action programs, be they binding or voluntary. Member state tactics generally follow a simple line of reasoning: Proposals that enhance national interests should be supported, and those that are considered harmful should be opposed. Because of the one-state–one-vote system, a member state, by itself, is unable to adopt or defeat policy proposals; that is, it needs support from like-minded member states. Nevertheless, it is harder to get a proposal adopted in the UN than it is to defeat one.

In diplomacy, as in warfare, those on the offensive have the tactical advantage of initiative, whereas "defenders" have the benefit of having more tactical options. As Kaufmann points out, proponents can only strive for adoption, whereas opponents can choose between outright defeat and the subtle tactic of deferment (Kaufmann 1980, 143). The more member states there are, the more complex the situation often is regarding issues before the UN.

Although a member state's representatives do not act on their own, since they receive instructions from their capital, more often than not a delegation may select its own tactics in a UN debate. In essence, negotiation is the art of convincing other parties that one's own opinion is the right one and that they will be better off when they adopt it as their own. The most obvious way of doing this is through plain reasoning, or as Kaufmann puts it, "intellectual arguments" (Kaufmann 1980, 144). Representatives will simply try to explain the position of their country and its merits to their colleagues. If this approach proves to be ineffective, a delegation might use less subtle tactics, like promises of economic, financial, or political rewards. When these methods do not work either, harsher techniques—warnings and threats—are often applied. These tactics are the opposite of pledges in that they promise not a better but a worse situation for one or more parties in the negotiations. A threat, however, will have sufficient force only if the delegation making the threat performs a crucial role in the decisionmaking process. A threat becomes even more convincing when it entails financial or economic repercussions, either bilaterally or as part of a UN program. Clearly, Indonesia's withdrawing (temporarily) from the United Nations in 1965, for example, had less serious consequences for the organization than the withdrawal of the United States and the United Kingdom from UNESCO in 1984.

In an organization dealing with diverse issues such as the UN, only the most affluent countries with the widest scope of interests can afford to spend the substantial human and financial resources needed to cover every topic in depth. The result is that, apart from the most pressing issues like peace, security, and development, many delegations have come to occupy some comfortable niche areas in which they can develop their own policies together with like-minded states and can present resolutions on a regular basis that are often adopted without a vote.

The Future

The world has changed dramatically since the end of the Cold War. Although "the conventional mechanisms of diplomacy have survived" (Hamilton and Langhorne 1995, 233), new problems, such as intrastate conflicts, failed states, resurgent irredentism, terrorism, global threats to the environment, and deteriorating socioeconomic conditions, have been added to the diplomat's agenda. The real challenges of the diplomatic profession derive from the tendency to bypass and even reject multilateral institutions and organizations, the addition of new actors to the global political arena (from the often constructive role played by NGOs to the always destructive role played by terrorists), and the general scrutiny which diplomats and diplomatic transactions are subjected to by the public, mostly through the global media. But the greatest threat that the UN system faces in the coming years may be the political and economic abandonment by its most important member state, which would undermine the credibility of the system as a whole.

References

Aurisch, Klaus L. (1989) "The Art of Preparing a Multilateral Conference," *Negotiation Journal*, July, pp. 279–288.

Cox, Robert W. (1997) "An Alternative Approach to Multilateralism for the Twenty-first Century," *Global Governance*, Vol. 3, No. 1, pp. 103–116.

De Wilde, Jaap. (1996) "Europa's Nieuwe Slagvelden. Machtsstrijd over Internationale Organisaties," *Internationale Spectator*, Vol. 12, pp. 574–578.

Fomerand, Jacques. (1996) "UN Conferences: Media Events or Genuine Diplomacy?" *Global Governance*, Vol. 2, No. 3, pp. 361–375.

Hamilton, Keith and Richard Langhorne. (1995) *The Practice of Diplomacy: Its Evolution, Theory and Administration* (London: Routledge).

Jonkman, P.J.H. (1992) "Inleiding Internationaal Onderhandelen." Lecture held in the Peace Palace, The Hague, September 25.

Kaufmann, Johan. (1980) *United Nations Decision Making* (Alphen aan den Rijn: Sijthoff & Noordhoff).

_____. (1996) *Conference Diplomacy* (London: Macmillan).

Kissinger, Henry A. (1994) *Diplomacy* (New York: Touchstone).

Kok, A. (1990) *Internationaal Onderhandelen: Problemen bij Internationaal Zakendoen*. (Deventer, The Netherlands: Kluwer Bedrijpswetenschappen).

Mastenbroek, Willem. (1990) "The Development of Negotiating Skills," *International Negotiations: Analysis, Approaches, Issues*, Edited by V. A. Kremenyuk (San Francisco: Jossey-Bass).

Mingst, Karen A. and Craig P. Warkentin. (1996) "What Difference Does Culture Make in Multilateral Negotiations?" *Global Governance*, Vol. 2, No. 2, pp. 169–188.

Ministry of Foreign Affairs. (1995) *The Foreign Policy of the Netherlands: A Review* (The Hague: Ministry of Foreign Affairs).

Parsons, Anthony. (1995) *From Cold War to Hot Peace: UN Interventions 1947–1994* (London: Penguin).

CITIZEN DIPLOMACY

Shelton L. Williams

In the original edition of this book my task was to reflect on multilateral diplomacy in arms control by recounting my experiences as a US delegate to the 1995 Nuclear Non-Proliferation Treaty (NPT) Review and Extension Conference. I limited my comments in that volume to the issues and events surrounding that particular conference. That is impossible to do on this occasion, for not only did I go on to work on another major arms control effort, the Comprehensive Test Ban Treaty (CTBT), after the NPT Conference, but in 2003 the NPT, the CTBT, and even multilateralism itself have been under siege in recent years. I regret to say that the US government for which I worked in the 1990s is at least in part (and in large part, I must say) responsible for the precarious state these core treaties are in today. Nevertheless, the assault on arms control and multilateralism transcends these treaties, so I must perforce broaden my comments to deal with other critical issues.

Again, I shall begin by recounting my personal experience as an arms controller. Upon the conclusion of the NPT Review Conference in May 1995, I received my second posting as a William C. Foster Visiting Fellow to return to Washington, D.C., to become the "special advisor" to the deputy director of the Arms Control and Disarmament Agency. The euphoria of the NPT indefinite extension was still high when the interagency process rendered a decision in July 1995 to decline a NAM-demand at the Conference on Disarmament (CD) in Geneva to create an ad hoc committee on the issue of nuclear disarmament. I have no idea at what level the decision was made, but I do know that there was a consensus among the agencies that such a committee was not the correct next step in the disarmament process. "More practical" step-by-step measures were preferred, and pursuing the cut-off of the production of fissile materials was the emphasis the United States favored. I differed with my boss, with my agency, and with my government on this decision. I did not anticipate that an ad hoc committee in Geneva would result in a nuclear disarmament treaty or even that such a committee could quickly establish an agenda, but I believed that the states who had opposed, or who had reluctantly endorsed, NPT extension and who were visibly bitter at the outcome of the NPT Extension Conference would react harshly to a decision not to establish a nuclear disarmament committee that they saw as part of the nuclear weapons states' (NWSs)–NPT Article VI obligation to "negotiate in good faith the conclusion of the arms race."

The United States and Nuclear Disarmament

The United States has continued to remain opposed to the establishment of the nuclear disarmament ad hoc committee since 1995. At the CD in Geneva for seven years the atmosphere has been tense, the process has been sluggish, and a "New Agenda Coalition" (Egypt, Ireland, New Zealand, South Africa, Sweden, and Brazil) has arisen to demand that the United States and other NWSs create an ad hoc committee on nuclear disarmament to fulfill in part their Article VI commitments. The United States has rejected this proposal and has remained firm in its assertion that this would not be consistent with a step-by-step approach. However, at the 2000 NPT Review Conference the United States agreed, with reservations, to the "Thirteen Steps" demands of the New Agenda Coalition.[1] The 2000 NPT Review Conference ended on an upbeat note with a consensus statement by the body, but the United States objected to the passage of another "Middle East Resolution" similar to the one passed in 1995 (see above). The US assertion was that such a resolution would complicate the Middle East Peace Process, so it did not happen. The reason for this stance was obvious. In 1995, the Middle East Resolution called on all parties in the region who had not done so to sign and ratify the NPT. In 1995, those parties were Israel, the United Arab Emirates, Djibouti, and Oman. By 2000, Israel stood alone as the only party in the region not to have ratified the NPT. Thus, the US objection to "another" Middle East Resolution fuels Arab frustration at the United States' "double standard" in the Middle East. Similarly the United States rejects the Egyptian calls for legally binding security assurances[2] and the creation of an ad hoc committee on nuclear disarmament at the CD.

Middle Eastern states are not alone in making demands and in criticizing the United States, but the prominence of the Middle East in arms control heightens these differences. This is naturally true after September 11 and the Bush administration's assertions that Iraq and Iran have ignored a range of arms control agreements while developing chemical, biological, and nuclear weapons-capable programs. Of course, the Bush administration's posture regarding arms control conventions, ranging from opposition to ratification of the CTBT, unilateral abrogation of the ABM Treaty, hostility to the continuation of the Biological Weapons Convention (BWC) Ad Hoc Committee talks on a verification protocol at the CD, and deprecating statements about the arms control process by the Assistant Secretary of State for Arms Control and International Security, John Bolton[3]—all preceded 9/11. Since 9/11 the administration has also bashed the International Atomic Energy Agency (IAEA) and the UN Monitoring, Verification and Inspection Commission's (UNMOVIC) inability to find weapons of mass destruction (WMDs) in Iraq; has hinted at the development of the United States' new nuclear weapon capabilities to strike targets in "rogue states"; and has floated an offer to the Democratic People's Republic of Korea (North Korea) (DPRK) for a written guarantee not to invade or attack it (seemingly rewarding the DPRK with a negative security assurance for violating the NPT while it denies Arab NPT parties that right from Israel). The administration, however, still refers to the NPT as the "cornerstone of the nonproliferation regime"; it still calls on all parties to adhere to the NPT; and it still argues that it favors Article VI.

The administration's sole case for Article VI compliance hangs on the the Strategic Offensive Reductions Treaty (SORT) with Russia, but NGOs and nuclear nonweapons states (NNWSs) critics pointedly note that the SORT agreement violates the principles of the Thirteen Steps in a variety of ways. SORT does not require the dismantling of a single strategic delivery launcher or nuclear warhead, nor does it provide any additional verification mechanisms.[4]

The United States is not totally isolated in its nonproliferation positions, especially regarding two of the most critical challenges facing the international community, Iran and North Korea. Iran's pursuit of a nuclear program that involves uranium enrichment and its resistance heretofore to submission to the 1997 additional protocol for enhanced IAEA safeguards (for challenge and/or surprise inspections) have been worrisome to the European Union, Japan, and even to the NAM as well.

For its part, Iran declares its nuclear program to be "peaceful, transparent, and independent" (The title of a speech to a NPT PrepCom by Vice President Reza Aghazadeh, May 6, 2003). Russia has contended that its nuclear sales to Iran are within the spirit and letter of the NPT, but the IAEA's discoveries of enriched uranium and other disturbing revelations make the case for Iran's need to sign the additional protocol all the more pressing. On September 12, 2003, the IAEA board of governors gave Iran until October 31, 2003, to agree to sign the additional protocol. Iran's ambiguous statement on October 21, 2003, that it would indeed sign the protocol may end the crisis, but at the writing of this piece, it is simply too soon to tell. However, if the Iranian crisis is resolved, at first blush it seems likely to be the result of European diplomacy rather than the harsh and confrontational US diplomacy. Initial reports indicate that the EU succeeded in gaining Iranian cooperation by offering balanced incentives of trade deals and technical assistance along with disincentives of possible sanctions and Iranian diplomatic isolation. What, if any, coordination occurred between the United States and the EU is unknown at this time, but if the deal sticks, it will be a great success for the nonproliferation regime.

North Korea

The situation with North Korea is clearly the most serious proliferation threat the international community has faced since the Iraqi program of the late 1980s and early 1990s. The DPRK's attempted withdrawal from the NPT in 1993, of course, led to the 1994 Framework Agreement that many Bush officials criticized when they were out of power.[5] The Framework Agreement froze the North Korean plutonium production program in Yongbyon in exchange for immediate energy supplies and a commitment by the Korean Peninsula Energy Development Organization (KEDO) to build two light water reactors under IAEA safeguards. After President Bush's "Axis of Evil" speech in January 2002, North Korea evidentially decided to engage in nuclear brinksmanship with the United States to secure a "nonaggression pact" in exchange for a renewed commitment not to develop nuclear weapons. In a series of revelations, innuendos, pronouncements, and eventually negotiations, North Korea withdrew from the NPT on April 10, 2003; admitted to and then bragged about having a nuclear weapons program; demanded face-to-face talks with the United States; agreed to hold talks with Japan, China, Russia, South Korea, and the United States; refused to continue the talks with Japan on the grounds of "renewed Japanese militarism"; and rejected, and then tentatively agreed to review, a US offer of a written security assurance. Where this zigzag affair will end is unclear, but if the DPRK accepts the US offer of security assurances and follows through with the verifiable dismantling of its plutonium and its nascent uranium enrichment programs, historians will analyze whether the Bush administration could have gotten the deal earlier and whether it could have been attained at all without China's involvement and threatened sanctions.

The 2005 NPT Review Conference

The outcome of these events will form the backdrop for the final PrepCom for the 2005 NPT Review Conference and the conference itself. By 2005, these issues and the discovery or nondiscovery of WMDs in Iraq will no doubt color the outcome of the conference. Indeed the 2004 US presidential election may itself in part be a referendum on the administration's support of and commitment to multilateralism. Unless the Bush administration does a radical about-face on its approach to multilateral arms control, the prospects for a smooth conference, much less a consensus statement, seem unlikely at this writing. Why this is true can be seen in how the administration has dealt with the CTBT.

A comprehensive test ban has been a symbol for decades of the NWSs' commitment to Article VI. The Clinton administration pledged to complete a CTBT prior to entering the 1995 NPT Review Conference, and although the CD could not reach consensus and report out a treaty, the UN General Assembly did so on September 10, 1996. Although the United States has seen no need to test a nuclear device since 1992, the elaboration of a binding treaty was a major factor in demonstrating that the NWSs are living up to their end of the NPT bargain. The Clinton administration's August 1995 decision to agree to a "zero yield" test was a breakthrough in the forty-year quest for a test ban, and it delivered on a major NPT promise to the other parties to the treaty. Although the Clinton position gained some criticisms from NNWSs and NGOs for allowing possible loopholes in the treaty, for the most part only conservative elements of the US political culture have found the treaty objectionable.

Even though the organization implementing the CTBT (the CTBTO) and the rules governing the "trigger mechanisms" for on-site inspections were largely US creations; even though the entry into force of the treaty would depend on the adherence of 44 particular states, some of whom were unlikely to do so; and even though the US Congress generously funded the "Stockpile Stewardship Program" that will allow the United States nonexplosive testing, evaluation, and maintenance of the existing nuclear arsenal and supercomputer simulation and warhead remanufacturing (and, according to some, even the development of new weapons), the US Congress ultimately rejected the CTBT in October 1999. Critics have argued that the Clinton administration failed to secure consent to ratification of the CTBT by not properly consulting Congress and by not negotiating adequate inspections provisions. Whether or not the Clinton administration consulted with Republican congressional leaders frequently enough or at the highest levels may be open to question, but as a Foster Fellow I participated in at least one such briefing and handled several congressional inquiries. It was clear even in the summer of 1996 that the treaty was in for rough sledding.

The Republicans Take Control

Perhaps the domestic political fallout of the Republican take-over of the Congress in 1994 and Clinton's personal difficulties undermined any chance that the Senate would consent to ratify the CTBT between 1997 and 1999. Nevertheless, in the presidential campaign of 2000 and after taking office, Bush and his administration have chosen not simply to accept the Senate's decision and move on. They have pressed for shortening the readiness posture of the Nevada Test Site in the event that testing might resume, have stopped funding the CTBTO preparations for on-site inspections, and have initiated new research on new and modified types of nuclear weapons that could require explosive proof-testing. Although it has not withdrawn its signature from the CTBT, it has, as recently as September 2003, boycotted the Third Conference on Facilitating the Entry into Force of the Comprehensive Nuclear-Test-Ban Treaty, held in Vienna. Little does it matter that an expert nonpartisan panel from the National Academy of Sciences examined the treaty and found it enforceable, verifiable, and compatible with US national interests to impede the proliferation of nuclear weapons (July 2001).[6] The Bush administration has nevertheless castigated the CTBT as inconsistent with US national interests and has positioned the United States as a critic of one of the most crucial multilateral treaties in the history of arms control.

In addition to the administration's assault on the CTBT, it has also taken positions at the CD demonstrating that US arms control interests and arguments will be pursued vigorously, but seemingly, only those multilateral treaties serving narrow US interests will be honored by the United States itself. The ABM Treaty and the CTBT, so very important to so many states, can be shunted aside while the parts of the NPT that matter most, compliance by NNWSs, will be the focus of US diplomacy. Criticisms that the SORT agreement does not comply with the Thirteen Steps or that the CTBT is an important part of NWSs' Article VI commitments are brushed aside as "old thinking" by US diplomats at the CD or at the NPT PrepComs. The administration argues that these stances reflect the strategic realties in the era of a war on terrorism, but the long-term structural value of a world free of nuclear weapons proliferation threats remains compelling.

It is not "old thinking" to say that the NPT is part and parcel of a "regime" of agreements, actors, and principles that have evolved over thirty years. The "logic" of proliferation still exists. This is obvious in the India-Pakistan standoff. India acquires nuclear weapons and cites China's possession of them as its excuse. Consequently Pakistan acquires them. Israel's possession spurs Iraq and Iran. North Korea? Japan? Others? The chain of proliferation could regenerate if there are other proliferators and would no doubt engender even more withdrawals from the NPT. The United States has always taken the lead on advancing the NPT, but our success at the 1995 NPT Review Conference consisted mostly in being able to convince states that a multilateral treaty with universal adherence could best provide them the security they need to forego nuclear weapons. This proposition will be a tougher sale in 2005 if the Middle East peace process has not generated more security in the region and Israel maintains its nuclear arsenal, if India and Pakistan still believe that nuclear weapons protect them, and if Iran or North Korea has withdrawn from the treaty. In my opinion, it will also be a tougher sale if the United States continues to assert that the NPT is the cornerstone of nonproliferation but that the only binding parts of the treaty are the limitation and constraint of others' programs while not accepting any constraints on itself or its allies.

Notes

1. The conference agrees on the following practical steps for the systematic and progressive efforts to implement Article VI of the Treaty on the Non-Proliferation of Nuclear Weapons and paragraphs 3 and 4(c) of the 1995 Decision on "Principles and Objectives for Nuclear Non-Proliferation and Disarmament":

1. The importance and urgency of signatures and ratifications, without delay and without conditions and in accordance with constitutional processes, to achieve the early entry into force of the Comprehensive Nuclear-Test-Ban Treaty.

2. A moratorium on nuclear-weapon-test explosions or any other nuclear explosions pending entry into force of that Treaty.

3. The necessity of negotiations in the Conference on Disarmament on a non-discriminatory, multilateral and internationally and effectively verifiable treaty banning the production of fissile material for nuclear weapons or other nuclear explosive devices in accordance with the statement of the

Special Coordinator in 1995 and the mandate contained therein, taking into consideration both nuclear disarmament and nuclear non-proliferation objectives. The Conference on Disarmament is urged to agree on a program of work, which includes the immediate commencement of negotiations on such a treaty with a view to their conclusion within five years.

4. The necessity of establishing in the Conference on Disarmament an appropriate subsidiary body with a mandate to deal with nuclear disarmament. The Conference on Disarmament is urged to agree on a program of work, which includes the immediate establishment of such a body.

5. The principle of irreversibility to apply to nuclear disarmament, nuclear and other related arms control and reduction measures.

6. An unequivocal undertaking by the nuclear weapon States to accomplish the total elimination of their nuclear arsenals leading to nuclear disarmament to which all States parties are committed under Article VI.

7. The early entry into force and full implementation of START II and the conclusion of START III as soon as possible while preserving and strengthening the ABM Treaty as a cornerstone of strategic stability and as a basis for further reductions of strategic offensive weapons, in accordance with its provisions.

8. The completion and implementation of the Trilateral Initiative between the United States of America, the Russian Federation and the International Atomic Energy Agency.

9. Steps by all the nuclear-weapon States leading to nuclear disarmament in a way that promotes international stability, and based on the principle of undiminished security for all:
   · Further efforts by the nuclear-weapon States to reduce their nuclear arsenals unilaterally
   · Increased transparency by the nuclear-weapon States with regard to the nuclear weapons capabilities and the implementation of agreements pursuant to Article VI and as a voluntary confidence-building measure to support further progress on nuclear disarmament.
   · The further reduction of non-strategic nuclear weapons, based on unilateral initiatives and as an integral part of the nuclear arms reduction and disarmament process
   · Concrete agreed measures to further reduce the operational status of nuclear weapons systems
   · A diminishing role for nuclear weapons in security policies to minimize the risk that these weapons ever be used and to facilitate the process of their total elimination
   · The engagement as soon as appropriate of all the nuclear-weapon States in the process leading to the total elimination of their nuclear weapons

10. Arrangements by all nuclear-weapon States to place, as soon as practicable, fissile material designated by each of them as no longer required for

military purposes under IAEA or other relevant international verification and arrangements for the disposition of such material for peaceful purposes, to ensure that such material remains permanently outside of military programs.

11. Reaffirmation that the ultimate objective of the efforts of States in the disarmament process is general and complete disarmament under effective international control.

12. Regular reports, within the framework of the NPT strengthened review process, by all States parties on the implementation of Article VI and paragraph 4(c) of the 1995 Decision on "Principles and Objectives for Nuclear Non-Proliferation and Disarmament," and recalling the Advisory Opinion of the International Court of Justice of 8 July 1996.

13. The further development of the verification capabilities that will be required to provide assurance of compliance with nuclear disarmament agreements for the achievement and maintenance of a nuclear-weapon-free world.

2. This has long been an Egyptian goal, but see in particular the statements that Nabil el Araby made in Security Council Resolution 984 in 1995 and that various Egyptian statesmen have made at the 2000 NPT Review Conference and the CD since.

3. Source: *Interview – Under Secretary John Bolton on US Arms Control Policy,* Washington File, August 14. Could you explain and elaborate a little more on a recent statement you made—"From little acorns, bad treaties may grow"? MR. BOLTON: . . . And I said to the U.N. press corps, you of all people ought to know how it works here, where you start off with half of a sentence in a preambular paragraph in an obscure resolution in an obscure conference on an obscure subject, and over time the half of a sentence becomes an operative paragraph in another resolution, then it becomes the subject of a General Assembly resolution, then it becomes the subject of communiqués, then it becomes the subject of a major international conference, and then it becomes the subject of a treaty document, which, it turns out, we find is unacceptable and we have to reject it. And people say, "But everybody else accepts this treaty. For 10 years this has been going on and you never expressed objection to it." And that's what I meant by "bad treaties from little acorns grow." So my idea is to deal with the acorn at the beginning, and to make sure that people understand what our substantive position is.

4. *Disarmament Diplomacy,* Issue No. 71, June-July 2003. NPT Report: "Rogues and Rhetoric: The 2003 NPT PrepCom Slides Backwards," by Rebecca Johnson: Though acknowledging that the Strategic Offensive Reductions Treaty (SORT, or more simply the Moscow Treaty) was a positive step in defining a new US-Russian relationship, the New Agenda questioned the measure's contribution to disarmament, noting that it ignores non-operational warheads, requires the destruction of no warheads or delivery systems, and contains no verification provisions. Referring to the 13 Steps, Caughley called for the application of the principles of

irreversibility (step 5), increased transparency (step 9), and verification (steps 10 and 13) to be applied to all agreements, including the Moscow Treaty. Warning that "reductions in the numbers of deployed strategic nuclear warheads are not a substitute for irreversible cuts in, and the total elimination of, nuclear weapons", the New Agenda in its opening statement called on the US and Russia to make the Moscow treaty "an irreversible and verifiable instrument on nuclear disarmament".

5. *Disarmament Diplomacy*, Issue No. 41, June 1999.

6. *Disarmament Diplomacy*, Issue No. 46, May 2000.

North-South Issues at the 2002 Monterrey Conference on Finance for Development: *Plus ça change . . . ?*[1]

Jacques Fomerand

Introduction

On April 22, 2002, the Secretary-General addressed the Economic and Social Council as it met with the Bretton Woods institutions in New York City. Commenting on the International Conference on Finance for Development (FfD), which had just wound up its work a month earlier in Monterrey, Mexico, Kofi Annan described the event as a real "achievement" which had instilled "new and timely life to the noble quest for international cooperation for development."[2] His words were echoed by the Deputy Managing Director of the IMF. He, too, welcomed "the sense of solidarity with which the international community had worked together to take decisive actions to maintain financial stability to strengthen the recovery under way" and concluded that the "agenda ahead . . . was rich, challenging and encouraging."[3] The Deputy Managing Director of the World Bank also concurred, stating that he was "impressed" by the degree of consensus and convergence that had emerged in Monterrey.[4]

There were words of caution, however. Referring to the "Monterrey Consensus", the main document outcome which had in fact been agreed on several weeks before the March 18–22, 2002, conference, the Secretary-General went on to state that "Monterrey was not an end in itself." The challenge now was to maintain the political momentum and positive spirit that had led to the Monterrey Consensus and to translate it into real and meaningful implementation.[5] The president of ECOSOC made a similar observation, stressing that the Monterrey Conference had been "an important first step" and a "massive effort was now required to mobilize more and better cooperation for development and to build an international economic system that was more conducive to the development of the poor."[6]

Outside the felted walls of United Nations meeting rooms, the tone of the debate was more contrasted. Whereas the International Chamber of Commerce and other business groups expressed their satisfaction with the outcome of the conference,[7] many NGOs viewed it as yet another manifestation of a collusion between governments and multilateral financial and trade organizations. A group of European NGOs blasted the Monterrey Consensus for being "void of any concrete commitment for raising the finances needed to meet the Millennium Development Goals by 2015" and for failing "to address the structural problems that prevent the realization of a sustainable, gender-sensitive and equitable globalization."[8] The World Council of Churches condemned the Monterrey Consensus as an uncritical neoliberal model which "holds out no real hope for eliminating or even reducing poverty, but rather continues to exacerbate it."[9] Women's groups protested that the Monterrey Consensus was not "their" consensus and that "the UN [was] eaten for breakfast by the Bretton Woods Institutions [and] the lethal mix of free market nostrums, free trade propaganda, 'structural adjustment' and privatization they dispense."[10]

Contrasted opinions do indeed abound about the Monterrey Consensus, which revolve around one basic question: Did the Monterrey Consensus legitimize the agendas of the Group of 7, the WTO, and the Bretton Woods institutions (BWIs), together with an unmanaged opening of markets and the unregulated role of the private sector in development? Or did it foreshadow a new dawn of development efforts based on greater corporate accountability, the democratization of the international financial institutions (IFIs), and firmer political commitments in support of development? The purpose of this paper is to provide some tentative answers to these questions. As shall be argued, the picture emerging from Monterrey has more gray tones than is usually acknowledged, a state of affairs which warrants neither unbridled enthusiasm nor existential despair but rather a cautious and guarded prognosis.

Monterrey in the Cycle of UN Global Conferences

Global conferences are a long-standing characteristic of multilateral diplomacy, the origins of which may be traced back to the economic conferences organized in the early 1930s by the League of Nations. From its inception, the United Nations further broadened this practice, which culminated in a series of major conferences taking place in the 1990s on a variety of development issues ranging from gender, population, the environment, and social development to human settlements, natural disaster prevention, and human rights. Each of these gatherings follows a now well-established ritual beginning with the establishment of a preparatory body by the General Assembly which hammers out a draft document for consideration by the conference, a procession of high-level government dignitaries making high-flown statements, side events including "interactive dialogues" among "stakeholders," parallel "forums" that most frequently bring together vocal nongovernmental organizations, and the issuance of an Action Plan and/or a Programme of Action laboriously finalized in committee rooms.[11]

The Monterrey Conference roughly followed the same pattern. On December 22, 1999, the General Assembly decided to convene a "high-level intergovernmental event of political decision makers" on financing for development, and it set up a preparatory committee opened to all states to carry out the substantive preparations for the "event." The mandate of the committee was broad and far-reaching as its purpose was to address national, international, and systemic issues relative to financing for development in a holistic manner in the context of globalization and interdependence and to identify means for ensuring the availability of sufficient financial resources to reach the major goals set by United Nations global conferences and summits in the 1990s, in particular, poverty eradication.[12] The preparatory committee labored through four sessions, focusing its agenda on six major interrelated themes: mobilizing domestic financial resources, foreign direct investment and other private flows, international trade as an engine for development, increasing international technical and financial cooperation for development, external debt, and enhancing the coherence and consistency of the international monetary, financial, and trading systems. On February 15, the committee completed its work with the formal adoption of a draft text to be submitted for adoption by the conference.

Over fifty heads of state or government and more than two hundred ministers, senior officials of the UN, and other multilateral organizations converged on Monterrey on March 18, 2002. Fifty-five side events took place during the conference, including twelve roundtables involving eight hundred participants. Independent forums were organized by civil society, parliamentarians, and local authorities. The pageantry came to an end with the formal adoption on March 22 of the Monterrey Consensus, the lean and relatively short document that had been adopted a month earlier by the preparatory committee in New York City.[13]

Like past UN global conferences, Monterrey drew the familiar cast of heads of state and foreign ministers. More unusual was the fact that it brought together a large array of players hitherto estranged from UN processes. Highly unusual in meetings generally overshadowed by foreign affairs officials was the brisk participation of many ministers of finance, trade, and development cooperation. The heads of the IMF and the World Bank, flanked by their highest senior staffs, as well as governors of central banks and regional banks, were conspicuously present. The director-general of the World Trade Organization (WTO) was also actively engaged. Equally if not more visible was the presence of business organizations representing investment banks, consulting firms, leasing services, and advocacy groups promoting private-sector participation and support for the United Nations among business leaders. With the International Chamber of Commerce leading the pack, business representatives also held a one-day-long forum and participated in the roundtables organized by the Secretariat. Monterrey was the first-ever UN-sponsored conference based on the participation of not only governments and civil society but also the business community and the Bretton Woods institutions, and its preparatory process had also been marked by similar extensive informal interactions on each element of its agenda.

Drawing these new "stakeholders" into UN processes was necessary to ensure a modicum of political success at Monterrey. But this was no mean task in light of past historical experience, assumptions about who was doing what in the promotion of development, and the political divisiveness of the issues.

Virtually since their creation, all multilateral institutions comprising the UN system have been concerned with development. But the division of labor which developed and prevailed placed them on separate and diverging tracks. The focus of the UN was on development "with a human face" and more specifically on the linkages between social, economic, and environmentally sustainable development. The approach of the BWIs, GATT, and its successor organization WTO was to promote the globalization of the world economy through market-based trade and investment policies as means to achieve higher levels of welfare. Whether Monterrey bridged that long-standing ideological and programmatic gap remains to be seen. But for the first time, the United Nations was staging a major conference on questions hitherto considered the closely guarded preserve of finance ministries and the Bretton Woods institutions and the WTO. And Monterrey did treat development finance issues—to use the conference jargon—in a "holistic manner," that is to say, in their linkages with other developmental issues.

More to the point, development finance had for decades been a stumbling block in the North-South dialogue. The question had been on the agenda of the UN since the early 1950s in one form or the other. In the 1950s, the battle lines between North and South had formed around the creation of a capital development fund under the aegis of the United Nations, which developing countries deemed indispensable to sustaining their drive toward industrialization. Developed countries, led by the United States, countered and sought to placate Southern pressures through the establishment of the International Finance Corporation (IFC) and the International Development Association (IDA) as two affiliates of the World Bank where they would not be steered by "tyrannical majorities." This did not put the issue of development finance to rest. Still at the insistence of developing countries, the General Assembly in 1970 endorsed the notion that developed countries should earmark 0.7 percent of their GDP for official development assistance (ODA) purposes, a norm which received first grudging acceptance and then wider recognition, with the notable exception of the United States. Developing countries' pressures did not slacken as they sought to further legitimize their demands for ODA and private finance through the NIEO, the 1975 declaration on international economic cooperation, and the successive development decades proclaimed by the UN. With the onset of the 1980s, development finance receded as attention focused on debt and neoliberalism acquired the status of "conventional wisdom" in the following decade. But the issue of development finance continued to lurk under the surface of apparently more tranquil political waters and kept resurfacing each year in the General Assembly and UNCTAD as well as in all the global conferences organized by the United Nations throughout the 1990s.

Moving Toward Monterrey

Against such a background, the convening of a UN conference on finance for development was nothing short of a political coup. Not surprisingly, the road to Monterrey was long, rocky, and tortuous. Negotiations over the agenda of Monterrey reflected long-standing deep differences between the industrial countries and the G–77. Developed countries pressed for discussions to be limited to fulfilling the commitments made at UN conferences, whereas the G–77 was intent on broadening the agenda to include not only issues of development finance such as official development assistance but also their linkages to trade, debt, their participation in the governance of the international financial architecture, and the management of financial crises. Reaching an agreement on the scope and agenda of the conference took no less than two years from June 1997, when the General Assembly adopted an Agenda for Development and set up an open working group to formulate recommendations on the scope of an international meeting on finance for development finance until the endorsement of the group's report by the General Assembly in the fall of 1999 and the establishment of a preparatory committee.[14] All throughout this process, the projected conference was merely referred to as an "event," reflecting the hesitations of industrial countries over the wisdom and desirability of yet another UN global conclave that could provide developing countries with an opportunity to reopen a host of outstanding development issues from the perspective of finance and to legitimize their demand for international regime change.

These widely contrasted approaches continued to clash throughout the proceedings of the preparatory committee. In fact, the United States initially rejected the earliest draft under negotiation and took issue with its references to the notions of inequitable globalization, increasing polarization, and international responsibilities for global development and social governance. Calling the assertion of a right to development an "illusion" and reminding every one that governments had no role in income distribution and should not interfere with market operations, the US representative hammered the points that basic financial resources for development must come from within countries and that the goal of the FfD process was not to bring about changes in the capitalist system but to integrate all countries within it. Going a step further, he took the position that the primary outcome of the "event" should be a one-page-long political declaration simply expressing a commitment to freedom, capitalism, and democracy and the willingness and commitment of all the stakeholders concerned to continue the dialogue that they had initiated in the previous months. Meanwhile, the developing countries acknowledged that development was their primary responsibility but also stressed that the international community had to create an environment "supportive" of their efforts to strengthen the domestic financial sector through the implementation of multilaterally agreed-on financial standards, the development of their capital markets, and the creation of financial instruments to promote savings. The European Union agreed in principle but insisted that the developing countries' national responsibilities had to be spelled out in the context of transparency, the rule of law, respect for human rights, and, more broadly, good governance.[15]

All the other individual items of the committee's agenda elicited similarly contrasted views. In regard to the mobilization of international private resources for development, small island, land-locked and the least-developed developing countries questioned how foreign direct investment (FDI) could be attracted to "risk" or unattractive economies. Reflecting these concerns, the G–77 underlined the need to broaden the number of FDI recipients. One of the cross-cutting preoccupations of the group was to strengthen international instruments ensuring corporate social and environmental responsibility. In contrast, the European Union argued that bringing in international investment was the prime responsibility of its recipients and that the OECD guidelines on multinational corporations and the UN Global Compact were sufficient and adequate tools to prompt responsible corporate behavior and policy. Official development assistance was another bone of contention. The G–77 expressed its readiness to explore new, alternative sources of development finance but insisted on the need for timelines for the doubling of ODA in order to reach the Millennium Development Goals adopted at the 2000 Millennium Summit as well as binding commitments to reach the 0.7 percent target. Another one of the group's demands was the elimination of tied aid and the increased use of grants. "Partnerships" based on "shared responsibility" and a broader involvement of civil society organizations were the motto of the European Union on this point. Although not adverse to the idea of exploring new sources of financing and expressing support for ODA's targets and halving poverty by 2015, the EU emphasized the importance of sound domestic responsibilities and took the position that the recently introduced practice of the World Bank of preparing poverty reduction papers should be the prime vehicle for ownership and coordination of international aid for poverty eradication. The untying of aid was the province of the OECD's Development Assistance Committee (OECD-DAC), and no timetable was necessary to achieve the ODA target. Japan also recommended against the setting of ODA targets because of the donors' tense financial situation and emphasized the primacy of private resources which surpass ODA. The United States was even more trenchant: Aid targets were conceptually flawed and did not meet the needs of developing countries. Improving the effectiveness of ODA and shifting the focus to corporate sources of finance were the real issues, not the availability of funds.

On the sensitive debt issue, the G–77 asked for immediate debt relief for the poorest countries, debt moratoriums or cancellations in some circumstances, and marked improvements in the operation of the Heavily Indebted

Poor Countries (HIPC) initiative. Debt swaps were an avenue that could possibly be explored as well as the creation of arbitration mechanisms and US-type bankruptcy codes. From the standpoint of the European Union, debt was only one issue in a wider set of issues related to economic management. The scope available under HIPC should be fully utilized before the idea is entertained of moving to a new phase, although special allowances could be made to countries affected by unforeseen factors beyond their control. In any event, the idea should not be construed as an automatic entitlement for HIPC status, and bilateral initiatives in support of HIPC, although welcome, should be considered against the background of fair burden sharing. This viewpoint was even more forcefully argued by the United States, which underlined the importance of economic reform and poverty reduction efforts as the main determinants of debt relief.

The elimination of trade barriers and the use of subsidies which limited their ability to be fully engaged in the international trading system were other key demands of the G–77. In the group's view, environmental and labor concerns needed to be addressed, but as separate and distinct issues to be dealt with in "appropriate" institutions. For the United States, agricultural policies and the trade-related intellectual property rights (TRIPS) were of no concern to the preparatory committee. They properly belonged to the WTO. The European Union agreed, pointing to the fact that the launching of a new trade negotiation round at the WTO ministerial meeting in Doha was designed to deal with these matters. In addition, the elimination of agricultural subsidies did not take account of food security implications that could have negative effects on the net food importing of developing countries. In any case, trade could not automatically bring growth and development without adequate income distribution policies and a diversification of the trade exports of developing countries.

The so-called systemic issues, the last and perhaps the most controversial item on the preparatory committee's agenda predictably triggered polarized views. For the G–77, the distribution of the costs of financial crises still needed to be addressed as debt standstills and voluntary mediation and arbitration were woefully inadequate. The United Nations should play a key role in improving the coherence of the governance of international finance. Greater coordination in tax matters was desirable, though not necessarily in the form of a new institution like an International Tax Organization. Follow-up mechanisms should be set up to monitor and follow up on the outcome of the conference. The idea of assigning to the FfD process the purpose of deciding on changes in the international financial architecture ran into opposition by the European Union. Strengthening existing institutions rather than establishing new ones was of the essence, and the follow-up to FfD should be part of the regular proceedings of ECOSOC.

Reconciling these widely contrasting approaches was the task of the cochairs of the preparatory committee (one from the North, the other from the South) and of a "facilitator," who issued successive periodic "working papers" reflecting the progress made toward a consensus document.[16] Inevitably, the final product—a negotiated text—was modest and fraught with ambiguities.

The Monterrey Consensus (MC) is a comparatively short and lean document. One chapter underlines the challenges of development financing in the context of globalization, stressing the need for a holistic approach. A second chapter identifies "leading actions" in the areas identified by the preparatory committee. A third and final chapter specifies modalities for "staying engaged." But all throughout the text, the language is primarily exhortatory and mildly prescriptive. Words like *encourage, invite,* and *stress the need* abound without further clarification. A stronger terminology appears in the trade chapter, in which the parties to the MC *urge, affirm, will implement, will ensure,* and *resolve.* But the chapter simply reaffirms decisions agreed to earlier at Doha.

Radical proposals aired out in the course of the preparatory process were deleted because of US pressures, supported by a few other developed countries such as Japan and Australia, and sometimes by the EU. Such was the case of some of the proposals of the High Level Panel on Financing for Development chaired by the former president of Mexico, Ernesto Zedillo. The panel, which consisted of top financial leaders, had been set up by the Secretary-General to advise him on policy issues that he could submit at the Monterrey Conference. Released in June 2001, the Zedillo report argued that an improved governance of the global economic system, significantly higher levels of aid, and freer markets would go a long way toward achieving the international development goals and summits of the 1990s. Among its proposals which were set aside were convening a global economic governance summit by the UN with the possibility of establishing an economic and security council, shifting aid to a "common pool" that would finance the recipient development strategy, exploring the possibility of securing an adequate tax source to finance public goods, a study on the feasibility of a Tobin-style tax, a tax on carbon emissions, the consolidation of environmental institutions into a global environment organization, and the creation of an international tax organization. Likewise, the MC avoids questions of institutional reform and leaves untouched the balance of power between the UN and the BWIs and the WTO. The suggestion of doubling ODA together with proposals for debt relief was dropped.

Over all, the MC juxtaposes Northern and Southern visions of development, placing perhaps greater emphasis on the former than the latter. The primary focus of the document is on the mobilization of domestic rather

than international financial resources for development and on the responsibilities of developing countries in this process. One key responsibility of developing countries is to lay down the conditions for "good governance"
and "sound economic policies," in the absence of which international financial flows are unlikely to materialize. The role of the international community is limited to that of a supportive crew, and the MC thus devotes
more attention to enhancing the effectiveness of ODA than to higher levels
of aid.

At the same time, the MC does acknowledge a number of issues of concern to developing countries. It recognizes that many developing countries
have been or can be adversely affected by trade liberalization. They should
have the freedom and flexibility to protect themselves against import surges
and should be entitled to special and differential treatment in multilateral
trade liberalization agreements. Similarly, the MC concedes that trade-dis-
torting subsidies in agriculture, the abuse of antidumping measures, and
trade barriers in textiles and clothing need to be curbed and rolled back in
order to enable developing countries to expand their shares of export markets. In regard to debt, the MC stresses that "external debt relief can play a
key role in liberating sources for sustainable growth and development" and
welcomes "initiatives that have been undertaken to reduce outstanding in-
debtedness and invite further national and international measures in that
regard, *including . . . debt cancellation*" (italics added). In brief, while concentrating on market-based development policies and stressing the importance of domestic resource mobilization and international trade and foreign
investment as engines of growth and development in line with the Doha
Ministerial Declaration, the MC also gives a stamp of legitimization to the
demands of developing countries. To use the language of the UNDP admin-
istrator, the Monterrey Consensus is in effect a "contract," a "compact"
between North and South whereby the developing countries should implement reform measures and mobilize more of their own resources. In return,
the rich countries should give more official aid, open their markets, and encourage foreign investment.

What Did Monterrey Achieve?

Taking into account the persisting lack of consensus over development policies and over the role of the UN in them, it is not surprising that the Monterrey Conference, like its predecessor conferences, should have been used
by different constituencies to legitimize their conflicting claims. It is not
surprising either that the outcome of the Monterrey Conference should be a
highly ambiguous consensus lending itself to conflicting interpretations.

What meaning, then, should be assigned to the Monterrey Consensus? On this point, the following tentative observations can be made.

In the first place, Monterrey must be contextualized and seen as part of an ongoing long-term process. As pointed out earlier, the issue of development finance is not new. But for the first time ever, Northern countries allowed substantive discussion of economic and financial policy issues in the UN system outside the Bretton Woods institutions, which they control. Monterrey thus provided a unique opportunity to air out and discuss at the highest levels and among key financial policymakers contentious issues such as the reform of the international financial institutions, biases in the trade regime, a new issue of special drawing rights to be allocated to developing countries, improved cooperation among national taxation authorities to reduce tax avoidance and evasion, the establishment of a debt mediation facility, and detailed proposals for innovative ways of mobilizing private finance presented at the Business Forum, many involving partnership between public and private sectors. Like the General Assembly, which can make only recommendations, UN global conferences are not instruments of authoritative decisionmaking. At best, they are incubators of ideas and approximate a global version of the general will of the international community. No "concrete" action was thus taken on these questions, but again, this is not the business of UN global conferences.

Nor could the Monterrey Conference be expected to bring an end to the political process which drives the defining and redefining of development policies. But it certainly underlined a degree of convergence in development thinking. Since the mid–1980s and particularly since the end of the Cold War, the political economy of global trade, finance, and development has changed dramatically. The hold of the Washington consensus is no longer as strong as it was in the last two decades of the twentieth century. The BWIs are on the defensive as they were shattered by the financial crises of the 1990s. The IMF has been faulted for repeated financial misdiagnoses and policy prescriptions. The Bush administration has put forth a proposal that would reduce the power of the World Bank, converting up to 50 percent of the Bank's loans to grants for specific projects such as health, education, and sanitation. Both institutions have thus reviewed their development approaches and now place poverty reduction, the provision of safety nets in times of crises, and good governance at the core of their policies. The introduction of the Poverty Reduction Growth Facility administered by the IMF (now the primary source of funding for poverty eradication strategies) is an instance of incremental change. The UN—one of the main institutional normative critics of the Bretton Woods institutions—is also changing. Without losing altogether its fundamentally less-orthodox approach to development, the organization has since about the mid–1990s endeavored to build bridges with academia, nongovernmental organizations, and the private sector. The Global Compact, an initiative of the Secretary-General is perhaps the most visible manifestation of the UN's new pragmatism. Relations between the BWIs and the UN have also evolved. Since 1996, when the General Assembly passed a resolution calling for greater consultation between them, there has been an unprecedented frequency of contacts between UN agencies and the BWIs, including high-level meetings between ECOSOC ambassadors, the IMF, and the World Bank; ad hoc meetings between individual officials; and an official visit of the UN Secretary-General to the Bank. In June 2000, on the opening day of the World Summit for Social Development, the OECD, the UN, and the Bank and the IMF launched a joint publication of *A Better World for All*. As noted before, one of the most innovative features of the preparations for Monterrey was the inclusion of the Bank and the IMF in the process. Perhaps even more striking was the fact that several organizations, including the BWIs, seconded senior-level staff to serve alongside UN officials in the UN technical and substantive secretariat for FfD.

Against this backdrop, Monterrey stands out as a pragmatic acknowledgment that developing countries cannot change the balance of international economic and political power, that ODA increases are illusory, that financing for development cannot be based only on ODA, and that new sources of financing must be tapped, notably from the private sector. Monterrey was not a pledging conference, but it did result in concrete financial commitments by several countries and in particular the United States and the European Union. The European Union announced that it would increase its average ODA to 0.39 percent of GNP by 2006, with all member countries aiming for a minimum of 0.33 percent by the same year. This will increase the EU's annual aid by 8 billion euros by 2006, in addition to the current 27 billion Euros. The United States plans to increase its current ODA of $10 billion by $1.6 billion in fiscal 2004, $3.2 billion in 2005, and $5 billion in 2006, and to maintain that level thereafter. If Monterrey has any significance, it may be viewed as the point where donor aid began to edge upward after reaching its lowest levels in years. But the point should not be overstressed. Development aid has never been large, and donors have often used aid labeled for development to advance their own foreign policy goals or to promote their own exports. President George W. Bush made it clear that increased US ODA would be tied to political, legal, and economic reforms and would be doled out to nations that "governed justly, invested in their people and encouraged economic freedom."[17] In fact, some suggested that his proposal had come in exchange for the omission of an explicit commitment to fulfill the 0.7 percent target in the outcome document. Others suggested that the change in US policy came in part because

President Bush made a direct connection between poverty and terrorism. In any case, even these anticipated increases will leave the United States as the lowest per capita donor, and the prevalence of a security agenda over development in US foreign policy since September 11 does not bode well for the future. Skeptics also point to the fact that nine months earlier, at the UN and the Genoa G-8, enthusiasm for a $10 billion annual world health fund to combat AIDS, malaria, and tuberculosis was considerable. But pledges so far amount to less than one fifth of the target. Similarly, achieving the Millennium Development Goals for poverty reduction would mean doubling donor aid, a politically unrealistic objective.

Have developing countries tangibly benefited from the Monterrey Consensus? Answering this question may be premature, but many of the MC's normative injunctions that are supportive of developing countries' interests continue to go unheeded. Since the Conference, the United States has increased various agricultural subsidies. The EU has taken no action on its agricultural tariffs and farm spending. Stiffer tariffs still affect textile and clothing products. At the twelfth general review of quotas, the participation of developing countries and transition economies in IMF decisionmaking as well as the level of IMF resources to respond to crises was discussed without modification of levels of the distribution of existing quotas. Additional resources to strengthen the HIPC have not been forthcoming and the record is far from satisfactory, since only eight countries had reached the completion point as of November 2003. The MC acknowledges the need for the IMF to make quick decisions for temporary issues of special drawing rights (SDRs) to assist member countries experiencing international liquidity crises. The matter appears to have fallen into oblivion.

Concluding Thoughts

The Monterrey Consensus is a consensus less about substance than about a process based on general policy principles. At Monterrey, it was recognized that a number of issues were simply intractable but could be taken up at a later stage, in the words of the MC, by "staying engaged." On this point, the follow-up to the Monterrey Conference is different from that to previous UN conferences in the sense that it calls for the involvement of a whole range of actors extending beyond states. Their involvement was critical during the preparatory process and will continue to be crucial in the post-Monterrey process. In this regard, Monterrey in effect sanctioned a new model of international cooperation based on a "partnership" between developed and developing countries, international organizations, business, and NGOs.[18]

In this negotiating space occupied by new actors, how will the issues left outstanding at Monterrey be tackled and resolved? Will they be dealt with on the basis of the neoliberal policies of the BWIs and WTO, the UN's concerns for human rights, labor and environmental standards, or a combination of these approaches? Many believe that the UN will be pushed aside by its wealthier and weightier partners and that the true leveragers in the post-Monterrey process will be the Bretton Woods institutions and the industrialized nations of the North. It is also true that the implementation of the Monterrey Consensus and the further consideration of the undecided issues are now up to donor and developing countries, to international organizations (notably the WTO), to business, and to civil society. But the MC establishes clear linkages with the implementation of the outcomes of UN global conferences, including the Millennium Development Goals, which aim to significantly reduce poverty, improve access to education and health care, and stop the spread of contagious diseases. The entire UN system is now mobilized toward the realization of the MDGs. Reports highlighting progress (or lack of progress) toward their achievement are due each year to the General Assembly and can be expected to build pressures for further change. Meanwhile, the structured engagement of business organizations and NGOs continues as planned within the General Assembly and ECOSOC. "Dialogues" and "hearings" took place in March 2003 in preparation for the ECOSOC and Bretton Woods/WTO meeting on April 14 and in the fall of 2003 in preparation for the October high-level dialogue on financing for development in the General Assembly. Clearly, Monterrey may not have resolved all North-South issues. But it certainly gave further impetus to a process that requires a greater degree of accountability by all parties concerned to the extent that they all claim to have adopted poverty eradication as a normative goal and to have accepted the notion that the economic, social, and financial dimensions of development must be dealt with in an integrated manner.

Notes

1. This article first appeared in *Development and Finance (Fejlesztés és Finanszírozás), Quarterly Hungarian Economic Review*, No. 3 (2003), pp. 60–68. Reprinted with permission of the publisher—Ecoforum Ltd/Strategic Advisory Board of Hungarian Development Bank, Budapest.

2. UNDPI Press Release ECOSOC 6001.

3. Ibid.

4. Ibid.

5. UN Document E/2002/13.

6.UNDPI ECOSOC/6001.

7.See United Nations, *Financing for Development: Building on Monterrey* (New York: United Nations, 2002), pp. 313–317.

8."Where Is the International Coalition Against Poverty?" globalpolicy@globalpolicy.org.

9. "WCC-Monterrey Consensus Fails to Provide," retrieved from smm@wcc-coe.org.

10. "An Equitable World Is Possible and Necessary," retrievable from wide@gn.apc.org.

11. For a useful overview of UN global conferences, see Michael G. Schechter (ed.), *United Nations Sponsored World Conferences: Focus on Impact and Follow Up* (Tokyo: United Nations University Press, 2001).

12. General Assembly Resolution A/54/196 of December 22, 1999.

13. United Nations, *Outcome of the International Conference on Financing for Development*, Report of the Secretary-General, A/57/344, August 23, 2002.

14. The report of the group may be found in UN document A/54/28 of May 28, 1999.

15. The following account is based on the "roundup" summaries of the preparatory committees, prepared by the NGLS and retrievable from www.unsystem.org/ngls/documents. See, for example, the first working paper of the facilitator in document A/AC.254/24, April 2001.

16. See, for example, the first working paper of the Facilitator in document A/AC254/24, April 2001.

17. See www.un.org/ffd/pressrel/22b.htm.

18. For a summary of proposals from the private sector on financing for development, see the website of the Business Council for the United Nations [www.bcun.org].

Chapter SIX

PROSPECTS OF MULTILATERAL DIPLOMACY

Multilateral Diplomacy in the Twenty-First Century

Earl Sullivan

Multilateral diplomacy is as old as the Westphalian order of independent territorial states. Even though there has been considerable growth in the number and significance of multilateral institutions and non-state actors, the state-centric Westphalian system is intact. Multilateral diplomacy is distinct from traditional bilateral diplomacy by virtue of the environment or arena in which it is conducted. This arena includes, but is not necessarily restricted to, public international organizations, international nongovernmental organizations (NGOs), international conferences, and summit meetings. The multilateral diplomatic environment provides diplomats who operate within it with a framework that in some ways limits and in others expands how they operate.

Contemporary multilateral diplomacy evolved over many centuries to take the form it has today. From the Peace of Westphalia to the Congress of Vienna to the conferences that established the first international organizations to those conferences that settled the great wars of the twentieth century, the use of multilateral diplomacy has increased in frequency and significance. For most of the period of the Westphalian order, multilateral diplomatic activity took place largely in occasional meetings convened to deal with specific issues such as postwar settlements. In the contemporary world, most multilateral diplomacy occurs in institutionalized settings such as the United Nations, NATO, and the World Trade Organization (WTO).

Several factors help account for the increased salience of multilateral diplomacy in today's world. One is the growth in the number and importance of international organizations, especially since the end of World War II. Another element in the multilateral diplomatic equation is the increase in the number and significance of NGOs that have an international agenda and membership. Also important, especially in the post–Cold War era, is the phenomenon known as globalization. Finally, the Cold War itself had a profound impact on the growth of multilateral diplomacy.

During the Cold War, multilateral diplomacy, often institutionalized in international organizations, became more the norm than the exception. One aspect of the Cold War was that both superpowers sought allies in their contest with each other, and this search led to the creation of new international organizations such as NATO and the Warsaw Pact. Furthermore, the Cold War era also witnessed the emergence of large numbers of newly independent states whose formal entry into the Westphalian order was typically marked by membership in the United Nations and other international organizations. In addition, some of these states also formed international organizations of their own, such as the Arab League, the Organization of African Unity, and the more global Group of 77. These organizations added a North-South dimension to the East-West orientation of the Cold War. They also augmented the significance of multilateral diplomacy.

In one sense, the Cold War froze all diplomacy in place, including the multilateral variant, as many conflicts, even those traditionally said to be within the exclusive jurisdiction of the sovereign state, were linked to the Manichean struggle between the superpowers. One consequence was that the traditional distinction between domestic and international issues became blurred. Thus, to cite only one example, a struggle for power within the newly independent state of the Congo in the early 1960s quickly became enmeshed in the global conflict between the Soviets and the Americans, the United Nations becoming part of the battlefield.[1] If anything, this blurring has increased in the post–Cold War era of accelerated globalization.

Globalization in all of its dimensions, but particularly the spread of capitalism to virtually all corners of the world, has accelerated in the wake of the collapse of the Soviet Union and the end of the Cold War. As globalization has increased, so, too, has the growth in the number, complexity, and importance of international transactions. The bankruptcy of a leading financial institution in Japan creates ripples in the many countries in which it served as a major source of loans. Decisions of the WTO may affect employment and investment around the world. Similarly, a decision to send UN forces to a troubled state or region affects lives and budgets in countries far removed from the field of battle, as personnel and equipment are moved, funds are spent, and complex UN-sponsored activities are undertaken. Globalization means that domestic political concerns reverberate internationally and that international politics becomes more intertwined with local politics. Thus, although globalization enhances the significance of multilateral diplomacy, it also increases its complexity. However, multilateral diplomacy is much more suited to dealing with the problems that attend globalization than is traditional bilateral diplomatic activity. Many if not all of the most serious contemporary issues involve large numbers of states as well as the numerous intergovernmental organizations (IGOs) that have been created. As pointed out in the introduction to this volume, most IGOs have been established since the end of World War II, reflecting the growing need for such institutions and hence the increased salience of multilateral diplomatic venues.

The actors on the multilateral diplomatic stage today are not all representatives of states. Officials from multinational corporations and NGOs jostle for power and influence in the corridors of the UN and other international organizations along with professional diplomats, politicians, and international bureaucrats. The large numbers of nonstate actors such as these have contributed to the environment within which multilateral diplomacy is conducted. For example, many NGOs call for global conferences to be held, and when they are, the NGOs lobby governments, the press, and officials of international organizations on issues that concern them. They also provide diplomats with technical data and advice, a factor of special importance to diplomats representing poor countries that are unable to generate technical studies on their own.[2]

One special type of multilateral diplomacy occurs when summit meetings involving more than two states take place. As argued in Chapter 5, some diplomatists may wish to do without summit diplomacy, perhaps because they fear that the leaders of states would not do as good a job of negotiating the interests of the country as professional diplomats themselves. Avoiding summit meetings is no longer possible, however; the supposedly risky séances take place with considerable frequency, and many, if not most, are now multilateral events. Thus, meetings of the heads of state or governments of the Group of 7 (G-7), plus Russia,[3] are now at least annual events, as are summits of the members of NATO, the European Union, and the Association of Southeast Asian Nations (ASEAN) to name only a few. The passing of the Cold War accelerated this process, as bilateral summits became less common than those involving three or more states. During the Cold War, the term *summit* inevitably referred to a meeting between the leaders of the Soviet Union and the United States, while the rest of the world waited and watched. By the mid-1990s, however, multilateral summits were the norm rather than the exception, and this is a trend that is likely to continue.

In the preceding chapters of this book, several concepts related to multilateral diplomacy have been explored. One recurrent theme is that multilateral diplomacy and bilateral diplomacy, although sharing important features, are somehow distinct and that the differences between them matter. This chapter continues and expands that exploration. One dissimilarity between the two modes of diplomacy is related to the knowledge base required in each case. In traditional diplomacy, diplomats representing their country in the capital of another country need to have a firm grasp of the national interests of both places. They need to know where the interests of the two overlap and where they are at variance. In order to be effective, they must understand the political system and political culture of the country as well as the individuals who count in the local political, economic, and even cultural life. In a multilateral setting, successful diplomats must also develop an acute awareness of the players. However, the issues dealt with are often particular to the specific multilateral arena in question; even if they are the same as those discussed in bilateral diplomacy, they are approached in a different way. For example, negotiations regarding a trade question in a traditional setting might focus on the specific bilateral issues between two countries, whereas at the United Nations or the WTO, discussion would focus on broad issues of policy and trade law. Furthermore, just as diplomats in a traditional setting must understand the political culture of the country to which they are accredited, multilateral diplomats must realize that international organizations also have a political system and political culture. Additionally, in multilateral diplomacy diplomats must acclimatize themselves to a political arena in which people speak several languages and in which the national interests of a large number of countries must be accommodated.

As pointed out in Chapter 1, multilateral diplomacy typically involves daily personal contact with a large number of people. It is not surprising, therefore, that the ability to get along with people, regardless of political, economic, or cultural differences, is probably more important in the multilateral setting than in bilateral diplomacy, where the political and military weight of the two countries may be more decisive than ideological or cultural variances. Important in this regard is the ability to convey genuine respect for the religious and cultural diversity represented at the United Nations. Delegates who are not respectful and tolerant of this diversity may be unable to convince others to accommodate their views and may find themselves outside the UN consensus. By contrast, those who respect the religion and culture of others will be likely to give more weight to what other delegates say than those who don't. Consequently, they are likely to try to find a way to use language that is not offensive to the culture or religion of others when drafting resolutions.[4]

Contemporary multilateral diplomacy takes place in the environment of the "new diplomacy" referred to in this book's introduction. This new diplomacy is much more public than was the old diplomacy of preceding centuries. It also includes many nonstate actors in addition to the usual representatives of states. As a consequence, successful contemporary diplomats must master, whether in bilateral or multilateral settings, the skill of dealing with news media. However, as pointed out in Chapter 1, diplomats in multilateral venues, regardless of their nationality, must pay special attention to the US media, because so much multilateral diplomatic activity revolves around the UN headquarters in New York City.

Another distinguishing factor of diplomatic activity in international organizations is that it involves public speaking and the ability to master the rules of parliamentary procedure that are adhered to by these bodies. Multilateral organizations have decisionmaking structures that are similar to those of many parliamentary bodies. Divergent views are debated in public, many questions are settled by voting, and meetings are conducted according to established rules of procedure. Furthermore, in international conference diplomacy, as in many national legislative bodies, participants are "accustomed to finding solutions, often in the form of compromises, for difficult problems" (Kaufmann 1988, 145). Thus, experience in parliamentary politics and parliamentary procedure probably constitutes good training for wheeling and dealing at the UN (Kaufmann 1988, 142 and 144–145).

There are some important differences between many national legislatures and most international organizations. For example, no UN official, including the Secretary-General, has power comparable to that of the British prime minister or the Speaker of the House in the US Congress. Furthermore, although there are voting blocs in the United Nations, there are no disciplined political parties, and states may defect from their bloc with relative impunity. Although in theory diplomats at the UN must vote according to instructions from their capitals, in practice they are often relatively more autonomous than diplomats in many bilateral settings; they have considerable latitude as they participate in the extensive and prolonged lobbying that is the hallmark of diplomacy at the UN and in multilateral conferences convened to deal with such issues as global warming and the law of the sea.

As mentioned frequently in this book, the pattern for diplomacy at the United Nations is to seek consensus. In the Security Council, consensus among the five permanent members is most important, whereas in the General Assembly a two-thirds majority, as distinct from a simple majority, is required to pass a resolution on an "important question" (Article 18, para. 2). Even in the Security Council, the votes of the nonpermanent members are important, as any sign of dissent would weaken the appearance of resolve, especially if action under Chapter VII of the Charter is to be undertaken.[5] Thus, in most international organizations that operate on the basis of one state, one vote, all, or virtually all, member states are important, and the wording of a resolution must satisfy the interests and needs of the vast majority of the members. One result is that diplomats representing small countries may have a large impact on the outcome of a debate or the content of a specific resolution. Sometimes this influence is due to specific knowledge they possess, but more often it is more related to rhetorical, bargaining, or resolution-writing skills than to substantive expertise.

Not all states choose to seek a broad consensus in multilateral arenas when vital interests are at stake. This is especially true of superpowers, which may prefer unilateral action or may prefer to ignore the UN altogether if possible. For example, faced with the prospect of a veto of its preferred outcome at the Security Council, the United States has the option of acting unilaterally and doing so with impunity because the other veto powers at the UN do not have the political or economic muscle to prevent the US from doing so.

The end of the Cold War marked the beginning of an era dominated by the United States of America as the world's single superpower. Its role as a global hegemon is such that it is able to determine what role, if any, will be allotted to the UN or other major international organizations. Consequently, as a result of American preferences, the UN does not play a central role in settling the conflicts over the fates of Palestine, Afghanistan, or Iraq. The UN's irrelevance in the earlier conflict over Vietnam is being repeated in all of the key conflicts of our time. Some scholars have argued that "the forceful and unilateral exercise of U.S. power . . . is the logical outcome of the current unrivaled U.S. position in the international system" (Jervis 2003, 84). Others take the position that an ideological preference for unilateralism is neither logical nor in the long-term interests of the superpower (Albright 2003; Tharoor 2003). For example, the United States could have responded unilaterally in 1990–1991 to the challenge to world order presented by Iraq's invasion of Kuwait. Instead, for pragmatic reasons that Bush administration decided to lower US human and financial costs and create a multilateral coalition including the UN and a large number of states. Furthermore, it made numerous concessions in order to secure the participation of allies in that coalition. In 2003 the situation was quite different, and the coalition assembled by the United Stated to invade Iraq was smaller, excluded the UN, and was quintessentially an American operation. Multilateralism broad enough to include the United Nations was eliminated as an option by that Bush administration, partly as the result of an ideological preference of the US government for unilateral action. This illustrates an important point. Superpowers dominated by elites with an ideological preference for unilateral action will make few if any concessions to secure the support of allies, even if to do so would reduce the costs to the superpower, and those allies who do ally with such a state will be little more than window dressing. Not surprisingly, most potential allies will refuse to accept this role (de Montbrial 2003).

US Secretary of State Colin Powell disputes the assertion of critics of the foreign policy of the Bush administration, who claim, unjustifiably in his view, that "U.S. strategy is widely accused of being unilateralist by design" (Powell 2004, 23). He has articulated a strategy of forming "partnerships" with allies in pursuit of common goals and argues that the pursuit of such partnerships is the hallmark of President George W. Bush's foreign policy. However, in so doing he made scant mention of the United Nations, except as an arena for the articulation and approval of US preferences (Powell 2004, 25), and no mention was made of the World Bank or the International Monetary Fund or most major multilateral arenas. The only multilateral organization mentioned in a positive tone is NATO. It is not surprising that a superpower would prefer to operate in bilateral frameworks, as they are the traditional arena for classical power politics. Nor is it surprising that a military alliance such as NATO, in which the United States can be expected to serve as primus inter pares would be preferred to the less manageable Security Council of the United Nations. The thrust of Colin Powell's argument, and of President Bush's foreign policy, is to stress the importance of bilateral relations with other states, particularly relations "among the world's major powers" (Powell 2004, 28). As a result of such go-it-alone tendencies, especially by the United States, the United Nations became increasingly marginalized in the early part of the twenty-first century, especially from a security perspective. As long as Washington is propelled by this logic, it is hard to avoid the conclusion that multilateral diplomacy, and multilateral organizations, will not play a central role in the diplomacy of the single superpower.

This chapter contains three essays, each of which expands on important themes related to multilateral diplomacy in contemporary global politics. The first, by Ambassador Chen Luzhi, focuses on sovereignty; the second, by Richard Langhorne, discusses relations between state and nonstate actors in the international arena; and the third, by Richard Reitano and Caleb Elfenbein, concentrates on the role of the United States in global politics following the tragic events of September 11, 2001.

All members of the United Nations are sovereign states. Sovereignty is one of the key defining characteristics of the Westphalian order of states, and normally, it is guarded jealously by them. Rienk Terpstra, whose essay on post–Cold War diplomacy appears in Chapter 5 of this book, refers to sovereignty as a "bargaining chip," that is, something that can be traded in return for something else. Chinese Ambassador Chen Luzhi articulates a strikingly different approach to the importance of sovereignty in his essay. In Chen's view, the sovereignty of states must be clear and unchallenged. Only if states are truly sovereign can they delegate meaningful authority to multinational institutions, and only if those institutions have real authority can they be truly effective. Sovereignty of individual states is the defining characteristic of the international system, and diplomacy that ignores or deemphasizes this is guaranteed to fail in Ambassador Chen's opinion. Even though the interdependence of states is increasingly obvious, and sovereignty of small states is often downplayed by large states, it remains the legal centerpiece of contemporary world order.

This state-centric perspective is challenged in part by the second essay in this chapter. The world in which we live may be dominated by states, especially those at or near the peak of the hierarchy of international power, but an increasing number and variety of nonstate transnational entities are crowding the stage. Furthermore, some of them have a greater economic, cultural, or political heft than many of the states in the developing world. Richard Langhorne points out that the multilateral arena is often the venue of choice or necessity for interactions between states and transnational actors. In his essay, he explores this theme in the context of providing an overview of the development of multilateral diplomacy since the nineteenth century and up to the present period. In the contemporary world, Langhorne argues, "three changes have taken and are taking place: First, states are acquiring a different and sometimes lesser scope of action. Second, associations of states are affected by the changing role of their progenitors and some have begun to move into a more unilateral global role, though remaining multilateral in their construction. Third, the tendency for weak states to collapse into uncontrollable internal conflict has brought a new importance to private organizations offering humanitarian, human rights, and developmental relief."

One of the most important aspects of Langhorne's essay is his elucidation of the salience of the recent changes in information and communications technology, a change he likens to a "revolution" that has enabled people all over the world to communicate instantly and globally, with little or no interference from states. In such a world, states are weaker than in a system in which the possession of territory trumps all other political factors. Borders are increasingly permeable, and what has come to be called globalization affects people and institutions everywhere in unprecedented ways. Multilateral organizations are among the organizations most affected by this revolution. Langhorne focuses much of his attention on multilateral economic institutions (MEIs) and argues that organizations such as the World Bank, with weighted voting benefiting its richest members, has to a considerable degree been superceded in importance by organizations such as the recently created World Trade Organization (WTO), whose "one country, one vote" system heralds the beginning of "a real redistribution of political power."

As states have been weakened, some have collapsed and others may follow in their chaotic wake. In such a world, conflict within weak states takes on global significance, giving added importance to multilateral diplomacy as well as to international NGOs that move in to fill the vacuum that results in these circumstances. According to Langhorne, we live in a world where multilateral diplomacy is necessary, but where "its results can be frustratingly evanescent."

A book such as this one must draw a careful balance between concentrating on theoretical material, which is likely to stand the test of time, and material that focuses on "current events" that may soon be out of date. However, the consequences for multilateral diplomacy of the foreign policy of US president George W. Bush are so sweeping and have such potentially long-term consequences that we would be remiss if the book did not address this issue directly. This task fell to Richard Reitano and Caleb Elfenbein. In the final essay in this volume, they focus on the fate of "Multilateral Diplomacy and the United Nations in the Aftermath of 9/11." Much of the essay is a critique of American diplomacy in this period and is especially concerned about the negative effect the American preference for unilateral action has had and will have on the multilateral arena and on the prospect for global peace and prosperity. A powerful subtheme is that globalization includes the "globalization of conflict," a theme also found in the essay by Richard Langhorne.

A hegemon can project power anywhere and for any reason it thinks sufficient. Few if any countervailing forces exist to constrain a superpower, but Reitano and Elfenbein suggest that the United Nations is a potential "collective counterweight to American power." This is a potentially dangerous role for the UN, as counterweights to superpowers may end up being regarded as enemies rather than as preferred partners. In the end, however, Reitano and Elfenbein conclude, "The UN may be unable to prevent the United States from engaging in military adventures, but it can remind the world (and most Americans) that diplomacy and the use of multilateral force are always preferable and that unilateral force is rarely a long-term solution to the most difficult problems."

If the international system is in the midst of a long-term trend toward preference for the unilateral exercise of power by its leading members, especially the United States, then multilateral organizations of all kinds may face an extended period of being marginalized. In this context, it will be necessary for the United Nations, as the preeminent multilateral arena, to survive and thus keep the concept of multilateral action alive, awaiting the eventual and perhaps inevitable ebb tide of the unilateral impulse.

In the future, hegemons with an ideological preference for unilateral action may be confronted by a broad coalition of states and other political actors whose only means of defense against the hegemon is to act collectively to constrain it. As the dean of Columbia's School of International and Public Affairs has observed, in the aftermath of September 11, the Bush "administration's unilateralist impulses and resistance to international institutions in pursuit of the 'war on terrorism' were constrained by virtually unanimous support among other governments and NGOs around the world for supra-national institutions like the United Nations" (Anderson 2003, 5). Paradoxically, therefore, a unilateralist superpower may stimulate a multilateral counterforce. It is too soon to tell if or when this will happen, but even the staunchest supporters of US supremacy must admit that it is a realistic possibility.

With the end of the Cold War, the world has moved from domination by a system of bipolarity to a world of unipolarity, with the United States as the "sole surviving superpower." Major initiatives in the Security Council or the International Monetary Fund, for example, cannot succeed without American support and leadership. However, as pointed out in Chapter 3, as the importance of economic issues increases in the age of globalization, so, too, does the (potential) weight of the European Union, Japan, and other current and future centers of international commerce. It is possible, therefore, that the unipolar aspects of the world that became increasingly apparent in the 1990s and the early twenty-first century will be succeeded by multipolarity. If so, multilateral meetings and conferences could become even more central to global politics than during the Cold War. Unilateral action by the single superpower may become less prominent, and joint action, negotiated in multilateral settings, will become more common. This does not necessarily mean, however, that a multipolar world system will come about soon or that it will lead inevitably to a more peaceful world.

While reflecting on prospects for multilateral diplomacy and the changes the world is undergoing, it is important to remember that new technology, the proliferation of international organizations and NGOs, and globalization have not (yet) rendered the nation-state obsolete. The fact that people all over the world can watch a political crisis or even a war unfold on television does not necessarily mean that the Security Council will act to resolve the crisis, or that if it does the action it undertakes will be effective. Multilateral diplomacy coexists with traditional diplomacy, globalization with nationalism, and the pursuit of the national interests of individual states with a search for the means to serve the often-inchoate interests of the global community. The appeal of multilateralism is strong, but the incentive for powerful states to act unilaterally and their ability to do so remain. The importance of multilateral diplomacy may increase, but as long as the Westphalian order survives, independent states will retain the ability and the legal right, enshrined in Article 51 of the UN Charter, to employ such traditional geopolitical stratagems as unilateral military action in what their leaders perceive to be their own national interest. There is no reason to believe that they will forsake that right in the near future.

Notes

1. Although the Congo crisis may have helped augment the role of multilateral diplomatic activity, it is perhaps best known for leading to the UN payments crisis of 1960–1965. See Morphet 1994, 197–200.

2. Yehia Auda of the Egyptian Mission to the United Nations, interview by author, September 5, 1997.

3. The G-7 consists of the United States, Great Britain, France, Germany, Italy, Japan, and Canada. Russian officials are often included as well.

4. Yehia Auda, interview.

5. For a review of the provisions of Chapter VII of the UN Charter, see Chapter 2.

References

Albright, Madeleine. (2003) "United Nations," *Foreign Policy*, No. 138, September-October, pp. 16–24.

Anderson, Lisa. 2003. *Pursuing Truth, Exercising Power: Social Science and Public Policy in the Twenty-first Century* (New York: Columbia University Press).

de Montbrial, Thierry. "Allies Must Be Able to Disagree," *International Herald Tribune*, September 23, 2003, p. 9.

Jervis, Robert. (2003) "The Compulsive Empire," *Foreign Policy*, No. 137, July-August, pp. 83–87.

Kaufmann, Johan. (1988) *Conference Diplomacy: An Introductory Analysis* (Dordrecht, The Netherlands: Martinus Nijhoff, United Nations Institute for Training and Research).

Morphet, Sally. (1994) "UN Peacekeeping and Election-Monitoring," in *United Nations, Divided World: The UN's Role in International Relations*, 2nd ed., edited By Adam Roberts and Benedict Kingsbury (Oxford: Oxford University Press), pp. 183–239.

Powell, Colin L. (2004) "A Strategy of Partnerships," *Foreign Affairs*, Vol. 83, No. 1, January-February, pp. 22–34.

Tharoor, Shashi. (2003) "Why America Still Needs the United Nations," *Foreign Affairs*, Vol. 82, No. 5, September-October, pp. 67–80.

Multilateral Diplomacy
in a Time of
"Relative" Sovereignty

Ambassador Chen Luzhi[1]

In academic, political, and business circles there has been much ado about making sense of the changes in international relations since the end of the Cold War. And one disturbing—and mistaken—conclusion is that the state system is seemingly irrelevant and sovereignty eroding. To say this is to suggest that there is not much of a future for multilateral diplomacy. But sovereignty is the defining principle of diplomacy, and a system of sovereign states is the organizing principle of multilateral diplomacy; without sovereign states there can be no multilateral diplomacy—or bilateral diplomacy, for that matter.

It is true the modern state system feels the pressure of the forces of globalization and is challenged by increasingly powerful nonstate actors in the post–Cold War period. But this is not necessarily a new development. "There has been a challenge to the sovereignty of the state dating to the founding of the United Nations, the rise of human rights claims, and continuing on through economic interdependence and environmental issues," notes J. Brian Hehir, in a 1996 lecture to the Woodrow Wilson Center in

Princeton, New Jersey. Nor is the notion of "relative" sovereignty anything new. In practical terms, sovereignty is never absolute, although, in theory, the sovereignty of states cannot be relative. From the very beginning of the modern state system in the seventeenth century, sovereign states have entered into multilateral agreements and created multilateral institutions that have "relativized" their sovereignty. The environment of international relations has clearly changed, but it is still inextricably and firmly tied to sovereignty and sovereign states.

So, what is really being discussed is how relations between sovereign states in the global political system should be conducted at a time when multilateralism has become the order of the day. What follows is an effort to explain how the uncertainty that abounds in the post–Cold War world affects multilateral diplomacy and the future international system of sovereign states.

Sovereignty, the State, and Multilateral Diplomacy

"Sovereignty" of states is the core principle of international law and the cornerstone of today's international state system. The concept of sovereignty and the sovereign state is the product of state building that occurred in Europe when medieval Christendom fractured under the combined impact of the Renaissance and the Reformation (Jackson 1990, 30). It owes much of its meaning to the "universal" authority or supreme power of Europe's rulers;[2] hence "sovereigns preceded sovereignty." In the sixteenth century, Jean Bodin defined sovereignty as "the supreme power of the state over citizens and subjects, unrestrained by law" or as a government which "can secure itself against external enemies or internal disorder" (Wang 1995). Bodin's *Six Books of the Commonwealth* explicitly touches upon two basic aspects of sovereignty: a legal status and an empirical reality, or a norm and a fact. This is an important distinction that is easily confused. The former makes sovereignty "a legal, absolute, and unitary condition," and the latter confirms the state as an independent reality in the world.

Legally, the state is the only locus of sovereignty, and sovereignty is the exclusive property of the state. According to Alan James, "In this matter, there can, in principle, be no half-way house, no question of relative sovereignty"(James 1986, 39). There is no entity (country) that is at the same time sovereign and nonsovereign, or something in between. James argues that sovereignty is an absolute condition: It is "either present or absent." Theoretically, sovereignty—the supreme authority of the state over its citizens, territory, and external relations—cannot be divided or shared. It is unimaginable that a state that has more than one supreme authority in dealing with internal and external affairs can still be regarded as a sovereign state. A state without sovereignty and sovereignty without a state are both legally unfounded.

But it is important to remember that "states historically were empirical realities before they were legal personalities" (Jackson 1990, 30). The legal status of the state in international law is an abstraction of the state in reality. States, physically, cannot be detached and isolated entities. They exist in the same world and have much in common with each other. All states have a bordered territory, a settled population, an effective government, and the ability to secure themselves against external enemies or internal disorders. Efficacy is regarded as the standard by which to judge the validity of a state (Kelsen 1945, 93–94). Capabilities or state functions, along with the physical attributes of a state, constitute the empirical reality of sovereignty. Obviously, the size and other particulars (i.e., military defenses, economy, political system) of sovereign states vary, but these differences do not impinge on the legal status of their sovereignty. Just as "a dwarf is still a man,"[3] a small or economically and militarily weaker state is still a sovereign entity, even if it is seen to exercise less clout in international relations than does a bigger or stronger state. Only in this empirical sense can one talk about relative sovereignty.

Multilateral diplomacy is the way sovereign states relate to each other in the global political system. As the state system grew larger and political interactions among sovereign states became more complex, international organizations were created to provide a structured framework for the conduct of multilateral diplomacy. The Peace of Westphalia (1648) pioneered the use of international conferences and negotiations to settle conflicts among sovereign states. The Concert of Europe, which came into being after the Congress of Vienna (1814–1815) ending the Napoleonic Wars, was the first attempt to institutionalize multilateral diplomacy. It reinforced the foundation of the system of congresses, meetings, and multilateral diplomatic negotiations designed to establish agreed-on policies among the powers. The League of Nations established after World War I was the first multipurpose international governmental organization that was, in principle, open to all sovereign states. In fact, the League was the first formal multilateral diplomatic institution ever to exist in the history of the world. The United Nations, which was created after World War II, is in many ways an improvement upon the League of Nations and is the only universal international organization in the world today.

All these multilateral institutions laid down rights and duties of the member states, and accordingly member states willingly and consciously permitted these institutions to restrict their sovereignty in select areas. The Concert of Europe powers were treaty-bound to intervene to suppress revo-

lutions that might "disturb the peace of Europe." The members of the
League of Nations undertook to "respect and preserve as against external
aggression the territorial integrity and the existing political independence of
all Members of the League." The United Nations Charter binds member
states to "settle their international disputes by peaceful means"; and "to refrain in their international relations from the threat or use of force against
the territorial integrity or political independence of any state." State sovereignty is restricted by multilateral institutions, but such institutions also uphold and preserve the sovereignty of states. As Erskine Childers and Brian
Urquhart point out, "The United Nations represents the inviolability of the
sovereign states and the instrument for the development of trans-sovereign
thinking and cooperation" (Childers and Urquhart 1994, 19–20).

When sovereign states create multilateral institutions, they entrust these
institutions to do something on their behalf. Multilateral institutions function only as instruments of sovereign states in order to regulate international relations—a vehicle of multilateral diplomacy. As is specified in the
UN Charter, the United Nations is a center for harmonizing the actions of
nations. How can a multilateral institution carry out this function? Obviously it is entrusted with this function by the sovereign states in its membership. The institution itself has no sovereign authority and power. It
derives its authority and power from the constituting sovereign states,
which collectively delegate specific aspects of their power and authority to
the institution and supervise its activities through accredited representatives. A sovereign state may quit the institution and cease to be its member,
but this cannot reduce the institution's authority and power. Of course, the
effectiveness and validity of its function will be seriously affected if a large
number of constituting sovereign states or a few key constituting sovereign
states withdraw from it. The League of Nations did not fulfill the hopes of
its founders, to a large extent because only Great Britain and France among
the great powers were members throughout the League's life. So long as the
multilateral institution remains effective and valid, its authority and the
power delegated to it by the members will stand.

According to Paul Streeten, "The state has become too big for the small
things, and too small for the big things. The small things call for delegation
downwards to the local level. . . . The big things call for delegation upwards,
for coordination between national policies, or for transnational institutions"
(Streeten 1992, 2). The relationship between sovereign states and multilateral institutions is mainly a form of delegation. It is no exaggeration to say
that without the delegation of part of sovereign states' power and authority,
no multilateral institution of sovereign states can work or even exist. To delegate means to entrust authority, power, and other properties to a person or
an institution acting as one's agent or representative. Although sovereign

states cannot share or divide their authority and power with other states, they can delegate part of their authority and power to an agent acting on their behalf. This is completely different from the so-called limitation, abridgment, or erosion of sovereignty, because the authority and power delegated to an institution can be taken back by sovereign states as they deem necessary. Even on the issues of the so-called global commons, such as law of the sea, climate control, and biodiversity treaties, sovereign states can still refuse to sign or can cease accession to them any time after signing. There are no multilateral institutions that can forbid this. The most a multilateral institution can do is suspend the membership of a sovereign state. Even under such circumstances the sovereignty of that state cannot be deprived. For example, China was unjustifiably deprived of its membership in the United Nations, yet China still acted as a fully sovereign state.

The delegation of authority and power of sovereign states to a multilateral agent can take various forms. In one form it consists of fulfilling the legal obligations set by treaties. By accepting the UN Charter, for example, UN members are under obligation to settle disputes by peaceful means, to refrain from the threat or use of force against the territorial integrity and political independence of any state, to refrain from giving assistance to any states against which the United Nations is taking preventive or enforcement action, and to ensure that nonmember states act in accordance with the Charter's principles. The UN members have delegated authority on all these matters to the United Nations because they entrust to the United Nations the job of maintaining international peace and security. As a sovereign state, any UN member state has the right and power to make war on its adversary but is willing to forgo this right because it has entrusted to the UN the task of settling its dispute with its adversary.

A second form of delegation of power and authority is a voluntary action taken by states involved in an international dispute or conflict. For instance, in all the three wars fought in the Middle East between Israel and the Arab states, the states directly involved, which were members of the UN, eventually accepted the intervention of the United Nations by giving consent to the dispatch of UN peacekeeping operations to the fighting areas—specifically, the United Nations Truce Supervision Organization, the First United Nations Emergency Forces, and the Second United Nations Emergency Forces. The United Nations acted upon and in accordance with the requests of the member states and the decisions of the Security Council.

A third form of delegation involves a formal request for UN action by one or more UN member states or by the Secretary-General. This is actually a request to the multilateral institution to employ the authority and power delegated to it by member states through formal agreements. The member states that raise such requests are also signatories of the agreements. Even though they may not be the parties directly concerned, they can take the action in the absence of a request from the parties that *are* directly concerned. Some of the UN peacekeeping operations, such as the United Nations Protection Force in the former Yugoslavia, have been initiated in this manner. In any case, what matters most in both multilateral diplomacy and multilateral institutions is the authority and power of sovereign states.

The founding of the UN marked a major turning point in modern international relations. It gave definition and a new direction to the international political system, which had just emerged from a devastating world war. It embodied the post–World War II world order based on the principles of the sovereign equality of states and nonintervention[4], the right to self-determination of territories under colonial rule, and respect for fundamental human rights. These principles were the underpinning of postwar multilateral diplomacy.

However, the postwar world had other features that distorted the international system and weakened state sovereignty. Soon after World War II ended, the alliance that won the war and created the UN broke down, a breakdown dividing the world into two adversarial camps of states and resulting in the fifty-year Cold War. A bipolar system of international relations was established with the United States leading a bloc of states in the West and the Soviet Union dominating another bloc in the East. These opposing "alliances" were defined by competing ideologies and distinct political and economic systems. International order was maintained by the military, political, and economic organizations of the respective blocs. And the peace was maintained by a precarious balance of power and mutual nuclear deterrence. Multilateral diplomacy reflected the ideologically colored and bloc-oriented behavior of states. The United Nations, too, was significantly affected by bloc politics, this effect limiting its utility for multilateral diplomacy and its effectiveness as a center for harmonizing the actions of sovereign states.

Multilateral diplomacy during the Cold War was significantly affected by the success of decolonization and the introduction of newly independent states into the international state system. Although recognized as sovereign states when they became members of the United Nations, these states were swept into the bloc politics of the Cold War, even though most of them were politically and economically underdeveloped and still dependent on other states. Their numerical superiority in the United Nations could not help them overcome their underdevelopment and the external dependencies that limited their sovereignty. Many of them had not undergone the essential state-building process before achieving independence. Western nation-state structures were grafted onto wholly different cultures. They were sustained by one side and then the other in the

Cold War, while outside military support was provided by one bloc or the other for strategic reasons (Childers and Urquhart 1994, 16). The bloc system categorized states. There were superpowers, satellite states or "henchmen" states, and developing states. Multilateral diplomacy became a complex pattern of interaction among and between groups of sovereign states—the Western, capitalist bloc; the Eastern, socialist bloc; and the so-called nonaligned, developing, Third World bloc—where sovereign states were legally equal, but practically very different.

The massive changes in the international political system when the Cold War ended appear to have convinced some scholars that the Western concept of the nation-state is beginning to erode, that key socioeconomic processes which operate beyond a state's control should be managed multilaterally, and that gradual limitations, abridgments, and cessions of sovereignty have been brought about (Childers and Urquhart 1994, 16–18). The implication is that there have been changes in the definition of sovereignty as a legal norm. But if the changes in the world have had a significant impact on states' ability to exercise their authority in the world, they do not and cannot alter (or diminish) their sovereignty in the legal sense. Former UN Secretary-General Boutros Boutros-Ghali clearly recognized this fact when he commented, "Respect for [the state's] fundamental sovereignty and integrity is crucial to any common international progress. The time of absolute and exclusive sovereignty, however, has passed; its theory was never matched by reality" (Boutros-Ghali 1992, 9). If sovereignty is undermined, then multilateral diplomacy has been undermined and the present world political system is destined to disintegrate, giving rise to widespread confusion and violence, perhaps even a another world conflagration.

Post–Cold War Multilateral Diplomacy

The end of the Cold War introduced considerable uncertainty in international relations and caused confusion in multilateral diplomacy. The collapse of the bipolar, ideologically defined international political structure and the accelerated forces of economic globalization brought to the surface conflicts and problems within states, which had been contained or suppressed by the Cold War. The United Nations was at a loss on how to respond to these new and unexpected problems. All indications seemed to suggest that the concept of sovereignty was outdated, the "erosion" of sovereignty was accelerating, and the sovereign state system was expected to change. It appeared that we had entered a period not only of "relative" sovereignty, but of "withering" sovereignty as well.

But on closer examination, a different interpretation is possible. Based on the analysis made by Erskine Childers and Brian Urquhart, there are four kinds of conflicts that have emerged since the end of the Cold War:

1. Civil wars that were left over from the Cold War and in which the superpowers had been actively involved, such as the civil wars in Afghanistan and Angola.

2. Ethnic conflicts that were held in limbo during the Cold War and erupted afterward, often fueled by the stockpiles of weapons the Cold War left behind, like the tragedies in Somalia and Rwanda.

3. Internal cultural and ethnic strife in the former Soviet Union that had been suppressed by Moscow but that now, in the absence of such restraint, has flared up (i.e., the conflict over the Nagorno-Karabakh region of Azerbaijan and the conflict in Abkhazia in the northwestern region of Georgia).

4. Hitherto quiescent conflict among communities that are now invoking the same right to self-determination as the former republics of the Soviet Union. The conflict in the former Yugoslavia is a good example.

In my opinion, these internal conflicts and civil wars reflect states' "deficient national structures and capabilities"(Boutros-Ghali 1992, 33), the result of the weakening of sovereignty during the Cold War period. Although the United Nations had dealt with intrastate conflicts during the Cold War—for example, the internal conflict in the newly independent Congo in 1960—these conflicts were limited in scale and, on the whole, were managed in accordance with the UN principles and international law. The majority of intrastate conflicts today are transitional and exceptional events for which there is little or no international law available to guide the reactions of sovereign states or multilateral institutions. No one knows for certain whether intrastate conflicts endanger international peace and security, whether foreign intervention can really solve the trouble, and whether such conflicts can be dealt with in accordance with the established UN principles and international law. But it is quite clear that "civil wars are no longer civil, and the carnage they inflict will not let the world remain indifferent."[5]
In recent years, proposals (and even action in a few situations) for restructuring international relations that fly in the face of the principle of sovereignty have emerged. The proposal that gained the greatest currency

within the international community was to recast intrastate conflicts (civil wars and internal strife) as threats to international peace and security, a status that had been reserved for conflicts between states. If intrastate conflicts were viewed in this light, foreign intervention could be justified in the name of maintaining international peace and security. This would amount to a reconceptualization of "threats to the peace." It is a far cry from the UN Charter's current notion of such threats and would change the purposes of the United Nations (Sellers 1996, 239).

Strictly speaking, intervention in intrastate conflicts has nothing to do with maintaining peace among sovereign states, which is the goal of the United Nations, although such interventions are peace-related (Kaufmann 1994, 2). Essentially, the role the United Nations has been asked to play in situations of internal strife or conflict is "to compensate for the shortage of (positive) sovereignty"[6] (Jackson 1990, 26–31), for an immaturity in the state-building process. The conflicts within a number of newly independent states of the former Soviet Union and states-in-transition in Eastern and Central Europe are basically state-building problems that cannot be resolved by the United Nations through traditional peacekeeping operations or the so-called second-generation peacekeeping operations that have been developed since the Cold War (NIIS 1994). As these internal conflicts are, at most, peace-related, they cannot be settled by UN peacekeeping, peace building, and peacemaking.

Furthermore, the United Nations lacks the authority and the capabilities to undertake state building or to assist in the transition to so-called liberal democracy.[7] Democratic institution building is certainly an important issue for each sovereign state. But it is the internal affair of the states concerned and should not be imposed upon them from outside. If the grafting of Western state structures onto different cultures has caused internal conflicts (as it most certainly did throughout Africa and Asia during the Cold War years), the imposition of Western liberal democracy upon states of different historical background now can create even more trouble. It is inappropriate and even dangerous to transform the United Nations into a tool for expanding "Western" democracy.

Likewise, it is wrong to turn human rights, which has always been a domestic matter, into an international peace and security issue and grounds for invoking UN enforcement action—so-called humanitarian intervention. Heretofore, UN intervention in the area of human rights has been largely related to decolonization and supporting the right of self-determination of the peoples under colonial rule. It is widely accepted that self-determination is "an essential condition for the effective guarantee and observance of individual rights" (Sellers 1996, 1). It was not randomly applied lest it cause global disorder. If human rights now is seen as an issue affecting peace and security in the world, this new perspective can also cause great disturbance. With this in mind, the UN General Assembly has adopted a number of resolutions since its forty-third session that affirm the right of populations affected by conflict and strife within states to humanitarian assistance, but that preserve the principle of the requirement of state consent to such assistance.

The United Nations is still an international organization of sovereign states; it is not authorized under the current Charter to help or intervene in state building, and multilateral diplomacy among sovereign states is not suited to intervene in such matters either. The failures on the ground and the internal divisions in the Security Council in connection with operations in Somalia, the former Yugoslavia, and Rwanda bear this out. This is the dilemma the post–Cold War United Nations and multilateral diplomacy are facing.

In principle, however, the United Nations and multilateral diplomacy can help relieve some of the pain of states in crisis or in transition to new political and economic systems. Since the United Nations by itself cannot choose the role of directorate or the right to turn states into protectorates, it can only seek to create a favorable environment for the positive transition of these states. The goal is to make them fully effective sovereign members of the United Nations and of the international society of states. When facilitating these kinds of transitions, the United Nations cannot display any hint of taking away sovereign rights from these states. On the contrary, respect for sovereignty must be ensured. Therefore, UN member states must develop appropriate approaches that will balance sovereignty and self-determination, sovereignty and humanitarian assistance, and sovereignty and institution building. The proper handling of these fundamental relationships is a challenge to the post–Cold War United Nations and multilateral diplomacy.

Rather than an indication of the erosion of state sovereignty, the conflicts within some states since the end of the Cold War signal the weakening and distorting of sovereignty and the sovereign state system during the Cold War period and the urgent need to compensate for it. The yearning of states suffering from internal troubles and of the peoples afflicted is for full sovereignty and genuine sovereign statehood so that they can play their effective roles in the society of nations. For them, this is not a time of "relative" sovereignty; it is a time of "revitalizing" sovereignty. To meet the needs of post–Cold War world, the United Nations must act more effectively as an organization of sovereign states. It is the sovereign member states of the United Nations alone that will decide how the UN adapts itself to the new situation.

Globalization and Multilateral Diplomacy

Globalization, an extremely complex phenomenon that is most evident in the development of today's global economy, is another factor of the post–Cold War world that is thought to undermine sovereignty and to cause the breakdown of the sovereign state system. It has become platitudinous to say that the growth of a global economy is changing institutions fundamental to effective governance and accountability in the modern state (Sassen 1996, xi). Opposite trends are apparently playing out at the same time; disintegration and integration are happening almost in parallel. Although some people see them as contradictory, actually these trends are two sides of the same coin.

Globalization magnifies shortages of sovereignty and, at the same time, enhances the capabilities of sovereign states. The growth of the global economy has brought about cross-border flows of production factors—capital and labor—which diminish the relevance of a bordered territory and a settled population to the definition of sovereign states. National borders are no longer an obstacle to the movement of capital around the world, which now happens almost instantaneously. And barriers to the international movement of labor are slowly being dismantled, too. At the same time, the global economy makes the actions of a sovereign state more dependent on events outside its territory and the actions of other states—as the 1997–1998 upheaval in Southeast Asia's financial markets demonstrates—and accentuates the economic differences that exist between states, often leading to conflicts. So even as the forces of globalization are limiting the effectiveness of the government of a sovereign state, the same state's increasing integration into the global economy is enhancing its capability to provide socioeconomic well-being for its citizens. International trade and foreign investment are increasingly important economic tools for sovereign states to achieve economic growth and prosperity.

Saskia Sassen contends that defining the nation-state and the global economy as mutually exclusive entities is highly problematic, that the strategic spaces where many global processes take place are often national, and that sovereignty and territory remain key features of the international system. Sassen points out that the mechanism through which the new legal forms necessary for globalization are implemented by and often part of state institutions, that the infrastructure that makes possible the hypermobility of financial capital at the global scale is situated in various national territories, and that the condition of the nation-state cannot be reduced to one of declining significance—even though sovereignty may be "decentered" and territory partly "denationalized" (Sassen 1996, 27–28). Globalization may push sovereign states to delegate more authority and power to multilateral institutions, but it certainly does not mean that sovereign states will be gradually swallowed up by globalization.

Conflicts caused by globalization simply mirror the growing economic disparities that exist among sovereign states. These conflicts have reached the point where new rules and norms are needed to regulate today's global economy. The future well-being of the international state system depends on successfully closing the economic gap between three groups of states:

the developed economies, the newly developed economies, and the developing economies. In order to achieve this, multilateral cooperation must be strengthened. This will become, if it isn't already, the primary job of multilateral diplomacy.

Conflicts in post–Cold War international relations and globalization have brought the issue of "shortages of sovereignty" to the forefront. Although it is the task of the sovereign states concerned to remedy this problem, multilateral institutions, particularly the United Nations, have an important role to play in this regard. Of course, the UN and other multilateral institutions need to be reformed in order to act as the effective agents of sovereign states in the post–Cold War world and to mitigate the consequences of globalization. Reforming the United Nations to meet the global challenges today and in the future will require that sovereign states delegate more authority and power to multilateral institutions. Sovereign states will do this more readily and effectively if they are not rendered "short" of sovereignty. In the end, world order today and in the twenty-first century depends upon the effective functioning of sovereign states. This is the challenge of multilateral diplomacy now and in the future.

Notes

1. The author expresses his thanks to Allen Carlson, a Ph.D. candidate at Yale University, for his comments on an earlier draft of this essay when he was in Beijing teaching and working on his dissertation.

2. A similar situation existed in the East. In China, the feudal emperors were regarded as sons of heaven. All the land under heaven belonged to them, and all the people living on the land were their subjects.

3. Emmerich de Vattel made this point in his book *Le Droit des Gens (The Law of Nations)* in 1758.

4. It is important to note that these two principles have been the foundation of international relations since the Treaty of Westphalia in 1648.

5. Secretary-General Boutros Boutros-Ghali, opening statement to the meeting at the level of heads of state and government of the Security Council, New York, January 31, 1992.

6. Jackson uses the right of nonintervention as a standard to distinguish positive sovereignty from negative sovereignty, describing the former as the freedom to deter intervention and the latter as freedom from intervention. In my view what matters is the capabilities of a sovereign state. These capabilities constitute properties of sovereign states, the shortage of which is, of course, the shortage of sovereignty as an empirical reality.

7. Phillipe Ch. A. Guillot argues the opposite in this regard in his essay "Human Rights, Democracy, and the Multidimensional Peace Operations" (Sellers 1996, 298).

References

Boutros-Ghali, Boutros. (1992) *An Agenda for Peace* (New York: United Nations).

Childers, Erskine and Brian Urquhart. (1994) *Renewing the United Nations System* (Uppsala, Sweden: Dag Hammarskjold Foundation).

Hehir, Bryan. (1996) "The Uses of Force in the Post Cold War World." Presentation delivered at a conference at the Woodrow Wilson Center, June 3, Princeton, N.J.

Jackson, Robert H. (1990) *Quasi-States: Sovereignty, International Relations and the Third World* (Cambridge: Cambridge University Press).

James, Alan. (1986) *Sovereign Statehood, The Basis of International Society* (London: Allen & Unwin).

Kaufmann, Johann. (1994) *The Evolving United Nations: Principles and Realities* (Providence, R.I.: Academic Council for the United Nations System).

Kelsen, Hans. (1945) *General Theory of Law and State* (Cambridge: Cambridge University Press).

Netherlands Institute of International Relations (NIIS). (1994) *Case Studies in Second Generation UN Peaecekeeping* (Clingendael: NIIS).

Sassen, Saskia. (1996) *Losing Control? Sovereignty in an Age of Globalization* (New York: Columbia University Press).

Sellers, Mortimer, ed. (1996) *The New World Order: Sovereignty, Human Rights and the Self-Determination of Peoples* (Washington, D.C.: Berg, Oxfors).

Streeten, Paul. (1992) *Monographs on International Governance* (UK: IDS, University of Sussex Silver Jubilee Papers).

Wang Shengzu, ed. (1995) *History of International Relations* (in Chinese). (Beijing: World Culture Press).

NEW DIRECTIONS OF MULTILATERAL DIPLOMACY

The Changing Roles of State and Nonstate Actors in Diplomatic Practice

Richard Langhorne

Introduction

Multilateral diplomacy is not new in itself. Its contemporary scale, how-ever, is and so is its significance. Any quick glance at the dialogues taking place on the global stage will show that the actors are now a large cast of very varied characters all exercising some kind of power and influence. The variety comes from two main sources: First, some of the characters are property owners—they have a territorial existence—but others are not and derive their significance from what they stand for and not where they sit. Another way of putting this is to say that some of the actors are states, or the governments of states, and some of them are not. Those that are not may be global organizations made up of a combination of states but having an independent role to play; others are transnational and represent ideas or causes; still others are equally transnational and provide humanitarian aid or other social relief. The second source of variety stems from the wide disparities of physical size and scope of activity, which apply to both kinds of actor. Entities which can be called states range from the barely functional to the United States, and nonstate actors range from the smallest provider of humanitarian aid to the global reach and power of the human rights defender, Amnesty International—to give just one example. This situation is bound to raise the significance of exchanges between these parties, and one of the commonest forms—though not the only one—of such exchanges is multilateral diplomacy.

Evolution

What has happened to bring about the contemporary change in the quantity and importance of multilateral diplomacy? Essentially three changes have taken and are taking place: First, states are acquiring a different and sometimes lesser scope of action. Second, associations of states are affected by the changing role of their progenitors, and some have begun to move into a more unilateral global role, though remaining multilateral in their construction. Third, the tendency for weak states to collapse into uncontrollable internal conflict has brought a new importance to private organizations offering humanitarian, human rights, and developmental relief. Each of these three changes has been affecting and increasing the conduct of multilateral diplomacy.

In discussing this further, let us ask whether there is any benefit in considering past examples. Associations of bankers the trading interests of the Hanseatic League do provide early examples in Europe of a kind of multilateral system. They, too, shared the stage with rulers and religious centers of power; but they did not share the ease of communication nor receive any significant inheritance from a previously predominant set of methods that characterizes the modern experience, nor did they survive the emergence of the sovereign state. So though they are intrinsically interesting and do give some indication of what can happen when there is a plurality of type among diplomatic actors, they do not represent the origin of the current arrangements. For that, the period of nation-state primacy was crucial.

From the seventeenth century onward, the state became the primary and then the only diplomatic actor in Europe, with the exception of the (persistently declining) Roman Catholic church. During the eighteenth and nineteenth centuries, the modes of behavior of the states system were extended over the rest of the world. The establishment of empires shrank the globe, and the expansion of the United States contributed to the effect. Where this did not happen—in China, Japan, Siam, and Abyssinia—the European norms were nonetheless successfully insisted upon. Where there was reluctance to join in, as in the Ottoman Empire, the requirements of reciprocity enforced compliance. The result was the steady development of an extraordinarily effective system of interstate diplomacy, with a mechanism of almost watchlike complexity, which was designed to serve the needs of a community of sovereign states.

Toward the end of the nineteenth century, the needs of sovereign states began to include the making of transnational arrangements. The cause was the increase of governmental scope and power in the aftermath of the industrial revolution. Developed societies expected to be able to control all sorts of human activities which had formerly been unregulated or just had not existed, and it soon became apparent that, for example, the control of disease required more than national legislation, since disease does not know about frontiers or sovereignty. Diplomacy had thus to accustom itself to the idea and practice that the defense of national sovereignty might in some cases be best achieved if its limitations were actually negotiated with other states. The form that this idea took, at least to begin with, was the emergence of regulating bodies, established by international treaty, administered by international civil servants, who were usually diplomats "borrowed" for the purpose and given powers and methods to resolve disputes. The International Sugar Convention of 1902 gave rise to a ruling body which was given the power actually to punish member states for any transgressions of the treaty. The making and maintaining of such entities involved multilateral diplomacy, and both the nature of states and their international primacy were necessary preconditions for the emergence of multilateral activity. (Pigman 1997)

The age of the dominant state system gave rise in the early twentieth century to a massive collapse of international security, which caused the 1903–1905 war in Asia and the 1914–1918 war in Europe. The shocking slaughter of the conflict brought a determination to end war after 1918, and this led to the establishment of the League of Nations—a multilateral organization created by prior and extensive multilateral diplomacy. It was an association of states and dealt only with states, but it nonetheless produced a sharp growth in the techniques of multilateral diplomacy, both in its dealing with member states and in the activities of its members before, during, and after meetings. In one sense these techniques were familiar from the functioning of the international administrative bodies set up in the preceding seventy-five years, but their overtly high political role at Geneva gave them a more significant place in the diplomatic armory than before. Other contemporary problems had similar and additional effects. Efforts at disarmament, attempts to resolve both the political and practical problems surrounding reparations payments or nonpayments, the related issues over the repayment of US wartime loans, and the need to combat the Great Depression after 1931—all extended both the resort to and the scope of multilateral diplomacy. Through all these events, the parties to multilateral negotiations were more-or-less universally states.

Nor did this change with the onset of the 1939–1945 war. The conduct of the war, like that of its predecessor and the wars against Napoleon of 1792–1814, involved a high degree of multilateral negotiation and planning, more on the Allied than the German or Japanese sides in the twentieth-century examples. The range of topics and activities grew more complex: Intelligence, funding the war, and justifying the war to publics that had now become, often tragically, full parties to the conflict all required attention as much as the strategy and tactics of actual fighting. In all this, the Red Cross remained the only party which was neither a state nor an association of states, having a separate, treaty-given, position in world politics. Much the same followed after the war. Setting up the United Nations was certainly intended to bring a more powerful multilateral institution into play, which would be host to many subsets for specific purposes, but its position as a creature of states was clearly spelled out, and it was plainly not anticipated in 1945 that the end of the global primacy of states was approaching. No provision was made for such a momentous change, and it is easy to see why not. The postwar period and the onset of the Cold War produced both military and nonmilitary multilateral bodies such as NATO, South East Asia Treaty Organization (SEATO), Central Treaty Organization (CENTO) briefly, the Warsaw Pact, the Council for Mutual Economic Assistance or Comecon, the OECD, the Western European Union (WEU), the Coal and Steel Community, the EEC, ASEAN, and the OAS, just to name a few. These, too, were associations of states. As they came and went—Africa saw many failed attempts to set up multilateral bodies—and the Cold War ran its course, other developments were quietly occurring which were to change the picture dramatically. (Hamilton and Langhorne 1995)

Contemporary Change

The chief propellant of change was a revolution in the technology of communications, and the consequences were so important for multilateral diplomacy that it is worth charting them carefully. Globalization has been the consequence of this revolution and is the latest stage in a long accumulation of technological advance which has given human beings the ability to conduct their affairs across the world without reference to nationality, government authority, time of day, or physical environment. These activities may be commercial, financial, religious, cultural, social, or political; nothing is barred. Technological advances in global communications have made globalization possible, and the fact of globalization itself is to be seen in the contemporary surge in human activities conducted globally. The effects of these activities on the whole range of humanity's expectations, systems, and structures have been and are a heady mixture: They have come and keep coming at different paces in different places; sometimes they create entirely new significant activities, sometimes they share them with older systems and structures; sometimes they induce adaptation, and sometimes they erode and destroy. They represent both opportunities and threats (Langhorne 2000).

For multilateral diplomacy the chief significance of this revolution lies in its external consequences. The relative position of states is weakened and some states collapse. A general condition that weakens states will weaken their associations also, unless those associations take on a new role, independent, or more independent, of their progenitors, as single actors on the global stage. This evolution can already be seen in the World Bank, the IMF, and the WTO which now look less like multilateral institutions than they once did as they respond to public pressures derived from anxiety about the management and distributive fairness of the global economy. These public pressures are instructive in themselves, for they originate in the perception, sometimes instinctive rather than worked out, that states and their governments are no longer able to control global economic and financial movements satisfactorily, either separately or in combination. The global political environment induced by this situation has begun to see alternatives to the state emerge in some areas of activity, and these alternatives are generally multilateral both in their internal arrangements and in their external relationships. The reason is either changing roles among pre-existing multilateral entities or the development of entirely new roles. As will now be seen, states have to respond differently to their interlocutors, new ways of handling multilaterality develop in both old and new multilateral entities, and the very nature of contemporary problems leads to a rising significance for multilateral responses.

Multilateral Economic Institutions (MEIs) and Diplomacy

After World War II the governments of the victorious powers established what was to have been a trio of MEIs to manage and administer key aspects of what had become an increasingly global economy, whose mismanagement in the 1930s was held to have been partly responsible for the rise of fascism. In the case of the so-called Bretton Woods twins, the International Monetary Fund was to handle monetary relations, and the World Bank Group, comprising a family of MEIs, was to encourage development. The intended International Trade Organization would have supervised international trade. The latter did not emerge until the GATT became the World Trade Organization in the mid-1990s. These three institutions together have dominated the field of nonstate economic entity (NSEE) activity, involve the largest number of member governments, and are engaged in the lion's share of NSEE-government diplomacy. Power within them has been weighted in favor of the largest stakeholders.

Other, more specialized institutions were also created. Regional development banks such as the Asian Development Bank, the Inter-American Development Bank, and the European Bank for Reconstruction and Development, paralleled the focus of the World Bank for their respective regions, but with power distributed more substantially to the recipient governments. Functionally specialized economic agencies of the United Nations, such as the UN Conference on Trade and Development (UNCTAD), the UN Development Program (UNDP), and the UN Educational, Scientific, and Cultural Organization (UNESCO), concentrated on particular, usually development-related, economic objectives. These agencies developed their own politics, institutional character and sense of mission, mechanisms of decisionmaking, and diplomatic channels. They operated more on the principle of members' voting equally, contrasting with the Bretton Woods method of weighted voting power according to capital contribution, and as a result, they had a wider constituency. Another type of NSEE is represented by the OECD, which is knowledge-generating and consultative, though it might have developed more direct functions had its proposed Multilateral Agreement on Investment been agreed on. The World Economic Forum (WEF), particularly since it broadened its invitation list following public protests that it helped to perpetuate global economic unfairness, has become a good example of the knowledge-generating, consultative NSEE but, in this case, entirely nongovernmental in its procedures and funding. The International Chamber of Commerce (ICC) was founded in 1919 and is a further important example. It promotes free flows of trade and capital, and it has taken up issues as different as war debts and reparations and curbing protectionism. The ICC provides a range of services to members, including panels of experts on areas such as intellectual property rights, taxation, and competition law, and in 1923 the ICC established the International Court of Arbitration to help member businesses resolve commercial disputes. In the 1980s the ICC introduced mechanisms to combat international commercial crime, and in the 1990s it produced standards of practice for sustainable development that have been widely endorsed.

These institutions require regularized working relationships with member country governments. The professional staffs of the MEIs in particular were often drawn from the foreign services of member states or else from finance ministries or other appropriate agencies. But NSEEs from the outset took seriously the need to construct their own professional, and hence diplomatic, identities by such measures as establishing rigid nationality quota systems for employment and setting higher employment standards than member governments in areas such as linguistic ability. In doing so they created a cosmopolitan cadre that came to differentiate itself and its objectives from the staffs of the governments from which many of its members originated.

Although NSEEs are fundamentally different from nation-states in their character, organization, and purpose, the evolving complexities of intergovernmental diplomacy affect NSEE representation to governments equally. Most NSEEs have small, relatively centralized professional staffs that tend to represent themselves as and where the need arises. In many organizations, the great majority of the professional staffs function as diplomats, either formally or informally, at least in the information-gathering and communications tasks. In terms of the institutional organization of representation, among the diverse range of NSEEs the MEIs are the most likely to represent themselves to governments through permanent or ongoing missions. MEI missions to and in client countries—developing countries—are the most similar to permanent diplomatic legations of governments. Annual general meetings of the World Bank, the IMF, and regional development banks, WTO ministerial conferences, WEF Davos Summits and the ICC World Council—these are analogous to intergovernmental summits.

The emergence of communications networks built around Internet communications has made it much easier for all sorts of other nonstate entities, ranging from global firms to NGOs, to interact with NSEEs directly, bypassing the state institutions that would previously have represented civil society interests at NSEEs. Intensive lobbying, publicity campaigns, and protest activities have forced MEIs to reconsider policies and change actual diplomatic procedures—for example, the location and timing of meetings, and security. The protests against the WTO at its 1999 Seattle conference not only forced delays and changes in the proposed multilateral trade round but also brought about changes in the way that the WTO and other NSEEs publicize themselves and their activities. The WEF has reacted similarly.

MEI representation to governments has also changed as particular MEIs have been reformed. In the case of the GATT/WTO, diplomacy between nation-states over international trade issues was institutionalized in a particular way by the political process that led to its creation and early development, particularly because the ad hoc GATT secretariat was perceived as weak relative to nation-state governments. However, the GATT-led process of trade liberalization helped to trigger a structural change in the global economy and thus changed the perceived identities and interests of GATT member governments, particularly in the form of a shift among major developing countries toward more protrade liberalization positions. This structural change in turn led to a transformation of the institution and its processes through the creation of the WTO, with its strengthened secretariat and its one-country–one-vote with supermajorities decisionmaking mechanism, which brought about a real redistribution of political power (Pigman 2003).

Contemporary Conflicts and Multilateral Diplomacy

A changing relationship between states and nonstate actors does not stop at economic issues and institutions. The factors contributing to a weakening of state authority discussed earlier can in some cases become structurally destructive. Those states which evolved over time have been altered by what has happened and, in some of their former roles, reduced in function. But for those states which have much shorter histories and arose as deliberate creations, only because no other form of organization for human society was conceivable, have suffered much more and in several important cases have collapsed entirely. It is in the consequences of these collapses that the most significant developments in multilateral diplomacy have occurred. The resulting violence has been particularly uncontrolled and cruel, thus engaging the world's attention via CNN and like disseminating media, and it is internal conflict which has become characteristic. So much is this the case that it has become commonplace to observe that traditional interstate conflict has been largely supplanted by communal warfare—in Africa, the Caucasus, the Balkans, and South and Southeast Asia. Dealing with these outbreaks has not been easy either for states, local or distant, or for international organizations because their traditional stances and in some cases their charters do not envisage this type of conflict. Into the breach have stepped private organizations whose justification for intervention lies in their mission to relieve humanitarian disasters, encourage economic development, or defend human rights, not to keep international order or preserve or restore peace. All of these missions are trampled on when civil strife develops. This kind of activity, however, is new for such organizations because their missions cannot be accomplished as an aid to an existing public administration and government, which was the familiar pattern, because both are likely to have collapsed. This means either providing alternative governance themselves or constantly negotiating with others to achieve at least enough of it to carry on. Inevitably, because of the different functions that private organizations exist to perform, there has to be a multilateral approach among them, and the commonly found surrounding political chaos—the remains of collapsed governments, would-be governments, warlords, neighbors, international organizations, former colonial proprietors are all likely contributors—means that the entities with which private organizations must deal are themselves multilateral to the highest degree. Here is where the formerly stable concept that multilaterality occurs among states or bodies set up by them has evolved into something much more complicated, reflecting the complexities of the global political and economic situation itself.

Given the complications, it is no surprise to find that recent humanitarian crises from Rwanda onward have yielded flurries of multilateral diplomacy on-site, in other countries, and at the UN. During the Rwanda crisis, for example, the private organizations involved removed themselves at one point to a conference in Amsterdam and excluded the UN from participation. At other times, the UN, in addition to responding structurally by recognizing private organizations, has constantly had to initiate multilateral activities, particularly at the instigation of special representatives of the Secretary-General. But it should be remembered that not all the actions of private organizations are multilateral even if most must be. Médecins sans Frontières (MSF) and the Red Cross have both found themselves having to deal in the most bilateral way with groups that have murdered and/or kidnapped their staff.

It is probable that the most striking increase in both quantity and type of multilateral diplomacy by nonstate actors occurs in humanitarian and human rights disasters, but it is by no means the only area of expansion. The considerable history of global "summits" on social and environmental issues is a case in point. The tag is an extraordinary tribute to the importance attached to them, since nothing less like a summit, at least as they became known after World War II, can be imagined than these vast multilateral assemblages of governments, private organizations, and sometimes even individual participants. They have largely ceased in recent years, partly because of the sheer difficulty of handling them, but more because the lack of any administrative power behind them has meant that governments have been seen to be responsible for implementing their conclusions, such as they might be, and have not done so, either for national reasons, or out of practical impossibility. This problem is undoubtedly going to persist, as it does in the area of global economic management, because of the insufficient development of effective representative capacity by nonstate actors, so that their diplomatic activity regularly falls short of their intrinsic importance and their ability to monitor decisions or to implement policy change is either slight or nonexistent. There are exceptions in the environmental field, where global environmental organizations have taken on the task of monitoring the decisions arising out of the Rio and Kyoto conferences (Langhorne 2000).

Thus, there is a situation in which there has to be multilateral diplomacy, but its results can be frustratingly evanescent, which may lead to an increase in the already significant amount of public protest on the streets, particularly associated with global social and economic governance. Despite the highly traditional format, if not motivation, of the war in Iraq, it is the interface within and between multilateral entities and the global community of states which is providing the most forceful evolution in contemporary diplomacy, and the results will be of profound importance for institutions of every type as well as individual human beings.

References

Cooper, Andrew and Brian Hocking. (2000) "Governments, Non-Governmental Organisations and the Re-Calibration of Diplomacy," *Global Society*, Vol. 14, No. 3, pp. 361–376.

Ford, Jane. (2002) "A Social Theory of Trade Regime Change: GATT to WTO," *International Studies Review*, Vol. 4, No. 3, pp. 115–138.

Gardner, Richard N. (1956) *Sterling-Dollar Diplomacy: Anglo-American Collaboration in the Reconstruction of Multilateral Trade* (Oxford: Clarendon Press).

Hamilton, Keith and Langhorne, Richard. (1995) *The Practice of Diplomacy* (London: Routledge).

Harvey, David. (1990) *The Condition of Postmodernity* (Oxford: Blackwell).

International Chamber of Commerce. (2003) [www.iccwbo.org] Accessed February 22.

International Monetary Fund. (2003) [www.imf.org] Accessed February 22.

Langhorne, Richard. (2000) *The Coming of Globalization*. (New York: Palgrave Macmillan).

_____. (2001) "Winds of Change: Evolving Representations from the European to a World System." Conference paper, International Studies Association Annual Conference, Chicago.

Lee, Donna and David Hudson. (2002) "Globalisation and Diplomacy: A Critical Approach." Conference paper, International Studies Association Annual Conference, New Orleans.

O'Brien, Robert, Anne Marie Goetz, Jan Aart Scholte, and Marc Williams. (2000) *Contesting Global Governance: Multilateral Economic Institutions and Global Social Movements*. (Cambridge: Cambridge University Press).

OneWorld. (2003) "Multilateral Agreement on Investment (MAI) Guides." [www.oneworld.net/guides/MAI]

Pigman, Geoffrey Allen. (1997) "Hegemony and Trade Liberalization Policy: Britain and the Brussels Sugar Convention of 1902," *Review of International Studies*, Vol. 23, April, pp. 185–210.

_____. (2003) "Making Room at the Negotiating Table: The Growth of Diplomacy Between Nation-State Governments and Non-State Economic Entities." Paper given at the International Studies Association Conference, Portland, Ore.

Strange, Susan. (1994) *States and Markets*, 2nd ed. (London: Pinter).

_____. (1996) *The Retreat of the State: The Diffusion of Power in the World Economy*. (Cambridge: Cambridge University Press).

Multilateral Diplomacy and the United Nations in the Aftermath of 9/11

Richard Reitano and Caleb Elfenbein

Prior to the events of September 11, 2001, many American academics, journalists, and policymakers argued with remarkable certainty that globalization pointed to a future in which multilateral cooperation would temper the dominant state-centered model of international relations. September 11 and the other events of the past few years, however, have shown that globalization is not a neat process of increasing international interdependence. In fact, these events, particularly for those living in the United States, have exposed many of the problems exacerbated by globalization:[1] increasing international economic inequality, backlashes against "cultural imperialism," the decreasing ability of states to monitor the transfer of large amounts of capital, and, of course, the proliferation of weapons capable of inflicting tremendous harm on civilian populations and physical infrastructures. Increasingly, groups dissatisfied with, or most adversely affected by, the "new international order" are voicing their opposition outside official institutions, often in response to the domination of those institutions by local elites or by a handful of powerful nations. Although globalization is often understood in terms of the transfer of populations, technology, and culture, as well as increased economic interdependence, it is no longer possible to ignore that globalization also involves the "global-ization of conflict." It is in this context that we will evaluate multilateral diplomacy and the role of the United Nations and other nonstate actors in global politics today.

In September 2002, the Bush administration issued a major foreign pol-icy and defense statement, "The National Security Strategy of the United States of America." In the document, the president observed, "Today the United States enjoys a position of unparalleled military strength and great economic and political influence. . . . The United States will use this mo-ment of opportunity to extend the benefits of freedom across the globe." The document did express support for "multilateral institutions," such as the United Nations, the World Trade Organization, and NATO (Bush 2002, Introduction).[2]

The critics of current US foreign policy argue, however, that the adminis-tration pays only lip service to multilateralism and has extended only tepid support to multilateral institutions and alliances, as well as international agreements. As evidence, they cite the administration's withdrawing from the 1972 ABM Treaty with the Russian government, "unsigning" the Rome Statute creating the International Criminal Court, rejecting the Kyoto Pro-tocol, "gutting" the chemical weapons treaty, disengaging from the Israeli-Palestinian conflict and from the Korean Peninsula until the conflicts became crises, declaring that the absence of German and French support for the war with Iraq reflects the "Old Europe," and, of course, pursuing an essentially unilateral war with Iraq based on a new Bush doctrine of "preemption."

Mr. Bush made it clear in his "National Security Strategy" that "while the United States will constantly strive to enlist the support of the interna-tional community, we will not hesitate to act alone, if necessary, to exercise our right of self-defense" (Bush 2002). When UN Security Council mem-bers expressed opposition to going beyond Resolution 1441 regarding Iraq, Mr. Bush stated that the organization may "fade into history as an ineffec-tive, irrelevant debating society" (quoted by Glennon 2003, 18).[3]

As authority is currently distributed within the United Nations, this very well might be the case. How does this perspective affect the prospects for effective multilateral diplomacy and for a more peaceful world? This ques-tion provides a framework for the discussion that follows.

Critics argue that America's resort to unilateralism is really nothing new, and that Bush is merely restating what has been the dominant model of in-ternational interaction since the inception of the modern state system. Given Bush's words, the old Kantian vision of a more peaceful and stable world based on a compact (or organization) among democratic states clearly *is* in serious trouble.[4] The perception, widely shared in Europe and elsewhere, is that the United States has decided to create a new world order based on American military might and the superiority of American economic power. The United States will promote liberal democratic capitalism as the only model for nations to follow, by persuasion or by force if necessary, ignoring self-determination if the outcome contradicts the American vision for the world.

Others argue, as John Fonte has, that "transnationalism" (or multilateralism) is the "next stage of multicultural ideology." Transnational advocates, according to Fonte, promote "global governance" because they believe the "nation-state and the idea of national citizenship are ill suited to deal with the global problems of the future." He believes that these transnational values, "group consciousness (as defined by international law)," contradict traditional American values, that is, "citizenship, patriotism . . . and the meaning of democracy itself." Consequently, the Bush administration is correct in rejecting "multilateralism" because it fosters ideological values and supports institutions and organizations that undermine the American value system. His greatest fear is that by accepting transnational values, the United States will become "post-constitutional, post-liberal, post-democratic, and post-American" (Fonte 2002, 9). Other scholars, such as Anette Ahrnens, suggest that the multilateral era after World War II was a way of "institutionalizing" American hegemony and that "elements of minilateralism and unilateralism always existed within seemingly multilateral arrangements, as for example, the great power veto in the UN Security Council" (Ahrnens 2003).

Ironically, for over half a century after the end of World War II, the United States was largely responsible for the creation of a world order based on multilateral institutions: the UN and various regional organizations. Many people everywhere relied on the United States for leadership, protection, support, and moral authority. (The Universal Declaration of Human Rights, the 1963 Limited Test Ban Treaty, the 1967 Outer Space Treaty, the 1970 Nuclear Non-Proliferation Treaty, and the Strategic Arms Limitation Treaty (SALT) Agreements and the Strategic Arms Reduction Talks (START) Treaties are only a few examples of US leadership and international cooperation, which have made the world a safer place.) In short, *whether their trust was well-founded or not,* people trusted the United States to do the right thing, and certainly, one of the major casualties of this war with Iraq is trust. And as Charles Kegley and Gregory Raymond observe, "Building trust among a welter of diverse state and non-state actors is crucial for laying the foundation of a just world order" (Kegley and Raymond 2002, 208).[5]

Scholars such as Robert Kagan dismiss this concern by suggesting that Americans are from Mars and Europeans are from Venus when he states, "America has no choice but to act unilaterally" because of a "weak" Europe and an anarchic world. (Kagan 2002, 1)[6] Conservative columnist Charles Krauthammer has written that what the world needs is a "unipolar era" with the United States, of course, at the center of world power (quoted by Daalder and Lindsay 2003, B9). But a "unipolar" world based on America's self-appointed role as "globocop" may produce more resentment, anger, and hostile actions against the United States and its allies and may result in an unintended consequence: more, not less, anarchy in the world.[7] Nevertheless, once the "unipolar" genie is out of the bottle, it may be impossible for the United States, as Michael Glennon suggests, to "resubmit to old constraints in new contexts" (Glennon 2003, 35).

The central question we identify within this debate is as follows: What kind of international society—including nongovernmental organizations, nation-states, and international organizations—is most capable of confronting the myriad of global issues that confront the world today?

The viability of an "international civil society" dealing with global issues necessitates above all else an equal distribution of perspectives. Solutions must come about as compromises, uniting the beliefs of organizations and people from differing traditions and ways of thinking. In many cases, from negotiating international treaties to addressing health and humanitarian crises, NGOs also play an essential role. Although the origins of NGOs have certainly been diversified in recent years, the extent to which they represent a true cross section of cultures and approaches is highly questionable. Many of the better-known organizations are based in the United States or in states with similar traditions. In addition, most NGOs are, at the very least, funded by the "West," and therefore it's questionable whether they can put forth solutions which contradict the "Western" ideal.

Ultimately, the work of nongovernmental organizations and other private-sector actors depends on the extent to which the international community is working toward common ends. Action by those outside the state proper, intergovernmental organizations (IGOs), regional organizations, and NGOs necessitates that governments trust that other states will act in concert, for the implementation of treaties and agreements depends on a regime's willingness to act.

Karen Mingst, Angela Van Berkel, and Margaret P. Karns point out in "Global Governance Meets AIDS" that the AIDS problem in South African demonstrates the importance of states in fighting the epidemic. They argue that neither IGOs nor NGOs had much leverage until the South African government's leadership acknowledged the problem (Mingst, Van Berkel, and Karns 2003). Uganda, by contrast, has been a relative success story in dealing with the AIDS pandemic because of the commitment by the government to work with NGOs, civil society, and other states. The conclusion is an important one: State support is crucial to the resolution of many problems affecting developing nations, and NGOs can accomplish much when the support is there, but their impact is limited when state support is lacking.

In spite of its institutional weaknesses, such as a near-crippling imbalance in the distribution of power, the United Nations is the sole organization capable of coordinating the efforts of "international civil society" in dealing with issues of health, the environment, conflict resolution, and economic development. In order to operate effectively in coordinating sustainable solutions to problems confronting the international community, the UN must be seen as a neutral actor capable of representing common interests.

In brief, we are speaking of the integrity of international law. The body of treaties and conventions that comprise international law attempt to construct a common code of behavior, thus reassuring inherently insecure states that they are safe to let their guard down in the face of international action. In "The False Promise of International Institutions," John Mearsheimer maintains that in the end, states will always act in their own interests, following the maxims of realism: maximizing benefits, while minimizing threats and costs. This point seems to be an accurate description of international relations, particularly Washington's foreign policy; and as the sole remaining superpower, the United States inevitably sets much of the international community's agenda. Nevertheless, US interests are served, more often than not, by acting in concert with allies and NGOs, and by working through IGOs.

With the horizontal proliferation of weapons of mass destruction and the increasing "ease" with which acts of terror are committed, the state still concentrates on security issues. In post–Cold War diplomacy, a stark reality therefore persists: States act in a self-interested fashion. And at times, these actions do coincide with humanitarian and environmental concerns. Consequently, talk of a power shift away from the state toward a decentralized network of essentially private diplomatic agents is quite unrealistic. There is no doubt that NGOs and IGOs do and will play a useful role in future diplomatic efforts, but this part will remain secondary to the traditional role of the state's interests as defined by the pressures existing on the domestic front. Civil society and UN-sponsored conferences will also continue to play an increasingly important role in focusing the world's attention on transnational issues, but the reality is that system transformation, at least for the foreseeable future, is a highly unlikely outcome of the increased participation by nonstate elements in the global political arena.

In 1995, the Fourth World Conference on Women, unofficially known as the Beijing Summit, for example, was convened to focus more specifically on women's rights. The conference produced the Beijing Declaration and the Platform for Action, which "consolidated five decades of legal advances aimed at securing the equality of women [and] built on political agreements reached at three previous global conferences" (United Nations 1996, Introduction). The Beijing summit was notable for several reasons: It was held in China, an appropriate site given the country's record on human rights; it was held in a developing nation where women's rights are more problematic than in developed nations; and it was attended by over thirty thousand delegates. The conference called for concrete actions on the part of governments to deal with issues affecting women, such as poverty, education and training, violence, health care, conflict, and unequal justice and economic standing. The Platform for Action contained specific recommendations for the 189 participating governments on a broad spectrum of problems. Critics accurately observed that although the conference addressed problems from "female genital mutilation" to "equal inheritance," the Platform made it very clear that "all [issues of] human rights and fundamental freedoms" would be evaluated in the context of "various religious and cultural backgrounds" and "the sovereign responsibility of each state" (United Nations 1996, 67–68).

The growth of civil society through the global proliferation of NGOs reflects another major change in the distribution of power and in the uses of multilateral diplomacy. The most widely cited figure is that there are about thirty-five thousand NGOs at work in the world today. As Jessica Mathews concludes, "Increasingly, NGOs are able to push around even the largest governments" (Mathews 1997, 53). The draft treaty banning landmines, agreed to by eighty-nine nations in Oslo in September 1997, is a good example of the increasing political clout exercised by NGOs.

The facts about landmines are indisputable and the consequences are clearly appalling. The International Campaign to Ban Landmines (ICBL), the umbrella NGO, led the successful effort to conclude the agreement signed in Ottawa in December 1997. The ICBL was begun in 1991 by several NGOs: the Vietnam Veterans of America Foundation, Medico International, and a German humanitarian organization. They were joined by other NGOs (about a thousand in all); eventually, Jody Williams, an individual without prior diplomatic experience, was chosen to head the International Campaign. In less than six years, the ICBL played a major role in raising global consciousness about the destructive and indiscriminate nature of landmines and in obtaining the Oslo agreement to ban their use globally. The agreement was achieved despite the opposition of the United States and the refusal of China and Russia (which changed its position) to sign the agreement as well. In October 1997, both the ICBL and Jody Williams were awarded the Nobel Peace Prize. NGOs have been more successful because they can effectively compete now with states in the dissemination of information; and they have become integral players in many government delegations by dispensing advice at international conferences. NGOs proselytize for a cause locally and globally, they monitor the results of any agreement, and they continue to advance other related causes.[8]

More than any other body, the UN also represents a collective counterweight to American power. While there are many who argue that the United States must now continue to use its power "assertively," we are reminded of the American imperial adventure in Vietnam. Minxin Pei recalls the disastrous war in Vietnam based on a "combination of the United States' (then) universalistic political values (anticommunism), triumphalist beliefs in U.S. power, and short national memory"[9] (Pei 2003, 35). The UN must therefore counterbalance those who advocate force as a "better option than diplomacy" (Glennon, 2003, 34). The UN may be unable to prevent the United States from engaging in military adventures, but it can remind the world (and most Americans) that diplomacy and the use of multilateral force are always preferable and that unilateral military force is rarely a long-term solution to even the most difficult global problems.

The UN must be there to pick up the pieces, particularly given the short attention span of many Americans, which is shared by most administrations in Washington. The Bush administration, for example, neglected to include Afghanistan in its 2003–2004 foreign aid requests until members of Congress raised the issue in the media. By all accounts, Afghanistan still has serious political, social, and economic problems, which can be adequately addressed only by appropriate UN agencies through their multicultural career professionals. Although the administration has deferred to the UN in Afghanistan on major nonsecurity problems, it has marginalized the UN's role in postwar reconstruction, mostly because the organization refused to legitimize the US war with Iraq. As the situation continues to remain unstable, however, the United States will rediscover a role for the United Nations to play in the rebuilding of Iraq.

According to the Pew Global Attitudes Project, the Bush administration's "go it alone" policies have had a serious impact on world public opinion and support for the United States, the UN, and even NATO. The project surveyed sixteen thousand people in twenty countries and the Palestinian Authority in May 2003. The conclusions: "The war (with Iraq) has widened the rift between Americans and Western Europeans, further inflamed the Muslim world, softened support for the war on terrorism, and significantly weakened global public support for the pillars of the post–World War II era—the U.N. and the North Atlantic Alliance" (Pew

Research Center 2003, 1).[10] Although there was strong support in the survey for democratic institutions, in all the publics surveyed, it is clear that the Bush doctrine has damaged, either intentionally or unintentionally, the post–World War II (and even post–Cold War) framework that produced what John Lewis Gaddis has called "the long peace," the avoidance of global war since 1945.

The UN must be part of a series of multilateral institutions, which collectively will ensure observance of the rule of law by the international community, decrease the violence that characterizes relations between states and the resolution of conflicts within states, and constrain the American temptation to respond unilaterally to every global crisis. The horrific events of September 11 should have served as a warning that, as the South African journalist Allister Sparks wrote in 1995,

> When people feel desperate, and when they feel their desperation is ignored, they tend to do desperate things to attract attention to their plight. They seize hostages, hijack planes, blow up the World Trade Center in New York. Or they develop apocalyptic visions and turn to religious fanaticism, sometimes with homicidal consequences. And desperate nations throw up fanatical leaders who do desperate things at the national level. (Sparks 1995, 11)

Instead, the Bush administration concluded that "might and right can deliver a world of peace and prosperity for all" (Daalder and Lindsay 2003, B11). The arrogance of power is an overwhelming temptation, especially as Paul Kennedy notes when "being the world's single superpower on the cheap is astonishing" (quoted by Daalder and Lindsay 2003, B11), but it is not a solution to what afflicts this very troubled world that we all must live in so early in the twenty-first century. As Russian president Putin has stated, "The international community has no other, let alone more universal mechanism" than the United Nations for resolving conflicts.

Ted Sorensen, special counsel (and chief speechwriter) for President John F. Kennedy, addressed a graduating class at American University in May 2003. In his remarks he said that the United States' "declared policy of preemptive strikes, without legal justification or evidence, is music to the ears of terrorist organizations that specialize in such strikes; but, if followed worldwide, it will create a lawless planet in which the law abiding will suffer the most" (Sorensen 2003) A world without the UN and a world based on unilateralism is a world where the Russians are free to invade neighboring Georgia because the Russians could claim that Georgia provides safe haven for Chechen terrorists. It is a world where China could invade Vietnam because of "aggression" committed by the Vietnamese against Chinese interests in the Spratly Islands. It is a world where Pakistan or India could stage a first strike against the other with nuclear weapons in order to "prevent" an attack by the other.

A world without the UN or a world where the UN is ignored is a world where unilateral use of force will be the weapon of choice in dealing with any and all global problems. In short, the nature of interaction among countries and the complex nature of global problems require a necessary and pragmatic use of multilateral diplomacy through the UN, and not the dissolution of the Westphalian system. Sorensen reminded the graduates at American University that a president had spoken to another graduating class at AU forty years earlier. The president observed then, "In the final analysis, we all inhabit this small planet. We all breathe the same air. We all cherish our children's future; and we are *all* mortal" (Sorenson 2003). John Kennedy's words are as relevant today as they were in 1963.

In his book *Rogue Nation*, Clyde Prestowitz raises a number of "what if" questions. Instead of the Bush response of "you're with us or against us" after September 11, and if he had not announced a new policy of "preemption," what if he had convened a global conference on the challenges and threats posed by international terrorism to all humanity? What if the United States had really worked with its allies and through the UN to force Saddam Hussein to disarm with verifiable disarmament mechanisms? Would Hussein have survived? Could the United States and Britain have then avoided a war with Iraq? What if the United States had ratified the Kyoto agreement, the treaties creating the International Criminal Court and banning landmines, the antigenocide agreements, and the agreement on the status of women? Would the world be a safer place? What if the United States had attempted to work with North Korean Present Kim Jong-Il to defuse the nuclear crisis on the Korean Peninsula instead of calling North Korea part of the "axis of evil" (Prestowitz 2003, 269–271)? Could the United States avoid unilateral confrontation with the North Koreans? What if the United States had acted cooperatively and multilaterally on all these issues? Would the outcomes have been different? What would the United States have gained? What would the United States have lost?

In *The Atlantic Monthly*, Robert Kaplan offered ten rules for governing the world based on maintaining an American "global empire." The rules include "Emulating Second Century Rome," "Use the Military to Promote Democracy" (an oxymoron), and "Fight on Every Front." The fact that this kind of analysis is being given serious consideration by American journalists (and the media) is an indication of how far the United States has come since September 11. Vietnam is forgotten, Somalia clearly a mistake, and the "quick victory" in Iraq an indication of the role the United States must play in the post-9/11 world. In our judgment, these so-called rules will create more opportunities for global conflict, will diminish whatever support for the United States remains in the world, and will undermine the United Nations, other intergovernmental organizations, other alliances, and the body of treaties and agreements that constitute international law.

Mr. Kaplan's rules are a prescription for a sea change in US foreign policy and for an end to multilateral diplomacy as the essential element in resolving civil, regional, and global conflicts. This US empire may or may not be short-lived, but it will not, as Kaplan maintains, bring "prosperity to distant parts of the world under America's soft imperial influence" (quoted by Prestowitz 2003, 274). As Prestowitz suggests, a US empire will not promote military security for Americans or their allies and clients. It will promote efforts to create countervailing power (one of the fundamental themes in the history of international relations); it will corrupt American character, values, and institutions and the rule of law in the United States; and it will undermine US sovereignty, not reinforce it (Prestowitz 2003, 275–276).

In 1784, Immanuel Kant wrote his essay *Idea for a Universal History from a Cosmopolitan Point of View*. He concluded that "nature has accordingly again used the unsociableness of men, and even of great societies and political bodies, her creatures of this kind, as a means to work out through their mutual Antagonism a condition of rest and Security. She works through wars, through the strain of never relaxed preparation for them. . . . And at last, after many devastations, overthrows, and even complete internal exhaustion of their powers, even without so much sad experience. This is none other than the advance out of the lawless state of savages and the entering into a Federation of Nations" (Hastie 1891, 16). A central assumption in Kant's vision is that people—or nations—will enter into a compact in which common interests prevail. Of course, the possibility of common interests implies cooperation among states in instituting and enforcing the international law resulting from that compact. Without this multilateral approach, the apocalyptic vision implied in Kant's words may very well come true.

Notes

1. Globalization has also been called Americanization by many of its harshest critics.

2. Although "The National Security Strategy of the United States" is a compilation of various speeches by George W. Bush, it is also a blueprint for the new doctrine of "preemption." In one of the speeches, "Strengthen Alliances to Defeat Global Terrorism," delivered on September 14, 2002, President Bush states, "We will disrupt and destroy terrorist organizations by . . . defending the United States, the American people, and our interests at home by identifying and destroying the

threat before it reaches our borders. While the United States will constantly strive to enlist the support of the international community, we will not hesitate to act alone, if necessary, to exercise our right of self-defense by acting preemptively against such terrorists." This is essentially the basis for the doctrine of preemptive war, which was used to justify the war with Iraq.

3. Michael J. Glennon's "Why the Security Council Failed" (2003) is a powerful argument in favor of the continuing use of American power. He argues that "the use of force was a better option than diplomacy in dealing with tyrants, from Milosevic to Hitler. It may, regrettably, sometimes emerge as the only and therefore the best way to deal with WMD proliferation. . . . That the world is at risk of cascading disorder places a greater rather than a lesser responsibility on the United States to use its power assertively to halt or slow the pace of disintegration." He also argues for a new "institutional framework" to replace the UN Security Council, which failed to deal with Saddam Hussein and Iraq's WMDs.

4. "Every State," Immanuel Kant wrote, "even the smallest, must thus rely for its safety and its rights, not on its own power, nor on its own judgment of right, but only on . . . the combined power of this league of states, and on the decision of the common will according to laws" (Kant, *Perpetual Peace*).

5. Kegley and Raymond offer a very powerful argument regarding the importance of "trust" in international politics. They believe that "limited cooperation can take place without trust, and treachery can occur among those who trust each other; however, building international trust is critical if we are to move beyond the . . . competitive system of politics that arose in the wake of Westphalia" (Kegley and Raymond 2002, 205). Certainly, distrust of the United States is at an all-time high. Russian president Vladimir Putin, for example, recently observed in an address, "Strong and well-armed national armies are used not to combat . . . terrorism . . . but to expand certain countries' zones of strategic influence" (Myers 2003, A3).

6. "Power and Weakness" by Robert Kagan is an indictment of Europe's weakness. Europeans criticize the United States for its "culture of death" but benefit from the uses of US power and influence throughout the world. He maintains Europeans "lacked the wherewithal to introduce and sustain a fighting force in potentially hostile territory. . . . The real division of labor (as some Europeans put it) consisted of the 'United States making the dinner' and the Europeans 'doing the dishes'" (Kagan 2002, 5).

7. Criticisms of the United Nations abound regarding the various peacekeeping activities that the UN has undertaken, especially those ordered since the end of the Cold War. The critics charge that the Security Council has acted irresponsibly because peacekeeping operations are decided without adequate consideration of finances, logistics, soldiers (numbers and the states providing them), and, most important, the mission. The arguments deserve to be taken seriously because of so-called mission expansion (or mission creep, according to the US military), which has caused serious problems and has resulted in casualties in countries such as Somalia

and the former Yugoslavia. In brief, many critics are uncomfortable with this aspect of multilateral diplomacy because they believe that these missions often lack the necessary political, diplomatic, financial, and moral support to succeed. The critics also point out that without support by the United States, the only remaining superpower, these missions face an uncertain future in a very dangerous world. In defense of the United Nations, former Secretary-General Boutros Boutros-Ghali states that "mandates given to the United Nations itself [must] be clear, realistic, and backed by the human resources required to complete the assigned task successfully" (Boutros-Ghali 1996, 95). He decries the tendency to "scapegoat" the organization and observes that "member states cannot use the United Nations to avoid a problem and then blame the United Nations for failing to solve [it]" (Boutros-Ghali 1996, 95). Those views are echoed by many who point out that the missions assigned to the UN are often complex. They do not lend themselves, therefore, to easy solutions, particularly given the increasing demands on the UN, the decreasing resources available to carry out its activities, and the inadequate political authority to make decisions truly binding on all member states.

8. John Fonte also describes the key concepts of transnationalism, the foundation for NGOs, as "the ascribed group over the individual . . .   A dichotomy of groups: oppressor v. victim groups . . . [and] group proportionalism to the goal of 'fairness'" (Fonte 2002, 3). These concepts, he maintains, undermine American democracy, which is based on majority rule, and redefine democracy as power sharing.

9. Pei (2003) believes that America's global role is motivated by nationalism, which it denies; yet it often fails to understand the power of nationalism abroad and its impact on international politics. Most Americans, for example, consider themselves extremely patriotic but deny that patriotism and nationalism are linked. And the United States rarely understands the importance of nationalism in keeping local dictators in power in regimes which it detests.

10. Muqtedar Khan, a visiting fellow at the Brookings Institution, has also warned that "growing anti-Americanism will not only undermine the war on terror, but its extreme manifestations in the Muslim World [will produce] new and numerous recruits to the ranks of Al Qaeda and their associates" (Khan 2003).

References

Ahrnens, Anette. (2003) "The Road from San Francisco: How Far Have We Come?" Unpublished paper prepared for the annual meeting of the Academic Council for the United Nations System (ACUNS).

Boutros-Ghali, Boutros. (1996) "Global Leadership After the Cold War," *Foreign Affairs*, Vol. 75, No. 2, March-April, pp. 86–98.

Bush, George W. (2002) "The National Security Strategy of the United States of America," September (Washington, D.C.: The White House). [www.white-house.gov/nsc/nss.html]

Daalder, Ivo H. and James M. Lindsay. "American Empire, Not 'If' But 'What Kind,'" *New York Times*, May 10, 2003, p. 39.

Fonte, John. (2002) "Liberal Democracy vs. Transnational Progressivism," *Orbis*, Summer, pp. 1–9.

Glennon, Michael J. (2003) "Why the Security Council Failed," *Foreign Affairs*, Vol. 82, No. 3, May-June, p. 16.

Hastie, W., ed. and trans. (1891) *Kant's Principles of Politics, Including His Essay on Perpetual Peace. A Contribution to Political Science* (Edinburgh: Clark).

Kagan, Robert. (2002) "Power and Weakness," *Policy Review*, June-July, pp. 1–23.

Kegley, Charles W. and Gregory A. Raymond. (2002) *Exorcising the Ghost of Westphalia* (Upper Saddle River, N.J.: Prentice Hall).

Khan, Muqtedar (2003) "Is American Foreign Policy a Threat to American Security?" *Al-Jazeerah*, June. [www.brook.edu/views/op-ed/fellows/khan2003060.htm]

Mathews, Jessica T. (1997) "Power Shift," *Foreign Affairs*, Vol. 76, No. 1, January-February, pp. 50–66.

Mearsheimer, John. J. (1994–1995) "The False Promise of International Institutions," *International Security*, Winter, pp. 5–49.

Mingst, Karen A., Angela Van Berkel, and Margaret P. Karns. (2003) "Global Governance Meets AIDS." Unpublished paper prepared for the annual meeting of the Academic Council for the United Nations System (ACUNS).

Myers, Steven Lee. (2003) "Putin Tells Russians of Clouds with Reform-Plan Lining," *New York Times*, May 17, p. A3.

Pei, Minxin. (2003) "The Paradoxes of American Nationalism," *Foreign Policy*, May-June, p. 31.

Pew Research Center. (2003) "Views of a Changing World June 2003," report of the Pew Global Attitudes Project. [www.people-press.org/reports/pdf/185.pdf]

Prestowitz, Clyde. (2003) *Rogue Nation* (New York: Perseus Books).

Sorensen, Theodore. (2003) "Strategy of Peace." Commencement address at American University, May 11.

Sparks, Allister. (1995) *Tomorrow Is Another Country* (New York: Hill and Wang).

United Nations. (1996) *The Advancement of Women, 1945–1996* (New York: United Nations).

ABOUT THE EDITORS

James P. Muldoon, Jr., is Senior Fellow with the Center for Global Change and Governance at Rutgers University, Newark, New Jersey. Prior to joining the center, he was Senior Research Fellow at the Carnegie Council on Ethics and International Affairs (1999–2000) and Visiting Scholar at the Shanghai Academy of Social Sciences in China (1996–1999). From 1986 to 1996, he was Director of Education Programs for the United Nations Association of the United States of America (UNA-USA) in New York City and the editor of the annual publication *A Guide to Delegate Preparation* (UNA-USA). His most recent publication is *The Architecture of Global Governance: An Introduction to the Study of International Organizations* (Boulder: Westview Press, 2003).

JoAnn Fagot Aviel is professor and chair of the International Relations Department at San Francisco State University, where she also serves as the faculty adviser of the Model United Nations program. She served as a Fulbright Professor in 1999 at the University of Costa Rica and in 1984 at the Diplomatic Academy of Peru. She received her Ph.D. from the Fletcher School of Law and Diplomacy, Tufts University. She has published numerous articles in comparative foreign policy and international relations.

Richard Reitano is professor of government at Dutchess Community College and adjunct professor of political science at Vassar College in Poughkeepsie, New York. His course on the Model United Nations, along with twenty other college courses nationwide, was recently selected by the Carnegie Foundation for the Advancement of Teaching for a three-year national study on political engagement. He most recently published "LBJ Goes to War" in the *OAH* (Organization of American Historians) *Magazine of History*.

Earl (Tim) Sullivan is professor of political science at the American University in Cairo and the founding adviser of the Cairo International Model United Nations and the Cairo International Model Arab League. He has served as the provost of the American University in Cairo since 1998. He is coeditor of *The Contemporary Study of the Arab World: Critical Perspectives on Arab Studies* (Edmonton and Calgary: University of Alberta Press, 1991) and has published several articles on Arab and Egyptian politics.

ABOUT THE CONTRIBUTORS

Amer Araim is adjunct professor on the Middle East at Diablo Valley College in California, the spiritual leader of the Dar-ur-Islam Mosque in Concord, California, and a member of the executive committee of the Interfaith Council of Contra Costa County. He is a former Iraqi diplomat (1964–1978) and Senior Political Affairs Officer with the United Nations (1978–1998) dealing with issues of apartheid and decolonization.

Henk-Jan Brinkman is a Senior Economic Affairs Officer in the Executive Office of the Secretary-General of the United Nations. He advises the Secretary-General and the Deputy Secretary-General on economic, social, and environmental issues. Previously, he was in the Department of Economic and Social Affairs of the United Nations Secretariat, where he contributed to the World Economic and Social Survey. He holds an M.A. in economics from the University of Groningen in the Netherlands and a Ph.D. in economics from the New School University in New York City. He has written on such topics as economic adjustment in Africa and human stature as a measure of the standard of living. He is the author of *Explaining Prices in the Global Economy: A Post-Keynesian Model* (Edward Elgar, 1999).

Pamela S. Chasek is an assistant professor of government and political science and director of the International Studies Program at Manhattan College in the Bronx, New York. She is also the cofounder and editor of the *Earth Negotiations Bulletin,* a reporting service on United Nations environment and development negotiations. She has published extensively on global environmental politics and multilateral negotiations.

Ambassador Chen Luzhi is vice chairman of the China National Committee for Pacific Economic Cooperation and a visiting professor to Peking University, Nankai University, and the Foreign Affairs College. He was a member of the UN Secretariat from 1977 to 1983, serving as Deputy Director of the Security Division of the Department of Political and Security Council Affairs; principal officer in the Secretary-General's office; and director of the office of the Under Secretary-General for Special Political Affairs. He has served as China's ambassador to Denmark and Iceland (1984–1987).

Caleb H. Elfenbein is a graduate of Vassar College and Harvard Divinity School. He is currently working on a Ph.D. in Middle East studies at the University of California at Santa Barbara.

Jacques Fomerand studied law and graduated in political science at the University of Aix-en-Provence, France, and earned a Ph.D. degree in political science at the City University of New York. In 1977, he joined the United Nations Secretariat, where he followed economic, social, and coordination questions in the Office of the Under Secretary-General of the Department of Economic and Social Affairs. From 1992 to June 2003, when he retired from United Nations service, he was director of the United Nations University Office in North America. Jacques Fomerand now teaches at John Jay College of the City University of New York and at Occidental College. He has widely published on matters related to the functioning of the United Nations and is currently completing a *Dictionary of the United Nations* to be published by Scarecrow Publishers.

Ambassador S. Azmat Hassan is a faculty associate at the John C. Whitehead School of Diplomacy, Seton Hall University. A former career diplomat for Pakistan, Hassan served as ambassador to Malaysia, Syria, and Morocco and as Deputy Permanent Representative of Pakistan to the United Nations in New York City.

Stephanie Hertz is a program assistant at America-Mideast Educational and Training Services, Inc. (AMIDEAST), providing support and assistance for a variety of scholarship and exchange programs funded by the United

States and foreign governments. She serves as a local adviser on higher education issues during exchange students' stay in the United States. She has several years of experience in education and the Middle East/North Africa region. Ms. Hertz earned a B.A. in anthropology from the University of Pennsylvania.

Richard Langhorne is professor of political science and has been founding director of the Center for Global Change and Governance at Rutgers University in Newark, New Jersey, since 1996. He was previously director of Wilton Park at the British Foreign and Commonwealth Office and has published several books on diplomacy and on global politics.

Ambassador Sergey Lavrov is foreign minister of the Russian Federation and former Permanent Representative of the Russian Federation to the United Nations.

Megan McIlwain completed her M.A. in international studies at the Graduate School of International Studies, University of Denver, as well as a Graduate Certificate in Conflict Resolution. After serving as an Everett Public Service Fellow at Search for Common Ground, Ms. McIlwain is now implementing behavior change communication programs in Uganda.

Gayle Meyers is director of Middle East Regional Security Projects at Search for Common Ground. Ms. Meyers served for five years in the US Office of the Secretary of Defense, first as a presidential management intern, and then as a foreign affairs specialist in the Office of Counterproliferation Policy. She is trained in mediation and negotiation and holds an M.A. from the Fletcher School of Law and Diplomacy and a B.A. from the University of Pennsylvania.

Ambassador Don Mills is former chairman of the board of the Commonwealth Foundation; a member of the Independent World Commission on the Oceans; and a member of the Privy Council, Judicial Services Commission, Board of Dispute Resolution Foundation, and the North-South Roundtable in Jamaica. His government service includes appointments as director of the Government Planning Agency; alternate executive director on the board of the International Monetary Fund; ambassador and Permanent Representative to the United Nations; chairman of the Group of 77; president of the UN Economic and Social Council; president of the UN Security Council; chairman of the Natural Resources Conservation Authority; and special adviser on international environmental matters. He was awarded the Order of Jamaica (O.J.) for services in the field of international affairs.

Ambassador Juan Somavia is director-general of the International Labor Organization and former Permanent Representative of Chile to the United Nations.

Carolyn M. Stephenson is assistant professor of political science at the University of Hawaii at Manoa. She teaches and writes on international organization, environment, security, and peace studies; is a member of the graduate faculty in population studies; and participates in the Program on Conflict Resolution. She also directs the Hawaii Model United Nations. She received a B.A. from Mount Holyoke College and a Ph.D. from Ohio State University (1980). Before coming to University of Hawaii in 1985, she was director of Peace Studies at Colgate University and a scholar-in-residence at Radcliffe. She held a Fulbright Fellowship to Cyprus on conflict resolution in 2002.

Jeremy S. Taylor is a graduate of the Fletcher School of Law and Diplomacy at Tufts University. His career has spanned twenty-five years and includes global corporate finance at Chase Manhattan and private banking for entrepreneurs at Citicorp. He was a founding partner of Portfolio Management Data LLC, now Standard and Poor's Leveraged Data and Commentary Group. He is now a writer living in Kathmandu, Nepal, on leave from Anthony Knerr and Associates, a firm that provides strategic counsel to leading nonprofit organizations in the United States and Europe.

Rienk W. Terpstra was the Netherlands' Youth Representative to the United Nations General Assembly in 1992. After his studies in contemporary history at Groningen University, he worked as a researcher with the Netherlands Defence Staff and the Parliamentary Investigative Committee on Srebrenica. He is currently working at Utrecht University and the Roosevelt Study Center on his dissertation on US-Dutch nuclear military relations during the Cold War.

Shelton L. Williams is currently the director of the Leadership Institute at Austin College and vice president of the American Center for International Policy Studies. In 1995–1996 he served as a William F. Foster Visiting Fellow in the US State Department and as a US delegate to the 1995 Nuclear Nonproliferation Treaty Review and Extension Conference. His latest work is a novel, *Washed in the Blood* (Bristol Press, 2004).

I. William Zartman is Jacob Blaustein Professor of Conflict Resolution and International Organization and director of the African Studies and Conflict Management programs at Johns Hopkins University's Paul H. Nitze School of Advanced International Studies. He is the author or coeditor of several articles and books, including *Conflict Resolution in Africa* (Washington, D.C.: Brookings Institution,1991) and *Elusive Peace* (Washington, D.C.: Brookings Institution,1995).

INDEX